`T0165130`

'Original, bang up-to-date, and impressive in its scholarship. This is a fine p[...] work from an experienced historian.'

Colin Heywood, University of Nottingham

'This is a superb book. David Vincent has mobilized texts that he has mastered over fifty years of scholarship and supplemented these – poetry, novels, memoirs, and autobiography – with a dazzling range of sources on everything from stamp-collecting to dog-walking to prison reform. He manages the intractable distinction between solitude and loneliness over a large domain. This will become the standard work on a topic of both academic and general interest.'

Thomas Laqueur, University of California at Berkeley

'This is a deeply researched book that sheds light on many aspects of modern history, from leisure to penology. While exploring rich historical cases, the book also provides an explicit backdrop for contemporary concerns about loneliness but also about modern barriers to achieving solitude. A real gem.'

Peter Stearns, George Mason University

'Are we living in a lonely age and, if so, when did it begin? In this riveting history, David Vincent tackles this timely question by bringing to light everyday experiences of solitude and loneliness from the late eighteenth century to the present. Here we meet solitary walkers, spiritual recluses, sailors on long solo voyages, but also men and women locked up in asylums or prisons where unremitting isolation broke minds and spirits. Solitude could be nourishing but it could also madden or even kill. Vincent gives us the stories in rich detail, in a pathbreaking book that will fascinate anyone interested in solitariness, past or present.'

Barbara Taylor, Queen Mary University of London

'In this well-judged history of a currently pressing preoccupation . . . Vincent performs a useful public service: he recognises the uniqueness of our contemporary problems, but gives them the calming and edifying perspective of context.'

Times Higher Education

'[An] elegantly written and acute history . . . It is characteristic of Vincent's insight that he detects mirrors everywhere.'

The Yorkshire Times

A HISTORY OF SOLITUDE

To the memory of Veronica Weedon, 1919–2017

A HISTORY OF SOLITUDE

DAVID VINCENT

polity

First published in 2020 by Polity Press
Paperback edition published in 2021 by Polity Press

Polity Press
65 Bridge Street
Cambridge CB2 1UR, UK

Polity Press
101 Station Landing
Suite 300
Medford, MA 02155, USA

ISBN-13: 978-1-5095-3658-0
ISBN-13: 978-1-5095-3659-7 (pb)

A catalogue record for this book is available from the British Library.

Library of Congress Cataloging-in-Publication Data

Names: Vincent, David, 1949- author.
Title: A history of solitude / David Vincent.
Description: Cambridge, UK ; Medford, MA : Polity, 2020. | Includes bibliographical references and index. | Summary: "A wide-ranging social history of why and how people have chosen to be alone"-- Provided by publisher.
Identifiers: LCCN 2019043747 (print) | LCCN 2019043748 (ebook) | ISBN 9781509536580 | ISBN 9781509536603 (epub)
Subjects: LCSH: Solitude.
Classification: LCC BJ1499.S65 V56 2020 (print) | LCC BJ1499.S65 (ebook) | DDC 155.9/2--dc23
LC record available at https://lccn.loc.gov/2019043747
LC ebook record available at https://lccn.loc.gov/2019043748

Typeset in 10.75 on 14 Adobe Janson by
Servis Filmsetting Ltd, Stockport, Cheshire

Cover illustration *Seated Figure, Seen from Behind* (Anna Hammershoi) 1884 (oil on canvas laid down on board), Hammershoi, Vilhelm (1864 –1916) / Private Collection / Photo © Connaught Brown, London / Bridgeman Images

Printed and bound in Great Britain by TJ Books Ltd, Padstow, Cornwall

referred to in this book are correct and active at the time of going to press. However, the publisher has no responsibility for the websites and can make no guarantee that a site will remain live or that the content is or will remain appropriate.

For further information on Polity, visit our website: politybooks.com

CONTENTS

Acknowledgements   vi

1 Introduction: Solitude Considered   1
2 Solitude, I'll Walk with Thee   31
3 Home Alone in the Nineteenth Century   71
4 Prayers, Convents, and Prisons   112
5 Solitude and Leisure in the Twentieth Century   153
6 The Spiritual Revival   182
7 The 'Epidemic of Loneliness' Revisited   220
8 Conclusion: Solitude in the Digital Era   247

Notes   260
Index   336

ACKNOWLEDGEMENTS

This book, as with any other historical enterprise, is the product of lone endeavour and collective support. I am particularly grateful to Barbara Taylor, both for the funded network she has established on the history of solitude and for sharing her own knowledge and expertise. Her forthcoming study of the subject in the early-modern era will be a necessary complement to this exercise. The 'Pathologies of Solitude' seminars have been a useful location for testing the ideas and conclusions of my work. John Naughton has supplied networked support through the projects of the Cambridge Centre for Research in the Arts, Social Sciences and Humanities. I thank him for his encouragement and hospitality, as well as his unrivalled expertise on the digital revolution and its implications. The visiting fellows at CRASSH have been a source of debate and information. Colleagues at the Open University have read and commented on draft chapters and made available their specialized knowledge, with particular thanks to Amanda Goodrich, Ros Crone, and John Wolffe. I have benefited from discussions with Patrick Joyce, Leslie Howsam, Kathryn Hughes, and Isabel Rivers. Andrew Mackenzie-McHarg and Anne Vila helped me understand Johann Zimmermann and his writings. Claudia Hammond lent me material from her impressive BBC/Welcome Trust collaborations. The progress of this project has been discussed in the generous company of

Brenda and James Gourley, and Seija and Graham Tattersall. Charlotte Vincent, as so often over so many years, has been a sustaining critic, arguing through the book's ideas, supporting its labour and reading every word for accurate expression. At Polity, Pascal Porcheron's persistent enthusiasm for this project has much to do with its completion. The care given by Justin Dyer to the preparation of this text has been exemplary.

This book has been researched in the deep quiet of the rare books rooms in the British Library and the Cambridge University Library, and I thank their staff for their patience and efficiency. As the project was commencing one Armistice Day, the public address system in the latter's Rare Books Room made the oddly unfeasible request of its readers that they observe a silence for the fallen. Even in the depths of a library, solitude has to be managed.

The book was written in a converted pigsty in my garden. It is twenty steps from my desk to my house, from my own company to that of my wife and the intermittent presence of children, grandchildren and friends. To be able to make that journey from one location to the other, from productive solitude to the most profound sociability, is the privilege of my life.

A History of Solitude is dedicated to Veronica Weedon née More, to whom I had the good fortune of being related by marriage. After an eventful war-service, which included work at Bletchley Park, she married and had a family, but was early widowed. Her subsequent life throughout nearly six decades, latterly in a mountain village in Majorca, was an exemplary demonstration of how to maintain a balance between her own company and a wide range of family, friends, and outside interests. She was a great reader, and in turn the author of four books, the first published when she was eighty-five. I hope she would have enjoyed this one.

Shrawardine, autumn 2019

1

INTRODUCTION: SOLITUDE CONSIDERED

'Zimmerman on Solitude'

In 1791, the first full-length study of solitude for more than four centuries was published in England. *Solitude Considered with Respect to its Dangerous Influence Upon the Mind and Heart* was a shortened translation of the four-volume *Über die Einsamkeit*, written in 1784 and 1785 by Johann Georg Zimmermann, personal physician to George III in Hanover and to the late Frederick the Great. The book was not universally welcomed. 'An essay on solitude, in 380 pages,' grumbled the *Gentleman's Magazine*, 'seems to require confinement in a solitary cell to read it.'[1] But there were plenty of purchasers prepared to undertake the challenge. It was an immediate publishing success, generating further editions and competing translations annually during the 1790s, and a scattering of reprints in the first third of the following century.[2] 'Zimmerman on Solitude', widely available on second-hand bookstalls, became part of the literary furniture of the modernizing society.[3]

The topic was inherently controversial. 'Various are the opinions concerning Solitude,' observed the *Critical Review* in its response to the publication. 'By some it is considered as the parent of all human excellence and felicity; by others, as the depraver of the faculties, and the source of disquietude: and those who can endure it have been

stated to be either above or below the standard of humanity.'⁴ Early
English versions of Zimmermann's book, which omitted much of the
criticism of solitude, led to a popular misconception that it was a mere
celebration of retirement.⁵ However Zimmermann's powerfully argued
treatise was a much more complex document. Throughout the book
he addressed the task of balancing 'all the comforts and blessings of
Society' with 'all the advantages of Seclusion'.⁶ Neither way of living
was sufficient in itself, or invulnerable to destruction by its opposite.
'When we scrutinise its calamitous operation in the cloister and the
desert,' Zimmermann wrote, 'we shall revolt with horror from the
lamentable and hateful spectacle; and acknowledge ourselves fully
persuaded, that, if the proper condition of man does not consist in a
promiscuous and dissipated commerce with the world, still less does he
fulfil the duties of his station, by a savage and stubborn renunciation of
their society.'⁷

The proper condition of man, and woman, is the subject of this
history. It seeks to understand how people over the last two centuries
have conducted themselves in the absence of company. Zimmermann's
treatise was a way station in a debate about social engagement and
disengagement that stretches back to classical times and has acquired
new urgency in our own era.⁸ Current anxieties about the 'loneliness
epidemic' and the fate of interpersonal relations in the digital culture
are reformulations of dilemmas that have surfaced in prose and verse
for more than two millennia. In selecting the topic of his *magnum opus*,
itself an expanded version of a shorter study of 1755–6, Zimmermann
made no claim to originality. He was engaging with a range of authorities, particularly Petrarch's *The Life of Solitude*, written between 1346
and 1356, and published as a book just over a century later.⁹ Petrarch
was conducting a discussion with early and pre-Christian authorities,
and Zimmermann in turn was seeking to re-focus rather than invent
the subject. He was a Swiss German with a French-speaking mother,
widely read in English as well as his native languages, and conversant
with the numerous eighteenth-century treatments of the topic in novels
and poetry.¹⁰ His book was rapidly translated because both its subject
matter and its evidential frame of reference were familiar to any educated European of the period. It stood in the mainstream of one of the
longest debates in Western culture and at the same time constituted a

critical reaction to a period of unprecedented change. Zimmermann was deeply immersed in the urban bourgeois society that was beginning to recognize itself as an historical force, and in his old age witnessed the French Revolution taking place on the other side of his native Jura.

The point of departure and return in *Solitude Considered* was what Zimmermann termed 'social and liberal intercourse'.[11] Despite a personal predilection for withdrawal, he was sympathetic to the Enlightenment endorsement of social exchange as the engine of cultural and mental progress. As one of Europe's leading medical practitioners, he was professionally committed to physical engagement with his patients. Theoretical explanations, learned and advanced in the closet, were not sufficient. Effective treatment of sickness required direct observation and accumulated practical experience.[12] Zimmermann's emphasis on social contact constituted a description of his own methods and achievement:

> The best and sagest moralists have ever sought to mix with mankind; to review every class of life; to study the virtues, and detect the vices, by which each are peculiarly marked. It has been by founding their disquisitions and essays on men and manners, upon actual observation, that they have owed much of the success, with which their virtuous efforts have been crowned.[13]

Two successful marriages and increasing worldly fame underpinned his broader analysis. 'Affectionate intercourse,' he wrote at the beginning of *Solitude Considered*, 'is an inexhaustible fund of delight and happiness. In the expression of our feelings, in the communication of our opinions, in the reciprocal interchange of ideas and sentiments, there lies a treasure of enjoyment, for which the solitary hermit, and even the surly misanthrope, continually sighs.'[14] Zimmermann shared with the intellectuals with whom he worked and corresponded across Europe the Enlightenment belief that human nature was essentially social, and that all other modes of living were either a deviation or a temporary respite from the pursuit of personal contentment and collective advancement.[15] 'Solitude must render the heart callous,' he observed in his collected *Aphorisms*. 'What has it whilst alone to pity, or to cherish? It makes no provision but for itself; there its care begins, there it terminates. Humanity is unknown to the Solitaire. Without it, and all the dear cares that it includes, of what worth is existence?'[16] Diderot's *Encyclopédie* debated the subject. Respect should be paid to the Carthusians, but their way of life belonged to much earlier centuries of church persecution. Times had changed. 'In our tranquil era,' the *Encyclopédie* argued, 'a truly robust virtue is one that walks firmly through obstacles, and not one that flees them. ... A *solitary* is, in regard to rest of mankind, like an inanimate being; his prayers and his contemplative life, which no one sees, have no influence on society which has more need of examples of virtue before its eyes than in the forests.'[17]

Duty and self-interest conspired to relegate solitude to the margins of useful living. Zimmermann's contemporary Christian Garve, an influential propagandist of the German Enlightenment, summarized the approach: 'Overall, and in the nature of things, society seems to be made for times of health, vivacity, and amusement; solitude, by contrast, seems to be the natural haven of the infirm, the grieved, and the stricken.'[18] There were classical precedents for this emphasis, but the more recent authorities with whom Zimmermann was debating had taken an alternative view. Petrarch was in flight from the corruption and distraction of urban commerce: 'And so, to dismiss the matter once for all,' he concluded, 'in my opinion practically every busy man is unhappy.'[19] In the late sixteenth century, Montaigne, in his 'Essay on Solitude', set out an essentially secular argument for withdrawal from the press of business. He presented a set of prescriptions for solitary self-sufficiency: 'Now since we are undertaking to live, without companions, by ourselves, let us make our happiness depend on ourselves; let us loose ourselves from the bonds which tie us to others; let us gain power over ourselves to live really and truly alone – and of doing so in contentment.'[20] His notion of retirement was not an intermission from public life but a permanent cessation.

By the later seventeenth century, the increasing prosperity and influence of the commercial classes were reflected in a new emphasis in the long-standing debate over the competing virtues of contemplation and action. John Evelyn, who in his private life found time for meditative retreat, adopted the case for sociable endeavour in both business and religion in response to a provocative essay by the Scottish lawyer

George Mackenzie.[21] In *Publick Employment and an Active Life Prefer'd to Solitude*, he argued against extreme forms of spiritual and secular withdrawal. 'Certainly,' he wrote, 'those who either know the value of themselves, or their imployments, may find *useful entertainments*, without *retiring* into *Wildernesses*, immuring themselves, *renouncing* the World, and deserting *publick affairs*.'[22] The free exchange of ideas was the driver of both personal and collective wealth. 'For, believe it Sir,' he insisted, 'the *Wisest men* are not made in *Chambers* and *Closets* crowded with *shelves*; but by *habitudes* and active *Conversations*.'[23] Periods of reflection were adjuncts to public life, not substitutes for it. The structures of commerce and politics were still vulnerable to the seductive appeal of escape from the demands and disciplines of collective discourse. 'The *result* of all is,' Evelyn's essay concluded, '*Solitude* produces *ignorance*, renders us *barbarous*, feeds *revenge*, disposes to *envy*, creates *Witches*, dispeoples the *World*, renders it a *desart*, and would soon *dissolve* it.'[24]

Amongst his contemporaries, Zimmermann was unusual in seeking to explore the range of circumstances that might cause an individual to retreat from the domestic and public structures of eighteenth-century life. His wide reading in several European languages and his professional engagement with illness and personal breakdown caused him to take seriously the possibilities of withdrawal. At its most benign, solitude was 'a tendency to self-collection and freedom'.[25] There was a tradition of seeking a retreat in order to think or engage in creative work. 'I may not deny,' admitted Robert Burton in his *Anatomy of Melancholy* of 1621, 'but that there is some profitable Meditation, Contemplation, and kinde of Solitarinesse to be embraced, which the Fathers so highly commend. ... [which] *Petrarch*, *Erasmus*, *Stella*, and other so much magnify in their bookes.'[26] During the eighteenth century, the attraction of such an avoidance of company was becoming more apparent. It was partly that the sheer noise and intensity of living in the bustling urban centres made ever more attractive the search for the peace and quiet in which thoughts might be collected. Some kind of time alone was required to write, or to plan new ventures. A place always had to be found, argued Zimmermann, for 'an enterprising and ardent mind' to retire 'from the uninteresting distractions of company, to digest and mature in solitude', that he might better formulate his 'adventurous and capacious projects'.[27] It was not a rejection of intercourse, but rather an escape from its more trivial and distracting aspects in order that more profound or ambitious interventions might be made in the intellectual or commercial life of the community.

Towards the end of the century, the implications of 'self-collection' were taking on a more focussed meaning, particularly in the writings of Jean-Jacques Rousseau, whose *Confessions* and *Reveries of the Solitary Walker* were posthumously published in 1782, just as Zimmermann was preparing to write his treatise. As *The Gentleman's Review* irreverently put it, 'Philosophers have just found out that the best way to bring a man to an acquaintance with himself, or, in short, to his senses, is to sequester himself into *solitude*.'[28] The search for a narrative identity, discoverable only through solitary self-analysis, opened a path towards a new genre of literary autobiography.[29] Rousseau explained the project of the *Solitary Walker*: 'It is in this state of mind that I resume the painstaking and sincere self-examination that I formerly called my *Confessions*. I am devoting my last days to studying myself and to preparing the account of myself which I shall soon have to render.'[30] Zimmermann was ambivalent about Rousseau's rejection of company in his search for self-knowledge. He was sympathetic to the personal sufferings that had forced the philosopher into retirement. His critics, he argued, were 'allowing nothing for the attack of human injustice and cruelty; nothing for the torments of penury; nothing for the ravages of sickness; the bloom and vigour of his genius is forgotten'.[31] But he had little confidence that the true self was only discoverable in the absence of society, and was convinced that the project to which Rousseau was committed in the closing years of his life could only lead to personal ruin: 'Every physician, however, who studies the history of Rousseau, will plainly perceive that the seeds of dejection, sadness and hypochondriacism, were sown in his frame of mind and temper.'[32]

Once he had negotiated the kind of withdrawal with which any writer was familiar, Zimmermann's catalogue of solitude became increasingly negative. At best he had an understanding of the circumstances that could cause a rejection of society, at worst he was wholly critical of both motive and outcome. He lived a life, like Montaigne before him, where the deaths of partners, children, and friends were a constant threat to the maintenance of any intimate relations.[33] According to Samuel-Auguste Tissot, a fellow Swiss doctor and lifelong friend, his first wife suffered 'a nervous disorder, which added infinitely to Zimmermann's sorrows, [and] made him wish more earnestly for retirement'.[34] He was later widowed and lost his daughter from his first marriage. Whilst he could scarcely commend the state, he was well aware of the presence of what in our own time would be termed bereavement: 'Solitude is often terrible to the mourner, whose happiness is buried in an untimely grave; who would give all the joys of earth, for one accent of the beloved voice, whose tuneful vibrations must never more fill his ear and heart with rapture; and who, when alone, languishes with the remembrance of his irreparable loss.'[35] Those connected with the sufferer could do what they could to ease them back to society; Zimmermann himself later remarried, and, claimed Tissot, 'the happiness of this union was never disturbed for a moment'.[36]

There were other kinds of misfortune which, as in the case of Rousseau, might propel the individual into retirement. 'A wounded spirit,' Zimmermann wrote, 'seeks shelter in the lenient repose of privacy, from the shocks of rivalry, the intrusion of misguided friendship, and malicious assaults of secret or avowed enmity.'[37] Such people, too, deserved sympathy, though not imitation. Beyond those forced into retreat through no fault of their own, there were the many individuals who were thrust into it by misconduct or inadvisably chose the condition. The most amorphous group were those who had failed to meet the ethical standards or behavioural demands of eighteenth-century society. It took a certain level of self-belief to participate in domestic, commercial, or political networks. Once this was lost by defeat or moral shortcoming, withdrawal was the looming prospect:

> Shame or remorse, a poignant sense of past follies, the regret of disappointed hope, or the lassitude of sickness, may so wound or enervate the soul, that it shall shrink from the sight and touch of its equals, and retire to bleed and languish, unmolested, except by its internal cares, in the coverts of solitude. In these instances, the disposition to retreat is not an active impulse of the mind to self-collection; but a fearful and pusillanimous aversion from the shocks and the attrition of society.[38]

In contrast to the elite souls who chose a temporary retreat the better to engage with the highest endeavours of their time, these were outcasts, driven from company by a sense of their own demerits.

The category of exile overlapped with the pathological condition of melancholy. In eighteenth-century intellectual culture, there were no hard boundaries between the sciences, literature, and philosophy. Zimmermann's excursions into poetry, political commentary, and guides to living were bound up with his principal occupational identity as a doctor. His first publication was a treatise on 'Irritability', referring not to short temper but to the functioning of the nerves of the heart. He brought to solitude his experience as a leading medical authority, and his discussion of melancholy was later cited by Jean-Étienne Dominique Esquirol, the mid-nineteenth-authority on mental illness, as a key contribution to the topic.[39] Melancholy had been a nosological term for two millennia, encompassing sadness, fear, and depression.[40] During Zimmermann's working life, the psychological causes were increasingly foregrounded over the physiological, which traditionally had been located in an excess of black bile.[41] A related category was that of hypochondria, or hypochondriasis, from which Tissot claimed Zimmermann himself intermittently suffered. This lacked the modern association of imaginary illness but referred instead to a collection of symptoms for which there were no evident physical causes.[42] The conditions were at the centre of a growing interest in the capacity of states of mind to generate bodily malfunctions. In his *Anatomy of Melancholy*, Burton observed that 'the Minde most effectually workes upon the Body, producing by his passions and perturbations, miraculous alterations, as Melancholy, Despaire, cruell diseases, and sometimes death it selfe'.[43] His speculation received increasing medical support. As Thomas Trotter excitedly wrote in 1812, 'at the beginning of the nineteenth century, we do not hesitate to affirm, that *nervous disorders* have now taken the place of fevers, and may be justly reckoned two thirds of the whole, with which civilized society is afflicted'.[44]

So broad a collection of ailments had no single diagnosis or prognosis, but a pronounced rejection of society featured in every account and at every stage of the illness. According to Zimmermann,

An unseasonable and ungovernable propensity to Solitude is one of the most general and unequivocal symptoms of melancholy: all those whose feelings are a prey to images of chagrin, regret, and disappointment, shun the light of heaven, and the aspect of man; incapable of attaching themselves to any ideas but those which torment and destroy them, they fly the necessity of efforts at once painful and ineffectual.[45]

The withdrawal from company was often the first visible sign of a looming mental crisis. 'When persons begin to be melancholy,' observed William Buchan's contemporary bestseller *Domestic Medicine*, 'they are dull, dejected, timorous, watchful, fond of solitude, fretful, fickle, captious, and inquisitive, solicitous about trifles, sometimes niggardly, at other times prodigal.'[46] Increasingly the sufferer could find no source of pleasure except in the denial of intercourse with those who might have been able to help them out of their deepening depression. Philippe Pinel's influential *Treatise on Insanity* of 1801, set out for the coming century the principal characteristics of the illness: 'The symptoms generally comprehended by the term melancholia are taciturnity, a thoughtful pensive air, gloomy suspicions, and a love of solitude.'[47] How an individual arranged his or her social life was now the legitimate concern of European doctors. Too much time alone immediately raised warning flags. Medical textbooks routinely devoted a section on solitude in their advice on the causes and treatment of the most pervasive form of mental illness. Pathological melancholy was distinguished from the increasingly fashionable 'white' melancholy, a condition professed by those with a pronounced literary sensibility, denoting a low-key withdrawal for the purpose of observing the lessons of nature and the rural world.[48] Thomas Gray, author of the most widely read poem on country life in the second half of the eighteenth century, mocked his own predilections:

> Mine, you are to know, is a white Melancholy, or rather Leucocholy for the most part; which though it seldom laughs or dances, not ever amounts to what calls Joy or Pleasure, yet is a good easy sort of a state, and *ca ne laisse que de s'amuser*. The only fault of it is insipidity; which is apt now and then to give a sort of Ennui.[49]

'Black' melancholy was altogether more serious, a one-way journey towards a complete breakdown of mental and physical health.

As a doctor, Zimmermann could take a practical view of the pathologies of solitary living, seeking to reduce their incidence through medical intervention and published writings. It was otherwise with his final category of negative solitude, which he treated with unremitting hostility throughout his treatise. His tour of the landscape concluded with its spiritual dimension:

> This long catalogue of the numerous causes which conduct to Solitude, is closed by Religion and Fanaticism. The former leads to the serenity and quiet of retirement, from the purest and noblest of considerations, the best propensities, and the finest energies. It is the passion of the strongest and best regulated minds. The latter is a rebellion against nature; a violation and perversion of reason; a renunciation of virtue; the folly and vice of narrow and oblique understandings; produced by a misapprehension of the Deity, and an ignorance of themselves.[50]

Zimmermann had no argument with religion itself. A Swiss Protestant, he was at ease with his denomination's mixed economy of private prayer and collective worship. His problem was with the eremitical tendency in the Catholic Church, whose influence had been curtailed but by no means obliterated by the Reformation. The objection was not just to current monastic practice, limited as it was even in the Catholic regions of Europe. Rather, Zimmermann was exercised by the broader status and moral authority of the tradition of seclusion rooted in the desert hermits of the fourth century, who in turn were seeking to replicate Christ's sojourn in the wilderness.[51] He aimed his fire directly at the founding fathers of the Catholic Church: 'So far were these madmen, who are deemed to be the stars of the infant Church, from understanding human nature, that they employed their knowledge to exact from themselves and their proselytes everything unnatural and impracticable.'[52] What he repeatedly termed 'fanaticism' had no place in the rational, sociable culture of late eighteenth-century urban Europe.[53]

Zimmermann's point of departure lay in his conception of how to live. Although an observant Christian, he had no sense that a silent, intensely personal communion with God was the ultimate purpose of man's time on earth. *Solitude Considered* was a treatise on the pursuit of happiness, centred on the individual's inherent sociability. The irreversible rejection of comfort and company represented a perversion of human nature. Zimmermann's problem was with those who, 'instigated by religious fervour, and perceiving nothing but corruption in the joys of social life, and sinful abomination in its virtues, retire from the spectacle to contemplate in the sacred gloom of the monastery, or the solitude of the cave and desert, a Being whose essence is unalterable purity, unlimited goodness and perfection'.[54] He took issue with a spiritual tradition that argued, in the words of the seventeenth-century Cistercian Cardinal Bona, that 'no one can find God except he is solitary, for God himself is alone and solitary'.[55] At best, such a public renunciation of society was a form of self-indulgence. Zimmermann was of the same view as John Evelyn that the practice trivialized rather than grounded Christian worship. 'Verily,' wrote Evelyn, 'there is more of *Ambition* and empty glory in some *Solitudes*, and affected *Retreats*, than in the most expos'd and conspicuous actions whatsoever: *Ambition* is not only in publick places, and pompous circumstances; but at *home*, and in the interior life; *Heremits* themselves are not recluse enough to seclude that subtile spirit, Vanity.'[56] At worst, it overlapped with other forms of insanity. 'Religious melancholy' was seen as a particularly lethal category of mental illness. 'All authors who have treated this subject,' noted John Haslam in his *Observations on Madness and Melancholy* of 1809, 'appear to agree respecting the difficulty of curing religious madness.'[57] The human mind was incapable of coping alone with the consequences of seeking out the most profound spiritual revelations. Christian observance was entirely beneficial, continued Haslam, 'but when an anxious curiosity leads us to unveil that which must ever be shrouded from our view, the despair, which always attends these impotent researches, will necessarily reduce us to the most calamitous state'.[58] This category of melancholy remained part of the diagnostic tool-kit of nineteenth-century doctors, and still featured in Krafft-Ebbing's compendious textbook on insanity in 1904.[59]

In his discussion of religious fanaticism, Zimmermann drew a distinction between continental Europe and its outlying nation, where the monasteries had not recovered from the Reformation. 'An Englishman,' he wrote, 'when melancholy, shoots himself; a melancholy Frenchman used to turn Carthusian.'[60] In a country where the only visible hermits were those employed to inhabit grottos for the entertainment of visitors to newly landscaped country estates, monastic seclusion did not appear an immediate threat to the good ordering of religious practice.[61] However, in Britain as elsewhere, Enlightenment rationalism was at odds in the eighteenth century with forms of religious enthusiasm that foregrounded a direct encounter with God by the impassioned believer. Anglican and nonconformist evangelicalism had yet to generate new institutional contexts for such personal communication, but the tradition of the desert fathers remained alive and towards the end of the eighteenth century was stimulating interest amongst theologians. While *Solitude Considered* was going through successive English editions in the 1790s, the Reverend James Milner began publishing his influential *History of the Church of Christ*, which sought to educate the clergy and laity in the lives and work of the early Christians. He argued for greater, though not uncritical, respect for the monastic tradition: 'We often hear it said, How ridiculous to think of pleasing God by austerities and solitude! Far be it from me to vindicate the superstitions of monks, and particularly the vows of celibacy. But the error is very natural, has been reprehended much too severely and the profaneness of men of the world is abundantly more dangerous.'[62] Alongside this cautious defence of religious solitude, popular interest in the 'superstitions' of the Catholic churches was heightened by the outbreak of war in 1793 with Britain's nearest Catholic neighbour. The outcome was the publication in 1796 of a novel still more sensational than Zimmermann's treatise.

Matthew Lewis's *The Monk* created a template for a category of vigorous, sometimes salacious attacks on enclosed religious institutions that was to flourish throughout much of the succeeding century in both fiction and non-fiction. The novel was written when its precocious author was still only nineteen, following a stay in Weimar to learn German.[63] Lewis met and translated Goethe, but there is no evidence that he encountered the Hanover-based Zimmermann either in person or in his writings. Although Lewis was widely accused of plagiarism, the sources were generally held to be the fertile German tradition of *Schauerromane* (shudder stories) together with home-grown gothic novels, particularly Horace Walpole's *Castle of Otranto* of 1764, and, more immediately, Ann Radcliffe's *Mysteries of Udolpho* of 1794.[64] His attack on the perversions inherent in monasteries and nunneries reflected a wider Enlightenment sensibility of which Zimmermann was merely a representative figure. Denis Diderot's *La Religieuse*, written in

1760 but not published until 1796, described in vivid detail the sufferings of a reluctant nun, confined to 'a little dark underground chamber,
where I was thrown on to a mat half-rotten with damp', when she
attempts to leave her convent.[65] Lewis's story soon took off into realms
of gothic fantasy that were entirely at odds with the ordered universe
of the Swiss doctor. But early in the novel he wrote a speech which
exactly captured Zimmermann's objection to eremitical living. The
eponymous Monk, Ambrosio, addresses a young man, Rosario (soon
to be revealed as the cross-dressing sorceress Matilda, the Monk's fatal
nemesis), who has taken up residence in a hermitage in the monastery
grounds:

> Disgusted at the guilt or absurdity of Mankind, the Misanthrope flies
> from it; He resolves to become an Hermit, and buries himself in the
> Cavern of some gloomy Rock. While Hate inflames his bosom, pos-
> sibly He may feel contented with his situation: But when his passions
> begin to cool; when Time has mellowed his sorrows, and healed those
> wounds which He bore with him to his solitude, think you that Content
> becomes his Companion? Ah! no Rosario. No longer sustained by the
> violence of his passions, He feels all the monotony of his way of living,
> and his heart becomes the prey of Ennui and weariness. He looks
> around and finds himself alone in the Universe: The love of society
> revives in his bosom, and He pants to return to that world which He
> has abandoned. Nature loses all her charms in his eyes: No one is
> near him to point out her beauties, or share in his admiration of her
> excellence and variety. Propped upon the fragment of some Rock He
> gazes upon the tumbling water-fall with a vacant eye. He views without
> emotion the glory of the setting Sun. He returns to his Cell at Evening,
> for no one there is anxious for his arrival; He has no comfort in his
> solitary unsavoury meal: He throws himself upon his couch of Moss
> despondent and dissatisfied, and wakes only to pass a day as joyless, as
> monotonous as the former.[66]

There was no sense of the youthful hermit being sustained by an unmediated encounter with God in the silence of his cell. Bereft of society, he
is incapable of preventing a collapse of spirit.

The Monk himself enjoys a reputation as a fashionable preacher, but

is portrayed as 'virtuous from vanity, not principle'.[67] Having sought
to rescue the young hermit from the dangers of solitude, he himself
falls into every kind of corruption, including rape and murder. The
instant success of the novel both created and destroyed the reputation
of its youthful author.[68] Criticism of the novel did nothing to harm
sales, however, and as with other popular successes in print or on the
stage in the Georgian era, it was rapidly translated into diverse cultural
forms, including plays and chapbooks, which ensured that its message
reached an audience well beyond the novel-reading public.[69] The issue
of 'religious fanaticism' became one of a range of arguments about
the merits and demerits of solitude that were given a new focus by the
late-eighteenth-century debate but in no sense brought to a conclusion.
As we shall see in Chapters 4 and 6 in particular, the function of solitary spiritual observance remained an area of controversy, innovation
and experiment in areas such as penal policy, revived monasticism and
evolving forms of private observance.

Zimmermann viewed solitude much as a doctor might consider
the human body. If health was the central objective, it was the business of the medical practitioner to engage with the frequent threats to
wellbeing and, where necessary, take action to prevent the outbreak
of personal illness or wider epidemics. There was always a need for
disciplined exercise by the individual to ensure moral and intellectual
fitness, particularly for those with highly tuned minds. Forms of personal relaxation needed to be monitored in case they undermined the
patient's constitution. In 1760, Zimmermann's colleague Tissot had
diagnosed a particular category of solitary behaviour in a text which
framed the debate on the subject until the twentieth century. Those
who committed the vice of onanism, he wrote, 'are all affected with
hypochondriac or hysterical complaints, and are overcome with the
accidents that accompany those grievous disorders, melancholy, sigh-
ing, tears, palpitations, suffocations, and faintings'.[70] The sequence of
events was a function of a more general withdrawal from company.
Once the individual began to obsess about a particular desire and ceased
to participate in the affairs of others, disaster beckoned. 'Nothing is
more pernicious', Zimmermann insisted, 'to people inclinable to be
devoted to a single idea, than idleness and inactivity; this is particularly
pernicious to our patients, and they cannot too assiduously avoid lazi-

ness and solitude. Rural exercise and agriculture are more particularly diverting than any others.'[71]

Two aspects in particular of Zimmermann's approach to his chosen topic were relevant to the history of solitude as the modern world took shape. The first was his conception of solitude as an event. The mere fact of physical isolation was of little interest. It was not whether but why a person was alone. What determined the impact of solitude both on the individual and on society was the state of mind that caused the retirement from company.[72] There was all the difference between the withdrawal to the closet or the countryside for the purpose of self-collection, and the retreat to the same spaces because of emotional defeat or misguided passion. As Zimmermann wrote,

> If the heart be pure, the disposition cheerful, and the understand-ing cultivated, temporary sequestrations from general or even private intercourse, will improve the virtues of the mind and conduce to hap-piness; but when the soul is corrupted, and myriads of depraved images and wishes swarm in the tainted imagination, Solitude only serves to confirm and aggravate the evil; and by keeping the mind free to brood over its rank and noxious conceptions, becomes the midwife and nurse of its unnatural and monstrous suggestions.[73]

The second feature of Zimmermann's approach has received insuf-ficient attention in subsequent writings on the subject. His treatise was not about solitude alone. The significance of the topic lay in the movement between the conditions of sociability and retreat. His liter-ary intervention was designed to achieve a world in which the 'benefits of Solitude and the advantages of Society may easily be reconciled and intermingled with each other'.[74] The key criterion for distinguishing between beneficial and malign withdrawal was the capacity to manage the transition between the two states. Solitude for self-recollection was acceptable if the individual possessed the strength of mind to take the gains from the period of reflection and rejoin the fray with an enhanced sense of purpose. The virtues gained in rational intercourse prior to the sojourn in solitude would guarantee a successful return to the world of debate and association. Those, however, who sought their own com-pany for essentially superficial or self-indulgent motives would re-enter society still in a state of moral infirmity. Other forms of retirement were increasingly dangerous because they appeared to cut off the path back to sociability altogether. 'Leisure and Solitude,' Zimmermann warned, 'to the imagination clouded by sorrow and despondence, do not expel, but on the contrary increase and aggravate, the evil they are fondly employed to eradicate.'[75] The 'victim of dejection' would never recover if he avoided the company of those who might sympathize with or understand his sufferings, which 'cannot but be aggravated and augmented in solitude'.[76] The presence of solitude as both a cause and a leading symptom of melancholy ensured that sufferers lacked the resources to make their own return to spiritual health and happiness. Their condition would feed on itself, eventually generating physical symptoms which would still further reduce the prospects of recovery: 'Solitude itself, far from mitigating, serves only to exasperate the misery of these unhappy mortals.'[77] The damage wrought by religious fanaticism began with the decision to reject collective observance and the authority of spiritual leaders. A monastic vow was a ticket to a one-way journey from which there could be no return. In the isolation of the cell, the imagination would run riot, deprived of any rational constraint. A silent God would offer no comfort: 'Solitude renders religious melancholy an earthly hell; for the imagination is thus suffered to dwell, uninterruptedly, on the terrific apprehension so inseparable from this sickness of the mind, that the soul is abandoned of God, and an outcast from Divine mercy.'[78]

States of mind in solitude and the capacity to make transitions between solitude and sociability were issues that had to be addressed by every following generation in the modernizing world. Zimmermann's own answers were of his time and conditioned by his identity as a Protestant, urban intellectual. The urgency of his treatise stemmed from a sense of the deep instability of the prevailing balance of solitude and sociability. There was a tension in *Solitude Considered* between an endorsement of the emerging urban civilization and a reaction against its trivializing effects that went back to Petrarch and Virgil and forward to successive cohorts of critics as populations in Western Europe increasingly clustered in towns and cities. The efficacy of the movement between society and solitude went both ways. Those who had 'their faculties narrowed by continual intercourse with vanity and nonsense',

Zimmermann observed, were in no fit state to 'relish the delights of seclusion'.[79] It was not just the major population centres. The treatise contains a heartfelt condemnation of the superficial dramas of provincial living, derived from its author's long and increasingly resented sojourn in Brugg, the small town near Zurich where he was born and to which he later returned as chief medical officer.[80] The danger derived from a sense that the elite culture of the period was hard-wired for retirement in the face of the excesses of urban civilization. Zimmermann both sympathized with this reaction and feared its consequences. It would be impossible to maintain the forward momentum of the associative project of the Enlightenment if its leading members were, like Rousseau, continually looking over their shoulders at the attractions of sylvan retreats.

The same was true of withdrawal for spiritual contemplation. The desert fathers and their medieval successors were in the bones of European religious sensibility. They constituted a common heritage of Catholic and Protestant alike, icons to be admired, celebrated and conceivably imitated. The ferocity of Zimmermann's attack on 'religious insanity' reflected his awareness of its continuing attraction. Despite the further damage caused to the surviving networks of monasteries by the French Revolution, both in France and in the countries to which the Revolution was exported, their way of life retained a fading glamour. What continued to appeal was the extremity of the experience. If the problem was the corrupting comfort of urban culture, the answer lay in a complete denial of ease and indulgence. If the obstacle to restorative contemplation was the press of other people, the solution was a total escape, whether temporary or, in specific circumstances, permanent. In this sense, the monastic ideal was at once a particular, if increasingly uncommon, institutional possibility, and a more general inspiration of varieties of spiritual retreat. Within the Christian tradition, there were those driving a religious revival who, unlike Zimmermann, believed that a direct, personal encounter with God was a feasible path to revelations unattainable in an increasingly secular and commercial society.

There was further unease about the disruptive role of the imagination. Zimmermann understood its new-found power and that it was particularly creative when individuals withdrew to consider their own thoughts.[81] 'Solitude,' he wrote, 'acts with continual and mighty force on the imagination, whose empire over the mind is almost always superior to that of the judgment.'[82] However it was precisely when the subject was alone that imagination was likely to overthrow judgement, unexposed as it was to the critique of rational discourse. English moralists such as the third Earl of Shaftesbury had debated whether, as Lawrence Klein writes, 'solitude bred phantasms of the mind, of which enthusiastic delusions were but one sort'.[83] Towards the end of the eighteenth century, the Romantic Movement proposed a means of focussing the imagination through an intense, frequently solitary engagement with nature. Although Zimmermann was well aware of the time-honoured duality of town and country, his discussion of the latter was perfunctory. He had limited interest in what might be termed the geography of solitude, the association of a state of retirement with a particular spatial, preferably natural, location. He came from a part of Europe that was becoming celebrated as the most awe-inspiring manifestation of the natural world, but in his own affairs he was more concerned with finding a suitable location for his medical career. Not for him the enthusiastic project of the English radical John Thelwall, who compiled *The Peripatetic; Or, Sketches of the Heart, of Nature and Society* three years after the first English translation of *Solitude Considered*:

> In one respect, at least, said I, after quitting the public road, in order to pursue a path, faintly tracked through the luxuriant herbage of the fields, and which left me at liberty to indulge the solitary reveries of a mind, to which the volume of nature is ever open at some page of instruction and delight; – In one respect, at least, I may boast of a resemblance to the simplicity of the ancient sages: I pursue my meditations on foot, and can find occasion for philosophic reflection, wherever yon fretted vault (the philosopher's best canopy) extends its glorious covering.[84]

Walking had become and would remain a critical element of the construction and practice of solitude. It will be the central issue in Chapter 2 on the nineteenth century and will be revisited in Chapter 5 on the twentieth.

The Modern History of Solitude

The long debate over solitude was given new urgency by the Enlightenment commitment to sociability. Personal exchange drove innovation but left insufficient space for intellectual exploration and self-discovery. Social interaction promoted creativity but might also distract and trivialize if there was no opportunity for retreat and reflection. A new balance had to be struck between engagement and seclusion in the pursuit of progress. At the same time, historical forms of withdrawal retained a dangerous attraction amidst the noise and materialism of an urbanizing society. The walled cloister or unpeopled nature had long been a cleansing alternative to the corrupting pressures of the contemporary world. Both threatened an irreversible rejection of vital structures of discourse and debate. Amidst these pressures there were evident casualties of social living. There was a growing apprehension, driven by the emerging medical profession, that the mental resilience of those charged with achieving change could not withstand the maelstrom of personal interactions. The more intense the demands of society, the larger the number of participants, the greater the risk of a descent into a potentially lethal melancholy.

The question of how to be alone has remained a lightning conductor in the response to modernity.[85] As European populations expanded and relocated from the country to the city after 1800, so new questions were asked in a host of contexts about the appropriate role of solitude. What James Vernon has characterized as 'a new society of strangers'[86] was faced with the task of redefining and remaking practices which could variously be seen as compounding the dangers or exploiting the strengths of more fragmented interpersonal relations. Over time, three distinct functions of solitude emerged, each of them a response to the opportunities and threats of increasingly crowded populations.

The first of these had a lineage stretching back to the Romantic Movement and thence to oppositional practices with which Zimmermann was concerned. In this discourse, solitude was a recurring, endlessly remodelled critique of whatever was conceived as modernity. The locus of unwelcome change was the expanding urban centres which corrupted human relations and threatened physical health. The principal arena of spiritual and bodily recovery was nature in as unspoilt a form as the

British Isles could supply. With the growth of international transport systems from the mid-nineteenth century onwards, it became possible to engage in person or through travel literature with truly wild land-scapes. What was required above all was an unmediated relationship not between one individual and another, but between the lone walker or explorer and some manifestation of God's original creation. This withdrawal from urban sociability is considered in Chapter 2, which is principally concerned with walking in the nineteenth century, Chapter 5, which discusses recreational encounters with the countryside in the twentieth century, and Chapter 6, which examines the increasingly exhausted practice of battling with extreme nature.

The second function of solitary behaviour was as a pathology of modernity. The licentious pursuit of material pleasure and individual satisfaction increasingly threatened healthy forms of sociability. Severe forms of physical or psychological morbidity were a direct, quantifiable measure of unmanageable contradictions in interpersonal relations. Over the period covered by this study, concerns coalesced around the emerging notion of loneliness. Before the modern era, the term was rarely deployed in isolation from emotional solitude more generally. Milton's 1643 tract on divorce argued that marriage was primarily 'a remedy against loneliness', and existed to provide 'the apt and cheerful conversation of man with woman, to comfort and refresh him against the evil of a solitary life'.[87] In the eighteenth century, lonely meant a state or more often a place of solitude. It began to appear more widely as a distinct negative emotion in the writings of the Romantic poets.[88] The disaffected wandering of Byron's *Childe Harold* takes him to the Alps, 'The palaces of Nature, whose vast walls, / Have pinnacled in clouds their snowy scalps, /And throned Eternity in icy halls / of cold sublimity.'[89] There was, however, 'too much of man' in Lac Leman and he renewed his quest for a form of bitter solitude: 'soon in me shall Loneliness renew / Thoughts hid, but not less cherish'd than of old.'[90]

The term 'loneliness' entered popular discourse during the nine-teenth century, although initially the concept was subsumed within the pathologies of solitude discussed by successive medical authorities and other writers.[91] In Charles Dickens's 1840 Christmas story, a deaf, elderly man is befriended on the festive day by the narrator, who seeks to draw him out of his melancholic isolation, described in the story not as loneliness but as a state of 'solitude'.[92] Gradually it became a separate condition, carrying with it a specific set of symptoms. Writing in 1930, G. K. Chesterton satirized the emergence of what appeared to be a particularly local phenomenon:

> One of the finer manifestations of an indefatigable patriotism has taken the form of an appeal to the nation on the subject of Loneliness. This complains that the individual is isolated in England, in a sense unknown in most other countries, and demands that something should be done at once to link up all these lonely individuals in a chain of sociability.[93]

Loneliness was embraced by the emerging discipline of psychology.[94] At its most intense it could cause outbreaks of psychotic illness. The diffuse concept of melancholy was reborn as a condition with interacting mental and physical symptoms. Chapter 7 will examine the post-1945 emergence of a public crisis of loneliness, culminating in the appointment of the world's first government minister for the phenomenon, and the publication of an official strategy to combat it.

The third change was the most pervasive yet the least recognized by contemporary commentators. The replacement of literary doctors by professional social scientists from the late Victorian period onwards did little to alter the marginal status of solitary behaviours. The first major study to place solitude as a normal and necessary aspect of living was written by the psychologist Anthony Storr as late as 1989. He mounted a case against the prevailing orthodoxy. 'It is widely believed,' he wrote in his Preface, 'that interpersonal relationships of an intimate kind are the chief, if not the only, source of human happiness.'[95] His book stimulated greater interest in the topic amongst social scientists, but as recently as 2016, Ira Cohen could still observe that 'while my fellow sociologists have made extraordinary progress in the study of how individuals engage in social interaction, they have seldom acknowledged that there is an entire realm of behaviors in which people engage when they are not involved in interpersonal encounters'.[96] Such activities, it will be argued in this history, were more than residual pastimes that have been obscured by the noise and energy of commercial progress. Rather, they were at once a product of modernity and a necessary condition of its success. From the early nineteenth century onwards, multiform improvements in material prosperity, consumer markets and communication networks made possible a wider range of solitary practices across the population. Solitude in its basic form as a site of fleeting leisure amidst hard-pressed lives became more available, especially for women and the labouring poor. It will be argued, particularly in Chapters 3 and 5, that at all stages of the life-course, and for all but the most dispossessed of society, these forms of solitary endeavour made a sustainable sociability possible.

The dynamics of change across these three functions have been obscured by a static conception of solitude as an activity. In Zimmermann's treatise, as more widely in his own time and subsequently, solitude was seen as a simple antonym of physical company. He insisted, as we have seen, that the motives for withdrawal were critical, but nonetheless assumed that in all circumstances he was dealing with the absence of another in a particular space. The modern debate about loneliness is still largely predicated on a binary opposition between face-to-face contact and non-communicative isolation. Whether in an unpeopled landscape or an empty room, the withdrawn figure is a key component of the experience and understanding of solitude throughout our period. Two further forms of solitude have, however, become increasingly significant. The first may be termed networked solitude, the engagement with others through print, correspondence or other media whilst otherwise alone.

In the late eighteenth century, particularly at the level of education and society that a medical practitioner occupied, there was already an intervening structure of virtual representation, whereby an individual could be both by himself or herself and in communication with another. In Britain, men and women of the gentry class had been using letters to conduct their affairs with distant relatives and business partners since the later middle ages.[97] By 1800, what Susan Whyman terms 'epistolary literacy' had reached as far down as the many literate members of the artisan community.[98] For a manual worker, the composition or receipt of a letter was a rare event, but leading scientists had long been accustomed to maintaining a network of correspondents across Europe and latterly with the New World. Zimmermann conducted not only his research on this basis but also his literary endeavours. 'His work upon Solitude,' recorded Tissot, 'was received with great *éclat*, not only in Germany, but wherever German is read, and procured him a correspondence which gratified him greatly.'[99] The subsequent expansion of European and global postal networks, founded on the flat-rate, pre-paid model of Britain's 1840 Penny Post, was designed to maintain connections between family members dispersed by the economic and demographic upheavals of the period.[100] The later inventions of the telephone and the internet, which will be discussed in the final chapter, supplied further means of managing physical isolation. Networked solitude both reduced the stress and enriched the experience of being alone. Through correspondence and the proliferating forms of printed media, it enabled solitary individuals to enjoy their own company and at the same time feel that they were in some sense part of a wider community.

The second alternative form has only lately become the subject of scholarly discussion.[101] Abstracted solitude was the capacity to be alone amidst company. It was the means by which individuals withdrew their attention and thoughts from those in close physical proximity. The long-standing concern with finding mental space within the press of people gained a new urgency in the rapidly expanding metropolitan civilization of the eighteenth century. In 1720, Daniel Defoe wrote a second sequel to his epochal novel of solitude.[102] Robinson Crusoe was now back in London, and anxious to draw a distinction between absolute physical isolation, whether chosen or enforced, and a temporary withdrawal from surrounding company. The returned castaway had no nostalgia for his former life. The solitude he had enjoyed was necessary to the wellbeing of his moral self, but artificial and unsafe when disconnected from the moral structures and constraining perspectives of educated society. The most profound forms of spiritual reflection were better undertaken in the midst of everyday activity. 'Divine Contemplations,' Crusoe insists, 'require a Composure of Soul, uninterrupted by any extraordinary Motions or Disorders of the Passions; and this, I say, is much easier to be obtained and enjoy'd in the ordinary Course of Life, than in Monkish Cells and forcible Retreats.'[103] The crowd, specifically that of the nation's capital, was a condition of disciplined, productive meditation, not its negation:

It is evident then, that as I see nothing but what is far from being retir'd, in the forced Retreat of an Island, the Thoughts being in no

Composure suitable to a retired Condition, no not for a great While; so I can affirm, that I enjoy much more Solitude in the Middle of the greatest Collection of Mankind in the World, I mean at *London*, while I am writing this, than ever I could say I enjoy'd in eight and twenty Years Confinement to a desolate Island.[104]

It was an argument about what was necessary and also what was feasible. Crusoe's creator had no doubt that abstracting himself at will from the complex networks in which he lived and worked was an entirely practical proposition. His hero insists that 'all the Parts of a compleat Solitude are to be as effectually enjoy'd, if we please, and sufficient Grace assisting, even in the most populous Cities, among the Hurries of Conversation, and Gallantry of a Court, or the Noise and Business of a Camp, as in the Desarts of *Arabia* and *Lybia*, or in the desolate Life of an uninhabited Island'.[105]

By its nature, abstracted solitude has left little record, but it may be argued that in the overcrowded domestic interiors in which most people lived for much of the time covered by this study, it was the principal means of achieving the benefits traditionally claimed for physical isolation. It required a degree of practised concentration, and could vary in time from a few snatched minutes of contemplation or day-dreaming to a prolonged immersion in a personal task or distraction. There was a frequent association with types of networked solitude, most obviously getting lost in a book whilst the noisy life of the household went on around the reader. In middle-class interiors it was visible in the ability of employing householders to consider themselves entirely alone whilst in the presence of toiling servants. Throughout the period it was influenced by technical change, and as Chapter 8 will argue, it reached its apotheosis with the arrival of the texting smartphone.

Common to the differing responses to modernity and the varying categories of solitude were questions of class and gender. Late eighteenth- and early nineteenth-century writers on the subject, as on melancholy more generally, were in no doubt that their principal concern was with well-educated men.[106] 'Close, and unremitted thinking', as Thomas Arnold argued, was a leading cause of insanity.[107] Only those with a mature, balanced mind were capable of withstanding the perils of isolation and returning to productive intercourse with society.

Conversely, those spending excessive hours in their studies were especially vulnerable to the pathologies of solitude, whereas the bulk of the population were shielded from them by their intellectual limitations. As William Buchan's *Domestic Medicine* of 1769 put it, 'The perpetual thinker seldom enjoys either health or spirits; while the person who can hardly be said to think at all, seldom fails to enjoy both.'[108] Men who worked with their hands were unlikely to suffer from disorders of the mind. Thomas Trotter's *View of the Nervous Temperament* of 1812 noted that 'I do not find that the pitmen in the coal-mines in this district are liable to any particular diseases; when temperate in drinking, they commonly live to a great age.'[109]

In most of the contemporary commentary, women were excluded from the benefits of the solitary state. The early eighteenth-century poet Mary Chudleigh regarded it as a 'masculine pleasure' for which reason '*Solitude* ought never to be our Choice, an active Life including in it much greater Perfection.'[110] There was a possibility of withdrawal 'in our Studies, in our Gardens, and in the silent lonely Retirement of a shady Grove', but 'none can be thus happy in *Solitude*, unless they have an inward Purity of Mind, their Desires contracted, and their Passions absolutely under the Government of their Reason'.[111] Zimmermann thought this display of virtues highly unlikely amongst women. Either they were simply too busy managing the affairs of the family ever to have the opportunity to enjoy their own company, or their particular exposure to the imaginative faculty rendered them incapable of withstanding its destructive effects. 'Solitude is still more prolific of visionary insanity in the minds of women,' he observed, 'than in those of men; since the imaginations of the latter are in general less governed by an irritable sensibility and more restrained by stability of judgment.'[112]

People with time to spare were held to require a certain level of education to make use of their leisure. The seventeenth-century poet Abraham Cowley observed in his essay 'Of Solitude' that he 'cannot much recommend Solitude to a man totally illiterate'.[113] Those encountering what he termed 'the little intervals of accidental Solitude, which frequently occurr in almost all conditions (except the very meanest of the people, who have business enough in the necessary provisions of life)', needed access to books or some form of 'Ingenious Art' to fill the empty hours.[114] It is possible to argue, however, that solitude has both an upper-case and a lower-case existence. There is an intertextual literary tradition, reviewed in Zimmermann's treatise and revisited in prose and poetry throughout the modern period. And there is a tradition of commonplace practices which have been and remain of critical importance to men and women of every level of society and education as they seek to balance their lives and find space for themselves amidst the demands of company.

Cowley's 'little intervals of accidental Solitude' were not the exclusive preserve of the privileged, whether male or female. For most of the population at the turn of the nineteenth century, even in urbanizing England, many of such opportunities as existed were to be found in the rural economy. In 1800, the labourer poet Robert Bloomfield wrote in *The Farmer's Boy* of the young lad tending a field of growing wheat and in the course of his daily labour enjoying 'his frequent intervals of lonely ease. ... Whence solitude derives peculiar charms'.[115] As Chapters 3 and 5 will explore, there were times in the working day when the demands of labour could be suspended, the more so before the imposition of factory-based time discipline. In the home there were again moments of escape, their incidence varying according to the numbers and ages of children. The density of company varied over the course of the day as men went out to labour and increasingly children left for school. And always, particularly but not only in rural areas, there were the gardens, lanes, and fields beyond the front door where it was possible for fleeting periods to be alone with yourself.[116]

Upper- and lower-case categories of solitude have to be seen in relation to each other. There needs to be a focus on the exchange between the literary discourse and everyday attitudes and practices. In his classic study of the related subject of the pastoral ideal in American life, Leo Marx argues that 'to appreciate the significance and power of our American fables it is necessary to understand the interplay between the literary imagination and what happens outside literature, in the general culture'.[117] Over the period from 1800, there were a series of fierce debates on topics, for instance, such as solitary confinement, which will be examined in Chapter 4, where there was complex movement between high-level theoretical arguments, some of which went back to the monastic tradition with which Zimmermann was so preoccupied, and the actual and perceived experiences of common criminals. By the same measure, as Chapter 7 argues, it is impossible to understand the emergence of the pathology of loneliness in a range of sociological, psychiatric and medical studies unless a clear view is kept of the basic features of demography, household structure and standards of living from the nineteenth century onwards. More generally, successive information revolutions, from the Penny Post to the internet, profoundly altered the sense of what solitude was and might be as a communicative experience.

At the same time, lower-case solitude remains a neglected topic in its own right. From Robert Bloomfield to our own era, opportunities for casual withdrawal from company have been sought and enjoyed. In his *Solitude: A Philosophical Encounter*, Philip Koch writes that, 'One of the most fervently celebrated virtues of solitude is its ability to provide a place of refuge from the beleaguered toils of social life.'[118] These may take the form of extended leaves of absence from daily rituals, but more often they are borrowed moments from pressured lives. For most of the population most of the time, solitude has been a snatched experience found in contexts where company and its absence are equal and overlapping possibilities. This will be the central concern of Chapter 3 on the nineteenth century, and Chapter 5 on the twentieth and early twenty-first centuries. Whilst the latter-day advocates of monasticism and long-term retreats who will be discussed in Chapter 6 sometimes presented the practices as a form of spiritual base-jumping, risking sanity in a high-risk encounter with prolonged silence and self-examination, the more general pattern has been to embrace solitude simply as a form of relaxation from work and family. In the words of Diana Senechal's *Republic of Noise*, 'Solitude contains great leisure. To be in solitude is to rest, even momentarily, from meeting the demands of others.'[119]

There is a need for what might be termed a quiet history of British society. Too little attention has been paid to the intermittently organized, often silent, re-creative practices that have been and remain a vital presence in the lives of most men and women in the modern world. Ira Cohen's *Solitary Action: Acting on Our Own in Everyday Life* catalogues the 'numerous . . . public sites where we find people engaged in solitary activities', together with 'our homes, where at various times of the day individuals find themselves alone or claim zones of solitude in order to do some housework or homework or recreate by themselves', and observes that 'this hitherto half-hidden realm of human behaviour' is 'a suitable subject for sociological enquiry'.[120] What is true of the present applies also to the past. Social historians, like social scientists more generally, have tended to focus on communal, noisy forms of activity. This is partly from a desire to emphasize the complexity of interactions at all levels of society and not just amongst the educated and privileged. It is partly from a sense that collective practices have been the locus of historical change. And it is also a matter of evidence. Bloomfield's farm boy enjoying his 'frequent intervals of lonely ease' left no mark on the public record, neither did the weary housewife stepping outside the house for a few moments of private peace. Even where historians have stooped to consider the pastimes of the common people, the tendency has been to concentrate on rough sports and commercialized mass entertainment which one way or another generated a trail of commentary and paperwork.[121]

There are, however, a number of historical sources which between them permit the creation of at least a patchwork quiet history. A fertile archive was generated by the continual expansion of networked solitude. As we shall see in the next two chapters, from the beginning of the period covered by this study, solitary pastimes called forth a literature of periodicals and monographs which serviced isolated practices. A year after Zimmermann's treatise first appeared in English, *The Sporting Magazine* began publication, carrying, amongst much else, information on long-distance solo walking against the clock, a popular constituent of the vibrant gambling culture of the era.[122] From the late eighteenth century through to the present day, the energetic and responsive publishing industry produced material on a proliferating range of private pastimes. Alongside these there were monographs on the most salient quiet recreations, such as fishing and gardening, although these infrequently addressed the breadth of popular participation. From the last quarter of the nineteenth century, practitioners of all kinds of unseen hobbies, from embroidery to stamp collecting, began to form themselves into associations which created their own archives and publications. During the more recent past, oral histories and social surveys have extended their scope to examine the quotidian lives of the mass of the population. Finally there are the commentators from within the everyday world in the form of memoirs and imaginative literature. A champion of Robert Bloomfield was John Clare, one of the very few writers of his own or any subsequent period capable of engaging with both upper- and lower-case solitude, and his poetry and prose will form the point of departure for the next chapter.

In Zimmermann's critical universe, solitude, for good or ill, was consciously practised by only a small minority of the population. The most striking change over the modern period was the expansion of the numbers of men and women who deliberately set aside time for themselves in the absence of company. Their behaviour was testament both to the growing demand for restorative withdrawal and the sustaining influence of material and communicative resources. As Chapters 7 and 8 will argue, persisting and in some cases deepening domestic poverty in the era of late modernity, together with growing disinvestment in public services, threatened to reverse these changes, generating a sense of crisis about the pathology of failed solitude in the form of loneliness. At the same time, the digital revolution in the last few years of this study seems likely to cause a significant disruption of the established patterns of networked solitude. Critical solitude, the search for alternative forms of spiritual truth in the face of corrupting social relations, had a fierce energy throughout this period, driven by the accelerating movement of the population from the countryside to the towns. But as will be discussed in Chapter 6, there were growing difficulties in maintaining the authority of the Christian retreat and the sanctity of nature as a refuge from urban civilization. The demand persisted, but in an increasingly diffuse and personalized form.

The Tally Ho Stakes

The posthumous life of *Solitude Considered* travelled far from its origins. 'Zimmerman on Solitude' became a cultural object in its own right, largely independent of the full text.[123] During the course of the nineteenth century, it was treated as a shorthand for an uncritical endorsement of the subject. A young man or woman seeking to be considered serious and soulful would like to be seen with a copy as they walked in the countryside or found space for quiet reading at home. As with other literary successes, it enjoyed an existence in diverse recreational forms, including, in this case, horse racing. In March 1845, Mr Wesley's three-year-old 'Solitude by Zimmerman' was entered for the Tally-Ho Stakes at the Northampton and Pytchley Hunt. It set off at a great pace, but at the first turn the horse bolted, leaving its rival, 'D'Egville', to build up a lead of three hundred yards.[124] Eventually the rider regained control of his steed. The newspaper report concluded: 'Solitude, however, made up for lost time on coming up the flat, and was only beaten by about three lengths.'[125]

2

SOLITUDE, I'LL WALK WITH THEE

Clare, Keats, and Solitude

In the spring of 1820, John Clare discussed his poem 'Solitude' with John Keats. They were unable to meet face to face. Clare had for the first time in his life travelled to London earlier in the year at the invitation of his publisher, John Taylor. He was anxious to meet Keats, who shared his literary manager, but in the event Keats was too unwell to attend the dinner arranged by Taylor. Clare was back home in Helpston by the time Keats's health temporarily improved, and to his great regret he was never to meet a man whom he greatly admired both as a poet and as 'a brother wanderer in the rough road of life & as one whose eye picks now & then a wild flower to cheer his solitary way'.[1] After Keats's death in Rome in February 1821, Clare wrote a sonnet in his memory.

As with all the material that was published in *The Village Minstrel* the following year, Clare's 'Solitude' was the product of toil. He explained to a correspondent early in 1820 that it 'was written by scraps last summer in all the bustle of hard labour',[2] and he looked forward to Keats's judgement. In the absence of a direct encounter, Taylor managed an epistolary conversation between his two young poets.[3] He showed the three-hundred-line poem to Keats and relayed his comments by letter, to which Clare responded. Taylor reported that Keats liked 'Solitude' but had reservations about the balance of the poem: 'When I read Solitude to [Keats] he observed that the Description too much prevailed over the Sentiment. – But never mind that – it is a good Fault – and besides you know I must have something to cut out, or "Othello's Occupation's gone" as the Play says.'[4] Keats's response reflected his more general view of Clare's work. In a further letter later in the year Taylor wrote to Clare that 'I think he wishes to say to you that your Images from Nature are too much introduced without being called for by a particular Sentiment.'[5]

It is not difficult to understand Keats's reaction. The poem's invocation of its topic appeared to be trying to rewrite 'Elegy Written in a Country Churchyard' from the perspective of Thomas Gray's 'plowman':

> Now as even's warning bell
> Rings the day's departing knell,
> Leaving me from labour free,
> Solitude, I'll walk with thee[6]

It took off into an extensive description of the life in the fields around Clare's home, deploying his precise observation of nature and his evocative local vocabulary:

> And the little chumbling mouse
> Gnarls the dead weed for her house,
> While the plough's unfeeling share
> Lays full many a dwelling bare[7]

From time to time Clare devoted a few more lines to his ostensible subject before returning to what Keats characterized as 'Description'.[8] The references to solitude borrowed from the long-standing characterizations of the oppressive urban world which the poet sought to escape. James Thomson's *The Seasons*, a profound influence on Clare as on every other working-class reader and writer of the early nineteenth century, wrote of 'these iron times / These dregs of life'.[9] It was a theme echoed by Peter Courtier, whose long poem 'The Pleasures of Solitude' enjoyed a success at the turn of the century: ''Tis sweet, escaping from the throng's turmoil, / To breathe the cooling freshness of the grove.'[10] In turn Clare found the most obvious rhyme for his topic: 'O thou soothing Solitude, / From the vain and from the rude.'[11] Solitude appeared to be a necessary summit for every aspiring poet to ascend, and in his concern to be taken seriously by established writers and their audience, it was one he could not ignore.

There is, however, another way of reading the poem, which brings the component parts into a single frame, notwithstanding the occasional descent into routine 'Sentiment'. The opening lines defined the topic as a process of movement: 'Solitude, I'll walk with thee.' The emotion was at once an external presence that accompanied Clare and a product of ambulatory observation. As with so much of his poetry, the narrative both described and was made possible by the writer walking along the paths around his home. Sometimes the journey itself constituted the subject. In his *Sketches in the Life of John Clare*, Clare described the beginning of his life as a poet. On his way to work he climbed over the wall of Burghley Park to read a book out of sight of his censorious neighbours:

> the Scenery around me was uncommonly beautiful at that time of the year and what with reading the book and beholding the beautys of artful nature in the park I got into a strain of descriptive rhyming on my journey home this was 'the morning walk' the first thing I commited to paper I afterwards wrote the evening walk and several descriptions of Local Spots in the fields which I had frequented for Pootys, flowers, or Nests in my early childhood.[12]

On other occasions the intense observations of the natural world arose from successive encounters as he proceeded around his deeply familiar but constantly surprising landscape. It was a bounded world. There were four visits to London at the height of his fame, and the confused, desperate attempt to walk home after the final move to the asylum in Essex, but otherwise his explorations were within a few miles of Helpston, as would be the case with any farm labourer of the period.[13] Some used public highways, but most perambulations were along tracks known only to the villagers and leading to destinations which had meaning only for the local population.[14] Clare's intense consciousness of the value of footpaths and the freedom to use them was at the centre of his bitter critique of enclosures. He wrote in the titular poem of *The Village Minstrel*:

> There once were lanes in nature's freedom dropt,
> There once were paths that every valley wound, –
> Inclosure came, and every path was stopt;
> Each tyrant fix'd his sign where paths were found,
> To hint a trespass now who cross'd the ground[15]

This is a chapter about walking as both a location of solitude and a means by which solitude was given form and meaning. The nineteenth century was the last great era of pedestrian travel. For most people in most locations, everyday movement was conducted on foot. Only the well-to-do made regular use of a horse, and only the seriously wealthy secluded themselves within their own carriage. The great communications revolution of the period, the steam train, displaced the stage-coach, but few of those who had previously walked long distances could regularly afford to purchase tickets. Although urban transport systems in the second half of the century began to offer alternatives to walking to work, the trains in and out of the main towns and cities also served to enlarge the possibilities of recreational walking, making accessible local beauty spots as well as more distant and wilder destinations. Not until the arrival of the bicycle and motor vehicles was the sovereignty of the footstep challenged.

Walking was the simplest means of escaping company, especially from the overcrowded domestic interiors of the period. As with other forms of solitude, there were fluid boundaries between solitary and social practice, with few forms of pedestrian locomotion exclusively private or necessarily collective. In general terms, as the next section will discuss, the poorer the pedestrian the more likely it was that their solitude was forced rather than chosen, particularly in respect of their work experience. Walking was the most ordinary and least considered of tasks and recreations, and at the same time an intensely literary experience. Clare was sharply aware of the conversations he was having with his textual predecessors and contemporaries, and over the succeeding century walkers took books with them to read in secluded locations and in turn contributed to the diversifying literature of pedestrian exercise. The speed of movement on foot was ideally suited to reflection on both the natural and the man-made environment. It offered the combination of a constantly changing perspective and a capacity to bring into focus what was discovered and seen. The undistracted, mobile gaze permitted immersion without capture whether the walker was exploring fields and woods, or pacing the streets of the rapidly expanding urban communities. Pedestrian solitude was at once physical and constructed. The middle-class trampers who will be considered in the third part of this chapter found solitude in a countryside that was teeming with agricultural labourers, and the urban explorers saw isolated pedestrians who were in practice attracted to the towns and cities because of the greater choice they offered in modes of association. Over the course of the century, as the final section will discuss, rail transport opened up new opportunities for extreme personal endeavour, where solitude was not so much a matter of physical company as individual risk-taking in the last unspoiled spaces of God's creation.

The Crusoe of His Lonely Fields

Whether alone or in company, the labouring classes walked either out of necessity, or as a fugitive activity amidst the requirements of housework and paid labour. Unless they were skilled artisans living over the shop, most working men had to begin and end their days on their feet, sometimes covering several miles before they could begin to earn their living. Those employed on farms travelled to and from different fields as the demands of cattle and seasonal crops varied. Clare gave an overview of rural mobility in 'The Shepherd's Calendar':

> Now maidens fresh as summer roses,
> Journey from the distant closes,
> Haste home with yokes and swinging pail;
> The thresher, too, sets by his flail
> And leaves the mice at peace again . . .
> Bearing his hood beneath his arm,
> The shepherd seeks the cottage warm;
> And, weary in the cold to roam[16]

The labourer returning home had long been a favourite topic of nature poets, combining sympathy and gratitude in an unthreatening image. 'Home, from his morning task,' wrote James Thomson, 'the swain retreats / His flock before him stepping to the fold: / While the full-udder'd mother lows around, / The cheerful cottage, then expecting food.'[17] There was a truth in the relief felt at the end of a day's toil, as Clare acknowledged, but the reality of the walk to and from work in every kind of weather, often in the gloom of winter months, was anything but romantic. The agricultural union leader Joseph Arch remembered his early days without affection: 'Many a time and oft in the dark and early hours of the morning has little Joe Arch, the ploughboy, trudged up the lane, "creeping like a snail unwillingly to work," with his satchel on his shoulder, containing, not books, but his food for the day.'[18] William Howitt's *Rural Life of England* painted a picture far from the conventional pastoral, where the labourers 'pass their lives in the solitude of the fields; and go to and fro between their homes and the scene of their duties, often through deep and lonesome dells, through deep, o'ershadowed lanes by night; by the cross-road, and over the dreary moor: all places of no good character'.[19] In the growing towns and cities, there was less variation in the destination of the walk to work, but it remained an additional physical task to the labour itself. 'Many a time,' recalled Charles Shaw as a child-worker in the Potteries, 'after fourteen and fifteen hours' work, I had to walk a mile and a half home with another weary little wretch, and we have nodded and budged against each other on the road, surprised to find our whereabouts.'[20]

For agricultural workers in particular, the walk to work could end with a day in solitude at the behest of an employer. Farming was much more labour-intensive than it has become in the mechanized era, but the ploughman and shepherd with only their horses or sheep to keep them company were familiar figures, as was the child marooned in a field all day keeping birds from the crops or preventing livestock from straying. The chief memory Alexander Somerville had of his early working life in the Scottish borders was of his own company:

> Long summers of my boyish life were spent amid these woods, and in the rocky ravine of the Ogle Burn, with the cows which I herded,

in almost unbroken solitude, with only the birds singing in the trees, and my dreamy thoughts, and the incessant invention of my organ of constructiveness to amuse me. In the farm fields, sheltered by those woods, I drove the harrows, and held the plough, when I grew out of the office of herding cows.[21]

This isolated apprenticeship to the world of labour began before the conclusion of such education as was available. 'From the time he was nine,' wrote Margaret Ashby of her father, 'Joseph would spend long, lonely days in school vacations and on Saturdays scaring crows off the short, green corn. He had a wooden clapper, but if he saw no one for hours he took to shouting so as to hear a human voice. This method had another convenience; you couldn't cry while you shouted.'[22]

In the lives of the labouring poor there was a porous distinction between walking and going for a walk. The everyday requirement of getting to work or going shopping for the most part rendered the exercise so commonplace as to be barely an event. In the distributed populations of the countryside, keeping the household economy supplied frequently meant lengthy journeys. Flora Thompson recalled that in her Oxfordshire hamlet 'it was thought nothing of then to walk six or seven miles to purchase a reel of cotton or a packet of tea, or sixpen'orth of pieces from the butcher to make a meat pudding for Sunday. Excepting the carrier's cart, which only came on certain days, there was no other way of travelling.'[23] The carrier was one of the few affordable means of transport, but the cost had to be set against a foregone expenditure on some necessity. In the towns the penny economy of most working families meant that a trip to the shop was part of the daily routine, bringing with it at least the opportunity of temporary release from cramped accommodation. A Swiss visitor observed of eighteenth-century London that walking was the most common outdoor recreation.[24] As with many forms of leisure, it was intrinsically neither sociable nor solitary. The activity fulfilled the requirement of an easy transition between the two states. In the nineteenth century, the last century in which pedestrian locomotion was the dominant mode of personal movement, the activity provided opportunities for every kind of social interaction, or none at all. It could be a means either of casually meeting neighbours on neutral territory or of escaping company of the household and finding time for yourself. Pedestrian solitude was at heart the most improvised of all the forms of taking personal time.

Where there was no practical purpose, simply taking a stroll along the street or out into the lanes and fields was, as it had been for centuries, the single most available and widely practised form of active leisure. It was what the modern philosopher of walking Frédéric Gros describes as 'the *suspensive* freedom that comes by walking, even a simple short stroll: throwing off the burden of cares, forgetting business for a time'.[25] As I have argued elsewhere, it was a particularly important means of enjoying privacy for the large majority of the population who lacked the domestic space to withdraw from the company of other members of their household.[26] The front door that kept strangers out could also release the occupants from each other's society. In the words of Miles Jebb, 'It provided a blessed moment of privacy in a life crammed communally into crowded rooms, and an intimate touch with the natural world in all its annual variety.'[27] This unrecorded, and largely unstudied, pedestrian recreation was the simplest, cheapest and least preventable means of relaxation in a toiling life. It was a precious exercise of choice as to whether company was embraced or escaped.[28]

At some point, the casual stroll became a definable walk. The factory bell was the fate of only a minority of the working population. Those engaged in casual labour, in artisan workshops or in agriculture would find spaces opening up during the year when they could make more extended pedestrian excursions, out of reach of their employers and other family commitments. Clare's *Journal* contains a series of entries which simply state 'Took a Walk in the fields' during or after the working day.[29] Skilled artisans rarely found themselves in continuous employment six days a week, month to month. In London the struggling journeyman breeches maker Francis Place took the opportunity of the frequent downturns in his business to walk out of what was still a compact city:

> In fine weather I used frequently to saunter into the fields and in these excursions I explored all the roads, lanes and paths within five or six miles of London, and to a greater distance in the County of Surrey. On these excursions I very seldom had a companion. I usually bought a twopenny loaf and ate it outside some road or lane side public house,

drinking half a pint of beer which cost a penny, and this was my dinner.[30]

Within work, two of the most emblematic new occupations of the nineteenth century were founded on walking. The measured and supervised 'beat' of the policeman and the postman's delivery round were aspirational jobs, requiring both a basic level of education and demonstrable physical fitness. If the strolling policeman was not always a figure of respect and affection, after 1840 the postman (or sometimes, as in Flora Thompson's case, postwoman) coming down the street with a bag of pre-paid letters was the single most visible representative of the state in the lives of the civilian population in every corner of the British Isles.[31]

Whatever their trade, Sunday was a day not so much of rest as of freedom from the demands of employers. Clare celebrated the change in his 'Sunday Walks' of 1818:

> A six-days' prisoner, life's support to earn
> From dusty cobwebs and the murky barn,
> The weary thresher meets the rest that's given,
> And thankful soothes him in the boon of heaven;
> But happier still in Sabbath-walks he feels,
> With love's sweet pledges poddling at his heels[32]

Processing to church or chapel was a public ritual, but just walking was the most common activity for the 'six-days' prisoner' and his family. Clare found himself in trouble when his footsteps took him away rather than towards the Sunday service: 'I got a bad name among the weekly church goers forsaking the "church going bell" and seeking the religion of the fields tho I did it for no dislike to church for I felt uncomfortable very often but my heart burnt over the pleasures of solitude & the restless revels of ryhme [sic].'[33] In the afternoons the Sunday walk was an established ritual for all members of the household. Well before cheap train excursions, ferries and steamers were carrying urban populations out of smoky towns for a day's gentle exercise. As early as 1833 twenty thousand people were crossing the Mersey on a Sunday to take a walk in the cleaner air of Cheshire.[34] Parents and children spent time together, and for those seeking to begin a marriage, stepping out on a

Sunday, as far as possible out of sight of inquisitive neighbours, was a crucial opportunity. Robert Bloomfield celebrated Sabbath courtship:

> Hither at times, with cheerfulness of soul,
> Sweet village Maids from neighbouring hamlets stroll,
> That like the light-heel'd does o'er lawns that rove,
> Look shyly curious; rip'ning into love[35]

During the nineteenth century, material improvements in communication were experienced across society.[36] The main thoroughfares became safer and increasingly better surfaced during the eighteenth century. While the fastest means of horse-drawn movement became obsolete, the transport arteries continued to improve. A series of legislative interventions, culminating in the Highways Act of 1835, enforced a standard pattern on the width and construction of roads. Within towns, better efforts were made to separate pedestrians and traffic, with regulations on the width of pavements. If nothing else, setting out on a journey by foot presented less of a threat to life and limb as the century progressed. There were increasing numbers of carts and other horse-drawn vehicles on the roads, but these rarely exposed pedestrians to the kind of mortal danger presented by a stage-coach travelling at full speed. Not until the arrival of the motor car, which killed its first pedestrian in England in 1896, did walkers once more have to take absolute care with what else was sharing their space. As Jo Guldi has argued, the long-term developments favoured the lone walker.[37] In earlier eras, travellers on the roads clustered together for collective defence against robbers or wild animals and mutual assistance on un-signposted, ill-maintained highways.[38] Now a national network of roads, the disappearance of toll-houses, a growing supply of maps, guidebooks, and signposts, and an increasing provision of inns, hotels, and lodging houses made it unnecessary to talk to anyone before reaching a destination.

Developments in transport systems introduced a greater element of time discipline in the practice of walking. All levels of society, from the gentlemen ramblers who will be discussed in the next section, to working people out for an excursion, began to pay more attention to planning their activities. Horse-drawn omnibuses, and during the second half of the century trams and suburban railway lines, supplied time-tabled means of traversing towns and cities. A measure of change in the period was the career of Richard Jefferies, John Clare's greatest successor in the nineteenth century as an observer of the natural world in England. The son of a failing small farmer, he was raised partly in the Wiltshire village of Coate and frequently returned to the landscapes of his childhood. However, the need to earn a living as a writer required him to spend much of his adult life in the south London suburbs. He became a commuter-naturalist, catching the train out of the city and returning at the day's end with the sights and smells of his explorations still about him. Thus his chosen path through the woods and fields is shaped by an inevitable destination:

> After rambling across furze and heath, or through dark fir woods; after lingering in the meadows among the buttercups, or by the copses where the pheasants crow; after gathering June roses, or, in later days, staining the lips with blackberries or cracking nuts, by and by the path brings you in sight of a railway station. And the railway station, through some process of mind, presently compels you to go up on the platform, and after a little puffing and revolution of wheels you emerge at Charing Cross or London Bridge, or Waterloo, or Ludgate Hill, and, with the freshness of the meadows still clinging to your coat, mingle with the crowd.[39]

So it was with the increasing volume of excursion walkers, some alone, some in the walking clubs that began to proliferate towards the end of the century. On the days freed from labour they stood on station platforms, holding tickets for a framed escape into the countryside.

There remained, however, major differences in how the prosperous and dispossessed exploited their opportunities for solitary pedestrian progress. This is most apparent in the description of distance. Thomas De Quincey, in an essay on the Lakeland poets, made a much-cited calculation that in spite of his indifferent legs, over his lifetime 'Wordsworth must have traversed a distance of 175,000 to 180,000 English miles – a mode of exertion which, to him, stood in the stead of alcohol and all other animal spirits.'[40] Everyday pedestrians proceeded at speeds varying from three and four miles an hour to barely visible movement. However, from the early eighteenth century onwards, feats of speed and endurance by walkers attracted increasing public interest. Shorter distances were accomplished at a pace of up to six miles an hour, and longer marches were undertaken at a consistent fifty to eighty miles a day. The driving force was gambling, which embraced the two fundamental modes of locomotion of the era, on horseback and on foot. William Thom's survey *Pedestrianism* of 1813 noted that 'Mr Foster Powell was the most celebrated pedestrian of his time; and in the performance of long journies has seldom been equalled. – In 1773, he walked from London to York, and back again, in six days, for a wager of one hundred guineas.'[41] The exploits were solitary endeavours, sometimes assisted by support teams, and at their conclusion were capable of generating large audiences. The richest event of the period was the attempt by the 'Celebrated Captain Barclay' in 1809 to walk a thousand miles in a thousand hours. The initial wager was a symmetrical thousand guineas, although immense side-bets were made, allegedly amounting in one case to £100,000.[42] The growing print media were integral to the culture, generating nationwide interest and accumulating lists of achievements to be celebrated or exceeded.

Over the course of the nineteenth century, walkers continued to compete against the clock. In the 1880s, 'go as you please' contests became popular, with bets being made on how far individuals could walk or run in six days on a circular track.[43] But the solo long-distance pedestrians never regained the level of national celebrity they had enjoyed in the era of Captain Barclay. It was partly that the railways transformed the interest in speed, and partly that the process of setting new times was undermined by increasing doubts about the boundary between walking and running. What connected these measured pedestrian feats was the absence of need.[44] The competitors walked for no other purpose than breaking records and winning wagers. Most covered measured distances between two locations, although Barclay's thousand miles went nowhere at all. His feat was undertaken in front of an increasingly large audience on a circular course marked out on Newmarket Heath and illuminated by seven gas lamps. Wordsworth had many reasons for his excursions, but none of them were critical to earning his daily bread.

By contrast, there are the narratives of walking that fill the pages of James Dawson Burn's *The Autobiography of a Beggar Boy*, published in 1855. As a child and a young man, he spent his days traversing the Scottish borders, with occasional excursions to Wales and the south of England. Under the control of his alcoholic stepfather, he was eking a living on the margins of the economy, sometimes as an itinerant dealer or as a casual labourer, and often as an outright beggar, seeking a meal and a bed as he arrived penniless in yet another strange village or town. The purpose of his walking was not a destination, but a living. Movement was inescapable, although there were periods when he settled to a few months' employment, and at one point he managed to serve part of an apprenticeship as a hatter. There was no point in keeping a precise record of such excursions. In his autobiography, Burn noted occasional epic journeys as matters of suffering rather than achievement. Effort brought no great reward. The 'hardest day's work I ever had in my life', he wrote, was a tramp of sixty-two miles to obtain what turned out to be three weeks' labour in the harvest.[45] Alexander Somerville decided to go to sea at the age of fourteen, walked a circuitous route from Branxton in the Scottish Borders to Berwick-on-Tweed to find a ship, changed his mind, and was back home, weary and footsore, by nightfall: 'The distance I had travelled over that day surprised them, as it may do many, considering the want of food; but the number of fifty-two miles is correct, including what I walked in the morning, before I turned.'[46]

As continuous journeys, setting out day after day until work eventually was found, these uneducated labourers entered Wordsworth's territory of long-distance walking, without a De Quincey to do the sums. In 1830, Burn found himself exposed to a general economic depression: 'I obtained employment in Glasgow, where I worked until 18th of October; having lost my work a second time through the slackness of business, I left my family, and went on tramp in search of employment. I travelled 1400 miles upon this occasion ere I could obtain work. At last I got shopped in Sherborne, in Dorsetshire.'[47] He remained there for two months, and then walked another 130 miles to look for a job in London. Skilled, unionized workers of the period enjoyed more income and status but were exposed to tramps of similar distance, particularly in years of bad trade. Elaborate systems of houses of call and living expenses were established to remove skilled workers from over-stocked local economies and enable them to find work elsewhere in the country. The detailed records kept by the Steam Engine Makers' Society between 1835 and 1846 indicate that the average annual tramp was 129.4 miles, rising to a peak of 333.8 in the bad year of 1841–2, with six of the Society's members travelling over a thousand miles.[48] The only rest permitted to their weary feet was occasional deck fares on coastal shipping. Where the occupations were too spatially concentrated to sustain long-distance tramping, there remained, as the mechanic Benjamin Shaw discovered, the task of walking between neighbouring towns in search of employment.[49]

The circumstances that caused labouring people to set out on pedestrian expeditions ranged from the most pressing necessity to the most casual pleasure. They walked because everyone in their community had always walked, but the function of such exercise was gaining a more literary form in this period. John Clare's pleasure in his explorations was both highly personal and widely shared amongst the writers who were developing what Anne Wallace terms the 'peripatetic' literary mode.[50] As he wrote, he had before him both the recollection of his own wanderings and a wide reading in the poetry and prose of rural exploration. James Thomson's *The Seasons* repeatedly returned to the necessity of the personal escape into the quiet of the countryside:

> Then is the time,
> For those whom Wisdom and whom Nature charm,
> To steal themselves from the degenerate crowd,
> And soar above this little scene of things . . .
> Thus solitary and in pensive guise,
> Oft let me wander o'er the russet mead.[51]

He invoked 'Inspiration' not from society but 'from thy hermit-seat / By mortal seldom found'.[52] By the end of the eighteenth century, such a generalized feeling, which in Thomson's hands referred neither to a specific landscape nor to a personalized walker, was gaining a sharper edge. Robert Bloomfield, whose flush of literary fame with *The Farmer's Boy* gave Clare the confidence to believe that it was possible for a self-taught poet to reach a national audience, transposed Thomson's sentiments into the hard detail of a Suffolk farm labourer's life. He wrote of a prelapsarian nature that was still accessible to the labourer's footsteps.[53] The development of the imagination required the capacity to find a kind of inner exile in the lanes and fields around his home:

> Fancy's fair buds, the germs of song,
> Unquicken'd midst the world's rude strife,
> Shall sweet retirement render strong,
> And morning silence bring to life.[54]

Clare embraced the notion of retirement and translated it into a way of feeling about the fields in which he walked around Helpston. The most compact statement of his experience was written in High Beech asylum sometime before 1856:

> There is a charm in Solitude that cheers
> A feeling that the world knows nothing of
> A green delight the wounded mind endears
> After the hustling world is broken off
> Whose whole delight was crime at good to scoff
> Green solitude his prison pleasure yields
> The bitch fox heeds him not – birds seem to laugh
> He lives the Crusoe of his lonely fields

Crusoe had accompanied Clare's footsteps since childhood: 'the Romance of "Robinson Crusoe",' he recalled, 'was the first book of any merit I got hold of after I coud read'.[55] The attraction of the story was as much as a source of adventure as of hardship: 'new ideas from the perusal of this book was now up in arms new Crusoes and new Islands of Solitude was continually mutterd over in my Journeys to and from school'.[56]

The presence of Defoe's hero in Clare's landscape reflected his immersion in the literature of the peripatetic and the solitary. He was also looking at his fields through the lens of the romantic poets, whom he read widely from the beginning of his career.[57] Wordsworth walked through a vividly described Lake District, and across half of Europe, glorying in the 'independence of the heart' that he achieved: 'And I was taught to feel, perhaps too much, / the self-sufficing power of Solitude.'[58] It was not enough to look out at a dramatic landscape from a fixed viewpoint. The act and the speed of solitary pedestrian locomotion sharpened every sense and opened the mind to deeper feeling. In *The Prelude* Wordsworth describes setting out for a walk in the quiet of the early morning:

> Thus did I steal along that silent road,
> My body from the stillness drinking in
> A restoration like the calm of sleep,
> But sweeter far. Above, before, behind,
> Around me, all was peace and solitude,
> I looked not round, nor did the solitude
> Speak to my eye; but was heard and felt.[59]

Clare was not alone in his enthusiasm for Crusoe. He had borrowed the battered book from another schoolboy, and Defoe's character was a staple figure in children's and adults' reading in the period. *Robinson Crusoe* was one of a handful of texts – Thomson's *Seasons* and Izaak Walton's *The Compleat Angler* were others – which, though the product of a specific cultural and temporal moment, floated free of their context and belonged fully to the nineteenth century, available in frequent new editions, or on second-hand bookstalls.[60] In Clare's case, as with many bright children in semi-literate communities, the act of reading was itself a form of exile, compounded by the further action of taking up a pen.[61] Further on in his memoir he recounted 'the laughs and jeers of those around me when they found out I was a poet'.[62] He described his condition in 'The Progress of Rhyme':

> The curse of the unfeeling throng,
> Their scorn had frowned upon the lay
> And hope and song had died away,
> And I with nothing to atone
> Had felt myself indeed alone.[63]

However, as John Goodridge has recently stressed, Clare's withdrawal from village culture was balanced by a continued mining of its imaginative resources.[64] His immediate response to John Taylor's communication of Keats's criticism of 'Solitude' is illuminating. Instead of appealing to some alternative literary standard, he cited the judgement of his own unlettered community:

> You talk of cutting me about in 'Solitude' I can only say have mercy I have provd your judgment & patiently submit – my lodge house I think will be above your thumbs & Keats too it is (past) undergone the Criticism of my father & mother & several rustic Neighbours of the town & all approve it you will agree they beat your polite Critics in that low nature which you never prove but by reading & which them & I have daily witnessed in its most subtle branches.[65]

In a sense, Clare's continual movement between the lower-case and upper-case cultures was like the act of walking that was so critical to the development of his imagination. Until he entered the asylum, it was always a return journey.[66] He took every opportunity to escape from his family and fellow labourers for the isolation of the fields and woods, but then he walked back home, or to the public house. It was a life of constant limitation, content neither with the sufficiency of the oral and printed resources of his community nor with his access to metropolitan literary circles, comfortable neither with the company of his peers nor with the freedom he could find in an increasingly enclosed landscape. What contained the tensions was the daily ability to make the transition between the social and the solitary, each in its way a grounded reality in the life of the 'Northamptonshire Peasant'.[67]

'There is a charm in Solitude that cheers' also captures the persisting ambiguity of the condition. It is part of a long tradition, stretching back to Petrarch and beyond, and forwards to twentieth-century writers, of opposing a broadly condemned urban society, 'the hustling world . . . / Whose whole delight was crime at good to scoff'. It embodies a sense of exile and impotence. There is no indication that 'green solitude' has the capacity to rectify the pressing evils of his times, or to heal the poet's 'wounded mind'. At the same time the poem is fundamentally a celebration. It describes an experience that is inherently personal and always accessible. Clare walks to his lonely fields at will, and there finds in the absence of company a pleasure that is both playful and profound.

Rambling

In the same year that Clare's 'Solitude' appeared in print, William Hazlitt published the single most influential essay on walking in the nineteenth century.[68] 'On Going a Journey' became a key point of reference for every subsequent attempt to define the purpose and mode of pedestrian locomotion by a new generation of gentlemen ramblers.[69] 'Never start on a walking tour,' advised G. M. Treveleyan, 'without an author whom you love.'[70] In practice, all of these educated walkers were accompanied by texts, whether or not they were carrying a book. Hazlitt debated with earlier authorities, particularly Dr Johnson, and those who continued the literary conversation cited not only 'On Going a Journey' but also a range of writers drawn from two millennia of European culture.

A new enthusiasm for exploring nature on foot was taking shape in the closing years of the eighteenth century and the early decades of the nineteenth. In 1835, Wordsworth was persuaded to add to the growing number of guides to the Lake District, whose landscape his poetry had done so much to bring to the notice of the reading public.[71] He was clear that his writing lifetime had coincided with a fundamental change in the mobility of the 'Persons of taste' whom he was addressing. He associated the change with a growing interest in 'Ornamental Gardening':

> In union with an admiration of this art, and in some instances in opposition to it, had been generated a relish for select parts of natural scenery: and Travellers, instead of confining their observations to Towns, Manufactories, or Mines, began (a thing till then unheard of) to wander over the island in search of sequestered spots, distinguished as they might accidentally have learned, for the sublimity or forms of Nature there to be seen.[72]

Historians of middle-class recreation and the literature of walking have endorsed this account.[73] As George Watson writes, 'the nineteenth century was entirely aware that it had a new and original sense of solitude: the lonely country walk was a conscious, innovative habit among Wordsworthians'.[74]

Whether inhabitants of the expanding towns and cities were transported to the 'sequestered spots' by the last of the stage-coaches or the
first of the steam trains, they were increasingly willing to spend long,
energetic days traversing fields and ascending the modest mountains of
the British landscape. As they did so, there was a sense that they were
for the first time participating in a common culture of mobility. In place
of the basic distinction between those on horseback and those on foot,
or, still more fundamentally, between those in a coach and those trudg-
ing along the dusty highways trying to avoid being run down, the rich
and privileged were now engaged in the same form of locomotion as the
humblest of labourers. The intellectually and morally serious among
them also liked to think that they were employing their feet as did the
ancient philosophers and early Christians. Not only were the respectable walkers adopting the pace of their inferiors, they also had the
opportunity to meet them in the open air, unencumbered by the rituals
of hospitality that protected the privacy of their homes. Wordsworth
possessed a copy of John Thelwall's *The Peripatetic* of 1793, which had
deployed the trope of the pedestrian journey as a means of encountering an 'unhappy rustic' and other labouring men and learning about
their sufferings.[75] Wordsworth's ideal walk comprised long stretches of
striding alone along a road, interspersed with random discussions with
local men and women, whose situations illuminated the stresses of the
expanding market economy.[76]

In the opening of his article, Hazlitt addressed the central question
of whether the activity was intrinsically solitary: 'One of the pleasantest
things in the world is going a journey; but I like to go by myself. I can
enjoy society in a room; but out of doors, nature is company enough
for me. I am then never less alone than when alone.'[77] Jeffrey Robinson
describes the essay as 'a Romantic's argument with Romanticism'.[78] It
took Wordsworth's imaginative release through the encounter with
nature and turned it inwards. The purpose of the walk was not to generate insights and imagery that could be translated into wider literary
communication, but to satisfy a need for personal freedom. 'The soul of
a journey is liberty,' wrote Hazlitt, 'perfect liberty, to think, feel, do just
as one pleases. We go a journey chiefly to be free of all impediments
and of all inconveniences; to leave ourselves behind, much more to get
rid of others.'[79] The footpath or country road was where people were

not, and where there was no prospect of the spoken word: 'mine is that undisturbed silence of the heart which alone is perfect eloquence'.[80] In that quiet it might be possible to reach into the confused body of thoughts and feelings that accumulated in the course of daily life and find meaning in what lay buried within: 'From the point of yonder rolling cloud,' continued Hazlitt, 'I plunge into my past being, and revel there, as the sun-burnt Indian plunges headlong into the wave that wafts him to his native shore. Then long-forgotten things, like "sunken wrack and sumless treasuries," burst upon my eager sight, and I begin to feel, think, and be myself again.'[81]

This combination of mysticism and misanthropy had a long future ahead of it. Half a century later, Robert Louis Stevenson laid out his pedestrian philosophy;

> Now, to be properly enjoyed, a walking tour should be gone upon alone. If you go in a company, or even in pairs, it is no longer a walking tour in anything but name; it is something else and more in the nature of a picnic. A walking tour should be gone upon alone, because freedom is of the essence; because you should be able to stop and go on, and follow this way or that, as the freak takes you; and because you must have your own pace, and neither trot alongside a champion walker, nor mince in time with a girl. And then you must be open to all impressions and let your thoughts take colour from what you see. You should be as a pipe for any wind to play upon.[82]

There was a hierarchy of excursion. It was of course possible to walk in company, and derive pleasure from the exercise. But it was a lesser experience. 'Silence is not enough,' insisted G. M. Treveleyan,

> I must have solitude for the perfect walk, which is very different from the Sunday tramp. When you are really *walking* the presence of a companion, involving such irksome considerations as whether the pace suits him, whether he wishes to go up by the rocks or down by the burn, still more the haunting fear that he may begin to talk, disturbs the harmony of body, mind, and soul when they stride along no longer conscious of their separate, jarring entities, made one together with the mystic union of the earth.[83]

Although most of the tramping took place through cultivated land-scapes, it was an experience divorced from the rural economy and its workforce, and indeed from the occupational world altogether, except insofar as the walk might have to take place at weekends or during annual holidays. The only tolerable presence of people was in the inn or hotel at the end of the day's strenuous exercise, where the staff would provide food and comfort while the travellers exchanged tales of their exploits.

The gentlemanly ramblers were preoccupied with personal endeav-our but not to the point of physical exhaustion. The increasing numbers of middle-class walkers prided themselves on the distance that they could cover in a single day without evident effort. For those educated at the English ancient seats of learning, it was a ritual achievement to stride the fifty-five miles from Carfax to London or the fifty-one miles from King's Parade to the capital. According to Treveleyan, 'Every aspiring Cantab or Oxonian ought to walk to the Marble Arch at a pace that will do credit to the college whence he starts at the break of day.'[84] 'And there is a harder test than that,' he wrote, 'if a man can walk the eighty miles from St Mary Oxon. to St Mary Cantab. in the twenty-four hours, he wins his place with Bowen and a very few more.'[85] Leslie Stephen famously celebrated two forms of strenuous exertion by walking from Cambridge to London in twelve hours for a dinner of the Alpine Club.[86] The effort represented a celebration of wilful physi-cal effort over speed and comfort. There were regular stage-coaches between Oxford, Cambridge, and London, and then train services,[87] but to travel by such means involved a submission to the social and organizational discipline of transport systems, and the enforced com-pany of other travellers. 'Free from all bothers of railway timetables and extraneous machinery,' wrote Stephen of walking more generally, 'you trust to your own legs, stop when you please, diverge into any track that takes your fancy, and drop in upon some quaint variety of human life at every inn where you put up for the night.'[88]

The capacity of ramblers to step out on their own was enhanced by the publishing industry. Guide-books and maps had begun to appear in the 1770s, and by the end of the following century provided a compre-hensive service for the individual rambler. W. H. Hudson, writing in 1909, described the change:

Guide-Books are so many that it seems probable we have more than any other country – possibly more than all the rest of the universe together. Every county has a little library of its own – guides to its towns, churches, abbeys, castles, rivers, mountains; finally, to the county as a whole. They are of all prices and all sizes. If any man can indulge in the luxury of a new up-to-date guide to any place, and gets rid of his old one (a rare thing to do), this will be snapped up by poorer men, who will treasure it and hand it down or on to others.[89]

The literature obviated the need to depend on the local rural population for advice and assistance. Walkers increasingly were isolated not from each other but from the communities through which they passed. The *Field-Path Rambles* series by 'Walker Miles', which began in 1892, supplied train times, maps, and minute descriptions of the prescribed route. The purpose was to reconcile adventure with security: 'To many it must have occurred that a day, or perhaps a week or more, spent among these lofty hills and the delightful open country beyond, would be the most enjoyable did one only know the direction to take and the points of interest to make for.'[90] Nothing was left to chance or inquiry: 'Leaving Lewes railway-station,' began one fourteen-mile itinerary, 'turn to the right and keep straight on uphill to the High-street. Gaining the latter, turn to the right, and avoiding a road forking to the left, follow on down School-hill . . . .'[91]

Over the course of the nineteenth century it became easier to engage in solitary tramping, but the boundary between collective and private walking remained unstable. Below the literary debate, social practice was reshaping the nature of rambling. A casual day's walk amongst fellow enthusiasts was proving attractive to a wider range of men and occasionally women. As the following chapter will discuss, the final quarter of the nineteenth century saw the creation of an extensive organizational framework for quiet recreational activity. Leslie Stephen's informal 'Sunday Tramps' who undertook walks of up to twenty miles in the countryside around London from 1879 onwards were followed by clubs catering for an increasingly diverse membership.[92] Many of these were offshoots of bodies formed for other purposes, such as the Manchester YMCA Rambling Club, which began in 1880, and various political and religious associations. By the end of the century, the upper reaches of the urban working class were extending the pedestrian activities in their daily lives to formal weekend walking expeditions into the rural areas outside the towns and cities.[93] In the larger conurbations the associations began to come together in bodies such as the London Federation of Rambling Clubs, formed in 1905, whose functions included the negotiation of cheaper excursion fares with the railway companies.

Equipped with a map and an open path, lone ramblers remained a familiar presence in the countryside, whether or not they were also members of an organization. The most fundamental hostility to their activities eventually came not from recalcitrant landowners but from within their own culture. Hazlitt's vision of the lone walker stood in opposition to the late Victorian and Edwardian enthusiasm for team sports as the source of physical and spiritual fitness. In the public schools and Oxbridge colleges from which men like Treveleyan and Stephen were drawn, there was increasing emphasis on the mutual dependence and physical contact inherent in organized games. Here were developed what would now be designated the soft skills of courage, co-operation and honour which would fit the individual for leadership of the world's largest empire. Arthur Hugh Sidgwick was from the same background as the solitary walkers. He was educated at Winchester and Balliol, the son a distinguished academic and in his turn a prize-winning scholar, poet, and senior civil servant. His interest in walking, was, however, diametrically opposed to the tradition derived from Hazlitt and his successors. In 1912, he made clear his position on the long debate about whether the tramping gentleman should seek or avoid companions:

> Walking alone is, of course, on a much lower moral plane than walking in company. It falls under the general ban on individual as opposed to communal pursuits. The solitary walker, like the golfer or sculler, is a selfish and limited being, unlike the rower, footballer, or cricketer, who is a member of a community. The point cannot be seriously argued.[94]

It was a matter of both personal morality and national identity. Walking by yourself was neither manly nor British: 'it is plainly better to do things in company than alone: and the solitary walker, if he is honest, will at once resign all claim to the halo of patriotism, disinterested devotion, esprit de corps and good citizenship which encircles the brow of the footballer'.[95]

Walkers venturing from the towns and cities into the countryside increasingly assumed an absence of people, despite the fact that wholly uncultivated, unpopulated landscapes could now only be found on the margins of Britain. They constructed a sense of solitude in the contrast between their striding figure and the empty rural scenes through which they passed. By contrast the urban peripatetic celebrated the experience of being alone through the deliberate refusal of intercourse with every other inhabitant who was passed in the street.[96] From at least as early as John Gay's *Trivia: or, the Art of Walking the Streets of London* of 1716, it had been assumed that the best way of understanding the rapidly expanding towns and cities, particularly the capital, was by engaging in frequent pedestrian excursions through what Gay called the 'long perplexing lanes untrod before'.[97] As the communities outgrew their early-modern limits, it became impossible to comprehend their cartography merely by going about the quotidian social business of labour, consumption, and recreation. Thomas De Quincey, whose youthful perambulations of London streets became a founding text of a literary genre, claimed for himself the status of a Columbus or Captain Cook: 'I could almost have believed, at times, that I must be the first discoverer of some of these *terrae incognita*, and doubted whether they had yet been laid down in the modern charts of London.'[98] The vision of the city as a wilderness awaiting mapping by intrepid explorers became a familiar theme in the writings of the era.[99] A Victorian guide to London insisted that 'no one can see the City properly who does not walk in it'.[100] The flâneur entered French and British literature in the early decades of the nineteenth century as a privileged male observer, restlessly mobile but never engaging with the people and activities that he observed.[101] This form of movement collapsed the mode and the subject of inquiry. The nineteenth-century city was viewed as a society of anonymous strangers, only knowable in the rapid passage of isolated individuals through streets whose by-laws increasingly discouraged loitering in groups.[102]

Those who observed the injunction to learn on their feet were as serious about their exercise as the long-distance rural walkers. Charles Dickens placed himself half-jokingly in the tradition of pedestrian record-breakers: 'So much of my travelling is done on foot, that if I cherished betting propensities, I should probably be found registered in sporting newspapers under some such title as the Elastic Novice, challenging all eleven-stone mankind to competition in walking.'[103] His fierce, fast, urban expeditions might cover twenty miles in a few hours and were a means, amongst much else, of finding physical release from the nervous, static labour of writing to recurring deadlines.[104] Sometimes he assembled a convivial party of friends whose jaunts ended with a dinner or a play. But the essential activity was undertaken alone, at once escaping from and nurturing his fiction and journalism. Like Hazlitt and Stevenson, he was wholly free to direct his own thoughts and footsteps. 'My walking is of two kinds,' he wrote, 'one straight on end to a definite goal at a round pace; one, objectless, loitering, and purely vagabond. In the latter state, no gipsy on earth is a greater vagabond than myself; it is so natural to me, and strong with me, that I think I must be the descendant, at no great distance, of some irreclaimable tramp.'[105] 'The London peripatetic', as he described himself,[106] observed, occasionally stopped to question, but always moved on. The refusal to rest in any one place, and the deliberate absence of system enabled him to map the complex social and economic boundaries in London that would not have been apparent to a static, organized observer:

> a single stride, and everything is entirely changed in grain and charac-
> ter. West of the stride, a table, or a chest of drawers on sale, shall be of
> mahogany and French-polished; east of the stride, it shall be of deal,
> smeared with a cheap counterfeit resembling lip-salve. West of the
> stride, a penny loaf or bun shall be compact and self-contained; east
> of the stride it shall be of a sprawling and splay-footed character, as
> seeking to make more of itself for the money.[107]

Lone urban walking was both curious about and separated from the mass of the population. The mobile observers were committed to expanding their knowledge of urban society but were never absorbed into it. It was an activity riven with class and gender distinction. Labouring men on their way to and from their place of work, or strolling to the public house at the end of the day, did not consider themselves embarked on a course of social investigation, nor were they seeking exercise beyond what their place in the economy imposed upon

them. The distinction between solitary and social walking was much
more fluid and improvised. At best, like Clare's villagers, they might
take the air of an evening or enjoy their free time on Sunday to visit a
green space within or on the edge of the city, with or without the rest of
their family. If a fast-moving, eleven-stone pedestrian stopped to talk to
them, he soon departed. Movement itself was less critical. Sometimes
they were in a hurry, sometimes not. Some days there was a job to go to,
on others their steps were aimless in a far more profound sense than the
gypsy urban rambler. Dickens was as apprehensive as any middle-class
householder of men out of doors for no apparent purpose.[108]

As public authorities sought to increase the speed of transit through
the urban streets, so they legislated to penalize those loitering with
no evident objective. The Vagrancy Act of 1824 specified that 'every
person wandering abroad and lodging in any barn or outhouse, or in
any deserted or unoccupied building, or in the open air, or under a tent,
or in any cart or waggon, not having any visible means of subsistence
and not giving a good account of himself or herself . . . shall be deemed
a rogue and vagabond'.[109] Working-class housewives were constantly
out and about in their neighbourhood, taking part in the local economy, making penny purchases in the nearby shop or just gossiping in
the street and keeping an eye on their playing children. But to be seen
standing still in a public place was immediately to invite the assumption
of immorality. 'Street-walking' was a description of an occupation, not
a mode of getting about. For much of the nineteenth century, respectable women could not be seen by themselves in the thoroughfares
of towns and cities. If they wanted to take a walk, they did so with a
protective male or at least with female companions. The development
of department stores in the 1850s and 1860s created the possibility of a
public destination outside the home that could be reached in company,
but it was not until the closing decades of the century that it began to
become acceptable for a well-bred woman to set out alone on foot for
her own private purpose.[110]

The most obvious solution to the suspicions surrounding lone urban
walking was to take an animal with you. Dog-walking became over the
century a quintessential urban practice. It was an activity circumscribed
by social distinction and legal regulation. The animal was coming to be
seen as an emotional support for the solitary person. In the words of

one of the earliest modern accounts of the value of the dog, it was 'an excellent companion when human society is wanting'.[111] More recent research has confirmed that one of the functions of a dog was to act as a companion animal to otherwise isolated individuals.[112] Amongst the increasing range of pets and breeds which will be examined in the following chapter, the dog stood out for its perceived capacity to engage with human emotions.[113] 'The dog,' claimed Samuel Beeton's survey of domestic livestock, 'far more than any other animal, becomes a humble friend and companion of man, often seeming actually to know and sympathise with the joys and sorrows of his master.'[114] The dog was becoming integral to the cultural and physical construct of the Victorian home, both protecting its inhabitants from intrusion and supplying them with unquestioning warmth and affection.[115]

Unlike most other pets, however, the dog needed to spend time out of doors. During the nineteenth century, an increasingly firm distinction was drawn between walking with a dog and dog-walking. The former implied no physical constraint on the movement of the animal. Merely heading in the same direction as your accompanying dog, which was otherwise free to explore passers-by, interesting smells and spaces, and any other animals in the vicinity, did not conform to the disciplined, purposeful movement that was now the subject of an increasing range of by-laws. Next to the immobile pedestrian, the greatest fear of polite town dwellers was the uncontrolled dog. It was at best a source of noise, pollution and unwanted physical contact for other pedestrians, and at worst a threat to life through the widely feared disease of hydrophobia, or rabies.[116] Dog-walking, on the other hand, implied control of the animal by means of a collar and leash, and, in the case of more aggressive breeds, also a muzzle. Taxing dogs, which began in 1796, was a means of policing their mainly urban owners.[117] Rural working dogs were exempt. By accepting ownership of an animal and paying an annual fee it was assumed that responsibility would also be exercised for its conduct in public places. There were complaints that the tax fell largely on the middle classes, whose careful management of their pets exposed them to the attention of the police, whilst poorer dog-keepers let their animals run free in every sense.[118] By the final third of the century, the numbers were large. Following reforms to the cost and efficiency of taxation in 1867, reliable records were kept.

By 1877, there were nearly 1.4 million licensed dogs in Britain, mostly in towns and cities.[119] At least as many owners again were believed to be avoiding the tax, and an unknown proportion of those will have kept control of their animals in public spaces.[120] But even if we assume that only those who held a licence possessed a collar and lead, the figures represent the single largest army of purposeful walkers of the later nineteenth century and beyond. In every street and urban open space there were solitary, mobile humans accompanied by disciplined and disciplining animals.

Solitary walking could also be justified as a heuristic device. For John Clare, unaccompanied movement on his feet was essential for the larger task of seeing and responding to the beauty and complexity of his natural surroundings. For the urban pedestrian, enclosed, self-sufficient street-tramping was the most appropriate way of understanding the nineteenth-century town or city as a society of strangers. This was both the strength and the limitation of the practice. The trope of urban ano-nymity has a persistent hold. Frédéric Gros in his recent *A Philosophy of Walking* writes of 'An unending succession of strangers' faces, a thick blanket of indifference which deepens moral solitude.'[121] There is some substance to this interpretation. For the migrant from the village or small town, a persistent attraction of the larger community was the ability to go about the streets without disclosing opinions or identity. Where strangers had caused immediate interest and frequently con-cern, now they were passed by without a thought beyond the need to avoid physical collision.

In even the most rapidly expanding cities, however, anonymity was a temporary moment. It was a characteristic of only some of the streets, some of the time. The flow of pedestrians in a main thoroughfare was of a different order to that in a narrow space between tightly built terraces or in a fetid enclosed court. In the busier arteries, the men and sometimes women were moving from one social environment to another, whether between the home and work, or the house and a recreational facility, or merely from the domestic interior to informal gatherings on the street or in a shop. At some distance from a point of departure or arrival, they might become complete strangers; nearer there would be a greater prospect of seeing and been seen by a familiar face. In the street outside their home, everyone was known: neighbours, playing children, nearby relatives, the postman, the frequent visiting tradesmen and street entertainers.

The truly solitary urban dweller, alone not only on the pavement but also at home, was a comparative rarity in the household structures of the period.[122] Migrants generally left their known community when they were confident of finding relatives or fellow villagers in a corner of a town or city. Those who did not travel with a ready-made family, or who failed to find immediate company, made for the uncomfortable society of a lodging house. In his early essay 'Thoughts about People', Dickens conjured the figure of a friendless clerk, working by himself in an office, walking through the streets, eating a solitary meal at five and going home to a 'little back room in Islington'.[123] Such people existed, but they expected that sooner or later they would develop their own networks. There was always a risk of failure, and many migrants made temporary or permanent return journeys to rediscover a familiarity of place and people they had yet to establish.

What motivated the migrants to take the chance was not the pleasure of anonymity itself, but the prospect of greater choice between degrees of solitude and sociability. In the city and the larger towns there were much finer gradations of knowing and being known. Whilst there remained many constraints on living, it was easier to get away from one kind of company and find another, to spend time in wholly familiar or completely strange surroundings, and to experience all points between the extremes. The greater the material success of the migrant, the more the chance of establishing and managing different worlds of privacy and public association. Those, therefore, who walked alone to meet those alone in the street discovered only a partial truth about their urban world. It took a further act of imagination, as Dickens displayed elsewhere, to take the roof off the homes to which the pedestrians returned and seek to understand the life that was led inside.[124]

The Wild

In 1812, Byron was translated from an impecunious minor aristocrat to a national literary sensation by the publication of the first two cantos of *Childe Harold's Pilgrimage*. The poem recorded the wandering journey of its hero, disillusioned with both himself and the European culture that was emerging in the final stages of the Napoleonic Wars. Restless movement across the wilder regions of decayed nations enabled the subject to reflect on his own fallen self and the direction in which modern civilization was travelling. Sublime perspectives, jagged mountains, rushing torrents, constituted a universe unpolluted by the moral and political failings of the age. In this landscape the individual was fundamentally alone and inescapably in company. In Canto II, Byron set out the contrasting forms of solitude which faced modern man. The melancholy pedestrian celebrated the absence of society and the sustaining moral resource of untrodden nature:

> To sit on rocks, to muse o'er flood and fell,
> To slowly trace the forest shady scene,
> Where things that own not man's dominion dwell,
> And mortal foot hath ne'er or rarely been;
> To climb the trackless mountain all unseen,
> With the wild flock that never needs a fold;
> Alone o'er steeps and foaming falls to lean,
> This is not solitude; 'tis but to hold
> Converse with Nature's charms, and view her stores unroll'd.[125]

Alternatively, true isolation was to be found amidst the press of people:

> But midst the crowd, the hum, the shock of men,
> To hear, to see, to feel, and to possess,
> And roam along, the world's tired denizen,
> With none who bless us, none whom we can bless;
> Minions of splendour shrinking from distress!
> None that, with kindred consciousness endued,
> If we were not, would seem to smile the less
> Of all that flatter'd, follow'd, sought, and sued;
> This is to be alone; this, this is solitude![126]

Byron sought celebrity but was nonetheless surprised at the scale of his success. Twenty thousand copies were sold of the first two cantos over the succeeding six years.[127] Given that the price of the book put it beyond the reach of those below the upper-middle class, it must have enjoyed near universal appeal amongst the more prosperous and intel-lectual reading public. There was and would remain in different forms a market for the high literary treatment of solitary experiences in distant wildernesses. The appeal of such reading matter lay in the capacity to work through the place of the self in a changing moral order without personally enduring the expense or physical discomfort of prolonged travel in difficult terrain. Extracting the individual from the toils of daily living and managed surroundings supplied drama, perspective and the chance of coming to terms with past failings and future challenges. The risk of the enterprise lay in the consequences of an imagination no longer tethered to specific social structures and the duties and respon-sibilities that they entailed.

Early in the nineteenth-century debate about solitary encounters with nature, two major texts were written from within Byron's literary circle about the dangers of abandoning, or being abandoned by, human contact. Percy Bysshe Shelley's *Alastor, or The Spirit of Solitude* was published in 1816, just as John Clare was beginning to find his literary feet. Its narrative embodied Shelley's fascination with the power of the imagination in seclusion.[128] Left alone, the mind was the source of imagery whose destructive consequences were beyond prediction or control. The subject of the poem is a poet who withdraws from society and makes a journey into wild, unpeopled nature:

> When early youth had past, he left
> His cold fireside and alienated home
> To seek strange truths in undiscovered lands.
> Many a wide waste and tangled wilderness
> Has lured his fearless steps[129]

The outcome is a desperate search for an unattainable love, increasing mental confusion and physical weakness, and an inevitable death. In case readers of the poem were themselves seduced by the myth of the lonely quest, Shelley attached a preface which summarized with clarity a message that Zimmermann would have fully endorsed:

> They who, deluded by no generous error, instigated by no sacred thirst of doubtful knowledge, duped by no illustrious superstition, loving nothing

on this earth and cherishing no hopes beyond, yet keep aloof from the sympathies with their kind, rejoicing neither in human joy nor mourning with human grief; these, and such as they, have their apportioned curse. They languish, because none feel with them their common nature. They are morally dead. They are neither friends, nor lovers, nor fathers, nor citizens of the world, nor benefactors of their country. Among those who attempt to exist without human sympathy, the pure and tender-hearted perish through the intensity and passion of their search after its communities, when the vacancy of their spirit suddenly makes itself felt. All else, selfish, blind, and torpid, are those unforeseeing multitudes who constitute, together with their own, the lasting misery and loneliness of the world. Those who love not their fellow-beings, live unfruitful lives, and prepare for their old age a miserable grave. [130]

In the year that *Alastor* appeared, Mary Shelley began work on a ghost story, subsequently published in 1818 with a preface by her husband. *Frankenstein, or the Modern Prometheus* is permeated with apprehension at the effects of extreme isolation and the inability of encounters with nature to relieve impending disaster. Victor Frankenstein and his monster pursue parallel paths to their early deaths. After a 'youth passed in solitude', the scientist turns away from his colleagues in pursuit of his intellectual obsession: 'In a solitary chamber, or rather cell, at the top of the house, and separated from all the other apartments by a gallery and staircase, I kept my workshop of filthy creation.'[131] His deepening depression at the consequences of his experiment is briefly lifted by a walking tour in Switzerland:

It was during an access of this kind that I suddenly left my home, and bending my steps towards the near Alpine valleys, sought in the magnificence, the eternity of such scenes, to forget myself and my ephemeral, because human, sorrows. . . . Ruined castles hanging on the precipices of piny mountains; the impetuous Arve, and cottages every here and there peeping forth from among the trees, formed a scene of singular beauty. But it was augmented and rendered sublime by the mighty Alps, whose white and shining pyramids and domes towered above all, as belonging to another earth, the habitations of another race of beings.[132]

However, the monster has tracked him to Mont Blanc and eventually he is forced to set up a new laboratory in a fruitless attempt to generate a mate for his creation. Once more he is 'immersed in a solitude where nothing could for an instant call my attention from the actual scene in which I engaged'.[133] With every person close to him murdered, Frankenstein expires on board a ship in the Arctic wastes.

The monster is a pitiless murderer who is himself pitifully alone. He has become a satanic destroyer because of the failure of his creator to nurture him and his subsequent rejection by everyone he encounters. 'Believe me, Frankenstein,' he protests, 'I was benevolent; my soul glowed with love and humanity: but am I not alone, miserably alone? You, my creator, abhor me; what hope can I gather from your fellow creatures, who owe me nothing? they spurn and hate me.'[134] He has had no childhood. 'No father had watched my infant days,' he laments, 'no mother had blessed me with smiles and caresses.'[135] As an instantly formed adult, he is prevented by his size and appearance from giving or receiving affection, however hard he tries. He wanders away from Frankenstein's laboratory and like his maker finds temporary solace in the natural world, celebrating the return of spring:

> The birds sang in more cheerful notes, and the leaves began to bud forth on the trees. Happy, happy earth! fit habitations for gods, which, so short a time before, was bleak, damp, and unwholesome. My spirits were elevated by the enchanting appearance of nature; the past was blotted from my memory, the present was tranquil, and the future gilded by bright rays of hope and anticipations of joy.[136]

But the release is temporary. It cannot compensate the monster for his repeated exclusion from society or inure him from its consequences. He is driven to a path of murder out of revenge for his isolation and as proof that he too can create desolation. Whilst to his victims he is an inexplicable horror, to himself he is the inevitable product of his utter loneliness. 'My vices,' he explains, 'are the children of a forced solitude that I abhor.'[137] He sets off on an ice-raft to 'the most northern extremity of the globe', where he will 'collect my funeral pile and consume to ashes this miserable frame'.[138]

In the decades following the misadventures of Alastor and

Frankenstein and his monster, the landscape through which they travelled took on a more benign if still dramatic function. Before the final third of the eighteenth century, 'a civilised being', wrote Leslie Stephen, 'might, if he pleased, regard the Alps with unmitigated horror'.[139] Gradually a new sensibility emerged, influenced by Rousseau's passion for the uncultivated scenery to which he and his fictional characters could retreat from the bruising world of urban civilization.[140] There was a celebration of the rocks and torrents and endless perspectives, and increasingly an emphasis on scaling the summits of the mountains rather than just enjoying their view from below. Mont Blanc was publicly climbed for the first time in 1786, and a literature of exploration began to emerge, celebrating notable ascents and providing guides for those seeking to make their own expeditions.[141] In the horse-drawn era, however, the alpine region remained out of reach to all but the handful of British travellers and writers who could afford to engage in long European tours. Everything changed with the construction of railways through France and, in 1844, into Switzerland itself. Now it became possible to fit a climbing expedition into the annual month's holiday available to lawyers, clergymen, academics, and the occasional active businessman. With most of the peaks still unconquered, the 'golden age' of Alpine exploration began.

In a physical sense, Victorian summit climbing was almost exclusively social rather than solitary. The railway termini were still some distance from the serious mountains, and there were opportunities for lengthy solo walks across the valleys to reach the base of the climbs.[142] The Scottish glaciologist James Forbes traversed the Alps twenty-seven times, generally alone, and celebrated the escape from his busy life:

> I always feel a satisfaction and a freedom from restraint when I approach these mountains and their exhilarating atmosphere, which dispel anxiety, and invite to sustained exertion. What a field, indeed, for those whom professional and other cares, and even the habits of the society which they frequent, leave, during a great portion of life, but a few hours together, never a whole day, which can be called their own, to find themselves transplanted to a new position – time at command – no interruptions – no calls, invitations, or engagements – no letters to write or receive but those which give pleasure – surrounded by nature

in its grandest forms, delighting the eye, yet affording far keener pleasure to the intellect, by the interest of the problems which it presents for solution![143]

No serious climber, however, attempted to reach a major summit by himself. The routes were too untried and the techniques and equipment too basic.[144] Furthermore, the certified local guides were well organized and did all they could to compel the increasing flow of English visitors to hire their services. The mountains were ascended by parties in several senses of the term. Groups of friends came out from England, met up with their local support and set off roped together, carrying between them not only their equipment but also plentiful supplies of food and alcohol to be consumed on the summit and other resting points. 'As far as my own experience goes,' wrote the barrister Thomas Hinchcliffe, 'and that of several of my more immediate friends, I can have not the least hesitation in saying that we have always found the processes of eating, drinking, and smoking go on with complete satisfaction on the highest peaks that we have attained.'[145] The climbers then descended to their hotels to celebrate in the company of wives and friends who during the day had stood on the balconies and watched their victorious endeavours through telescopes. The Victorian upper-middle-class male had found a new playground. With a few exceptions, their women merely waited for their safe return.[146]

Solitude on the mountains was a state of mind. It referred first of all to the emptiness of the landscape. The hardened climbers distanced themselves from the increasing crowds of tourists brought out by Thomas Cook and clustering in the valleys. The essence of the venture was to escape company and embrace 'the awful solitude of the Alps'.[147] No matter how busy the resorts, above the snow line everything was free of people and their material traces. There were as yet no cable-cars, no marked routes, and there was little or no detritus from earlier climbs. Here it was possible, as for Clare in the remnants of pre-enclosure Helpston, to encounter nature as it had been left at the Creation. The motive for leaving the cities for the mountains had echoes of the embrace of solitude by Petrarch, whose climb of Mount Ventoux in 1335 is held to be the first ascent merely for the view from the top.[148] The climbers were educated men with ready access to the literary marketplace. Their copious writings were framed by the contrast between their points of departure and destination. Each was driven by the need to escape the soft, corrupting culture of the overcrowded commercial civilization. 'We may turn with greater eagerness than ever,' wrote Leslie Stephen, 'from the increasing crowds of respectable human beings to savage rock and glacier, and the uncontaminated air of the High Alps.'[149] In 1859, *Blackwood's Edinburgh Magazine* reviewed the first set of mountaineering memoirs published by the newly formed Alpine Club. 'The scenes' where the activity is carried out, it concluded, supply the toiler in

> the over-civilised world the greatest attainable change. He is transported from the reek of cities and the dull air of plains, to regions of freshness and vitality, where the air itself seems to produce a kind of innocent intoxication. He is carried away by those railways, which are in general inimical to the hardy physical life, as by magic, in a few hours, and at small cost, into the grandest regions of the earth.[150]

The concomitant perspective was personal challenge. Whilst the climbing memoirs paid appropriate attention to the role of teams on successful ascents, their underlying theme was the risk taken by the narrator. The Alpine peak became a defining test of mid-Victorian manhood. 'It possesses the two great elements of hazard,' wrote *Blackwood's*, 'viz, danger and uncertainty, in the perils to which climbers of high mountains are liable, and the uncertainty of an undiscovered way, the discovery of which is the prize sought for.'[151] It was a particularly national attribute. Commentators celebrated the fact that most of the first ascents in the Alpine golden age were made by British mountaineers, despite the many European climbers in the region. Their achievement demonstrated why Britain had become the world's leading colonial power and supplied the best defence against a threatened decline into 'the mere performance of the duties of wealth and the relaxation of effeminate pleasure'.[152] The individual's willingness to expose himself to the extremes of discomfort and danger in pursuit of a mastery of nature at its most wild and hostile exemplified the importance of intense personal endeavour in mid-Victorian Britain. Towards the end of his account of his climbs, Edward Whymper summarized the particular intersection of landscape and character they displayed:

We glory in the physical regeneration which is the product of our exertions; we exult over the grandeur of the scenes that are brought before our eyes, the splendours of sunrise and sunset, and the beauties of hill, dale, lake, wood, and waterfall; but we value more highly the development of manliness, and the evolution, under the combat with difficulties, of those noble qualities of human nature – courage, patience, endurance, and fortitude.[153]

For as long as mountaineering was a function of both individual spirit and roped-up teamwork, it was possible to present the Alpine culture as an exemplary conjunction of solitary and social endeavour. There were, however, voices protesting at a narrative which sought to combine the ascetism of the desert fathers with the creature comforts of the mid-nineteenth-century bourgeois on holiday. John Ruskin, whose praise of the aesthetic grandeur of the mountains had done much to popularize their exploration, took a sharp view of the '[t]he extreme vanity of the modern Englishman in making a momentary Stylites of himself on the top of a Horn or an Aiguille, and his occasional confession of a charm in the solitude of the rocks, of which he modifies nevertheless the poignancy with his pocket newspaper, and from the prolongation of which he thankfully escapes to the nearest table-d'hôte'.[154] The critical debate gathered momentum with Whymper's disastrous first ascent of the Matterhorn in 1865. A party of four Englishmen and three guides reached the summit just ahead of a rival Italian team, but on the descent, four of the climbers fell to their deaths. It was the most famous climbing tragedy before Mallory and Irvine on Everest in 1924, generating a public inquiry in Switzerland and newspaper commentary across Europe.[155] The rope that broke when the least experienced of the English climbers lost his footing, pulling two other amateurs and a guide to their deaths, disconnected the element of personal risk from the culture of convivial enterprise.

The focus of attention now was on the justification of the individual's embrace of untamed nature. In its leader on the event, *The Times* mourned the loss of the three 'scholars and gentlemen' (the dead guide, Michel Croz, presumably fell into neither category), and attacked a form of bravery that was no longer appropriate to the Victorian civilization:

Every gentleman with a sphere of duties and a station in society requires courage and presence of mind, otherwise he is sure to be scorned and to become an object of civil contempt. . . . But this courage is not acquired in a succession of desperate adventures. The Age of Chivalry is over. A man does not now learn temperance by a toilsome journey through a desert.[156]

At issue was a particular definition of masculine character, and more generally the matter Johann Zimmermann had rehearsed and Percy and Mary Shelley dramatized of the permissible limits of extreme solitary endeavour. Whilst the Swiss guides were earning their living, the English climbers lacked the defence of necessity. In risking their lives on the mountains, they voluntarily exposed loved ones to the prospect of acute suffering. It fell to that redoubtable urban pedestrian explorer Charles Dickens to draw the most pointed contrast between self-indulgent and socially useful personal courage in an article in his periodical *All The Year Round*, two months after the disaster:

We shall be told that 'mountaineering' is a manly exercise. It is so, inasmuch as it is not womanly. But it is not noblemanly when it is selfish. Is it manly to expose a parent, a brother, a wife, to the chance of quite uncalled-for sorrow? To lead them into danger perhaps for the satisfaction of recovering our remains? To tempt hardworking guides, most family men, to expose their lives for no adequate object. . . . Nobody will say or believe that our countrymen (whether Irish, Scotch, or English) are afraid to face danger. But danger should be nobly faced. Compare the man who ascends Mount Cervin, 'prepared to conquer the mountain or die', as reported in the newspapers, with him who braves the cholera, or visits typhus patients.[157]

The golden age of Alpine climbing is held to have ended with the Matterhorn tragedy, but the questions it raised about the legitimacy of individual record-breaking at the edge of the wild, whether on land or water, would be asked again in different contexts, including mountaineering itself, throughout the succeeding century and a half.

A Life Apart from Other Things

Throughout the nineteenth century, walking was the most common-place means of experiencing solitude. 'There was a feeling that I must go somewhere, and be alone,' wrote Richard Jefferies in his autobiography. 'It was a necessity to have a few minutes of this separate life every day; my mind required to live its own life apart from other things.'[158] All but the aged and infirm could step out from their homes or their places of work and discover a means of balancing their existence. It was the essence of the quiet history of recreation, rarely recorded except in its extreme forms, largely unstructured until the rambling associations began to be formed towards the end of the nineteenth century. The activity was made possible by a particular moment in the history of mass communication, with the roads never better maintained and speed confined to the railway tracks. The coming of the motor car would change every calculation of where it was safe and desirable to set out on foot. Nonetheless, in an era when the population doubled and redoubled, the concept and practice of solitary perambulation could never be taken for granted.

In the sense that the wild was the place where humankind was not, a space which could itself be described as solitary, it was to be sought and found throughout the century. It was, for the most part, a micro-wilderness. There might be grand perspectives; determined travellers continued to find their way to the English Lakes, the Scottish Highlands or the Welsh mountains to enjoy scenery as drama. A tiny minority, with a large readership of their endeavours, ventured into the high Alps. But this was not the common ambition. The experience of what Thomas Miller described as 'the green solitudes of the country' rested not on the distance but the intensity of the view.[159] It required a capacity to examine with every sense what could be seen on a day's stroll away from urban homes and excursion destinations. During the week it was a matter of standing in a garden, or finding a moment to walk up the street to the municipal park, which was becoming more common in the second half of the century,[160] or stepping out to the fields which were still within sight of most of the northern manufacturing communities, and recollecting yourself in the face of some familiar fraction of nature. The quality of the gaze dissolved the distraction of other people. Amongst the increasingly energetic gentlemen ramblers this was taken a stage further. Equipped with maps and guidebooks, wearing special boots and clothing, they strode through a still heavily populated countryside and saw only the fields and landscapes that for the most part had been formed and were still maintained by human labour. Equally the urban flâneurs constructed themselves and those they passed as anonymous units in a society of strangers. Pedestrian solitude was as much a state of mind as a physical condition. Where it could not avoid contact with people, it required a particular form of abstraction, assisted, in the case of rural rambles and eventually urban explorations, by networks of print which avoided the necessity of actually speaking to those the walkers passed.

The avoidance of other people also generated its own forms of conflict. At one level, walking was so inconsequential an activity as to be barely noticed by contemporaries. Dog-walking, the one category of pedestrian exercise to be indirectly licensed by the state, grew into the largest single mode of casual solitary exercise with barely a comment by observers or journalists. Other behaviour, such as John Clare's Sunday walks, drew criticism for its rejection of sanctioned collective ritual. Walking without ostensible purpose in urban streets, or loitering between movement, attracted legal penalties. From the enclosures onwards there were legal disputes about the rights of walkers to pursue their paths across private property. More fundamental arguments were generated at the edges of pedestrian culture. The polarity insisted upon by writers from Hazlitt to Stevenson between going alone and going in company provoked resistance towards the end of the century from those proclaiming the virtues of team endeavour. Apprehension grew about the most extreme forms of solitary expedition. There was all the difference between departing with a day's provisions and a return train ticket and setting off on foot for an unpeopled wilderness with no guarantee of physical survival. There was a fascination, born of the Romantic Movement, with the idea of testing physical and emotional strength to destruction by striding away from soft civilization into uncharted wastes. This in turn provoked a reaction, visible in Zimmermann's cautions about non-returnable retreats into total solitude, and given new forms in the nineteenth century, about the irrational and irresponsible rejection of sociable life.

3

HOME ALONE IN THE NINETEENTH CENTURY

The Threat of Idleness

Towards the end of his high-minded treatise on solitude, Johann Zimmermann briefly turned his attention to women's domestic arts. 'It is strange perhaps, but certainly true,' he observed, 'that more bad passions have been calmed and prevented by sewing and knitting, than by all the precepts of prudence, or all the lessons of morality.'[1] His interest in such mundane tasks arose from a broader concern with the consequence of idleness in the absence of company. 'Nothing is so dangerous,' he wrote, 'as the want of some pursuit to interest the passions, to busy the imaginations, and to employ the faculties.'[2] The threat was specific to gender and class. Men were seen to be better able to manage their unbounded imaginations than women, and it was not to be supposed that the wives of the labouring poor were burdened by unfilled spare time. The saving grace of bourgeois home-makers was their long tradition of occupying their hands in activities that demanded sufficient attention to distract the mind from undisciplined thoughts.

The consolidation of the institution and ideal of the middle-class family during the nineteenth century should have extinguished any apprehension about hours spent alone at home. The rapid growth in the population and in urban living did little to disturb the established patterns of household structure. Few people lived by themselves. A range of demographic studies have established that about 95 per cent of households consisted of two or more people. Only 1 per cent of the total population were on their own. There was a limited variation around this average, with some parishes recording the complete absence of lone units when the census enumerator came calling.[3] Unlike the twentieth century, there was almost no change in this period in either the proportion of the elderly in society or their propensity to end their days without company.[4] At any time, around nineteen in twenty men of sixty-five and over and eighteen in twenty women were living with one or more people.[5] Detailed analysis of the co-location of relatives, particularly widowed parents and their children, did not begin until after 1945, but it is likely that in the nineteenth century, as later, many of those recorded as sleeping alone lived so close to supportive family as to be able to spend much of their waking hours with them.[6] The basic demographic patterns were reinforced by the increasingly entrenched ideology of the middle-class home. Although there remained opportunities for economic activity, wives and daughters less often lived over the shop or business, or played a direct part in the pursuit of the household income by their husbands and fathers. The emphasis was thrown onto their social function, preparing for and undertaking their role as mothers, and looking after their menfolk on their return from work.[7] The activities of the family were conducted in the presence of one or more live-in servants, and the daily routines of the home were supplemented by frequent visits to and from other families in the neighbourhood.

Yet the question of achieving an appropriate balance between solitary and sociable activity within the household could not easily be laid to rest. It was partly a matter of the immense variety of conditions concealed by the demographic averages. Whilst the experience of living alone was uncommon at any one moment, over a lifetime it was a larger prospect as individuals moved into initially unfamiliar communities or experienced sudden bereavements. Households frequently contained non-nuclear family members with whom there might be no better than distant relationships. Children required less contact with their mothers as they grew up, and as the boys increasingly were sent away from middle- and upper-class households to boarding school. Women who never married tended to have a marginal status, neither excluded from nor fully a part of the family's life. As a rule, wives and servants did not share household tasks or social time. An employing female could consider herself entirely alone whilst in the daily presence of one or more women who slept in the same house Conversely a young maid, moving out of her home to go into service in her early teens, could endure profound isolation in her garret bedroom. Strategies of sociability had continuously to be adjusted and remade, with no certainty that breakdowns could be avoided or overcome.

The physical theatre of domesticity defied generalization. There were immense variations in the internal arrangements of living accommodation. At the bottom end were cellar dwellings or single tenements in multi-occupied houses where every activity had to be conducted in the presence of another. These multiplied in areas in response to sharp population increases, but over the period there was a long-term growth in the number of rooms available to each household. When national surveys began to be made at the beginning of the twentieth century, it was revealed that only 1.6 per cent of the English and Welsh population were living in one room, whereas just over a fifth were occupying four rooms and three-fifths five or more.[8] In Scotland, where units were traditionally smaller, the percentage in single-room accommodation fell from 26.2 to 8.4 between 1861 and 1911.[9] The move from one to two rooms created a minimum choice of whom to associate with. English by-law housing in the last quarter of the century specified two rooms downstairs, increasingly with a separate scullery for cooking and washing, two or three bedrooms and an enclosed area at the back of the property. The range of spaces multiplied the opportunities for moving between levels of sociability. With everyone home, and the front parlour reserved for ritual family functions, it would be difficult to escape physical company.[10] But as occupants came and went, over the course of a day areas would open up, inside the house or in its yard or garden.

There was also a question of the evolving function of sewing and knitting, and a range of other domestic recreations that became ever more extensive as the century progressed. Activity was better than inactivity, but how the practitioner moved between its solitary and sociable forms, whether it was pursued with sufficient vigour and how far it merely gilded the cage within which many women lived were unresolved issues. In the early decades of the nineteenth century, there was a growing apprehension that the rising generation of women no longer possessed the self-discipline to persist with their needles or any other task. 'By far the greater portion of the young ladies (for they are no longer women) of the present day,' argued Sarah Stickney Ellis, 'are distinguished by a morbid listlessness of mind and body, except when under the influence of stimulus, a constant pining for excitement, and an eagerness to escape from everything like practical and individual duty.'[11] 'Morbid listlessness' had echoes of the all-embracing condition of melancholy, and its tendency to undermine effective social discourse. Jean-Étienne Esquirol's 1845 treatise on 'Lypemania or Melancholy' laid particular emphasis on the 'sedentary life of our women' as a cause of their isolation.[12]

By mid-century, however, voices began to be raised from within the community of educated women questioning the purpose of needlework and other forms of polite domestic recreation. Men did not knit, and only rarely engaged in high-end embroidery.[13] They did not make, and rarely attempted to mend, their own clothes. Florence Nightingale mused on an alternative universe:

> Suppose we were to see a number of men in the morning sitting round a table in the drawing-room, looking at prints, worsted work, and reading little books, how we should laugh! A member of the House of Commons was once known to do worsted work. . . . Why should we laugh if we were to see a parcel of men sitting round a drawing-room table in the morning, and think it all right if they are women? Is man's time more valuable than woman's? or is the difference between man and woman this, that woman has confessedly nothing to do?[14]

The more wives and daughters consumed their days in these activities, the more they appeared to waste their talents. The sheer volume of objects made in and usually for the middle-class home embodied the imprisonment of those who ran it. The sum of so much activity was the negation of women's claim to dignity and authority.[15] If sewing and knitting were all there was, what larger case could ever be made for their participation in wider realms of power and creativity?

The resolution of this debate was far from straightforward. Whilst many of the quiet, domestic recreations had a long heritage, there was in the nineteenth century a rapid expansion in their volume and variety. The range of practical pastimes in this period reflected their modernity. They were driven by unprecedented household prosperity, by changes in the availability of time within the home, by an energetic and responsive consumer economy, and, crucially, by the energetic use of mass communication. The outcome was not merely the filling of empty hours in pointless days; rather it may be argued that such activities fundamentally reshaped the balance between sociability and solitude. The Victorian middle-class family generated a wide range of solitary activities in order that it might balance itself. The variety of private practices, and the fluidity between their personal and collective forms, were crucial to the maintenance of the outwardly social nature of the bourgeois home. Further, the proliferation of print and of correspondence rapidly expanded the realm of virtual communities. For the women consumers and letter-writers of the period, the option was no longer one of face-to-face conversation or silence. Rather they could abstract themselves from the company of their household and take part in wider networks of practitioners who never entered the home or challenged its domestic rituals and structures of authority. Later in the century these networks began to coalesce into formal organizations, but these were only a bureaucratic focus for passions and pastimes conducted by individual enthusiasts. At the same time, as we shall see in the final section of this chapter, the equation of solitude and mental pathology began to be challenged by radical, creative women. Using invalidity as a reason or an excuse for withdrawing from domestic society was explored in a range of lives and accompanying writings. Here the technology of solitary domestic recreation became both a defence against enforced participation in household life and a channel for engagement in wider forms of intellectual or organizational endeavour.

Patience and Other Pastimes

We should perhaps begin with the pastime which belongs specifically to this era and which most obviously embodied the pleasures of solitary activity. As Janet Mullin has recently demonstrated in *A Sixpence at Whist*, card-playing for low stakes was an integral element of eighteenth-century middle-class domestic sociability.[16] Everyone knew the most popular games and could afford to bring out a well-worn pack when the family wanted to entertain itself or occasional visitors. The contests were open to young and old, men and women, and gave expression to accepted rules of polite conduct. The goal was not financial gain, but consuming time in often poorly lit interiors for mutually acceptable outcomes. Playing card games entirely by yourself appears to have developed as a pastime elsewhere in northern Europe. The first known manual on card solitaire, or Patience, was published in Moscow in 1824.[17] It became popular in France and Germany, and an early route into England may have been through Prince Albert, who played a game he had known in his childhood. By mid-century, packs of cards designed specifically for Patience were on sale in Europe.[18] The first British guide, Lady Adelaide Cadogan's *Illustrated Games of Patience* of 1874, described thirty-five games, many with their original German titles.[19] At the same time, Solitaire as a single-person board game in which the player removes all but one of thirty-two marbles or counters also entered the recreational culture, generating in turn its own literature.[20]

The manuals on the card games demonstrated that there was time not merely to play cards by yourself but also endlessly to learn or invent elaborations of the basic task of building up suits, often using two packs at a time. The modern *Penguin Book of Patience* lists two hundred and fifty games, and twice that number if known variations are included.[21] The new versions demanded serious attention. 'Hare and Hounds' in *Games of Patience Illustrated by Numerous Diagrams* began with the following instruction: 'Deal cards from left to right, singly, face upwards, to ten "Hare depôts," counting one to ten as the cards are dealt, taking to a separate packet (as "Hounds") any card – except 10's, knaves, queens, kings – the value of which tallies with the number of the "depôt" upon which it is dealt.'[22] Once the basic German forms had been incorporated, ingenious efforts were made to associate the game with other popular pastimes. Walter Wood's *The Book of Patience; or, Cards for a Single Player* of 1887, for instance, described how to play 'The Flower Garden' with one pack of cards:

> This is a pretty game, and not very difficult to win, if played with care. Deal out six packets of six cards each, face upwards, and expose them

fanwise, as in the illustration. These packets form the *garden beds*. Sixteen cards will remain, which you hold exposed fanwise in your hand, or lay down, face upwards, according to their value, beneath the garden beds, as in the illustration; these are termed *the bouquet*. The object of the game is to fill up the four aces, *following suit*, to kings, from the garden and bouquet.[23]

Whereas the sociable eighteenth-century practices relied on a common knowledge of a handful of games, now every player could express their own individual preference and mental ingenuity. Patience provided an answer to the empty spaces during the day, requiring only one or two packs of cards that could be bought for as little as a penny each. It required neither the company nor the oversight of other participants. Each isolated player was dependent on their personal moral discipline for observing or breaking the ever-more complex rules in pursuit of the reassembled pack.

From the outset the literary references to Patience emphasized the importance to the player of the withdrawal from company. An early account of the game in English occurs in Dickens's *Great Expectations* of 1860–1. Pip is looking after the escaped convict Magwitch, who bears in his figure 'the influences of his solitary hut-life' that he had led in Australia, and is now hiding in a room in London.[24] Solitude in this case is exactly a matter of life and death. Magwitch believes that as a returned convict he will be hanged if he is discovered. 'I doubt if a ghost could have been more terrible to me,' Pip recalls, 'up in those lonely rooms in the long evenings and long nights, with the wind and the rain always rushing by.' Left to his own devices, Magwitch occupies himself 'playing a complicated kind of Patience with a ragged pack of cards of his own – a game that I never saw before or since, and in which he recorded his winnings by sticking his jack-knife into the table'.[25]

Amongst the less stressed middle-class householders later in the century, the value of the card game lay in its contrast to all forms of labour, as Mary Whitmore Jones explained in her guide:

We know of ladies living alone who have sat through their solitary evenings reading, writing, or working, till their brains are dazed and fingers sore; and they have found it an immense relief to put books and works aside, get out the cards, and solace themselves with a game of Patience before going to bed. We know of hard-worked professional men who play it regularly every evening; it makes a break in their thoughts, and keeps them from dwelling at night on the business which has been absorbing them all day.[26]

The game was held to be particularly suitable as a diversion for those prevented by their health from participating in the life of the family: 'We know of invalids,' wrote Miss Whitmore Jones, 'condemned to lie on a dreary couch the live-long day, who look forward to their evening Patience as the most enjoyable time of their sad existence.'[27] Both the card game and the sister board game were also promoted as an antidote to long-distance travel, where increasingly the passenger was not expected to engage in social exchange. In the absence of conversation with strangers, occupation could be found for the hands and the mind.[28] Thanks to the inventive Miss Jones, travellers could lay out their cards during train journeys on the 'Chastleton' Portable Patience Board.

A second newly invented solitary pastime was the unexpected by-product of the communications revolution of the era. Whereas many Victorian recreations could trace their antecedents to earlier epochs of civilization, philately had an exact and recent date of origin. Its birth took place on 1 May 1840, when the first Penny Black was issued for sale. The speed with which stamp collecting took off as both a private hobby and a vibrant commercial and organizational practice reflected the energy of quiet recreation in this period. It was beginning to emerge as a recognized hobby by the middle of the 1840s and the first illustrated stamp catalogue in English was published in 1862.[29] By this time, it claimed, albums for storing and displaying collections were 'to be obtained of almost every stationer'.[30] The activity had a wide appeal. 'The collecting of Postage Stamps,' declared John Edward Gray in *The Illustrated Catalogue of Postage Stamps for the Use of Collectors* of 1865, 'is a fashion not confined to this country, or to a single class; for the collections are frequently to be seen in the drawing-room of the luxurious, the study of the enlightened, and the locker of the schoolboy.'[31] Its attraction was wide-ranging. The urge to collect could be satisfied without filling overcrowded domestic interiors with intrusive objects. Schoolchildren could learn history and geography; technically minded adults could trace innovations in paper, design, typography, water marks, perforation, engraving and printing techniques, and currency.[32]

As rarity was rapidly monetized, a new source of financial speculation was introduced. Above all, philately celebrated Britain's place in the international order. Together with the steam engine and the railways, Rowland Hill's creation of the Penny Post and the associated invention of the gummed stamp could be claimed as world-leading innovations. Philately became the most effective means of celebrating the concomitant growth of the British Empire. New colonies issued their own stamps, which could then be bought by enthusiasts in the mother country, many coming to specialize in the output of particular places. According to the historian of the leading stamp dealer Stanley Gibbons, its 'Imperial Album', first published in 1879, became, 'beyond all doubt, the best known and most popular stamp album in the world'.[33] The national status of the hobby was confirmed when it was taken up by royalty, initially in the person of the Duke of York, later George V.

As with correspondence itself, philately was a means of connecting a private individual with wider networks. At the core of the activity was the solitary collector, who seems largely though not exclusively to have been male in this period, sitting with his album and the paraphernalia of tweezers, mounts, magnifiers, and perforation gauges, examining his stamps, organizing his collection, reading catalogues, guides and journals, planning the expenditure of anything from spare pocket money to the £1,450 the Duke of York (by now Prince of Wales) invested in a Mauritius two-pence blue in 1904.[34] Its strength was its flexibility. The hobby could be practised in the interstices of a busy life. At most it required a desk or a temporary space at a table. There was no prescribed calendar of activity, no imposed routine. The only rule was the privacy of personal property and the capacity to protect the albums from damage or loss at the hands of other members of the household. The individual was free to define his collecting strategy and determine whether or not to show his albums to family and friends.

Like other quiet recreations, philately was solitude policed by concentration. What mattered was not the presence or absence of company, but the capacity to become immersed in the pursuit. As with Patience, it appealed particularly to those wearied by more strenuous mental tasks. A guide explained that, '[a]s stamp collecting may be indulged in by all ages, and at all seasons, it is becoming more and more the favourite indoor relaxation with brain-workers. It may be taken up or laid down at any time, and at any stage.'[35] It supplied both an absorbing abstraction from company and an engagement with a stimulating external context: 'an ever-increasing supply of new issues from one or other of the many groups of stamp-issuing countries periodically revives the interest of the flagging collector, and binds him afresh to the hobby of his choice'.[36]

At the same time, the lone collector was embedded in a fiercely energetic commercial, organizational and literary environment. Stanley Gibbons, who began stamp-dealing in his father's chemist's shop in Plymouth as early as 1856, was only one of numerous businesses that sprang up to meet the demand for individual specimens and unsorted packets together with all the accoutrements of collecting. As with the other firms, Gibbons both sold the by-products of correspondence and depended on it for his business: 'He used personally to edit all his albums and catalogues,' wrote his biographer, 'and in the busy seasons received from two to three hundred letters a day, all of which, with a very few exceptions, were answered the same day as received.'[37] Collectors formed themselves into organizations, beginning with the Philatelic Society of London in 1869.[38] Provincial societies followed, such as a group of Sheffield enthusiasts which met to hear presentations on splendidly arcane topics. In February 1895, J. H. Chapman showed 'The Private Frank Stamps of Spain – the issues of the Honorary Postman of Spain and the Colonies, Dr Thebussen.'[39] Above all there was print, in the form of catalogues, organizational proceedings and monographs on every aspect of the frail fragments of gummed paper. According to an excited survey of stamp collecting in 1902, 'Its literature is more abundant than that devoted to any other hobby.'[40]

As the male members of the household pored over their albums, the girls and women attended to their needles. There was a long tradition of embroidery, but as with so many domestic pastimes it underwent an explosive growth in this period.[41] Berlin wool-work dominated the practice of making pictures with threads during the second and third quarters of the nineteenth century. In essence it was sewing by numbers, and throughout its heyday was mocked for betraying the high art of classical embroidery. The process involved pieces of meshed canvas together with corresponding printed patterns on squared paper. It took its name from the original source of the wool, which was spun in Gotha and dyed in Berlin. The embroiderer selected the colours she wanted to use and copied the patterns onto the prepared material. Initially the kits were imported from Germany, with the British market expanding rapidly after the leading London needlework shop, Wilk's Warehouse of Regent Street, began stocking them in 1831. By 1840, it was estimated that 14,000 different designs were on sale. A flourishing second-hand trade developed, with purchasers selling back used patterns for half the original price.[42] The attraction was the guarantee of an artistic outcome without long training of the hand or eye. 'No real skill with the needle was required,' writes an historian of Victorian embroidery, 'merely an ability to count and an infinite amount of time and patience.'[43]

Most domestic recreations were heavily gendered, none more so than the production of sewn or decorated objects for wear or decoration. 'And if we look for that feminine employment which adds most absolutely to the comforts and the elegancies of life,' wrote Constance Wilton in 1841, 'to what other shall we refer than to NEEDLEWORK? The hemming of a pocket-handkerchief is a trivial thing in itself, yet it is a branch of an art which furnishes a useful, a graceful, and an agreeable occupation to one-half of the human race, and adds very materially to the comforts of the other half.'[44] The activity reinforced a stereotype of silent, productive service, at once creative and subordinate to the needs and tastes of the household. It was a practical art which lent itself to almost every visual surface of the domestic interior, including the dress of its male occupants. Berlin wool-work cloth was incorporated into hangings, curtains, upholstery, footstools, antimacassars, screens, mats, tablecloths, mantelpiece hangings, watch pockets, waistcoats, and slippers.[45] The pictures women chose to reproduce from the catalogues reflected the visual language of the middle-class household, encompassing flowers, gothic art, domestic animals, religion, and the royal family. The proponents of Berlin wool-work argued that in spite of the mass-produced designs and fool-proof techniques, it required artistic judgement to select the wools and patterns and persist until a satisfactory image was produced. A handbook of 1851 stoutly defended the craft:

It will, perhaps, be urged by some, that needlework, as practised at the present time, is but a mechanical, art; and the recent invention of Berlin patterns may somewhat favour the opinion. This, however, we entirely disown. No one, who regards the work of the mere copyist of these designs, (as commonly done for sale in Germany, where neither taste nor judgment are displayed in the selection of the colours, nor skill in the appropriation of them) can compare it with that of the talented needlewoman, who, even though she may have worked stitch for stitch from the same pattern, produces what may be justly termed – a 'painting with the needle'.[46]

An efficient, responsive consumer economy produced and distributed the designs, the wools and related items, and a proliferating range of periodicals and manuals offered encouragement and guidance. But at the heart of the activity was the individual, bent over her piece of cloth, preoccupied with sequences of stitches and colours. 'Embroidery is essentially a personal art,' wrote a late nineteenth-century manual, 'and this, perhaps, in addition to the fact of its adaptability, not only to daily domestic use and adornment, but also to ordinary conditions – not requiring special workshop or expensive plant for its production – has contributed to the success of its revived practice, which is due to the enthusiasm, taste, and patience of our countrywomen.'[47]

Time and patience were the common factors across a wide range of quiet domestic recreations. They consumed the spare minutes and hours, but rarely enjoyed a space fenced off from the needs of the family. The most productive activities were those that could be picked up and put down as circumstances permitted. They could be conducted in total physical solitude. Despite the crowded interiors of middle-class homes, it was often possible to find a temporarily unoccupied room, or, providing the servants were ignored, to enjoy the freedom of the whole house when the rest of its members were out at school or work, or retired to bed, or, in the case of the men, gone to their club. Or they could constitute a form of abstracted solitude, where the needle-worker was at once present in surrounding company and absent from it as she focussed on her picture.

At its most effective, needlework served to create an internal mental universe where the manipulation of the fingers permitted a reflective concentration that was otherwise unobtainable in the crowded daily round of the household. *The Ladies' Hand-book of Knitting, Netting, and Crochet* concluded that the various activities with a needle would lead women 'to the formation of habits of thought and reflection, which may issue in higher attainments than the knitting of a shawl or the netting of a purse'.[48] Mrs Beeton's *Household Treasury* drew an unexpected parallel with a practice that was still a largely male preserve: 'There is a peculiarly soothing influence about needle-work, which is, perhaps, rather similar to that experienced by lovers of "the weed" when under the influence of tobacco. If a woman is alone, sewing helps her to think.'[49]

The enjoyment of these forms of abstracted solitude was confined to those who used a needle for some form of recreational pleasure. The craze for Berlin wool-work, challenged towards the end of the century by the revival of art-embroidery, had little in common with the desperate struggle of many working-class wives to keep their family's clothing in a fit state to be used the following morning. Just before the First World War, Maud Pember Reeves carried out an early time-budget study, tracking how a sample of men and women occupied themselves during the course of a typical day. The housewives undertook sewing, often alone, but not from choice. They sat up by themselves after their children and husbands had gone to bed, mending divested items needed for school or work the next morning. Three diary entries for the evenings ran:

> 9.0. Mend husband's clothes, and go on with frock till ten.
> 8.30. Sew while husband goes to bed. 9.0. Send mother off. Get everything ready for the morning. Mend husband's clothes as soon as he gets them off.
> 8.0. Tidies up, washes husband's tea things, sweeps kitchen, and mends clothes, nurses baby, puts elder children to bed. 8.45. Gets husband's supper; mends clothes.[50]

Their withdrawal from the life of the household was a function of practical need not reflective abstraction. The dominant experience was not mental renewal but physical exhaustion.

Networked Solitude

The published guides to Patience, philately, and sewing were self-sufficient texts, not only describing but often also visually displaying various stages of the recreations. They were characteristic of a burgeoning literature of quiet leisure.[51] In 1852, Samuel Beeton created a new template for women's periodicals. *The Englishwoman's Domestic Magazine* promised to supply precise, practical information on a range of topics which included cookery, dress, embroidery, pets, amusements, and gardening.[52] The key to its success lay in the combination of accurate, applicable detail on the activity in question and the address to the readership, who were assumed to be both careful household managers and intelligent, articulate women. They were encouraged to write back to the magazine on both the craft skills they wished to practise and a host of literary and occupational topics.

The growth in periodical literature was accompanied by a diversification in the market for comprehensive manuals of quiet recreations. By the final third of the nineteenth century, the range of reference books was so extensive that entrepreneurial publishers could bring to market compendium volumes seeking to present distillations of printed wisdom for domestic consumers. Ventures such as Mrs Valentine's *The Home Book of Pleasure and Instruction*, Cassell's *Household Guide* and Mrs Beeton's *The Housewife's Treasury of Domestic Information* supplied information on cooking, all kinds of needlework, household arts, home entertainment, gardening, pets and fancy birds and animals, and other emerging hobbies such as photography and stamp collecting.[53]

The guides were based on two convictions. Firstly, it was assumed that there was no loss of caste in respectable men and particularly women making useful and decorative objects or managing livestock with their own hands. 'In these days of sewing-machines, paper models, and fashion magazines,' wrote Mrs Beeton, 'with their accompanying illustrations of the ever-changing mode, there can be no more reason why a lady should not employ her leisure time in making her own dresses, than there was in earlier days sitting at the distaff and manufacturing their own linen.'[54] Secondly, it was accepted that the oral transmission of skills from one generation to another was insufficient to meet the wealth of opportunities that presented themselves to the occupiers of middle-class homes. Just as polite householders would turn to religious literature for their spiritual improvement and to novels for their imaginative lives, so they would expect to seek knowledge from texts on arcane matters such as paper-flower making and modelling in cork.

The encyclopaedic guides inherited literary traditions that stretched back centuries and in some cases millennia. In the Victorian and Edwardian periods, publishers found a market not only for new guides to various activities, but also for bibliographies of the proliferating material. Osmund Lambert's *Angling Literature in England* of 1881 claimed to be the seventh such survey, and was followed by Walter Turrell's *Ancient Angling Authors* of 1910.[55] The literature on cooking became a literary form, the subject of studies by Carew Hazlitt (William's grandson) and by Arnold Oxford.[56] Hazlitt established an English literary lineage stretching back to Neckam of St Albans in the early twelfth century and Oxford located the first printed cookery book in English as early as 1500. Prior to Byron's *Childe Harold* the most successful book issued by the publisher John Murray was Maria Eliza Rundell's compendious *A New System of Domestic Cookery*. First published in 1806, it sold 58,000 copies by 1816, and was in its sixty-fourth edition by 1840, remaining in print for the remainder of the century.[57] Embroidery asserted its historical and literary identity in the Countess of Wilton's *The Art of Needlework*.[58] Cornelia Mee sold over 300,000 of her guides to crochet and knitting between the 1840s and 1870s.[59]

Fishing was unusual in that the growing literature was dominated by a single historical text, Isaak Walton's *The Compleat Angler*.[60] First published in 1653, it remained in print through the eighteenth century, enjoying a new lease of life as angling expanded as a sport.[61] At least four editions were published annually in most years from the 1830s onwards. Forty-three were issued between 1890 and 1899, two-thirds in Britain, the rest in the United States.[62] It continued to be read, despite manifold improvements in the techniques and technology of angling in the Victorian era.[63] Part of the charm of the book lay in its conversational style, with Walton talking not only to his readers but also with earlier writers.[64] 'I shall next give you some other directions for fly-fishing,' he wrote, 'such as are given by Mr Thomas Barker, a gentleman that hath spent much time in fishing: but I shall do so with a little variation.'[65] At the root of the English printed tradition was *The treatise of fysshynge wyth an Angle* of 1486, one of the earliest printed books on any secular topic. The text, which itself is held to be based on yet earlier monastic manuscripts, set out to perform exactly the same function as every subsequent guide.[66] It took as its subject the enthusiastic beginner and supplied him with all the information necessary to become a success at the chosen pastime: 'Yf ye whole be crafty in anglynge, ye must fyrste lerne to make your harnays. That is to wyte your rodde, your lynes of dyuers colours. After that ye must know how ye shall angle, in what place of the water, how depe, and what time of day, for what manere so fysshe, in what wedyr.'[67] By the end of the nineteenth century, in angling as in so many other pastimes, including, as we have seen, mountaineering, there existed an immeasurable ratio between those who owned texts in order to use them, and those content to sit alone in their armchairs and vicariously enjoy the trials and labour of others. 'Why add another volume to the already heavily-laden shelves of angling literature?' asked J. J. Manley, as he introduced his compendious *Notes on Fish and Fishing* in 1881. 'I have been told or read that there are no less than 500 persons in the United Kingdom who make a practice of buying every fresh addition to the literature of fishing.'[68]

The penetration of print into quiet recreation is illustrated by John Clare's library. Unlike the neophyte suburban gardeners for whom J. C. Loudon and his successors catered, here was a countryman who would seem to have little need of literary assistance. Yet gardening for Clare was a topic that increasingly exceeded the inherited wisdom of his community. He confessed in a letter that 'altho I know wild flowers tollerable well my knowledge of garden flowers is very limited'.[69] Over his lifetime he accumulated a shelf-full of texts to make good his ignorance and keep up with the latest developments.[70] The oldest manual in his collection was Thomas Tusser's *Five Hundred Points of Good Husbandry*, an instructional poem first published almost a century before *The Compleat Angler*, and intermittently in press ever since. A new edition appeared in 1812, just as Clare was beginning to make his way in the world.[71] This combined observations on various topics, such as how to grow herbs, with a calendar of tasks in the garden. The rest of Clare's gardening library was more modern. He owned some of the compendious manuals that began to appear in the middle of the eighteenth century as a commercial leisure market was developing.[72] Benjamin Whitmil's *Kalendarium Universale: or, The Gardiner's Universal Kalendar* of 1748 supplied 257 pages of monthly instructions together with lists of the best flowers and fruit trees.[73] John Abercrombie's *Every Man His Own Gardener*, first published in 1767, was regularly revised and enlarged into the nineteenth century.[74] The 1803 edition ran to 646 pages of monthly tasks, followed by another hundred pages cataloguing plants and then a thorough index.[75] Clare also had on his shelves an 1822 edition of James Maddock's late eighteenth-century guide, *The Florist's Directory*, which described groups of flowers and gave instructions on their cultivation, and James Edward Smith's *A Compendium of English Flora*, which supplied Latin names of flowers and guides to their pronunciation.[76] Clare's more modern texts dealt with individual species, including Thomas Hogg on the carnation, Isaac Emmerton on the auricula and Elizabeth Kent's guide to growing flowers in pots.[77]

Few labourers amassed so large a library, but whilst the texts were often expensive at the point of publication, so many had been on sale for so long that it was not difficult to pick them up on second-hand bookstalls, or to receive them as gifts from more prosperous superiors who had no further use for them.[78] During the first half of the nineteenth century, the market enlarged in different directions. The encyclopaedic manuals, which met all the functions of modern television or online guides, expanded to over a thousand pages.[79] Increasing attention was paid to specific groups of gardeners, especially those in the expanding towns and cities,[80] and to individual categories of plants. Beginning with J. C. Loudon's *The Gardener's Magazine* of 1826, a thriving periodical trade developed.[81] The literature was driven by the conviction that gardening, as much as any kind of manufacture, was a site of continuing innovation, as new plants were introduced by collectors or by domestic breeding, and new methods of horticulture were explored. As early as 1716, John Worlidge's *Compleat System of Husbandry and Gardening* promised 'many New Experiments and Observations'.[82] The first weekly periodical, *The Gardener's Chronicle*, launched in 1841 as a joint venture between Joseph Paxton and one of the publishers of the new *Punch* magazine, associated its subject matter with the spirit of the age: 'the art of Gardening would soon be deprived of all novelty and interest, if it were not for the daily discoveries of science, and the application of them as they arise to the practices of cultivation'.[83] The sense of inquiry and change generated an intellectual and practical excitement in the flow of publications, in which John Clare may have shared, and also enabled publishers endlessly to promote new ventures and editions on the grounds of the instant obsolescence of existing material.

The experimental culture united professionals and amateurs. A central function of the literature was maintaining a dialogue between the specialists and the increasing number of practising gardeners. At the beginning of the nineteenth century, John Abercrombie, the most prolific author of his time, used the publication of yet another edition of his standard manual to emphasize the creative role of his readers: 'as systems like this can never be absolutely complete, owing to the many new discoveries which are daily making in the different parts of Europe, he earnestly hopes that those persons who are engaged in the cultivation of gardens will continue to oblige him with such discoveries as may occur in the progress of their employment'.[84] Previous readers had 'favoured him with hints for its improvement',[85] and these had been incorporated in the new volume. Within their fenced patch of ground, gardeners both tended their plants and connected with a borderless community of enthusiasts. Through their consumption of the printed word they could derive wisdom and encouragement from the accumulated body of energy and expertise and feel themselves capable of making their own contribution to the ever-expanding body of knowledge.

The conduct of domestic pastimes increasingly depended on the reformed and expanding postal system. Newspapers and periodicals were delivered containing information and advertisements; scattered enthusiasts kept in touch with each other; items for the pursuit of a recreation were purchased through mail order. The communications revolution of the Victorian period had a transformative effect on the activities of the middle-class household. Correspondence and its attendant business of stamps, envelopes, steel pens, post boxes, and slots cut into front doors generated a changing relationship between the physically confined individual and broader social networks. Rowland Hill's reform of 1840 was designed to release epistolary communication from the constraints of scale and price. Flat-rate, pre-paid letters would create a virtual community of correspondents capable of embracing not only the educated middle and upper classes but also the products of the newly subsidized elementary school system. By the end of the eighteenth century, familiarity with a pen and the business of ink, paper, addresses, and seals had spread into the upper reaches of the labouring classes.[86] In the short term, the Penny Post proved a costly innovation, succeeding only in putting to an end the unofficial channels of carrying mail.[87] However, by the mid-1850s, the anticipated sixfold growth had been achieved, and over the remainder of the century volumes doubled every couple of decades, increasing annual per capita usage in an expanding population from eight in 1840 to sixty by 1900.[88] For all the ambition of the reformers, this category of networked intimacy remained largely the preserve of the middle and upper classes. Skilled artisans might deploy correspondence in the conduct of their business, but the labouring poor for the most part confined their letter-writing to family emergencies and occasional domestic transactions.

The Penny Post magnified the distinction between physical and virtual intimacy. Whereas the residents of a crowded household faced a choice of speech or silence, the postal system provided an alternative means of communication irrespective of distance. The walls of the home became increasingly porous.[89] The meaning of solitude evolved. Increasingly it was possible to be alone in the company of others and in easy, frequent contact with friends, relatives, and lovers. Whilst there remained a danger of a letter falling into the wrong hands, the etiquette of correspondence required that the contents of an envelope were for the eyes of the addressee only. The written words conjured the presence of the absent writer. In turn the respondent would seek a space for themselves in which to compose a reply.

Correspondence reflected the broader question of the relationship between mass communication and solitary pursuits within the family. As access to the printed word increased, so the fears expressed by eighteenth-century commentators about the vulnerability of the isolated mind, particularly that of young women, became more widespread. The growth of novel-reading in the middle-class home highlighted the risks of exercising the imagination without sufficient policing by moral guardians. A sentimental love tale, warned *The Lady's Magazine* in 1795, can become 'a dangerous study, unless such persons have some kind instructor who can teach them, like the bee, to extract the honey without being infected by the poison that often lurks beneath the foliage of many a seeming lovely flower'.[90] Solitude through abstraction from the life of the household was made destructive by exposure to the sensations of the printed page. The inflamed mind lost its bearings.[91] In *Northanger Abbey*, her cheerful satire on the female readership of the gothic novel, drafted soon after the publication of Ann Radcliffe's genre-defining best-seller, Jane Austen pictures her heroine, Catherine Morland, 'left to the luxury of a raised, restless, and frightened imagination over the pages of Udolpho, lost from all worldly concerns of dressing and dinner'.[92] At worst it could lead to a complete breakdown of the psyche. 'The passion of *novel reading* is intitled to a place here,' wrote a guide to mental disorders in 1812:

> In the present age it is one of the great causes of nervous disorders. The mind that can amuse itself with the love-sick trash of the most modern compositions of this kind, seeks enjoyment beneath the level of a rational being. ... To the female mind in particular, as being endued with finer feeling, this species of literary poison has often been fatal; and some of the most unfortunate of the sex have imputed their ruin chiefly to the reading of novels.[93]

The population at risk was defined by age and gender. The main concern was the girl who was old enough to find her own reading matter and rebellious enough to resist the advice of older members of the family. There was less debate about married women, either because they were thought to have too little free time for such indulgence, or because they were more directly subject to the control of their husbands.[94] The issue of the adolescent novel reader was a forerunner of recurrent panics in the following two centuries up to the present debate about teenagers and the digital revolution. At the centre of the drama was the immature mind capable of being permanently deformed by forms of communication beyond the supervision of the family circle.

A further assumption was that the trend was from the collective, vocal consumption of print to individualized, silent reading. What was new and threatening was the withdrawn figure, involved in the drama of other lives but no longer speaking to those around them. The spread of literacy and the growing availability of reading matter, combined with increases in spare time and ever greater domestic comforts, made it possible to detach one reader from another. Each could pursue their own literary journeys without the need to listen to the voices of others. The remedy for the perceived threat of the 'unrestrained private reading' of novels was for parents, particularly mothers, to read aloud to their children rather than let them commune with the printed page without moving their lips.[95]

Recent scholarship has qualified this thesis. It is argued that whilst there was a shift to silent reading during the eighteenth and nineteenth centuries, social consumption was still attractive.[96] Reading aloud performed a variety of moral and practical functions.[97] Scarcity and cost remained problems. A triple-decker novel was a luxury purchase, forcing all kinds of sharing strategies within and between households, and increasing the use of commercial and public libraries. Subsequent changes in the publishing industry reduced prices, but the appetite for new fiction continued to exceed the purchasing capacity of many middle-class readers. The uncertain grasp of literacy amongst the newly educated, together with the persistent problems of cost and scarcity for those seeking to become serious readers, meant that informal or structured collaboration with other consumers of the printed word remained a necessity throughout the century.

Rather than setting one direction of change against another, it is better to stress the increase in the range of available practices. As elsewhere in this study, the key issue was the fluidity between different registers of solitary and sociable behaviour. The more prosperous and the better educated found it easier than the mass of the reading public to engage in both silent and vocal reading, to consume print in mental isolation and in conversational company. Memoirs of middle-class children growing up in the Victorian period frequently dwell on the way print enabled them to escape the noise of the family. Reading was a means of making company bearable. 'To be alone was never unpleasant to me,' wrote Elizabeth Sewell. 'In the nursery my great pleasure was to sit by myself in a dark closet, opening into a room, with a little lanthorn by my side, and read a story, whilst my sisters played about. I enjoyed hearing their voices, but I did not wish to join them.'[98] Adults valued sitting with a book not only as a means of focussed concentration, but also as a sign to those around them that they wished to be left in peace.

Literature created space in crowded households. The more that was available, the greater the opportunity to find solitude in the midst of company. Sustained periods of reading might be more desirable than snatched minutes with a volume, but it was in the nature of the practice that books could be picked up and put down as the opportunity arose. It required no other equipment except possibly spectacles, no special clothing, no preparation. It was a resource for detached, inward amusement and contemplation that was becoming generally more available as the century progressed.

At the same time, readers continued to share the printed word, as listeners or as performers. Only the very wealthy conceived of books exclusively as private possessions. Readers recommended titles to each other and borrowed them from friends or family members. As more books were published and it became easier to transport them by rail and by post, the local lending libraries were translated into national ventures, particularly Mudie's Select Library from 1842 and W. H. Smith's rival operation from 1860. Within the home, books were still read aloud as the basis for social events or as a means of entertaining family members concentrating on some other activity such as sewing.

Aspects of the movement between solitary and social reading can be detected amongst the products of the expanding elementary school system. During the course of the nineteenth century, print of some kind became a more familiar presence in most households. Where once reading matter comprised, at best, rarely consulted religious texts or much-thumbed chapbooks, now a plenitude of tracts, serials, newspapers, and other ephemera found their way into the home. One of the witnesses to the *Family Life and Work Experience* (FLW) oral history survey spoke of growing up in the Edwardian period with print substituting for basic furnishing: 'usually,' he recalled, we 'were busy reading a newspaper when we were having our meals because that – that was the tablecloth. The tablecloth was made of newspapers – spread on the table.'[99]

Nonetheless the kind of transitions that were commonplace in middle-class families were much more difficult to achieve. The weight of practice was tipped towards the collective and away from the personal. In Alice Foley's Bolton household, a literate father read Dickens

and Eliot to his illiterate wife, whilst his schooled children read to
themselves the stock of the local library.[100] In these households, spare
moments of withdrawal with a text were at a premium, particularly for
women: 'Oh dad read a lot,' remembered another witness. 'And mum
did when she had time. But with her – her dressmaking and that sort
of thing and – and the housework and the cooking I mean she didn't
have a lot of time, although we were only three in the family.'[101] In such
circumstances, the most that could be hoped for was one adult with
sufficient time and skills reading to another absorbed in domestic tasks.
In the case of one FLW's family it was a matter of the father reading to
the mother 'when she was ironing'.[102]

Out of Doors

Recreational indoor solitude was in most of its forms a luxury conditioned by taste. A basic command of money, time, and domestic
space were essential requirements of withdrawal from company. At the
bottom of society, choice remained minimal. In 1883, the campaigning
journalist George Sims conducted 'a journey with pen and pencil into a
region which lies at our own doors – into a dark continent that is within
easy walking distance of the General Post Office'.[103] The slum life he
exposed offered no opportunity for any of the activities which filled the
pages of Beeton's or Cassell's contemporary compendiums. He visited
a household where the 'woman, her husband, and her six children live,
eat, and sleep in this one room, and for this they pay three shillings
a week.[104] The unrelenting labour of maintaining the family and the
physical impossibility of escaping its presence in the crowded accommodation excluded any prospect of enjoying moments of physical or
absorbed abstraction. There were no empty rooms, no spare minutes,
and there was no surplus income to buy the periodicals and the various
accoutrements that were now available for the proliferating domestic
pastimes.

All that was left for Sims' slum-dwellers was the universal privilege,
discussed in the previous chapter, of walking out of the front door and
away from the confines of accommodation. In its most basic and casual
aspect, this remained a free pleasure, more available for solitary women
amongst the working class than for their social superiors. Over the

course of the nineteenth century, leisure activities outside the home offered new possibilities of bodily withdrawal and mental abstraction. The most common form represented both an extension of the home and an escape from its confined space. The garden, as distinct from the country estate, was increasingly seen not just as an adjunct to the interior of accommodation but also as a defining element of domestic living.[105] A home included a piece of land, separated from another by the physical boundary of a hedge or a fence, which was just as important to the private realm of the family as the walls of the house. The members of the family unit had unimpeded access to the indoor and outdoor parts of their private domain.

Gardening offered a complex example of the uneven spread of quiet recreations and the possibilities of private and shared pleasures. The avalanche of horticultural print in this period enabled renewed consideration to be given to the function as well as the practice of raising flowers and vegetables. At their most expansive, the commentaries elevated the activity into an all-purpose retreat from the pressures of modern living. Thomas Hogg, author of a series of guides on species of plants, surveyed the broader purpose of his chosen activity:

> The Flower Garden – enter but which, the restless and turbulent passions which disturb and agitate the breasts of men, amidst the busy and active pursuits of life, subside into a calm, and give place to the milder and softer emotions of the soul: everything here is calculated to inspire serenity and delight. . . . To the man of leisure and retirement, horticulture is a pursuit at once rational and amusing; it unites the 'utile dulci', and gives health and recreation alike to the body and the mind; the spade, the hoe, and the rake, even in the hands of a gentleman, degrade not, when used for such beneficial ends. To the invalid and valetudinarian, as well as to the sufferer from mental distress and agony, it presents a solace and a balm that at times teem to abate pain, and give distress the languid smile of pleasure. Females, both young and old, derive the highest gratification from the flower-garden in particular, and the more refined the taste, the more exquisite the gratification. . . . The garden is likewise the private sanctuary of the pious man's devotions, and the scene of his meditations: the flower is to him at once a text and a sermon.[106]

The domestic garden inherited the monastic tradition of the early church fathers.[107] It was a place of spiritual reflection and renewal. Physical toil amidst God's bounty was a form of silent prayer. The varied activities during the annual gardening calendar absorbed the mind as well as exercising the body. Plants took the place of people. The withdrawal from company made possible the healthy return to society, once the earth was washed from your hands.

The solitude of gardening was at once essential and conditional. Two people could not dig the same patch of soil, but in wielding a spade the individual was taking part in a set of social interactions. As we have seen, the literature of gardening enabled the lone practitioner to engage with a wider community of enthusiasts and specialists. There were variations in practice by gender. Books had been published for women gardeners since at least the early seventeenth century, and as the nineteenth-century market became more specialized, they acquired their own literature, such as Mrs Loudon's *Instructions in Gardening for Ladies* of 1840.[108] According to *Every Lady Her Own Flower Gardener*, 'floriculture has become the dominant passion of the ladies of Great Britain'.[109] It was not, though, appropriate that respectable women should grow vegetables, and, according to Mrs Loudon's influential husband, there were as yet 'very few ladies who are competent to lay out a flower-garden',[110] as distinct from tending it. The division of labour was sharper amongst the working-class gardeners who were to be found throughout the countryside and in the expanding urban centres. Whilst women might grow flowers immediately around the house, their menfolk, who shared few of the tasks in the interior, were primarily responsible for outdoor labour, making a practical contribution to the household economy by supplying food for the table.

There were two major distinctions by class. The labouring poor were more vulnerable than their social superiors to the intensification of urban living in the nineteenth century. Those who could not afford to move out to the expanding suburbs suffered from the construction of terraces with, at best, small paved yards, and from the associated atmospheric pollution. 'In the musty courts and alleys,' wrote a manual on town gardens,

> wall-flowers, stocks, and musk-plants are purchased every spring, and
> set to flourish in broken teapots, saucepans, flower-pots – damned for

ever by green or brown paint – or rotten boxes filled with stuff called mould, but which looks like the dust of a perished mummy. These go black in the face in four days from the date of planting, and die three days after that from sheer suffocation, gasping up to the last moment for light and air.[111]

For working-class gardeners not able to afford the better class of artisan housing, the only alternative was the allotment on the edge of the urban centre. In one striking example, there were reckoned to be more than five thousand plots around the centre of Nottingham at mid-century, and following the Small Holdings Act of 1892, local councils were able to make systematic provision.[112] By 1910, there were over half a million allotments in England and Wales, although, given the general absence of sanitary facilities, they tended to reinforce the gender divisions amongst working-class gardeners.

The second distinction was that of collective practice. From the late eighteenth century, the ingrained working-class appetite for competition infused with gambling found expression in the host of gardening societies and flower shows across the country.[113] Clubs were defined by area, occupation, or particular flowers, and through intense cultivation, amounting at times to the innovative breeding of new plants, they competed vigorously for prizes (often in the form of copper kettles) and the esteem they brought.[114] A survey of the industrial north in 1826 identified fifty auricular and polyanthus shows annually, together with twenty-seven tulip, nine ranunculus, nineteen pink, and forty-eight carnation competitions.[115]

Competitive gardening represented a particular balance between social and solitary endeavour. The end product required agreed standards of merit and some form of collective viewing. In the case of the artisan flower shows, the judging and the prize-giving might be preceded by a formal dinner of club members. But the outcome was the end point of months of intense, focussed, personal labour. Day after day, before and after work when the light permitted, on chilly spring days or warm summer evenings, the lone artisan inspected and tended his plants, producing specimens for display as well as flowers and vegetables for decoration or consumption inside the home. Without the incentive of competition, or the satisfaction of meeting the household's

needs, the planting, watering, and weeding would have been harder
to sustain. Conversely, showing to club members or neighbours looking over the fence gained meaning from the knowledge of how much
disciplined effort and long-acquired individual skill each bloom or giant
tuber represented.

A similar movement between the contrasting forms of endeavour
is apparent in the growing engagement with various categories of the
'Fancy': the breeding for competitive display of birds and animals.
The notion of the Fancy was itself essentially collective. It embodied
a shift from a private pleasure in a particular pet or working animal
to a shared acceptance of standards of quality which over the course
of the nineteenth century were increasingly embodied in formal rules
policed by national organizations. Following the abolition of bear-
baiting and cock-fighting in 1835, a flourishing dog Fancy grew up in
which owners trained their animal at home and brought it to a public
house to compete with another to kill the largest number of rats in a
specified time.[116] Dog breeding began with producing specialist animals for farming and rural pastimes and developed into an ever more
complex set of variations and accompanying organizations and shows.
The Kennel Club was founded in 1873 to bring order and discipline
to the description and presentation of animals, and published the first
volume of its stud book a year later.[117] By 1890, there were nearly fifty
affiliated organizations for different breeds. It was biologically more
difficult to distinguish variations in breeds of cats, but a successful
show was held at Crystal Palace in 1871 and the National Cat Club
was formed in 1887.[118] 'Since these early days,' claimed Miss Francis
Simpson in 1907, 'the Cat Fancy has made rapid strides and local clubs
have been started in all parts of England and Scotland, and specialist societies for almost every breed are now in existence.' A similar
trajectory was followed by the pigeon breeders, and by enthusiasts
of all kinds of lesser birds and animals.[119] 'It will be news to most
readers,' wrote an Edwardian survey, 'that, taking the average, there is
an exhibition of rabbits held in the UK every day of the week (with a
large surplus).'[120] Nothing was too small to breed and display. 'An Old
Fancier' published in 1896 a manual on *Fancy Mice: Their Varieties,
Management and Breeding*.[121] As with larger animals, rarity generated
value: 'fancy mice always find a ready sale at from 8d. to 10s. 6d. per

pair, according to the markings, &c. In fact, we have had as much as 30s. for a pair of tortoiseshell mice.'[122]

With mice, as with every other Fancy, the cost of prize specimens impacted on the economic identity of participants. In common with all domestic pastimes, there were variations in wealth and expenditure within the practising community. The possession of a pedigree dog was itself a public statement of the owner's social status. 'It is a fact which can hardly be disputed,' observed an Edwardian manual, 'that nobody now who is anybody can afford to be followed about by a mongrel dog.'[123] Nonetheless, there was a general sense of a mass movement emerging in the last quarter of the nineteenth century. Anyone who could maintain some regularity in the management of their time and income could participate in the process of breeding and showing. Whilst the Kennel Club represented an assertion of authority by upper-class breeders, it was possible for working men to raise specimen animals to be judged according to the public, standardized rules of excellence.[124] In the case of cats and dogs, the shows themselves became large-scale spectator events, attended by owners curious about the possibilities of their species and entertained by the competitive drama.[125] Working men with minimal spare resources would make any sacrifice to maintain their passion. George Ure's 1889 monograph on pigeons embraced every level of keeping birds: 'I have known many a hard-working man rise by three o'clock in the morning to feed a nest of larks or linnets, and go to bed again, and to repeat this twice or thrice before the six o'clock bell rang.'[126]

In terms of sheer numbers, the most striking expansion of outdoor pursuits was on the river bank. As we have noted, angling had a long history both as a pastime and as a literary genre, but in the 1870s and 1880s it began its ascent into what became the single most popular form of participator sport.[127] A survey of 1881 claimed that

> in no country under the sun has fishing, as a sport, ever attained the popularity it enjoys at the present time in the British Isles. We are pre-eminently an angling nation more so now than ever we were, for I estimate that, in proportion to the increase of population, the number of anglers has increased by five hundred to a thousand per cent during the last quarter of a century.[128]

The combination of growing numbers and a fixed length of suitable streams, rivers, and canals accentuated the social divide between game and coarse fishing.[129] Those who had prospered in the professions or in business rented remote trout or salmon stretches for increasingly high fees.[130] By contrast, the lower orders clubbed together to organize excursion trains and to share the costs of fishing rights in pursuit of less prestigious catch. They fished not by the week but by the day, travelling out of towns and cities to the nearest stocked water and returning with their catch at nightfall. In Sheffield alone there were twenty thousand registered anglers by the end of the Victorian period.[131]

As with gardening, nurturing, or killing birds and animals involved complex transitions between social and solitary practices. In the case of the various forms of the Fancy, the moment of public display was merely the end of a journey. Each specimen was bred and cared for over months or years, either in the home in respect of small species, or outside in kennels, cages, and lofts. The larger domestic animals, particularly dogs, as we saw in the previous chapter, had to be regularly walked in streets and open spaces and the pigeons allowed flight. Everything depended on a solitary relationship between owner and creature. However much advice could be secured from publications or fellow club members, individuals invested most of their time as breeders in close communion with their livestock, often at the expense of money, practical help, or conversation that might have been devoted to the rest of their family. The wives of working-class pigeon racers complained that their husbands spent more on their birds than on their families, and talked more to them. [132] The care and the communication was between a single enthusiast and one or more representatives of the particular breed. It was a means of expressing skill, knowledge, ambition, and a form of nurturing that had value only for the committed member of the particular Fancy. Meaning and achievement were obtained by turning away from human exchange within the social unit of the household. Then at an appropriate moment the bird or animal was transferred to a mobile cage to be transported to a club or a show where the owners could then socialize with other members of the Fancy. The means of conveying the specimens from the solitary to the social realm was itself an issue of specialized equipment. Take, for example, the vigorous proletarian recreation of competitive bird-singing. Cassell's compendium of pastimes reported that it was the custom for owners to make small cages, seven and a half inches high, six inches long and four inches deep, which they carried 'in handkerchiefs to various public houses, to which great numbers of goldfinches and linnets are taken'.[133] Bets were laid and prizes awarded for the bird which uttered the most notes in a fifteen-minute period.

Amongst the breeders of higher status and more expensive birds, such as the almond tumbler, the intense solitary experience of caring for the bird was ascribed the same meaning as other forms of escape from demanding intellectual labour. John Matthews Eaton's *A Treatise on the Art of Breeding and Managing the Almond Tumbler* of 1851 explained that the hobby 'is an innocent amusement and recreation, well adapted to the professional gentleman of law, physic, and divinity, or any other person engaged in long continued and excessive exertion of the intellectual faculties'.[134] Eaton was rehearsing the eighteenth-century conviction that those working with their minds were especially prone to forms of melancholy and mental illness. Periods of disciplined, purposeful solitude that retained a creative relationship to social endeavour were the surest remedy. 'I am of opinion,' he wrote, 'that many of the brightest luminaries that have suddenly been lost to society, would not have been so, had they been engaged in this Fancy, by way of recreation or relief to the mind. I have known some very old gentlemen in the Fancy, but never yet knew a Fancier that was troubled with hippochondriasis.'[135]

The same claim was made for the rapidly expanding sport of fishing. 'As a recreation for professional men,' wrote T. F. Salter's *Angler's Guide* of 1825, 'the brain-workers of the human tribe, those who are liable to mental exhaustion in callings which involve continuous attention at a high pressure, and not infrequently induce mental depression, there is in my opinion nothing to be compared with fishing.'[136] In common with many of the nineteenth-century texts, Salter was rephrasing the claims of Walton's *Compleat Angler*. In the revised 1665 edition, Walton had written,

No life, my honest Scholer, no life so happie and so pleasant, as the life of a well governed Angler; for when the Lawyer is swallowed up with businesse, and the States-man is preventing or contriving plots, we sit on Cowslip banks, hear the Birds sing, and possesse our selves with as much quietnesse as these silver streams which we now see glide by us.[137]

Of all the nineteenth-century recreations, angling laid the most insistent claim to quiet. Walton relocated the early hermits to the river bank, evoking 'that simplicity which was usually found in the primitive Christians, who were, as most Anglers are, quiet men, and followers of peace'.[138] The stained-glass window celebrating his writings in Winchester Cathedral bears the line 'Study to be Quiet'. Every account emphasized both the body of knowledge required by the successful fisherman and the fundamental absence of noise on the river bank. Walton wrote that for the practitioner the sport was 'a rest to his mind, a cheerer of his spirits, a diverter of sadness, a calmer of unquiet thoughts, a moderator of passions, a procurer of contentedness; and that it begat habits of peace and patience in those that professed and practised it'.[139]

The concentrated application of knowledge about which equipment to use, which bait to deploy, which part of the stream to fish, how the ecology of the river and its banks functioned, allowed the mind to wander away from the hard intellectual labour of business or a profession.[140] In a famous mid-nineteenth-century essay, Charles Kingsley evoked 'the angler's most delicate enjoyment, that dreamy, contemplative repose, broken by just enough amusement to keep his body active, while his mind is quietly taking in every sight and sound of nature'.[141] Most of those following Walton assumed the gains were greatest for the weary middle classes, but as William Howitt argued, the same pleasure in escape from occupational toil was sought by those who laboured with their hands: "The weight of the poor man's life – the cares of poverty – the striving of huge cities, visit him as he sits by the beautiful stream – beautiful as a dream of eternity, and translucent as the everlasting canopy of heaven above him; – they come – but he casts them off for the time.'[142]

As with other recreations, the greater the income, the easier it was to escape from company. Those who could afford to spend a week at a time on a rented Highland salmon stream were demonstrably more alone than working-class anglers who joined a club in order to afford to travel to a day's fishing in the surrounding countryside. Nonetheless the contrast between the two levels of activity should not be over-drawn.[143] Physical space between one angler and another was axiomatic at all levels of the sport, whether game or coarse. In the informal world of early nineteenth-century fishing, there existed an unwritten convention about how close one fisherman should be to another. 'To prevent disputes,' wrote T. F. Salter, 'it is generally understood and agreed to among Anglers . . . that a distance the length of a rod and line, or thirty feet, shall be kept between each person, while angling.'[144] The growth of rule-based clubs and the increasing numbers of participants in competitions made it all the more important that such regulations were specified and policed. The late nineteenth-century matches placed the pegs for competitors eight to ten yards apart.[145] Rather than permitting crowds, the clubs subsequently endorsed Salter's convention. Modern angling associations demand at least fifteen and preferably twenty yards between competitors, with each angler required to stay within a yard either side of his peg as he goes about his business.[146] The need to manage numbers made the match-fishermen more jealous of their own space than the less-organized game fishermen.

Angling was in this sense a microcosm of quiet recreations more generally. Those who fished alone were acutely aware of their membership of a textual community, most prominently in the writings and imitations of Izaak Walton, and later in the century of their connection to bureaucratic organizations. Rising prosperity permitted increasing investment in the paraphernalia of the sport and enabled more of the urban working class to put aside time and money to pursue their pastime. The mass communication networks were crucial to the expansion of fishing at all levels of society, carrying the lawyers, academics, and businessmen to remote game rivers and the lower orders to competitions around towns and cities. In the late 1860s, the 'Piscatorial Correspondent to the "Field" Journal' began publishing a series entitled *The Rail and the Rod* which linked railway timetables to the fishing streams around London.[147] Once on the river bank, the fishermen sought both physical and abstracted solitude. They kept at least a minimum distance from each other, observed conventions of silence and withdrew into themselves, concentrating entirely on the complexities of their sport and the intricate natural world of which they had for a while become a part.

The Invalid in the Home

Ill-health presented a particular challenge to the balance between solitude and sociability in the home. Invalids fill the pages of nineteenth-century fiction, their presence a reflection of both the prevailing standards of health and the fertile opportunities for creating and resolving crises of character and relationships.[148] For all but the least prosperous, illness and dying were domestic events. Hospitals were too bleak and too dangerous to risk entry.[149] Sufferers were confined to their bedroom, at once integral to the business of the household and apart from its daily routines. Their condition, and the course of their health, raised continual questions about the boundary between belonging and separation. The bedroom was both a private space and an open thoroughfare as healthy spouses and children, servants, nurses, doctors, clergy, and sympathizing visitors came and went. The authority of patients was compromised by their limited ability to exercise physical control over parts of the home from which they were now excluded, and by the intervention and advice of trained professionals.

There were conflicting views about how patients should engage with those about them. The dominant religious interpretation of invalidity was that it was a time of retreat from secular affairs. 'How important,' urged the *Christian Meditations; or The Believer's Companion in Solitude*, 'oh! how all-important is the question, – Am I prepared to die? Have I fled for refuge to Jesus, the sinner's friend?'[150] The sufferer should either draw upon reserves of prayer and contemplation or hasten to make up for past neglect. 'When we are afflicted,' wrote G. W. Mylne in *The Sick Room*, 'it is God knocking at our door, because He has something to say to us. God is now knocking at *your* door. . . . Perhaps it is to tell you that you have never thought seriously about your soul, and that you must now begin to do so without delay.'[151] It was all too likely that when patients came face to face with their mortality, they would find their spiritual warehouse insufficiently stocked. As *The Solace of an Invalid* advised, 'The hour of sickness and solitude (although, from the absence of all external impulses, most favourable to reflection) is not the time to collect our materials; they must have been previously stored.'[152] Amongst the '13 Uses of Affliction' listed in John Thornton's *A Companion for the Sick Chamber* were 'to excite serious and most earnest concern about the salvation of the soul in those who have been totally negligent', 'to move us at once to make a solemn surrender and dedication of ourselves and all we have to God without any reserve or delay' and 'to weaken our attachment to inferior objects and pursuits'.[153] All forms of occupational endeavour, and all the distractions of domestic recreation, should now be put aside. 'If, while you enjoyed health,' abjured Thornton, 'you were too much immersed in business, in literary study, or in any other earthly pursuit, turn, Oh turn away from the things which perish in the using, and enter the gracious presence-chamber of the King of kings.'[154]

This body of literary advice, reinforced by visits to a now captive audience by officers of the church, contrasted with the growing concern about the causes and treatment of melancholia. It was broadly accepted that there was some kind of continuum between states of mind and the progress of physical decline and recovery. Further, it was recognized that there was a body of sufferers, particularly women, who took to their beds for all or some part of the day because of a decline in spirits. In these cases, as we have seen, the emerging discipline of psychological analysis stressed that a withdrawal from secular company was at the root of the problem.[155] 'Society calls upon them importunately,' wrote Esquirol in *Mental Maladies*, 'but they fly from it; preferring solitude, in which their imagination and affection can exercise themselves without disturbance.'[156] The particularly feminine malady of hysteria was, as Elaine Showalter has written, explained by '"unnatural" desires for privacy and independence'.[157] The road to recovery was through renewed interactions with society within and beyond the home, and the avoidance of those forms of recreation which turned the mind in upon itself.

The central issue was the function of solitude in the life of the invalid. At a practical level, the enforced withdrawal from domestic routines placed renewed emphasis on all the recreational distractions, from Patience to sewing to reading, with which members of the household defended and exploited their own time and space. Pain and the approach of death sharpened the debate about the ways in which so many women occupied themselves in the absence of a career outside the home. 'Young ladies,' wrote Dinah Craik, 'tis worth a grave thought – what, if called away at eighteen, twenty, or thirty, the most of you would leave behind you when you die? Much embroidery, doubtless; various pleasant, kindly, illegible letters; a moderate store of good deeds; and a cart-load of good intentions. Nothing else – save your name on a tombstone, or lingering for a few more years in family or friendly memory.[158]

The most powerful response to this debate came from a rented room in a house in Tynemouth in 1844. Harriet Martineau, already established as a writer on political economy, had taken to her bed in the autumn of 1839 at the age of thirty-seven.[159] As with another famous female invalid of the nineteenth century, Florence Nightingale, who also collapsed in her late thirties, there has been debate about the substance of the ill-health. Retrospective medical diagnosis is an uncertain science, but it is now accepted that both had real illnesses which they put to strategic use as they continued to manage their public lives.[160] Martineau appears to have suffered from a prolapsed uterus and an ovarian cyst, and remained unwell for five years before making a recovery which she attributed in large part to the new science of mesmerism.[161] Although destined to live long lives, the two women believed they were dying at various junctures, a reflection not so much of hypochondria as of the realistic pessimism of any patient in this era faced with uncertain diagnostic techniques and a paucity of effective therapeutic interventions. They corresponded about their health in 1858: 'Every stroke of work is more likely than not to be the last. Yet I may go on, as I *have* gone on, – much longer than could be expected,' wrote Martineau, to which Nightingale replied, 'I too have "no future" & must do what I can without delay.'[162]

Confined to her room, Martineau reflected on her condition. As she began to recover, she wrote at great speed *Life in the Sick-Room: Essays by an Invalid*. It sold rapidly, a reflection of both the breadth of contemporary interest in the topic and the force of her argument.[163] Her central thesis was the need of the invalid to manage access to their room, and the lasting value of the solitude that could then be enjoyed:

I cannot but wish that more consideration was given to the comfort of being alone in illness. This is so far from being understood, that, though the cases are numerous of sufferers who prefer, and earnestly endeavour to procure solitude, they are, if not resisted, wondered at, and humoured for a supposed peculiarity, rather than seen to be reasonable; whereas, if they are listened to as the best judges of their own comforts, it may be found that they have reason on their side. In a house full of relations, it may be unnatural for an invalid to pass many hours alone; but where, as is the case with numbers who belong to the middle and working classes of society, all the other members of the family have occupations and duties – regular business in life – without the charge of the invalid, it does appear to me, and is felt by me through experience, to be incomparably the happiest plan for the sick one to live alone.[164]

As with middle-class householders more generally, the concept of being alone embraced the presence of live-in assistance. Towards the end of *Mansfield Park*, Jane Austen describes the plight of the dissolute Tom Bertram:

> Tom had gone from London with a party of young men to Newmarket, where a neglected fall, and a good deal of drinking, had brought on a fever; and when the party broke up, being unable to move, had been left by himself at the house of one of these young men to the comforts of sickness and solitude, and the attendance only of servants.[165]

In the same way the somewhat more disciplined Martineau contemplated a future that was both isolated and in company: 'I need not say that this plan of solitude in pain,' she explained, 'supposes sufficient and kindly attendance; but for a permanence, (though I know it to be otherwise in short illnesses,) there is no attendance to be compared with that of a servant.'[166] Then and later, Martineau treated her maids with great kindness, but at a certain level they did not count as people. Solitude was a matter of control. The servant was just an employee, as were nurses and doctors. There were regular visits from a nearby general practitioner, but against the claims of the rising medical profession, Martineau did not view him as the manager of her health.[167]

It was axiomatic that visitors, however well intentioned, were admitted not as a right but at the discretion of the patient. As Anthony

Thomson wrote in his *The Domestic Management of the Sick Room* of 1841, 'a decided salutary effect may be gained from well-regulated society, even when the invalid is yet incapable of leaving his room. Great discretion, however, is requisite in the choice of those who are intended to cheer and amuse him.'[168] Martineau was particularly irritated by the relentlessly optimistic discourse of the bedside attendant. The invalid did not wish to be told over and again that recovery was certain and imminent, when she knew well enough that this was not the case. 'Everything but truth,' she wrote, 'becomes loathed in a sick-room.'[169] The point was taken up by Florence Nightingale in her manual on nursing: 'I really believe there is scarcely a greater worry which invalids have to endure than the incurable hopes of their friends. . . . I would appeal most seriously to all friends, visitors, and attendants of the sick to leave off this practice of attempting to "cheer" the sick by making light of their danger and by exaggerating their probabilities of recovery.'[170]

Martineau wanted to turn the moment of physical infirmity into an assertion of power over space. She found that in her Tynemouth lodgings, far from the London homes of many of her friends, it was easier to enforce her isolation in the darker half of the year. 'Now for about seven months,' she told Henry Crabbe Robinson, '(if I live) my days will pass in the deepest repose that can be had in this world by any but hermits. I shall see scarcely a face but those of my Doctor and maid, till June . . . this loneliness is altogether a matter of choice. I have at last persuaded my friends to indulge me in it.'[171] Self-professed invalidity permitted the sufferer to practise a form of polite incivility, courteously refusing company, however pressing the request. Thus Elizabeth Barrett dealt with a persistent enquirer:

> Dear Sir, I hasten to reply to the request with which you honour me, and beg to assure you that I should have pleasure besides, in receiving your visit and making our acquaintance personal, if it was not that my weak health makes it necessary for me to live comparatively alone, and confined for the most part to one room. It is my only chance for being better ultimately, but I keep myself very quiet now, and this forces me despite of courtesy to say that I cannot see you as indeed I have to answer to others, day by day.[172]

Harriet Martineau was a largely secular hermit. At this juncture she retained enough of her declining Unitarian faith to find spiritual meaning in suffering, but she had no regard for the Christian emphasis on deathbed review and repentance. Although *Life in the Sick-Room* was subsequently filleted to provide entries in literary companions to dying, she was resolutely opposed to the culture of morbid introspection. 'To think no more of death than is necessary for the winding up of the business of life,' she wrote, 'and to dwell no more upon sickness than is necessary for its treatment, or to learn to prevent it, seems to me the simple wisdom of the case, — totally opposite as this is to the sentiment and method of the religious world.'[173] If the sick-bed was a form of imprisonment, it was also an opportunity for greater creative insight into society and its affairs. Bodily frailty was compensated for by the uninterrupted time that was rarely available in the busy life of a healthy woman, whether managing a household or forging a career as a public intellectual. 'By living quite alone,' Martineau wrote to Anna Jameson, 'I am able to write, slowly, the book I told you lay near my heart.'[174] The more she embraced her mortality, the more intellectually alive she felt.[175] She arrived at a basic endorsement of solitude as a necessary retreat for concentrated, creative thought. 'By our being withdrawn from the disturbing bustles of life in the world,' she wrote, 'by our leisure for reading and contemplation of various sides of questions, and by our singular opportunities for quiet reflection, we must, almost necessarily, see further than we used to do, and further than many others do on subjects of interest, which involve general principles.'[176]

In common with other forms of domestic solitude, the viability of the condition was partly dependent on maintaining forms of networked association. Out on the north-east coast, Martineau was supplied with all the books she could read, and felt herself fully engaged with the intellectual currents of her time. Whilst she rigorously policed physical invasion of her space, she kept up an extensive correspondence with relatives, friends and colleagues. Her period as an invalid coincided with the introduction of the Penny Post. She agitated for reform prior to 1840, and described its moral influence as 'unspeakably important'.[177] Down in Torquay, a similarly bed-ridden Elizabeth Barrett described the reformed system as 'the most successful revolution' of the period.[178] It was not merely a matter of maintaining flows of information and sentiment. Letters permitted a level of control of communication. Martineau could read them when she felt up to the task, and amidst fluctuations in her energies and spirits she could reply when most able to present a positive construction of herself. 'It becomes a habit,' she explained, 'from the recurrence of this feeling, to write letters in one's best mood; to give an account of one's self in one's best hours; to present one's most cheerful aspect abroad; and keep one's miseries close at home, under lock and key.'[179]

As was the case with Zimmermann and every networked writer of the era, correspondence was a means of gathering and refining material for a book, and once it was published (and the authorship belatedly acknowledged), *Life in the Sick-Room* itself became a generator of extensive epistolary conversation.[180] Furthermore, although Martineau was physically imprisoned by her health, her room had windows and she was equipped with a stand telescope.[181] This she used to reconnect herself with both the natural world and the everyday life of the seaside town. She looked out at the waves breaking on the shore and into the 'two or three little courts and gardens' she could see behind her house.[182] Although she had the grace to be concerned at the threat to their privacy, stating firmly that 'nothing of the spy shall mix itself with my relations to neighbours who have been ever kind to me',[183] her ability to immerse herself in the humdrum, healthy lives of others whilst remaining alone in her room was a continual source of small epiphanies. She found herself gazing at someone feeding pigs in a nearby market garden: 'the pains of all those hours were annihilated – as completely vanished as if they had never been; while the momentary peep behind the window-curtain made me possessor of this radiant picture for evermore'.[184]

Martineau's embrace of domestic solitude covered the quiet recreational activities as well as her professional writing. It was commonly believed that women made better invalids because they had a wider range of solitary recreational skills than their husbands. 'Another reason why women are more patient than men during sickness,' observed Lynn Linton,

> is that they can amuse themselves better. One gets tired of reading all day long with the aching eyes and weary brain of weakness; yet how few

things a man can do to amuse himself without too great an effort, and without being dependent on others! But women have a thousand pretty little devices for whiling away the heavy hours.[185]

Providing she could still think and write, Martineau practised various handicrafts both as a relief from intellectual endeavour and as a pleasure in their own right. She wrote to a friend at the end 1841, celebrating the completion of a literary project:

> O! my dear friend, you cannot imagine how I enjoy my rest from the pen. I corrected my very last proof on Sunday night, & I feel pretty thoroughly sure that I shall never write again. You w^d be amused to see me, day after day, making baby-things for my sister Ellen, – reading all manner of books that I have wanted to read for years past, – growing narcissus, tulips, hyacinths & crocuses in my window, – studying Euclid, &c, when sufficiently alone, drawing, at my best hours.[186]

She shared in the leisure activities of her time. Although she had no family of her own, she was a doting aunt, making clothes for a succession of nephews and nieces. As her letter indicated, she gardened insofar as her health and her tiny patch of earth permitted. She was fully immersed in the prevailing enthusiasm for Berlin wool-work. In common with other needle-workers, her pictures were destined for sales of work, given a political twist in her case by the donation of profits to the anti-slavery movement.[187]

Control was everything. In middle-class households more generally there was constant movement between solitary and sociable activity, sustained both by growing material prosperity and by developments in consumer markets and communication networks. Recreational solitude was a complement to domestic sociability as much as an escape from its pressures. Amidst endless demands on time and space there were choices to make through the day, with physical or abstracted solitude snatched from other duties and responsibilities. The Victorian invalid was in this case a privileged instance of a more general set of conditions. Properly managed, as Martineau argued, periods of ill-health enabled transitions to be more freely made between solitude and company. She was aware of voices arguing that embroidery and related pastimes were symbols of the constructed exclusion of women from the world of male endeavour, but where they could be combined with the opportunities for female intellectual practice, they were welcome elements of a complete life. As she explained in her autobiography, working quietly with her hands was a way of giving voice to her mind:

Then, – I have always had some piece of fancy-work on hand, – usually for the benefit of the Abolition fund in America; and I have a thoroughly womanish love of needle-work, – yes, even ('I own the soft impeachment') of wool-work, many a square yard of which is all invisibly embossed with thoughts of mine wrought in, under the various moods and experiences of a long series of years. It is with singular alacrity that, in winter evenings, I light the lamp, and unroll my wool-work, and meditate or dream till the arrival of the newspaper tells me that the tea has stood long enough.[188]

4

PRAYERS, CONVENTS, AND PRISONS

Solitary Spiritual Communication

In the Sermon on the Mount, Jesus gave instruction on how to pray: 'when thou prayest, enter into thy closet, and when thou hast shut thy door, pray to thy Father which is in secret; and thy Father which seeth in secret shall reward thee openly'.[1] The translators working on the King James Bible at the start of the seventeenth century rendered a vague term for a secluded place into a particular room that was becoming more common in the homes of the gentry and prosperous town dwellers.[2] Solitary communion with God required a physical location from which other members of the household could be excluded. With the destruction of the monasteries at the Reformation, there were no longer any specifically constructed spaces for individual spiritual meditation.[3] Churches were for collective worship and observance. Only the tiny Quaker sect emerging in the mid-seventeenth century encouraged silence and unstructured speech in a specialized location. Private prayer, whether as a means of complementing the weekly services or as a direct conversation with God, had to be undertaken in the home, or perhaps, if it were available, in a spacious and well-tended garden.[4]

During the eighteenth century, an accommodation had been made between the sometimes intense conversations with a hidden God in the midst of the domestic routine and the Sabbath rituals and sermons. But as the religious revival gained momentum in the early decades of the following century, the role of solitary spiritual communication became more complex and in several contexts much more contested. There were three separate issues. The first arose from the attempt to turn the family, particularly the bourgeois domestic unit, into a miniature religious community. At its most rigorous, the Protestant household was to become a monastery with carpets, a physical retreat with comfortable furnishings and a mixed community of men, women, children, and servants. Piety was to be rehearsed daily, with text-based observations led by the head of the family, who combined the roles of spiritual and secular leader. The role of private prayer in this collective worship became increasingly unclear. The conversation with 'thy Father which is in secret' was a matter for the individual alone as he, or she, drew up a spiritual balance sheet and sought the promised reward. How physical and moral energy was found in order to move between the registers of solitary and social communion posed a major problem for the host of manuals on domestic religion which poured from the presses in this period.

The second issue was the revival from the 1840s onwards of the built religious community, Protestant and Catholic, male and female. For the first time in three hundred years Britain possessed a network of monasteries and convents. Their founding unleashed a ferocious debate about enclosed orders, whose demerits Zimmermann had summarized at the end of the previous century and Lewis had translated into gothic melodrama. Here solitude was salient less as an actual practice and more as an alleged abuse. The image of the lone penitent, separated from his, and in particular her, family, locked in a bare cell, exposed to secret mistreatment by religious superiors and God, encapsulated all that was deforming about the walled community. The imagined destructive power of solitude altered the rules of evidence and accusation. Anything could be believed unless the privacy-seeking communities or their often embarrassed church hierarchies could supply alternative narratives.

The third issue also centred on the dangerous power of spiritual solitude. The religious revival of the early nineteenth century represented a new partnership between the denominations, particularly the

Anglican Church, and the emerging democratic state. The first sign of a practical collaboration was the decision in the tense aftermath of the Napoleonic Wars to invest in a major church-building programme. A grant of a million pounds was made in 1818, followed by another half million six years later. During the years of the Reform Bill crisis and Chartism, churches were being built in every corner of the country, and new parishes were being created with better-paid clergy. These initiatives were designed to enable the Anglican Church to perform its traditional function, which was threatened by the rapid expansion of urban communities. A more ambitious agenda involved the church playing the leading role in a new and still more expensive alliance with the state in the maintenance of public order.

The debate about penal policy which began in the final quarter of the eighteenth century eventually led to a major prison-building programme by Reform Act governments. At the centre of the first model penitentiary, opened in the same decade as the earliest monasteries and convents, was clergy-supervised solitary confinement. The last great push by the churches to regain their spiritual and social hegemony in Britain was founded on the figure of the prisoner alone in his cell, exposed to a prolonged, personal conversation with his Maker.

Where private prayer in the household functioned as an adjunct to the spiritual life of the family, the exposure of the penitent individual to God was the driving force in the process of punishment and rehabilitation. The maintenance of law and order in a society apparently faced with the collapse of all forms of moral discipline rested on a redefined notion of prayer in a space which, if not as well appointed as a middle-class closet or study, was better built, heated, and serviced than the accommodation most of the prisoners had enjoyed in the world outside. The essence of the joint enterprise between church and state, whose trajectory will be traced in the fourth part of this chapter, was the fearful experience of enforced isolation. The originators of the new penal policy were in no doubt about its negative effects. From first to last, the default argument for solitary confinement was that if it did no good, its deterrent effect would keep down the prison population. Imposed solitude was seen as a high-risk strategy, requiring close monitoring to prevent the destruction of the prisoner's sanity. The proffered gain was a combination of punishment and rehabilitation. The unmediated encounter between the convict and God would lead to the total reconstruction of the convict's moral sense and his re-entry into society as a useful, law-abiding citizen.

Enter into Thy Closet

In 1829, William Roberts welcomed a new era in Christian worship. 'We seem,' he wrote, 'at length, by God's peculiar blessing, to have arrived in this country at a period in its religious advancement, when family worship at the beginning and end of each day is quite of course among all professing Christians who have any right apprehension of what that name imports.'[5] The domestic unit could be seen as the essential building block of a religious society. 'The nation is but an aggregate of families,' wrote the Reverend John Frere in 1851. 'The religion therefore of families is the best security for the religion of the nation.'[6] As in the Anglican Church, the spiritual unit was also an authority structure. 'Let a parent execute,' continued Frere, 'as it were, an episcopal office in his own home.'[7] Male heads of the household had a particular responsibility. Their privilege, as explained in *Ten Minutes Recommendation of Private Prayer*, was accompanied by a heavy duty, as they were responsible not only 'for their own everlasting welfare, but for the welfare of those immortal souls over whom they exercise a kind of spiritual guardianship'.[8] The model was that of a miniature religious community, in which the principal accepted the burden of leadership and the dependent members gave him unquestioning obedience. 'It is in his power,' explained Frere,

> and therefore it must be his duty, to set his household forward in the way to heaven. Every Christian ought to be the head and guide of the Church in his own house; to instruct, admonish, and encourage all its inmates to the zealous performance of their duty to their common Lord and Master. Oh, what a blessed thing would it be for this Christian country, if this principle were acted up to, and every family were made a seminary of religious principles and habits![9]

There was a division of labour within the seminary, but the outcome was essentially communal. All its members, including the servants, would lead a disciplined Christian life and in turn the aggregate society would constitute a morally ordered whole.

There remained the question of private prayer. Heads of the households would supervise daily worship, based on the devotional literature that the Society for the Promotion of Christian Knowledge and the Religious Tract Society were vigorously distributing to every home they could reach. As Arthur Benoni Evans advised in *Personal Piety, Or Aids to Private Prayer for Individuals of All Classes*, 'they have only to select for themselves out of hundreds of publications drawn up for that express purpose, by pious members of our own Church'.[10] Each domestic unit was seen as a reading as well as a praying community, with those more advanced in their literacy able to guide and instruct those still learning their letters. But as had been the case at least since the Reformation, there was opportunity for the observant Christian to converse directly with God. The Reverend F. O. Morris stressed the difference between 'that prayer which is held solely between a man and his Maker, as distinguished from prayer in public, or in the family, or with friends'.[11] Whilst the bulk of the printed material on domestic piety emphasized social practice, there were a growing number of manuals giving advice on what they argued was the greater task of personal conversation with the Supreme Being. This spiritual exercise should precede any other. 'Your first of duties, then,' wrote Evans, 'is to make regular practice of thus holding "heart-communion" with God, in order that your minds should be always so prayerfully inclined, as often, even at your work, in your vocations, and at your daily occupation.'[12] A time of concentrated private prayer, in preparation for the day and at its conclusion, would supply the spiritual resource for every encounter with man's fallen state, within and beyond the walls of the home.

This mode of solitude offered the truest form of company. 'Here is friendship, indeed,' proclaimed *Ten Minutes Recommendation of Private Prayer*, 'as far transcending all human friendships as the heavens are higher than the earth! The one permanent, pure, and eternal; the other fluctuating, mingled with much corruption, and of a day.'[13] Kneeling by themselves in a closet, or if that were unavailable, in a bedroom emptied of other occupants, the individual could not be less alone. Through private prayer they could unburden their heart to God, who knew their strengths and weaknesses better than any other relation or friend. As F. O. Morris explained, 'A Christian has, through Christ, the Son of God, the everlasting Son of the everlasting Father, a personal relation to God. He has his own obligations, and, above all, his own wants, and it is both his duty and his privilege to go to God and to speak to Him alone.'[14] The conversation might be silent, but in this discourse God would make clear his response, directly or indirectly. The dialogue was hidden from the rest of the household and was able to supply moral and practical succour beyond the capacities of other family members, however close the relationship. It was at once the foundation of domestic piety and a deeper and more complete spiritual experience. 'The Christian can in secret give free vent to every desire,' wrote the Reverend Edward Bickersteth,

> vary his requests according to the present state of his mind, or the present necessities of the day or hour in which he is living; he can dwell on his personal wants; and, in short, give full scope to his feelings, and pour out his whole soul to God. Prayer in secret forms a line of distinction between the Christian and the mere Professor.[15]

At one level, private prayer was a further example of the process traced in the previous chapter of solitary activity created by the same forces that sustained the sociable event of the middle-class family. It gained force from the emphasis on the domestic unit as a spiritual entity, and it was made possible by the material comfort of the bourgeois household. As with so many other isolated activities, it depended upon and in turn generated a proliferating literature which sustained lone practitioners and connected them to a wider community. It was recognized that, left to their own devices outside the conducted formularies of the Sunday service, the observant Christian might find their daily prayers difficult to articulate. As Mrs Dawson warned in *Communion with God or Aids to Prayer*, 'there are times when communion with God is difficult, when thoughts flow with sluggish pace, and when the needed words refuse to come'.[16] However serious the intent, the untrained, unsupervised penitent could not guarantee a necessary fluency or appropriate vocabulary of prayer. 'Man is upon his knees,' wrote the Reverend R. C. Moberly. 'He tries to lift up his soul and speak to God. But too soon the tongue falters, mists gather before the sight, sounds of this world come floating through the ears, the mind wanders dreamily on, the stammered words have become monotonous, unmeaning, or have died altogether away.'[17] The proliferating tracts supplied advice and encouragement. They offered specimen texts of their own and a general endorsement of the use of the standard Protestant literature, particularly the Bible and Prayer Book.

There were, however, persisting tensions between the solitary and the social in the realm of spiritual observance. Although the manuals on private prayer were careful not to dismiss the value of domestic observance, in practice their emphasis was on the enclosed conversation with God. H. C. G. Moule's *Private Prayer* insisted that 'it is the occasion of all others for cultivating a deep individual insight into yourself and your personal needs, and into the Lord Jesus Christ, into God in Christ, in all His glory and grace *for you*'.[18] The withdrawal from the life of the household was fundamental to both the purpose and the practice of the activity. The day was framed by periods of intense focus on the inward soul. 'You will find in short,' continued Moule, 'that you as an individual sinner, an individual believer, cannot minimize your solitary, secret, individual seasons of confession, petition and praise, without the results that are to be expected.'[19] The process began and ended with a review not of the family or social relations more generally, but of the bounded inner self. 'I would recommend it to those, who use these Prayers,' wrote Sir James Stonhouse in his frequently reprinted *Prayers for the Use of Private Persons*, that before their devotions, 'they spend a few Minutes *in examining* themselves. . . . Without such a daily *Endeavour* their Prayers are Formality, Insincerity, and an Abomination to the Lord.'[20]

Whilst there was a diffuse sense that private prayer would better equip the individual for communal spiritual duties, the manuals were preoccupied with the fate of the persons conducting the conversation with God. They alone could prepare themselves for the dialogue, and they primarily reaped the benefit. As befitted an increasingly commercial society, they were encouraged to look for an identifiable return on the investment of their time and energy. One of the more practical manuals, Charles Harford-Battersby's *Daily: A Help to Private Prayer*, supplied a form of double-entry spiritual book-keeping. The bulk of the pages were blank apart from a heading. On the left-hand page the user entered 'Special Subjects for Prayer' with a column for the date that the request was made. On the matching right-hand page the user recorded 'Answers to Prayer', again with a date indicating when the Almighty made his response.[21]

Furthermore, there were serious practical conflicts between the mission of the solitary prayer and the busy life of the household. It was far from easy to achieve the form of spatial and mental withdrawal that private spiritual observations demanded. 'There are, however, PECULIAR DIFFICULTIES in maintaining constant, and fervent, secret prayer,' warned the Reverend Edward Bickersteth,

> ... besides the opposition of a corrupt nature within, the temptations of the world without, continually draw and allure us from our duty. Our great enemy Satan also uses every temptation to keep us from secret prayer. We do not find it so difficult to read the Bible, go to church or hear sermons, as we do to persevere in constant, fervent, and believing private prayer.[22]

In this context, Satan adopted mundane but nonetheless deeply obstructive forms. Even if, for instance, there did exist a closet or similar specialized room, there was no means of preventing the life of the household from trying to intrude, whether in the form of an incautious servant, an ill-advised wife or ill-disciplined children. 'It is true, indeed,' observed *Ten Minutes Recommendation of Private Prayer*,

> there is no retreat so sacred, none so retired, that the man of God can find in the present world, but it is exposed to·interruption, and liable to be broken in upon. You cannot enter the closet so secretly, not shut to the door so immediately, but what some enemy to devotion will observe, and either press in with you, or importunately knock afterwards for admission.[23]

For all the appropriation of the form and function of religious observance, a house was not a church, but a multi-functional entity with a host of demands on every individual and furnished space throughout every waking hour of every day.

The guides to private prayer were permeated with concern about backsliding. It was too often the case that good intentions were undone by external pressures or inner failings. In the monastic cloister, the distant model for the religious household, there were supportive rituals to maintain the discipline of spiritual observation.[24] In the middle-class home, bells did not chime to summon members of the domestic community to Lauds and the six successive services throughout the canonical day. Instead of the hard bed in a cell and the procession along stone floors to the chapel, there was a comfortable mattress and linen, and a host of secular concerns as the morning began. 'Amid the distractions of a busy life,' observed Charles Harford-Battersby, 'it is easy for prayer to be neglected.'[25] It was essential that resolve was stiffened by routine, at least in the form of concentrated private prayer at the beginning and the end of the day. Otherwise it was too easy to find excuses for lapsed observance. 'It is impossible to speak too strongly of the absolute necessity of saying your Morning and Evening Prayers,' wrote Carter in *A Book of Private Prayer*. 'It is not too much to say that upon the fulfilment of this duty hangs your salvation. It is all-important. Look upon it therefore as a matter of life and death, and never be tempted by idleness or *fancied* want of time to neglect it.'[26]

The sheer complexity of bourgeois family life, inside and outside the home, was a constant difficulty. Withdrawal was intrinsically less appealing than participation. However genuine the intention to spend time alone with God, there were always competing responsibilities and tempting diversions. A principal function of the multitude of manuals was to reinforce self-discipline. Alfred Dale wrote in *Looking Upward: A Little Hand-book of Prayer for Private or Family Use* that his publication was 'chiefly for anyone who has forsaken, or thought too lightly of, the sacred altar of personal or domestic prayer'.[27] The need for such literature was readily apparent. 'Therefore, to each of you let me put the question,' wrote Morris in *Plain Services for Plain People*, 'are you in the habit and love of frequent private prayers? Have you some stated daily times for the exercise of the duty, and do you make occasions for yourself? Or does the pursuit of pleasure, the care of a family, or the necessity of business, mistakenly supposed to be a hindrance, prevent you from the privilege.'[28]

Whereas the solitary recreations interwoven with the social life of the household were for the most part alternative ways of enjoying middle-class prosperity, private prayer was intrinsically a rejection of ease and self-indulgence. If the substance of the prayers might involve thanks for blessings already received and requests for further gifts, the process of making the intercessions required a temporary cessation of comfort. Moule's *Secret Prayer* left the reader in no doubt about the sacrifices that had to be made: 'The warm bed when we wake, the bright fire in the late evening, the allurements of book, or conversation, or whatever it is that *must give way* if we are to set ourselves to seek the King's face before we sleep.'[29] Solitude was both a condition of the intense conversation with God and a means of escaping the oversight of other members of the household. Once the closet or bedroom door was closed, there was no knowing what the professed penitent was actually doing. As Moule observed, there was a 'peculiar temptation to laxity and indolence in the practice, just because it is secret'.[30] A well-furnished bedroom offered all the wrong incentives. Much ink was spilled in the manuals on the practical issue of where to pray. At the very beginning and end of the day the obvious location was the bed itself, or, if time were short, whilst the individual was getting dressed or undressed. But physical warmth and relaxation was held to be inimical to the demands of the activity. Better be wearing a minimum of clothing and to be on the hard floor, whether or not it was carpeted. How the body was arranged was intrinsic to how the spiritual dialogue took place. 'When you are dressed,' advised the Reverend Edwin Hobson, 'kneel down in the place in your room where you can do so most conveniently and reverently; if by your bedside, avoid a lounging posture, remembering that a lazy, self-indulgent way of kneeling will be sure to lead to sluggish and languid praying.'[31]

A certain level of income made the conduct of private prayer both feasible and more difficult. Prayerful solitude was real labour made possible by increasing prosperity. The manuals were written by professional clergy for middle-class homes. It was recognized that the rituals of withdrawal that they specified were conditional on a certain quality of housing. Less fortunate families were either ignored, or advised to find locations for their communion with God outside their crowded accommodation. 'Poor persons, who have but one apartment,' wrote the Reverend Bickersteth, 'may enter the spirit of this direction by praying wherever they can be retired. Isaac's closet was the field.'[32] This was scarcely a relevant analogy for those crammed into the expanding

towns and cities. If comfort rendered solitary observance more stress-
ful, its absence made it virtually impossible.

Sisterhoods and Convents

Private prayer was a means of nurturing a Christian faith amidst the distractions of family life. A more radical response was to withdraw from
the domestic unit altogether. Nineteenth-century Britain inherited
a deeply ingrained hostility towards enclosed religious communities.
The epochal Catholic Emancipation Act of 1829 excluded monasteries
from its provisions. It remained illegal to conduct such institutions,
and any member of an overseas order found in the country was to
be deported.[33] Although they were not specifically penalized, Catholic
nunneries were assumed to be covered by the same prohibition, and
it appeared unlikely that the Protestant denominations would adopt a
practice so redolent of the worst excesses of the Papist religion. Within
little more than a decade, however, both the established church and
its Romish rival were creating walled institutions that had not been
seen in Britain since the days of Thomas Cromwell. The first religious
house to be opened in England since the Reformation was founded
by the Sisters of Mercy in Bermondsey in 1839.[34] Building work on
the Cistercian Mount St Bernard was completed in 1844, and a year
later the Anglo-Catholic Park Village Sisterhood was founded in the
slums around King's Cross.[35] Following the restoration of the Catholic
hierarchy in 1850, Cardinal Wiseman created fifteen male and twenty-
three female communities.[36] Nunneries continued to be established at
a greater rate, and by the mid-1870s it was calculated that there were
over two hundred Catholic convents in the United Kingdom housing three thousand nuns.[37] In the Anglican Church there was again a
greater investment in women's communities, with more than ninety
sisterhoods or similar bodies in existence by 1900. Since the founding
of Park Village, over ten thousand women had at some point in their
lives left their families to join an enclosed Protestant order.[38]

The proponents of the new institutions viewed personal isolation
not as an outcome but as a cause of the rejection of family life. A
sympathetic Anglican bishop, A. P. Forbes, explored the driving force
behind the growth of the sisterhoods:

Thousands and thousands have no relations; others have been abandoned by unnatural parents; others have had those they leant on, taken away by death; others have been desolated by their natural protectors forming new ties. All up through the different grades of society, this state of things more or less exists. In all there are persons who by circumstances are detached from home connections, or whose ties are so slight as to make a legitimate occupation which carries with it the sympathy and love of many and the sisterly relation of the holy and the pure, a real blessing. Till one meditates upon it, one can hardly conceive the quantity of solitariness that exists in this country, from these things; and we hesitate not to assert, that, comparing it with the other nations of Europe, there is none in which a home and refuge such as these Sisterhoods afford, would be such a blessing as here.[39]

By 'solitariness', Forbes meant a condition akin to a more modern notion of loneliness, which will be discussed in Chapter 7. These were not women who had chosen to withdraw from company. Rather they were forced by demography, social convention, and occupational prohibition to live lives bereft of intimate relations or purposeful institutional involvement. The 1851 census put a figure on a long-suspected fact, that there were many more women in Victorian society than could ever fulfil a destiny of marriage and motherhood.[40] A surplus of over half a million females in an adult population of some twenty million created an inescapable future of lives spent at best on the margins of other relatives' families.

For these women, as for those who saw little prospect of satisfying their intellect or their moral drive even if they did find a husband, the notion of a formal sisterhood seemed an increasingly attractive proposition.[41] It proffered a defined, supportive community, an expression of their Christian faith and for the first time the capacity to acquire a professional skill which could be put to the service of a society so obviously threatened by poverty and associated forms of deprivation. Anna Jameson explained the project:

There are thousands and thousands of women who have no protection, no guide, no help, no home; – who are absolutely driven by circumstance and necessity, if not by impulse and inclination, to carry out into the larger community the sympathies, the domestic instincts, the active administrative capabilities with which God has endowed them; but these instincts, sympathies, capabilities, require, first, to be properly developed, then properly trained, and then directed into large and useful channels, according to the individual tendencies.[42]

The search for an alternative destiny for those who had no place in the conventional Victorian home was driven by the same motives that led Harriet Martineau and Florence Nightingale to embrace the managed solitude of the sick-room that we saw in the previous chapter.[43] In both cases there was a desire for a controlled space in which aspiration and activity were not determined by male authority. In 1851, the thirty-one-year-old Florence Nightingale made a long visit to the Protestant deaconess community at Kaiserswerth in Germany, which was an influ-ential model for the formation of the English sisterhoods.[44] She was deeply impressed by the range of work that was being undertaken, which embraced hospitals, lunatic asylums, poor houses, orphanages, and normal schools; by the skills that the women were taught; and by the respect with which they were treated by the community they had joined.[45] On her return to England she wrote her first publication, a description of the life at Kaiserswerth with a preface which explained the need for such institutions: 'If . . . there are many women who live unmarried, and many more who pass the third of the usual term of life unmarried, and if intellectual occupation is not meant to be their end in life, what are they to do with that thirst for action, useful action, which every woman feels who is not diseased in mind or body?'[46]

Nightingale was ambivalent about the religious framing of the work at Kaiserswerth and the subsequent British communities. She respected the quality of the skills taught in the institutions and made use of nurses trained by the Sisters of Mercy in the Crimea, but in general she depre-cated any subordination of her professional mission to spiritual motives and structures. Her views remained, nonetheless, comparatively sympathetic set against the hostility aroused by the reintroduction of enclosed communities in Britain.[47] Throughout the remainder of the nineteenth century, it was argued in pamphlets, articles, public meet-ings, and Parliamentary debates that those who passed through the doors of the convents were exchanging solitariness for solitude at its most destructive and irreversible. Cardinal Wiseman summarized the popular characterization of a woman entering the communities he was setting up:

> A young, imaginative creature, disappointed in a sincere affection; a romantic enthusiast dwelling on ideal perfection, and craving after 'the pensive cell,' and its 'heavenly contemplation;' an early mourner, drooping under the loss of every one dear, and coldly looked upon in a borrowed home; such are supposed to be the staple of supply to the conventual life, where it is embraced by choice.[48]

The 'pensive cell' was to become the focus of repeated attempts to expose the enclosed orders to inspection by both secular institutions and critical religious groups.[49]

The scale of the controversy was partly a function of a freighted past. If the new communities were a response to the particular social problems of mid-Victorian Britain, they were also a conscious revival of the institutions of the early church. The very idea of enclosed orders, male or female, immediately invoked centuries of hostility to the abuses that were alleged to have taken place within them. The proponents of their restoration argued that the controversies which were such a vivid presence in the writings of eighteenth-century Protestants could be discounted. It was possible to reach over the failings of the last millennium and invoke the behaviour of the founders of the Christian religion. James Milner, whose writings, as we noted in Chapter 1, had begun the revival of interest in early Christianity, simply by-passed the subsequent history. 'The enormous evils of Monasticism', he explained, 'are to be ascribed to its degeneracy in after-times, not to its first institution.'[50] As John Henry Newman wrote in his influential *The Church of the Fathers*, monastic life 'had nothing in it, surely but what was perfectly Christian, and, under circumstances, exemplary'.[51] The Oxford Movement, which was a driving force in the introduction of walled societies in the Anglican Church, had little time for any organizational or theological developments since the sixth century.[52] Its critics were not so forgiving. An attack on convents in *Fraser's Magazine* claimed that 'the judgement of the nation at large on monastic life has undergone no change since the period of the Reformation'.[53] The debate over the merits of the walled societies began in a state of heightened emotion. A survey of the first sisterhoods in the *Edinburgh Review* anticipated the level of discourse that would greet them:

> We do not fear reason nor enquiry. But what we do fear – we confess it – is a cry; a cry, against which neither reason nor charity nor religion are of the slightest service. Protestantism may be in danger! The Papists are coming! Because a certain number of single women have agreed to live in one house, put on one dress, and join their earnings and efforts into one common stock for the relief of certain acknowledged social evils, the whole Apocalypse is likely enough to be ransacked for the millionth time, to prove that the mark of the beast is upon them.[54]

The first sisterhoods were founded as popular anti-Popery gained momentum, fuelled by the increase in Irish immigration after the Famine and the re-establishment of the Catholic hierarchy in Britain.[55] The Catholic orders were condemned as reversions to a corrupt past, the Protestant as vehicles of a future takeover of the Anglican Church.[56] As Anna Jameson observed in 1855, 'The subject has suddenly taken a form which appeals to popular sympathies. Names and deeds have, of late, been sounded through the brazen trumpet of publicity, and mixed up, unhappily, with party and sectarian discord.'[57] Solitude, as a repressive and destructive experience, brought into focus layers of hostility to the new institutions. At the outset, the association of enclosed religious communities with withdrawal from everyday social interaction put them on the wrong side of history. In the midst of the threats and dislocations of the new industrial society, what was required above all was lay participation, not spiritual retreat.[58] 'Thus sinful and sorrowing humanity,' wrote Alfred Wishart in his history of monasticism, 'needing the guidance and comfort that holy men can furnish, was forgotten in the desire for personal peace and future salvation.'[59] The argument was made from within the established church as much as from outside. The Anglican periodical *The English Churchman* attacked the idea of solitude just as the first sisterhood was established:

> Whatever may have been the circumstances which, in former times, justified certain blessed Saints in leading a life of Solitude – God forbid

that we should say they were not justified – we apprehend that, in our day, when so much ignorance, vice, poverty, misery, and sorrow prevails on all sides, Solitude, except in very peculiar cases, is selfish and sinful. Christian men and women must be up and *doing*. If they have no duties at home, or among their kindred and acquaintance, they have duties abroad, among the ignorant, the poor, and the afflicted.[60]

The offence was compounded by the physical presence of the proliferating communities, each of which required the construction or conversion of its own building, with lockable doors, walled grounds and, so it was claimed, barred windows. As we shall see in the next part of this chapter, the first modern model prison at Pentonville, with its solitary confinement in separate cells, opened just three years before the first convent, and there was a wholesale transfer of imagery between the two projects. 'Why are they so like prisons,' asked an article on 'The Convents of the United Kingdom', 'and so unlike private dwelling-houses, or even unlike the public institutions of English towns?'[61] The notion of vulnerable young women being 'immured' in convents became a literal and metaphorical representation of their suffering.[62] The semi-pornographic tradition of monastic revelation commenced by Matthew Lewis generated *The Awful Disclosures of Maria Monk*, first published in America in 1836, and widely circulated in Britain.[63] It featured nuns gagged and locked in punishment cells.[64] Constant parallels were drawn between the two building programmes. 'They have all the same characteristics which we observe in the bridewells, the penitentiaries, and the prisons of our own land,' wrote Hobart Seymour. 'There are the same lofty walls, the same massive gates, the same barred windows, and the same grated openings; the same dull, sombre, cheerless aspect, the same uninviting, repelling, lifeless exterior, the same inaccessibility from without, the same precluded possibility of escape from within.'[65] Intent was read into architecture. Convents that had no ambition of locking up inmates in cells, it was argued, would not have constructed them in the first place. 'If no one is imprisoned,' speculated the author of *English Convents, What Are They?* '– if novices are not chained to their dens – why that gothic thickness of a wall, those bolts, those bars, and gratings, those mysteries of silence and seclusion, those inveterate attempts to cut an inmate off from the sound of a relative's voice, or the sight of a letter from "the outside world"?'[66] Conventional domestic spaces took on a new meaning. John Henry Newman had to write to *The Times* to insist that the underground rooms in the Colwich Nunnery were merely for storing wine, and then was forced to defend the cellars at the Oratory in Birmingham, which, he explained, were for deliveries of coal.

Particular attention was paid to the management of modern communications systems. In the period when the Penny Post was beginning to expand the category of networked solitude, the means by which individuals could be by themselves but easily in contact with others, the closed orders sought not only to limit visits from outside family and friends but also to control the receipt and composition of letters.[67] A critical survey of *Sisterhoods in the Church of England* deplored 'the fact that these conventual establishments are closed against all unwelcome visitation, and that any of the inmates may be secluded from all intercourse and communication with their family and friends'.[68] At every turn the ability of inmates to relieve their sense of physical isolation was frustrated. Correspondence was censored, with obvious parallels to prison mail, and books were limited in volume and content. It was a two-way exclusion: inmates could not tell outsiders about their lives; visitors could not freely enter the premises to find out for themselves. The least that was required, argued critics of both female and male communities, was the extension of the newly invented device of government inspectors. 'If monasteries and convents are to exist in all this free country,' argued the author of *English Convents, What are They?*, 'it must be under the same condition as asylums and prisons.'[69] A series of attempts were made in Parliament to create an inspectorate of enclosed orders, all of which foundered on the objection that they were private religious houses, subject to the management of the appropriate church hierarchies. The religious orders also managed to evade an alternative route of inspection by the Charity Commission which was set up in 1853.[70]

'The truth is,' wrote Hobart Seymour's *Nunneries* of 1852, 'there is a veil spread over all the inner life of the conventual system; and secrecy, and mystery, and concealment, are essentials of its nature.'[71] Within this opaque world, any vice could flourish, particularly where it involved impressionable girls separated from the natural authority of

their parents. In both the supposedly factual inquiries and the proliferating sensational fiction, there was a prurient obsession with repressed
sexuality. Beautiful young women were seduced from their families and
exposed to hidden temptation and abuse behind the walls and locked
doors.[72] General Sir Richard Phayre's *Monasticism Unveiled* of 1890
summarized more than four decades of critical commentary. Once the
noviates had taken their vows of obedience, poverty, and chastity they
were vulnerable to a repressive regime, 'enforced by the free use of
the cells and dungeons and the inhuman severities and tortures of the
system, which, in the course of a very few years, drive thousands of
young girls who are subjected to them either into lunacy or a premature
grave'.[73] The distinction between the meditative cell of the historic
monastery and the punishment cell of the modern prison was easily
blurred. The combination of spiritual tyranny and physical isolation in
the locked rooms within the buildings posed a fundamental threat to
the mental stability of young women, whom it was assumed were much
less able to withstand such pressures than male noviates.

The general condemnation of the sisterhoods was periodically reinforced by local scandals which were eagerly taken up by the national
press. In 1852, Henrietta Griffiths escaped from the Norwood Nunnery,
where, she claimed,

> I was kept in the closet for three weeks, from four in the morning till
> nine at night, and I was not allowed to go out for any purpose. My food
> was brought to me. The closet was only large enough to contain a chair
> and a table, but neither one nor other was in it, and I was obliged to
> lie on the floor. There was a window, but it was closed, and I was in
> darkness all the time.[74]

The closet of the Sermon on the Mount was now being put a more
malign purpose. Catherine Selby climbed over the wall of Colwich
Nunnery in 1865, and in the ensuing debate it was claimed that a
local carpenter had been employed to construct 'underground apartments only dimly lighted' for suspicious use. Four years later there was
a prolonged public controversy when Susanna Mary Saurin sued the
mother superior of a convent near Hull for false imprisonment after
relations had broken down within the community. It was stated that

'during her final seven months in the convent, after she had steadfastly refused to depart, she was condemned to complete silence, restricted to a single room, and assigned to a bed with too few blankets'.[75] For the *Times* the experience was doubly gendered. An enclosed community of women was uniquely exposed to unequal power relationships. Susanna Saurin had suffered 'for a long period a series of hardships, ignominies and insults, and vexatious annoyances that none but women could inflict, and none but women, it must be admitted, could endure'.[76] The 'escaped nun', breaking out of the locked cell and the walled convent to tell her story to the world, became an established literary genre. As late as the 1880s, the former American nun Edith O'Gorman became an international celebrity, lecturing across North America, England, and the Colonies about her imprisonment, and becoming involved in a controversy with Ellen Golding, 'the rescued nun'.[77] The cover of an English 1913 edition of O'Gorman's account depicted a nun's face gazing forlornly through the barred window of a door.[78] At the extreme end of the tradition was the figure of the 'walled-up nun', condemned to die in a bricked-in cell for an infraction of the convent's rules.[79]

With so many communities founded in Britain during the second half of the nineteenth century, largely escaping external inspection or legal intervention, there can be no certainty about the abuse that may have taken place. At a more general level, the small, bounded societies are likely to have been the site of low-level tension and conflicts between their members. But, as Florence Nightingale mordantly observed, this was yet more common in the celebrated domestic unit. 'I have known a good deal of convents,' she wrote, 'and of the petty, grinding tyrannies supposed to be exercised there, but I know nothing like the petty, grinding tyranny of the good English family.'[80] In large part the obsession with lone penitents, willingly or otherwise confined to their cells, was a function of myth rather than reality. It stemmed from the long-standing tension between eremitical (solitary) and cenobitic (communal) monasticism. The etymology of monk – *monachus* or alone – raised the vision of the ascetic hermit, rejecting all company in his search for communion with God.[81] But however much the desert fathers were celebrated by the early church, the construction of permanent communities, particularly at the beginning of the second millennium, required a balance between the two tendencies. Individual meditation, apart from not only wider society but also other penitents in the order, remained a powerful requirement. In its extreme tendency it was seen as an inherently unstable condition, dangerously detached from all forms of what had become a highly structured church hierarchy. The solution in the founding Rule of St Bernard was a kind of *via media* between the two forms of bearing witness.[82] Monks spent long periods at prayer in their cells, but joined together in the seven liturgical devotions throughout the day, and accepted the authority of the head of the community. Different orders placed themselves at particular points along the cenobitic–eremitical continuum, but none endorsed the complete withdrawal into a cell or some form of wilderness.

The revival of monasticism in an urbanizing and industrializing country forced a reconsideration of the balance between the solitary and the social. John Henry Newman, who had done so much to encourage the interest of Anglicans in religious societies while he was a leading member of the Oxford Movement, had the opportunity to establish his own institution when he crossed to Rome.[83] He chose a model based on the Oratory of St Philip Neri for his community in Birmingham.[84] This allowed space for private prayer, but the leading characteristic of the community was that of an Oxbridge college, where educated gentlemen could study and debate Catholic theology, and in their spare time engage in pastoral work in the surrounding city. The new sisterhoods were faced with a similar choice.[85] There was considerable debate in the initial Park Hall community about where to place the emphasis between a life of contemplation and a mission of good works in the community. Most of the subsequent orders made provision within their daily routines for individual prayer in the cells in which the women slept, as well as communal worship, but in practice their engagement in the alleviation of deprivation and suffering in the outside world left little time or energy for solitary meditation or even private reading. 'Another absolute rule of the ideal Sisterhood,' wrote Diana Craik, 'must be work. In this nineteenth century we cannot go back to medieval notions of ecstatic mysticism or corporeal penitences.'[86] The common pattern was for the vows of poverty, chastity, and obedience to be supplemented by a commitment to service, although some Catholic institutions remained suspicious of any activities which distracted from religious observance.[87]

A sympathetic commentator referred with little hyperbole to 'the hand-to-hand struggle with poverty, crime, and disease, into which English Sisters have thrown themselves during the last thirty years'.[88] They were required to learn increasingly rigorous professional skills in fields such as nursing and teaching and implement them for no income and little more than a basic, if regular, diet. Exhaustion, rather than solitude, was the leading condition of their lives. In compensation they had a sense of social and spiritual purpose and membership of an essentially supportive and enabling community of women. It is difficult to draw up a precise balance sheet. For the daughters of middle-class households who formed the majority of the noviates, the mothers and sisters they left behind probably enjoyed greater opportunities for solitude in their daily lives, as the previous chapter explored. In the final resort the state intervened not to inspect or discipline, but gradually to create secular caring professions. These enabled women to acquire and practise occupational competencies without requiring them to abandon their families for religious orders, although they remained faced with a choice between a career and marriage until well into the twentieth century.[89]

The Terrors of Solitude

The energy of the debate about enclosed orders was exceeded only by the ferocity of the arguments generated by the parallel reform of the penal system. There was a similar combination of contested evidence, mistrusted motives and disputed outcomes. In both cases the Christian concept of solitude lay at the heart of the controversy, at once powerful, dangerous and fundamentally unknowable in its consequences. With the opening of Pentonville Prison in 1842, a long debate was finally embodied in a purpose-built institution. It had become apparent during the late eighteenth and early nineteenth centuries that there was a need for a systematic alternative to the combination of corrupt, squalid, short-term prisons, and the degrading theatre of capital punishment.[90] To an increasing number of commentators, the solution lay in a general revival of Christianity and the application of one of its most profound practices.

The sense of crisis in penal policy was common to the modernizing states of Europe. A promising model at the beginning of the eighteenth century borrowed the routine of a Catholic monastery. The *Casa di Correzione* of San Michel a Ripa opened in Rome in 1703 following an initiative by the reforming Pope Innocent XII.[91] It was a purpose-built prison for juvenile delinquents based on the principles of hygiene and silence. The boys were held in clean cells, sleeping alone and forbidden to talk whilst at their tasks during the day. The regime embodied a new antithesis between solitude and sociability. Conversation between the inmates was held to be hostile to their rehabilitation. The reformative effect of a prolonged sentence was constantly undermined by extended opportunity for intercourse between the inmates. The more criminal infected the less, and as a group the prisoners would constitute an unsupervised school for vice.

In the European debate, silence became more than just the absence of verbal intercourse. Interest grew in the positive function of preventing conversation. John Howard, the first systematic English prison reformer, collected information on a range of international models, including cell-based institutions in the United Provinces and Germany.[92] He reflected on the constructive effect of isolation on inmates in a prison setting. 'Solitude and silence are favourable to reflection,' he wrote, 'and may possibly lead them to repentance.'[93] In the *Casa di Correzione*, prohibition on conversation was seen as a form of penance, and the spiritual function of sustained, unspoken meditation was explored further in the writings on prisons by the Dominican monk Dom Mabillion, posthumously published in 1724. The eremitical tradition he drew upon was a common heritage of both Catholic and Protestant churches, and strongly influenced the author of the single most important blueprint for prison reform published in England in the eighteenth century.

Jonas Hanway was an Evangelical social reformer, interested in a range of topics associated with poverty and the moral decay of his times. In the case of prisons, he was aware that he was joining a multi-vocal debate. 'Every one has a plan,' he began his account in 1776, 'and a favourite system; mine is *solitude in imprisonment*.'[94] His vision stemmed from his analysis of the ills of his society: 'The first consideration is, Whether infidelity and neglect of religion are not the ruling cause of the calamity we complain of?'[95] The rich were ceasing to give moral leadership, the churches had retreated to the margins of people's lives, and the disciplinary institutions of the state were worse than useless. In the case of prisons, Hanway shared the assumption of earlier reformers that talk was hostile to rehabilitation. 'If the safest way to preserve a *prisoner* from being infected by the poisoned breath of companions in wickedness,' he wrote, 'and to drag him from his evil courses, is to deprive him of all possibility of evil communication, can it be a question of whether we shall do it or not?'[96]

Once a prisoner was confined to a separate cell, he could begin to experience the profound benefits of enforced reflection. '*Solitude*,' wrote Hanway, 'will thus accomplish the work, not in a *vague, formal*, and *unmeaning* manner, but by creating a real change in the heart, to raise them that are fallen; and guard those who are most subject to be assailed.'[97] The essence of the punishment was that rather than dismissing the prisoner as a man fallen beyond recall, it recognized him as a fellow Christian, no less capable of redemption through reason and prayer than any other individual. The solitary prisoner experienced time in a new way. A life characterized by thoughtless action would be replaced by one of disciplined calculation. The long days in the cell compelled contemplation. In that elevated state the prisoner would reflect on his past and be forced to consider his future in this life and the next. Hanway, a devout Evangelical, sought to create the conditions in which the prisoners would replicate his own daily observances: 'Let a man be placed in circumstances that he can hardly avoid examining the state of his own soul; and he will look forward to the regions beyond the grave; not only in hopes of *good*, but in fear of *evil to come*.'[98]

Solitary confinement combined the most benign and the most punitive response to the criminal. It offered the prisoner the opportunity of sustained reflection that in society at large was so often only available to the secure and wealthy. At the same time, prolonged compulsory isolation was the most fearful prospect, where the prisoner would be driven to God by the pain of his condition. 'Reflection cannot lose all its power,' Hanway observed, 'nor can the heart of man be so petrified, but the consideration of his *immortal* part, under the terrors of solitude, will *open his mind*. He will feel his situation as an intermediate state between both worlds, and as a preparative for either.'[99]

In the light of the controversy caused by the delayed implementation

of Hanway's blueprint, it is important to note that he and other reformers were fully aware of the destructive possibilities of their system.[100]
Half a century before critics launched their attacks, they were asking
themselves whether the human mind could withstand the proposed
punishment. Hanway faced the issue head on: '*The punishment is too
terrible: May not the horror of solitary confinement, drive the prisoner to
suicide?*' He had two answers to the possibility. The first was to appeal
to the inherently supportive nature of periods of reflection, so often
the means of saving the individual from rash actions that could lead to
self-destruction.[101] The second was to invoke the assistance of religious
professionals. New kinds of built spaces needed to be accompanied by
new levels of personal intervention. At every turn the prisoner should
be able to look to the support and guidance of capable spiritual advisers.
Just as the lay staff of the prison should be salaried officials, no longer
dependent on bribery and extortion, so also their religious colleagues
should be offered a new career structure. Chaplains should become the
key figures in ensuring that solitary imprisonment realized its objectives and contained its terrors.

In the short term, Hanway made little impression on the construction and management of prisons. The 1779 Penitentiary Act embodied
a nominal commitment to solitary confinement at least at night, but
during the day the prisoners were to be so occupied with manual tasks
that they would have little time for spiritual contemplation. It took a
further half-century of debate, including the diversion of Bentham's
Panopticon, before the state invested in Hanway's project. Pentonville,
the first model prison of the modern era, was a posthumous embodiment
of virtually all his proposals, including such detail as the replacement
of prisoners' names by numbers and wearing masks in the chapel and
schoolroom to prevent conversation between them. However, before
his blueprint could be translated into bricks and mortar, a fierce controversy about a short-lived innovation on the other side of the Atlantic
rendered the term 'solitary' so toxic that it had to be abandoned as the
key descriptor of his system.

In 1821, the New York State prison in Auburn opened a new wing
containing eighty cells in which prisoners were confined in total solitude, with no exercise, no human contact of any kind, and insufficient
light and food. Penal reform was by now a subject of international

debate, and although the regime at Auburn was modified after only two years, the consequences were widely reported. An influential account was written by Gustave de Beaumont and Alexis de Tocqueville, first published in English in 1833. Their conclusion could not have been more damning:

> This trial, from which so happy a result had been anticipated, was fatal to the greater part of the convicts: in order to reform them, they had been submitted to complete isolation; but this absolute solitude, if nothing interrupt it, is beyond the strength of man; it destroys the criminal without intermission and without pity; it does not reform, it kills.[102]

This verdict became a key point of reference in the contemporary discourse about punishment.[103] As the *Quarterly Review* later wrote, 'Mind and body were crushed under this clumsy and barbarous experiment; some died, many were driven mad, twenty-six were pardoned, and the rest were removed at the end of the year. This disastrous American expedient has had the greatest influence in modifying the various theories of prison discipline.'[104]

There were two reasons why the Auburn trial had such an impact. The first was the tone of debate. The stakes were high in terms of the future roles of the state and organized religion, potential levels of public expenditure and the consequences of failure for law-abiding citizens increasingly apprehensive about the growing ineffectiveness of face-to-face discipline in the industrializing society. There was no accepted evidence base and no agreement on the psychological theories involved. The categories of behaviour that were in play, including surveillance, social interaction, and solitude itself, were so profound that the dispute rapidly took the form of a zero-sum game with neither side willing to find virtue in the other's arguments.[105]

The second reason was the predictable outcome of the New York experiment. The brief attempt to impose a total, entirely secular, experience merely confirmed how dangerous solitude was. The lesson forced a change in language. Solitude carried with it so many known risks and so much long-term cultural freight that in the post-Reform Act era it jeopardized the whole task of securing public consent. By the time Parliament sanctioned the construction of Pentonville, 'solitary' had become 'separate'. The new term foregrounded the prevention of interaction between prisoners whilst allowing regular intervention by prison staff. According to the *Prison Regulations* of 1843, the prisoner in the separate cell was to receive a stream of intruders:

> He shall be daily visited in his cell by the governor, chaplain, and surgeon; and by the schoolmaster at such times as may be prescribed by the chaplain; and each prisoner shall also be daily visited by a subordinate officer for the purpose of serving each meal, and also at such other times, daily, as may be necessary to superintend his employment.[106]

To many of those who had followed the debate on Hanway's blueprint, the distinction was meaningless. Prisoners would still spend most of their days and all of their nights completely alone in what were intended to be sound-proof cells. In his attack on the version introduced at Reading Gaol, Sir Richard Vyvyan wrote that 'the punishment is so nearly that of solitary confinement, that special pleading alone could satisfactorily define a difference'.[107] However much the advocates of the Pentonville model insisted on a new label, the older meanings lingered on in popular discourse. In their survey of London prisons, Henry Mayhew and John Binny noted that 'it is often condemned as being another form of solitary confinement, the idea of which is so closely connected in the public mind with the dark dungeons and oppressive cruelty of the Middle Ages, as to be sufficient to excite the strongest emotions of abhorrence in every English bosom'.[108]

The linguistic change made it all the more important that the role of the chaplains was fully implemented. Since Hanway's time, the religious staff had become increasingly important figures in the penal system. Their role was formalized by the 1823 Gaol Act, which gave them powers of surveillance over all the prison staff, including the governor, and the responsibility of transmitting shortcomings to relevant authorities.[109] During the following quarter of a century, the leading chaplains became public figures. They regarded the teachers of literacy as integral to their own project and regularly reported on their work.[110] 'In separate confinement,' explained the Commissioners for Pentonville, 'the solitude is relieved by more frequent intercourse with moral and religious

instructors, and by a more liberal use of the means of improvement.'[111]
If the 'terrors of solitude' were to act as a deterrent to those tempted
to break the law but not as a threat to the mental wellbeing of those
who had been convicted, interaction with professional men of God was
essential. Surveying the range of American experiments, de Beaumont
and de Tocqueville had no doubts about their importance. 'Can there be
a combination more powerful for reformation,' they wrote,

> than that of a prison which hands over the prisoner to all the trials of
> solitude, leads him through reflection to remorse, through religion
> to hope; makes him industrious by the burden of idleness, and which,
> whilst it inflicts the torments of solitude, makes him find a charm in
> the converse of pious men, whom otherwise he would have seen with
> indifference, and heard without pleasure?[112]

They were dubious about whether the new systems were transferrable
to their own country because they did not believe that the Catholic
clergy in France had sufficient interest in penal reform to commit their
time and energy to its operation.[113]

It was a two-way trade. Separate confinement facilitated the work
of the chaplains, who in turn ensured that the benefits of solitude
outweighed its dangers. John Clay, chaplain of Preston Prison, wrote
that 'it gives to the prisoner many solemn and uninterrupted hours for
inwardly digesting what he may have learned in the daily and Sabbath
services of the Chapel. It is clear, then, that the cell, though useless, if not injurious, unaccompanied by Christian ministrations, is the
best auxiliary which the Christian teacher can possess in a prison.'[114]
The traditional Sunday services remained important. As the chaplains
discovered when they sat down with individual prisoners, the level of
knowledge of the basic tenets of Christianity was for the most part so
low that it was difficult to conduct any kind of spiritual discourse. For
the remainder of the week, the confinement of prisoners to individual
cells made it easier for the clergy to do their job. The chaplains could
demand the attention of each of their charges, secure in the knowledge
that they would not be interrupted. 'In the quiet of the prison cell,'
argued the leading proponents of separate confinement, '– and when
humbled by correction – the warnings, promises, and consolations of

the Gospel come home to the conscience with redoubled force. There is no feature in the Separate System which more favourably distinguishes it than the facility which it affords to the minister of religion in the discharge of the various duties of his sacred office.'[115]

The chaplains had a further role. Pentonville was described as a trial. It was a site of learning. A disorderly body of anecdote and *a priori* assertion was to be replaced by long-term evidence about what worked and what did not.[116] A prison inspectorate was established in 1835 to act as the principal means of summarizing and analysing information generated by those charged with implementing government reforms.[117] After Lord John Russell had formally committed the state to separate confinement by sanctioning the construction of Pentonville, the reporting process gained a new focus. The central question was whether and how the experience of solitude could be measured, either by narrative evaluation or by numbers.

In the year that Pentonville opened, Charles Dickens set the tone for the ensuing debate about the effects of prison reform. His American tour took him to the Eastern Penitentiary in Philadelphia. 'The system here,' he reported, 'is rigid, strict, and hopeless solitary confinement. I believe it, in its effects, to be cruel and wrong.'[118] He argued that no outsider could fully comprehend the consequence of the punishment. The faces of the convicts bore witness to 'a depth of terrible endurance in it which none but the sufferers themselves can fathom, and which no man has a right to inflict upon his fellow creature'.[119] The harm was a product of social isolation. Occasional visits by prison staff could not replicate the complexity of human relations that sustained a normal life. Dickens wrote of an inmate:

> He never hears of wife or children; home or friends; the life or death of any single creature. He sees the prison-officers, but with that exception he never looks upon a human countenance, or hears a human voice. He is a man buried alive; to be dug out in the slow round of years; and in the mean time dead to everything but torturing anxieties and horrible despair.[120]

The popularity and timing of *American Notes* generated an immediate response. It was a matter of evidence. Dickens was attacked for basing his sweeping condemnation on a visit which lasted just two hours and involved minimal contact with the convicts themselves.[121] Further, his account confused the role of the novelist with that of the professional observer. Joseph Adshead condemned the whole exercise:

> The flights of fancy may take what altitude they please in works of fiction; the imagination may range discursively in the regions of romance; but the public ought not to be deceived by misstatements in matters of vital importance to the well-being and regulation of society; however pleasing the style, or fascinating the language, if a narrative *which should have the impress of truth* be marked by a departure from it, much as genius may be admired, it must be [a] matter of regret that talent should thus defeat its more noble purpose.[122]

Dickens stood his ground not just on his preference for the silent system but also on the way in which the effects of punishment were discovered and communicated. He argued in *Household Words* in 1850 that the process by which the prison professionals reported on their work was hopelessly naïve. On the basis of frequent visits to the London prisons he argued that the inmates displayed 'a pattern penitence, of a particular form, shape, limits and dimensions, like the cells'.[123] There was every incentive for the convicts to present themselves in the image that the chaplains desired, a 'tendency to hypocrisy; the dread of death not being present, and their being every possible inducement, either to feign contrition, or set up an unreliable semblance of it'.[124] Dickens then showed how a novelist could memorably make the same point. At the end of *David Copperfield*, also published in 1850, the hero and his friends make a visit to a lightly disguised Pentonville Prison, which, in defiance of the official vocabulary, is described as practising 'solitary confinement'.[125] Guided by the former tyrannical schoolteacher Mr Creakle, now translated into a Middlesex magistrate, the visitors begin to engage with the penitent prisoners. 'I found,' narrates Copperfield, 'that the most professing men were the greatest objects of interest: and that their conceit, their vanity, their want of excitement, and their love of deception . . . all prompted to these professions, and were all gratified by them.'[126] The group is taken to visit the prison's 'Model Prisoner', 'Number Twenty Seven', who is found in his cell reading a hymn book.

To their great surprise, and as a pleasingly neat conclusion to the novel, it turns out to be none other than Uriah Heep, who had earlier been imprisoned for an attempted fraud on the Bank of England. This monument to manipulative deference perfectly illustrates Dickens's larger point: '"Well, Twenty Seven," said Mr Creakle, mournfully admiring him. "How do you find yourself to-day?" "I am very umble, sir!" replied Uriah Heep. "You are always so, Twenty Seven," said Mr Creakle.'[127] The group asks after his wellbeing. 'Far more comfortable here, than ever I was outside,' replies Heep. 'I see my follies now, sir. That's what makes me comfortable.'[128]

The charge of hypocrisy persisted throughout the debate. De Beaumont and de Tocqueville had warned against it in their epochal report on the American experience.[129] Sir Peter Laurie protested in 1846 that he couldn't read the reports of the chaplains 'without feelings of disgust at the sickening and audacious hypocrisy exhibited by many of the prisoners; and without surprise at the amiable simplicity which could credit, far less chronicle, such unmitigated and transparent cant'.[130] As late as 1860, Mayhew and Binny in their survey of London prisons warned that 'so long as we seek by our present mode of prison discipline to make saints of thieves, just so long shall we continue to produce a thousand canting hypocrites to one *real* convert'.[131] Experienced clergy disputed the charge of credulity. They were under instruction to 'pay particular attention to the state of mind of every prisoner' and believed that they could do so.[132] Joseph Kingsmill, the long-serving chaplain at Pentonville, claimed to have made, by 1854, 'more than one hundred thousand visits for conversation' to prisoners in their cells and had no doubt that he could recognize a manufactured conversion on the rare occasion it was attempted.[133] He observed that 'it is commonly thought that there is a great deal of hypocrisy amongst prisoners; and no doubt, some bad men will put on the garb of religion, like the one referred to, for base purposes. But it requires more than ordinary knowledge, ability, and wickedness, to be an actor of this kind with any success.'[134] Dickens's 'pattern penitence' could be seen for what it was by those whose business it was to comprehend character and motive inside the prison walls.

The more intractable problem was not deception but self-deception. What worried Kingsmill and the other chaplains was the difficulty the prisoners themselves had in understanding the experience of enforced penal isolation. The problem was one not of motive but of perspective. As Kingsmill explained:

> That a great many deceive themselves, like persons on a sick-bed, into the belief that they have become true Christians, when they are not, mistaking depression of spirits and remorse for the consequences of their evil course of life, for godly sorrow, or an enlightened understanding for the renewing of the heart by the Holy Ghost, is very certain; but to accuse such persons of hypocrisy is most unjust.[135]

It was impossible for the inmate to comprehend the effects of solitude whilst still in solitude. On the one hand, the backwash of their prior criminal career and conviction prevented a clear reaction to guided meditation in a lonely cell. On the other, the truths reached in seclusion had no substance until they were applied to the world outside, with all its pressures and complexities. As Hepworth Dixon observed in his prison survey of 1850, 'can a man learn to restrain his passions in the cell? He is subject to no temptations there.'[136] Unless there was free and frequent movement between solitary and social experience, every spiritual self-review was provisional. Over time the verdicts of the chaplains became increasingly hesitant. 'It is difficult, and indeed almost impossible,' concluded the *Report of the Directors of Convict Prisons* for 1866, 'to express any decided opinion upon the real amount of good effected upon the minds of the convicts by the efforts made for their reformation. Secluded as they are from the world, they are more parts of a machine than free agents, and the ordinary temptations of the outside world are removed from them.'[137]

A further difficulty was the extent to which total solitude could ever be achieved. All penal reformers were committed to preventing the prisoners from talking to each other. The proponents of the silent system argued that they could achieve this objective without the expense of constructing cells and the risk of driving the inmates insane. Their opponents believed that maintaining silence in association was physically impossible. Attempts to impose it could only generate a second tier of punishment on top of the initial court sentence.[138] Better to remove all temptation to talk by confinement to a specially constructed cell.

In the event, the new regimes generated an illuminating case history of the unstoppable human desire for social exchange. It soon became apparent that the basic ambition of silent isolation was not working. 'While in the prison,' wrote Hepworth Dixon of inmates in 1850, 'they are supposed not to see or know each other. This innocent delusion they themselves try to keep up. But the fact is – they know each other perfectly, and communicate both in voice and writing.'[139] It transpired that not only the silent but also the separate system was creating an immense disciplinary problem. In 1854, for instance, with the Pentonville experiment fully mature, the list of internal offences was dominated by determined attempts by inmates to make contact with each other. There were only a handful of the infractions that might be expected in any prison, such as nine cases of assaulting officers and another nine escape attempts. Instead, the governor spent his time dealing with energetic and ingenious attempts by his charges to break out of their silent world. Thirty-seven inmates were punished for 'communicating by writing'; ninety-five for 'talking in exercise, and in corridors'; thirty-nine for talking 'through water taps, and by knocking, &c; on walls'; seventy-three for 'talking, whistling, shouting, and other misconduct in school'; thirty-two for 'obscene communications, obscene figures, and drawings on books and chapel stalls'; thirty-three for 'misconduct in chapel during divine service, talking aloud, laughing and mimicking Chaplain'; and two for 'attempting clandestinely to send letters out of the prison'.[140]

In the silent system, such offences could be punished by periods in solitary confinement. This option was not available at Pentonville. 'The zero of the Silent System is a cell,' Sir Peter Laurie pointed out, 'any aggravation is therefore confined to darkness and punishment diet; for, of course, the stricter the ordinary, the more severe must be the extraordinary discipline.'[141] The only way of making solitude more unpleasant was to remove light and food. In the mid-1850s, nearly 90 per cent of internal disciplinary sentences were for a number of days in a 'dark cell', over half on bread and water. This recourse to a version of a medieval dungeon had little deterrent effect. Masks and boxed-in cells had to be removed from the chapels because they served only to prevent the warders seeing what the prisoners were doing and who was talking to whom. From the outset, prisoners had resisted rules of silence by developing their own telegraph systems.[142] Memoirs and investigations throughout the remainder of the century revealed attempts at communication, if only by tapping on the plumbing or the cell walls.[143] There was a persistent problem at one of the most secure prisons, Dartmoor, caused by the materials out of which the cells were constructed. It was reported to the Kimberley Commission in 1879 that:

> Besides the inferiority of the iron cells in other respects, the partitions are so thin that the prisoners can make themselves heard through them; and it appears that, in spite of the constant supervision of the warders, communications take place to some extent in this manner. Moreover, even when the attempt is checked, the result is to increase petty offences and to render more difficult the maintenance of discipline.[144]

Solitude and silence were less compatible than the prison reformers had once supposed.

At the beginning of the Pentonville experiment, the clergy hoped that they could engage with the discourse of numbers that was coming to characterize government initiatives.[145] The legislation of the Reform Act Parliaments was accompanied by what Ian Hacking terms 'an avalanche of numbers'.[146] The term 'statistics', which in the eighteenth century had referred to all information describing a state, gained a more focussed meaning. Figures became the sensory organs of government, describing both the need for intervention and its consequences. The capacity to count separated the old order of untrained officials and amateur philanthropists from the new regime of professional public servants.[147] Thus in their early reports, the chaplains sought to measure the impact of their labours. 'We have a pleasing fact to cite,' wrote the Commissioners for Pentonville in 1848, 'in reference to the influence of religious instruction; – out of 1500 prisoners, the number admitted to the Holy Communion has been about 300; and of these 300 men, not 20 have committed any offence whatever, and not 10 have committed any immoral act after quitting our walls, so far as the chaplain has been able to ascertain.'[148] Such figures were, however, difficult to assemble into a time series, and bore at best an indirect relation to the central process of repentance and reform through solitary communion with God. The numbers at Holy Communion reflected some kind of journey through the formularies of Anglican religion but took no account of either the inmate's spiritual condition before entering the prison, or the relation between nominal observance and true repentance.

The demand for figures eroded the standing of the chaplains. Whilst their reports soon became confined to narrative commentary, other officials responded to the new culture of public administration by publishing increasingly detailed tables of performance. Progress in literacy was measured, the products of labour in the cells were listed from aprons to handkerchiefs to jackets.[149] Much of this was counting for counting's sake, but it gave the impression of purposeful, progressive effort on the part of the relevant officials. In the case of enforced solitude, all that was systematically recorded was failure. The medical officers, rather than the chaplains, listed and sought to explain the one or two suicides in Pentonville each year; the three or four attempted suicides (most of which were deemed bogus); the removals to Bethlem and later asylums; and the twenty or thirty prisoners who were annually returned to 'association' in the prison because of concerns about the impact of solitude on their mental or physical condition. As diagnostic techniques improved, they were able to provide tables of bodily or psychological ailments amongst the prison population. The data served to demonstrate the claimed strength of the separate system. As a consequence of regular visits to the cells, the wellbeing of prisoners was monitored according to the medical standards of the time, and action was taken to remove those deemed unable to withstand the rigours of prolonged solitude. But the numbers also provided ample ammunition to critics. In 1846, the chairman of Bethlem Hospital, Sir Peter Laurie, used the official reports to make a coruscating attack on the regime, entitled *'Killing No Murder'; or, The Effects of Separate Confinement on the Bodily and Mental Condition of Prisoners in the Government Prisons*. 'I assert,' he charged, 'that this system has consigned a large number of Prisoners as Lunatics to Bethlem Hospital, and has been attended with an extent of mortality and disease not to be found in Prisons conducted on the Silent System.'[150]

Over time, the chaplains abandoned any attempt to quantify the repentance of inmates through solitary spiritual communion with themselves and God. 'To depict with anything like certainty the results of efforts made in various ways to convince the criminal of sin, and to effect reformation in his life, would be impossible; to speculate or conjecture seems fruitless,' wrote the chaplain in the *Report of the Prison Directors* for 1862.[151] The closer they looked at the prisoners, the more struck they were by the difference between them. At the heart of the statistical movement was the search for what its most influential advocate, the Belgian Adolphe Quetelet, termed '*l'homme moyen*', the average man, in whom, 'under the influence of certain causes, regular effects are produced, which oscillate, as it were, around a fixed mean point without undergoing any sensible alterations'.[152] Much of the dialogue about penal reform had at its centre a standard prisoner who would respond in a predictable way to a specific regime, whether solitary, surveillance, silent, or separate. However, the more the chaplains sought to understand the impact of solitude, the more variety they found. Some prisoners through their physique or character were evidently more capable of withstanding isolation than others, either by stubborn resilience or by active rebellion. Conversely, failure had many parents. 'The longer the period of separation,' warned Joshua Jebb, the architect of the cellular prison system, 'the more watchful must be the exercise of medical superintendence, to guard against the failure of mental or physical health, which should always be anticipated as a possible result with prisoners of certain temperaments and dispositions, and in proportion to the keenness with which they feel their punishment.'[153]

For the chaplains and doctors it was increasingly obvious that the outcome of punishment lay in the interaction between the period in the cell and the history and perceived prospects of the prisoner. 'Thus,' argued the *Report of the Directors of Convict Prisons* for 1854, 'a difference either in the moral character of the subject of separate confinement – the length of his sentence – the nature of the prospects held out to him on liberation – the time of his natural life, and the degree of his physical strength, many be expected to produce, when viewed in large numbers, a corresponding difference in effects upon the mind.'[154] It was borne in on the prison professionals that poor mental health was a cause as much as a consequence of incarceration. Whether through genetic infirmity or acquired debility, those who were convicted of serious crimes brought into their cells an immense range of vulnerabilities.[155] 'The religious and moral condition of 1515 prisoners,' wrote the chaplain in the 1869 *Reports of the Directors of Convict Prisons*, 'if minutely and statistically tabulated, would occupy many sheets.'[156]

Any given cohort of inmates defied generalization, the more so after Pentonville ceased taking a specially selected group of prisoners in 1849, and housed instead a cross-section of the entire convict population. It was in several senses a question of time. Although they worked themselves to the point of exhaustion, the chaplains, even with assistants and lay scripture readers, could rarely afford more than a short visit to each cell every few weeks as they moved around the hundreds of inmates.[157] The vision of a prolonged spiritual conversation with each prisoner as they underwent the rigours of solitary self-examination was unattainable.[158] Where contact was made, the chaplains were faced with a multitude of biographies which stretched back beyond their vision, and forwards to perceived and possible futures. Measuring the experience of solitary confinement in a prison population poses acute methodological problems even for modern investigators, as the impact of social isolation, loss of control over daily lives and absence of environmental stimulation has to be assessed in the context of the varied and often acute morbidity of any group of inmates.[159] The problem was all the more challenging for the mid-nineteenth-century chaplains because at the heart of their enterprise was a distinctly secular conception of mental suffering. Although the regime of enforced isolation was founded on the openness of God to private discourse, from Hanway onwards there was no sense of divine protection for those undergoing the terrors of solitary confinement. The phalanx of professional Christians took a view of the dangers of the experience which was little different from that of the emerging discipline of psychology. As the debate over the Pentonville experiment was reaching a climax, John Bucknill and Daniel Tuke published a compendious *Manual of Psychological Medicine* which summarized the state of research in the field for the use of practising doctors. So far from prolonged spiritual devotion being a cure for this condition, they listed, as had earlier manuals, 'religious melancholy' as a distinct form of insanity, particularly prevalent amongst those who separated themselves from collective worship in pursuit of a personal programme of salvation.[160]

It proved impossible to shake off the association of solitary, or separate, confinement with insanity. 'Silence profound and terrible mostly tames them,' wrote a critique of Pentonville in 1879, 'and occasionally drives one to seek refuge in death.'[161] There was a growing literature of prisoner memoirs. As with wars, the accounts were written by the survivors. They largely featured well-educated, white-collar convicts.[162] Those who suffered total mental collapse under the regime were in no state to compose a coherent account of their experience. The one group that made a consistent case for resistance was the new generation of political prisoners. The Fenians who entered the convict system from the late 1860s displayed a truth that was to be repeated throughout the twentieth century, that the best defence against the terrors of solitude lay in the state of mind that had caused the incarceration. As Thomas Clarke observed in his *Glimpses of an Irish Felon's Prison Life*, 'the person who goes into prison with a mind well stocked with healthy ideas will take longer to break down than the person ill-educated, or who carries in with him comparatively few ideas'.[163] Where the punishment was for a larger cause and the punitive regime was framed as another tool of the enemy, it was possible both to come through the event and to turn it to larger advantage.

Michael Davitt was arrested in 1870 following the raid on Chester Castle in 1867 and encountered solitary confinement at Dartmoor and Millbank. On his release he combined his continuing struggle for Irish independence with a public profile as an authority on prisons, writing a number of publications and giving evidence to the 1895 Gladstone Committee.[164] Although he could countenance very brief periods of isolation, there was in his view only one outcome of prolonged solitude.

> One other very strong objection to nine months' solitary punishment in probation, is, that I think it produces insanity. I have seen several men in Millbank Prison go insane during my nine months' experience there, and I attribute it to the terrible punishment of being shut up in cold silent cells for 23 hours out of every 24 during that period.[165]

His fellow Irish republican Jeremiah O'Donovan Rossa got through his sentence by going to war with the warders and their rules, undergoing four months' bread and water solitude as a punishment for smuggling letters out of the prison.[166]

As a punishment, solitary confinement lingered longer in Britain than in many other European countries.[167] It was reduced to three months for recidivists and one month for first-time offenders by Churchill in 1910–11 and it faded out of the system between the wars. However, it had lost its association with a religiously driven reform of the prisoner long before. As early as the 1856 House of Lords Select Committee, the aspiration of moral reconstruction through prolonged reflection was weakening.[168] By the 1860s, the power of the chaplains was waning, and they were formally subordinated to the prison governors in convict and local prisons. Increasingly the function of solitary confinement was limited to the secondary objectives of preventing corrupting conversation between prisoners, and acting as a deterrent to those yet to commit crimes or as a punishment for those who had done so. The Convict Directors' Report of 1886 tried to remain optimistic:

> On the one hand, no evil results have followed since the less severe isolation and the more limited time were adopted; and, on the other, although a complete moral reformation is no longer expected to be the usual result, the separation undoubtedly prevents prisoners mutually contaminating each other, good influences have an opportunity of acting on them, and it has been found of the highest advantage as a training and discipline preparatory to the subsequent stages of a sentence of penal servitude.[169]

What remained was the impact of the terror. Edward Du Cane, who dominated penal policy in the last quarter of the nineteenth century, assured the Gladstone Committee that the 'separate confinement to which convicts sentenced to penal servitude are, in the first instance, subjected seems to be regarded with great dislike by most of them, and especially by those who are criminals by profession'.[170] As their great ambition faded, the clergymen clung to their theology less as a project and more as a consolation. 'And depressing indeed, utterly hopeless would be the attempt,' wrote the chaplain in the 1875 Convict Directors' Report, 'if we had not faith in the power and mercy of God, knowing that nothing is impossible with Him, and that "He has devised means for the restoration of his banished ones," we apply the means, sedulously, and leave the issue with Him.'[171] In the end, it was not for mere mortals to know the outcome of lonely, personal conversations with the Almighty.

To be Alone with Him

Of all the nineteenth-century sects and denominations, the Quakers thought most consistently about solitude and spiritual observance. In his *Observations on the Religious Peculiarities of the Society of Friends* of 1824, Joseph John Gurney, brother and fellow campaigner of the prison reformer Elizabeth Fry, set out the distinctive nature of his faith. At the centre of Quaker practice was a withdrawal from the noise of domestic and commercial life. Gurney explained that 'waiting upon God, as well as prostration and subjection before his Divine Majesty, is, in the Holy Scriptures, expressly recognized as connected with a state of *silence*'.[172] Whilst the good Christian should always be looking for moments of quiet reflection during the working day, it was impractical to suppose, as did contemporary Evangelicals, that the middle-class households in which most of the Quakers lived could conform to a domestic version of monastic ritual. The bedroom and the closet remained too exposed to the surrounding life to fulfil the expectations that were held for them. Neither was it feasible to suppose that private contemplation was of itself a sufficiently rigorous activity. Thoughts would wander, fleshly concerns would intrude. As the late nineteenth-century Quaker Caroline Stephens wrote, 'in order clearly to hear the Divine voice thus speaking to us we need to be still; to be alone with Him in the secret place of His Presence; that all flesh should keep silence before Him'.[173] Solitary contemplation was essentially difficult. As Stephens explained, 'silence is assuredly an art to be acquired, a discipline to be steadily practised, before it can become the instinctive habit and unfailing resource of the soul'.[174] It required the rigorous social context of the weekly Meeting, where what she termed the 'united stillness' of the gathering of Friends would enable the penitent to channel their thoughts into a spiritual communication with God.[175]

The necessity of finding an appropriate balance between solitude and sociability was evident in the campaigns of Elizabeth Fry, the most informed critic of the early nineteenth-century prison system.[176] She shared the conviction of contemporary reformers that Christian teaching delivered by professional chaplains and amateur visitors was critical to the process of reforming criminals. She assured the 1818 Select Committee on Prisons that reading the Bible to prisoners and giving simple explanations of its teachings were having an 'astonishing effect' on hardened inmates.[177] She did not believe, however, that requiring female prisoners to conduct their own spiritual journey alone in a cell was humane or productive. 'Solitary confinement,' she wrote in her manifesto of reform, 'which is useful in extreme cases, is, in my opinion, a punishment far too severe to be resorted to on any light and trivial occasion.'[178] What was required during the daytime was the collective experience of religious education, reinforced by communal labour on tasks such as sewing. After hours, by contrast, it was better that the inmates were locked up alone to avoid the contagion of unsupervised communication with each other. She explained that,

> I should prefer a prison where women were allowed to work together in companies, under proper superintendence; to have their meals together, under proper superintendence, and their recreation also; but I would always have them separated in the night; I believe it would conduce to the health, both of body and mind. Their being in companies during the day, tends, under proper regulations, to the advancement of principle and industry; for it affords a stimulus. I should think solitary confinement proper only in very atrocious cases.[179]

Fry was also insistent on the moral tone of reform. 'I am anxious,' she told the 1835 House of Lords Select Committee, 'that Punishments should be always consistent with the general Spirit that exists in this Country. I hope we always shall be a benevolent People, and we must shew it towards Offenders.'[180] In the event, limited benevolence was displayed to the prisoners, and still less between different factions of campaigners. Equally those seeking new institutional forms of voluntary spiritual withdrawal in the nineteenth century were exposed to virulent hostility. The failure to live up to the Quaker prescription, itself born of a long history of dealing with persecution, was partly a function of the nature of social withdrawal. Solitude sits on the borderline between privacy and secrecy. It can be a powerful means by which individuals explore themselves and develop their identity. It can also be a device for excluding others from what they are thinking or doing, or is being done to them. The balance is determined by the trust invested in the individual and their circumstances. In the atmosphere of seething hostility that characterized popular anti-Catholicism in the period, solitude was readily interpreted as an arena of wilful misconduct or imposed suffering.[181] The absence of direct evidence, attributed to the inspection-resistant churches and the locked doors of their institutions, became a cause of further suspicion rather than a caution against judgement.

The bitterness of the debate was also a consequence of the stressed nature of the condition. The distinction that was drawn in Chapter 1 between solitude as an adjunct of successful sociability and as a pathology of failed social intercourse was far from stable. Under the pressures of managing a rapidly urbanizing society, it was unclear which was the prevailing circumstance. The attempts by the churches to appropriate solitary spiritual reflection as a key defence against the breakdown of communal discipline succeeded only in exposing the deep uncertainties about the consequences of lone meditation. The history of penal reform in the nineteenth century can best be viewed as a long process of action research in which much was learned about the effects of enforced deprivation of company. The immediate outcome was the retreat of organized religion from the front line of state-sponsored reform. Only the Quakers remained certain about the function of sociable and solitary meditation, although even in their case the aspirations they had once held for prison chaplains and Bible-reading visitors had lost their much of purchase by the end of the century.

5

SOLITUDE AND LEISURE IN THE TWENTIETH CENTURY

Peace and Quietness

Amongst the witnesses in Margery Spring Rice's 1939 study of working-class wives was 'Mrs E. of Forest Gate, East London', who was thirty-eight years old. The toil of raising six children left her little time for conscious relaxation. 'She says firmly,' reported Spring Rice, 'that she gets no leisure till the evening when the children are in bed and then "I just sit still and say, at last a bit of peace and quietness."'[1] For many of the labouring poor, just taking a moment's time to themselves out of the round of daily labour constituted the summit of their expectation. This was particularly so in the case of married women, for whom, as Claire Langhamer has argued, the experience of continuous, unpaid housework made it difficult to conceive, let alone enjoy, structured recreational activity.[2]

A generation later, in the midst of the post-war economic boom, Pearl Jephcott visited an east London community. 'In a very poor area like Bermondsey,' she discovered,

the women have always expected to be over-occupied. It is still a novelty to have any regular stretch of free time, and they hardly know what to do with it. Leisure is still equated with physical rest, work with physical effort. 'Just sit', 'put your feet up', 'drop off', 'have a lay down', were phrases used to describe how the wife used her leisure.[3]

Their menfolk might have a pub or a club to visit outside working hours, but where there was no employment and no money to spend on any pleasure, the default activity was doing more or less nothing by themselves.[4] 'Ignorance and poverty,' wrote Robert Roberts in his *Classic Slum*, 'combined to breed, for the most part, tedium, a dumb accidie of the back streets. . . . How familiar one grew in childhood with those silent figures leaning against door jambs, staring into vacancy waiting for bedtime.'[5] E. Wight Bakke paid particular attention to the unemployed workers of the 1930s, who so concerned middle-class observers by standing around in public spaces without any apparent purpose. 'As a matter of fact,' he insisted, 'one of the outstanding features of the loafing in Greenwich was the lack of conversation. Men stood alone more often than in groups. The young men were more sociable; so were the older men who, I suppose, were pensioners. The middle-aged men were perfectly willing to talk when I approached them, but more often than not I found them alone.'[6]

Amidst the increasing noise and vitality of popular recreation in the twentieth century, the persistence and value of solitary 'peace and quietness' should not be underestimated. It was how most people at most times in the past had sought to recover from physical labour and prepare themselves for the tasks that lay ahead. Outside the home, as Chapter 2 discussed, casual walking in the neighbouring streets or fields served a similar function. The sociable alternative was equally unstructured and inconsequential conversation where that was available. However, change was taking place. The specific recreational activities that were examined in Chapter 3 were beginning to spread into the upper reaches of the working class, and then unevenly by income, age, and gender across the labouring population as a whole. There was generally a cost involved in the widening range of pastimes and hobbies. Money had to be spent on materials and tools, on the associated magazines and books, and perhaps on the membership of a society of fellow enthusiasts. Indirectly all of these practices required a level of household comfort and adequate management of time and space within or outside the home. During the twentieth and early twenty-first centuries, the pursuit of unstructured quietness never completely disappeared, as will be discussed in the next chapter, but for a growing proportion of the population it was accompanied by an increasing range of separate pastimes.

The process of change foregrounded the first of the three functions of solitude in the response to modernity. In general terms it both accompanied and enabled proliferating forms of personal choice and companionate domesticity. Both were driven by the twin forces of change in this arena: domestic living standards and mass communication. Increasingly it became possible to move between divergent forms of sociable and solitary recreation as taste permitted. There were iconic activities that were performed always alone or in company. Patience as a card game, which continued to develop new versions after 1900, might be an example of the former; team sports an example of the latter. But in many cases it was possible to move between contrasting registers of association according to the profile of the pastime and the desire of the practitioner. Some long-established collective pursuits took on more solitary forms, such as the consumption of alcohol following the rapid growth of home-consumed canned beer from the 1960s and the increasing availability of wine and spirits in off-licences and supermarkets.[7] Within the home, different leisure activities created a territory for shared endeavour on a scale rarely feasible in earlier periods at any level of society. At the same time, they established space within which a husband and wife, a parent and child, could retreat from each other's company and find personal expression and fulfilment. There was a further extension of the networked solitude that had begun to take shape in the previous century. Mass communication firstly in the traditional but highly innovative category of the printed word, and then in cinema and the electronic media, extended and reconfigured the ways in which an individual could associate with a larger community in the consumption of pleasure. The final transformation in this respect, the digital revolution, will be the subject of the concluding chapter.

Comfort and Communication

The prospect of solitary leisure was increased after 1900 by two long-term and often uneven developments. The most obvious was domestic space. In her famous essay of 1929, Virginia Woolf was clear-sighted not only about the necessity of 'a room with a lock on the door' but also about the cost, which she calculated to be at least 'five hundred a year'.[8] This placed the privilege out of reach of any householder below the upper reaches of the middle class. Kathleen Dayus, growing up in Edwardian Birmingham, described her experience of a family crammed into two sleeping spaces with one downstairs room for all the daily life of parents and children:

> My mum and dad slept in the main bedroom over the living-room and my brothers, Jonathan and Charlie, slept in another bed in the same room. My other brother, Francis or Frankie, and my sister, Liza, and I slept in the attic over the bedroom and my eldest sister, Mary, had her bed in the other corner of the attic facing ours. Mary was twenty and was going to be married soon, when she was twenty-one.[9]

In her world, only in the short child-free periods at the beginning and end of a married life might there be a possibility of more rooms than occupants. Private, lockable space was a dream not only of aspiring writers, but of all adolescent children. Few teenagers at the beginning of the century could slam their bedroom door in the face of a protesting parent.

If permanent use of a private room was out of reach, opportunities for retreat from the company of others were growing. The Tudor Walters report of November 1918 consolidated the improvements of post-1875 by-law housing and set the standards for the forthcoming programme of estate construction. It confirmed the expectation of two downstairs rooms plus a scullery, and two or three bedrooms, and tentatively explored the use of the parlour for purposes other than formal gatherings. Such a space, the report suggested, could be employed 'in cases of sickness in the house, as a quiet room for convalescent members of the family, or for any who may be suffering from long-continued illness or weakness'.[10] More positively, with complete nominal literacy amongst those of marrying age lately achieved, and an expanding education system, it envisaged that the parlour might be 'generally required for home lessons by the children of school age, or for similar work of study, serious reading, or writing, on the part of any member of the family'.[11]

The subsequent transformation was a function of both accommodation and demography. Public and private builders constructed four million houses according to basic standards between the wars and a further seven million in the quarter of a century following 1945.[12] At the same time, families of six children, which Kathleen Dayus had experienced, became increasingly uncommon. By the end of the inter-war period, the working class were beginning to display the same reproductive behaviour as their social superiors. Completed family size rapidly fell towards the current average of 1.91. As the period of a marriage devoted to child-rearing shortened and life expectancy increased, the proportion of households containing no more than two people began to grow. By 1961, just over two-fifths contained less than three occupants, a figure rising to two-thirds in the 2011 census. The most dramatic change, which more than any other separated modern domestic living from any preceding era, was in the numbers of people living alone. The early twentieth century inherited a tradition of no more than one in twenty single-person households, comprising 1 per cent of the population. The incidence of lone households had grown to 17 per cent by the mid-1960s, and to 31 per cent by 2011, embracing some eight million people.[13]

The graphs of change conceal significant variations in experience and behaviour over the period. Social investigators continued to discover overcrowding and inadequate provision of basic services until well into the third quarter of the twentieth century. Electricity did not become a near-universal provision until the 1970s.[14] The working-class wives examined by Marjory Spring Rice in 1939 and by Hannah Gavron in 1966 contained in their midst levels of domestic discomfort that were common in their grandparents' generation.[15] Programmes of slum clearance left substantial minorities living in officially condemned accommodation, such as the home in which the future Labour cabinet minister Alan Johnson was raised in the London of the 1950s.[16] In the middle decades of the century, the range of conditions within the working class was probably greater than at any time in history, with persistent numbers living in Dickensian squalor whilst their more fortunate contemporaries enjoyed the space, warmth, and domestic appliances which had become the birthright of their social superiors.[17]

A critical turning point was the Parker Morris report of 1961, which set out new official standards for private as well as public housing.

The central recommendation of *Homes for Today & Tomorrow* was that domestic space at every level of income needed to permit both social and solitary activities. Post-war prosperity had created 'a social and economic revolution' which foregrounded what the report termed the 'dual tendency in family life'.[18] It was no longer sufficient to supply basic shelter for the collective household. The essence of the modern home was movement between degrees of sociability determined by personal inclination and the family life cycle. Appropriately designed and heated space should enable the occupants to exercise choice about when and how they interacted with each other. 'Family life is both communal and individual,' explained the report. 'There is the process of coming together for activities in which the family joins as a whole – meals, conversation, common pursuits, and so on; and there is the need for privacy to pursue individual activities such as reading, writing, and following particular hobbies.'[19] The direction of change was towards more opportunity for withdrawal from the company of others. It applied not only to the increasing numbers of households of one or two people, but also to parents with growing children. 'This desire to live their own lives for an increasing part of the time they spend at home is spreading through the family as a whole,' wrote Parker Morris.

> Teenagers wanting to listen to records; someone else wanting to watch the television; someone going in for do-it-yourself; all these and homework too mean that the individual members of the family are more and more wanting to be free to move away from the fireside to somewhere else in the home – if only (in winter at any rate) they can keep warm.[20]

A common thread running through the evolving pattern of recreation was the consumption of mass communication. At one level it was the further development of practices which, as we saw in Chapter 3, were becoming commonplace in middle-class homes in the nineteenth century and through a flourishing second-hand market were frequently visible in poorer households. The change was partly a function of the late attainment of universal literacy. The achievements of the Victorian schools had left cohorts of older men and women in the population whose command of the written word had been fixed by earlier shortcomings in educational opportunity.[21] The need for the young to read to their parents or grandparents did not disappear until the end of the inter-war period. After 1945 the elderly increasingly turned to reading as a pastime.[22]

The further decline in the cost of full-length texts, accompanied by the continuing growth of public libraries, finally tipped the balance away from collective to personal consumption of literature. The newspaper press reached a peak national circulation in 1951, and the weekly periodicals began to embrace a socially inclusive readership before and after the Second World War.[23] In some form the written word was now available to anyone in a household who sought to entertain or improve themselves, however fleetingly. Whilst a minority of serious men and women engaged in sustained reading of full texts, the attraction for most consumers of print, particularly the hard-pressed household managers, was that it could be picked up and put down in what the *Social Survey of Merseyside* referred to as 'the bits of time left over from doing other things'.[24] Electric light, still a novelty for the wealthy at the beginning of the century, was being installed as standard in inter-war council houses and had reached three-quarters of the population by the time the post-war slum-clearance programme commenced. Reading no longer demanded the concentrated abstraction from the noisy life of the home clustered around the fireplace. Together with the improved heating that Parker Morris thought so important, it was now increasingly possible to find a private space in which to lose yourself in the realm of print.

Mass communication also continued to develop its symbiotic relationship with domestic pastimes and what increasingly were referred to as 'hobbies'. Established patterns of supporting individual practitioners through networks of publications became more extensive. 'The literature of this hobby,' wrote a guide in 1915, 'is undoubtedly the most extensive and complete ever devoted to a scientific pastime, though philately is at the most only just over sixty years old.'[25] As the market became more commercial, entrepreneurs became publishers, selling their products not just by advertising in other periodicals, but also by launching their own to promote their brand, introduce new items and connect users working away in secluded corners of their homes. The first magazine to carry the title *Hobbies* was launched in 1895 by an East Anglian manufacturer of fretwork tools and supplies. By the turn of the century, it had reached a circulation of 50,000, expanding its coverage to collecting coins and stamps, book binding, electrical devices, experimental chemistry and 'novel kinds of fancy work' for women.[26] The great innovator in toys for children and their parents, Frank Hornby, invested money and effort in the literature of his products, beginning with the *Meccano Magazine* in 1916, and repeating the process when he expanded into model trains.[27] His periodicals were designed not merely as a sales catalogue and as an advertising medium for suppliers in related fields, but also as a means of creating a conscious community of enthusiasts. Hornby valued his 'organ' for 'the opportunity it affords its readers of discussing not only their models, but also their own aims and ambitions, with the Editor and his staff, whose interest in their lives has given the Magazine great social importance'.[28] His audience should feel that it had a personal relationship with Hornby himself and his team of writers.

A similar ambition drove the expansion of magazines for women, which continued to offer advice and information on a range of domestic pastimes. *Woman* reached a circulation of three and a half million by the late 1950s on the basis of a deliberate strategy of 'reader identification'.[29] Through a combination of the tone and subject matter of the articles and the extensive use of correspondence pages, it sought to engage each purchaser as a particular friend. The intimacy of immediate family and neighbourhood was to be replicated by communication with the voice of the writer and participation in the broader network of readers.

The pervasive presence of print was centuries in the making. Electronic communication had a much shorter history and at first sight a much more dramatic impact on the social organization of the household. The wireless was a universal presence in homes with electricity by 1939, although receivers were too large and expensive for most households to install them in more than one room. Experiments in the transmission of moving images were halted by the outbreak of war but resumed with the return of peace. Television sets were installed in almost half of households by the mid-1950s, and reached near saturation coverage by the early 1960s.[30] The new media had the apparent effect of relocating recreation from the streets and public arenas into the home, and, within the domestic interior, of providing a virtual fireplace around which family members clustered to enjoy their entertainment.

Television presented the most dramatic narrative. Its introduction was faster as the purchase of sets led the post-war consumer boom. And its impact was highly visible as what had become the most popular form of public recreation, the cinema, was immediately driven into a long-term decline.[31] It was intrinsically a more attention-demanding medium than radio. The latter could readily be used to accompany rather than displace more solitary practices. Housework and repetitive leisure activities such as knitting or sewing or minor household repairs were combined with listening to a programme. Music might be playing while reading or during other activities requiring greater concentration. Television, on the other hand, invited the attention of the eyes as well as the ears, placing it intrinsically in opposition to the conduct of any other task or recreation. In the very early years, the sets were so rare and exciting that neighbours and friends would gather in the home fortunate enough to possess them, most notably for the 1953 Coronation. where the broadcast was watched by ten times more people than actually had a licence.[32] As television, whether owned or rented, became universal, and viewing figures climbed towards an average of twenty-four hours a week, it threatened an epochal change in the spatial and social organization of leisure.[33]

In retrospect, however, the effect was both less radical and more transient than at first seemed likely. By the 1980s, with television available on competing channels, social investigators were beginning to look more closely at what actually happened in the living room. Laurie Taylor and Bob Mullan were amongst the first to discover that the attention paid to the screen was considerably at variance with the expectations of the broadcasters and the fears of critics. The television tended to be switched on permanently, providing the same kind of generalized warmth as the fireplace, but otherwise disregarded unless a particularly popular programme brought the family together. For the most part the life of the household went on much as before, with its members occupied with their particular concerns. Taylor and Mullan cited the response to their inquiry of a thirty-one-year-old housewife: 'We have it on but we don't sit watching it. We turn it on first thing in the morning when we come down and it's on till late at night. I'm out in the garden, doing the gardening, going back and forth – I'm not watching telly all the time – it's just there and it's on.'[34]

As had always been the case in households before electricity, the pursuit of any available pleasure was in part dependent on a capacity for abstraction from whatever else was being said or done. The essence of home life was movement between alternate states of collective and private activity. The flickering screen merely added a layer of complication to this task. 'All this,' Taylor and Mullan concluded, 'is a long way from the silent rows of people sitting in semi-darkness on their television chairs. Today's television may be lucky to win itself a glance from people who are busy rushing past it on their way to other business.'[35] Where a member of the family did look out for a particular programme, this was not necessarily at the expense of other interests. In the early days of television, popular figures such as Philip Harben on cooking, Barry Bucknell on do-it-yourself and Percy Thrower on gardening expanded rather than confined the personal interests of individuals within the household.

Furthermore, the era of the exclusive radio receiver in the living room was coming to an end while its effects were still being assessed. Portable radios were introduced in the late 1950s, enabling programmes to be listened to in kitchens, bedrooms or out of doors.[36] The motor car was ceasing to be a privilege of the middle class, providing a new arena of private space, increasingly equipped with a radio. By the time of Taylor and Mullan's survey in the mid-1980s, a third of households had four or more transistors, and there were eleven million car radios on the road. Televisions were becoming sufficiently small and cheap for additional sets to be installed in other rooms in the house. Video recorders were on sale from the mid-1970s, freeing viewers from the tyranny of the programme schedules. The most revolutionary innovation of the final quarter of the century shifted the balance of recreation decisively towards the solitary consumer. In 1979, the Sony Walkman ushered in the world of fully mobile, wholly personalized, high-quality entertainment. Whether within the house or out of doors, surrounding noise and conversation could be diminished whilst the wearers were immersed in their own soundscape. Conversely, the use of a small earphone reduced the interference that one person's pleasure might cause to another. The tradename emphasized the ancient pleasure of pedestrian locomotion and it soon became associated with the increasing enthusiasm for jogging. It was equally usable when sedentary at home or in the garden. In that the Walkman enabled any kind of music to be listened to at any time in any space, it was a genuinely innovative product, a multi-million-selling forerunner of the iPhone and other portable digital media. But in another sense it was just a technical solution to a task that had faced the members of crowded households down the generations: how to tune out the noise of others in order to concentrate on a personal recreational project; if still expensive, it was now so much easier.

The Pleasures of Solitude

In the mid-1920s a pastime crossed the Atlantic from the United States, where it had lately become a craze. It was initially described as a 'new form of puzzle in the shape of a word square'.[37] Games with words had long distracted the educated, particularly the acrostic, which was a favourite of Queen Victoria.[38] The crossword, as it became known, rapidly established itself as the pre-eminent literary pastime. Britain's contribution was the cryptic clue, introduced in the *Observer* in 1926 by Edward Powys Mather, who took his penname from the figure of Tomás de Torquemada, the late fifteenth-century Dominican and Grand Inquisitor of Spain, who tortured and burned around two thousand alleged heretics who failed to give correct answers to his questions. In 1930, the *Times* finally recognized the popularity of the puzzle and began publishing what became the most famous of all the newspaper crosswords. As with many other recreations, the crossword was at once a solitary endeavour and a social enterprise. The puzzle solver was essentially alone with a pencil and a page of the newspaper, or a collection of games anthologized in book form. Completion was a personal achievement, whether or not it was undertaken within the mythical target of the four-minute boiling of an egg set by a former Provost of Eton. But conversation ensued with other members of the family, or colleagues at work, when faced with a difficult clue. For the expanding newspaper industry, the daily or weekly crossword was its most interactive element, more extensive than the correspondence column.[39] The games were presented as competitions, with small cash prizes or appropriate gifts of a literary artefact such as a dictionary. Like stamp collecting, the new passion was given a royal seal of approval in the person of Queen Mary, and as with popular pastimes from the late Victorian period onwards, the growing number of enthusiasts was translated into organizational form as the National Crossword Puzzle Association.

The crossword was suited to the rhythms of a mature capitalist society. It was a challenge requiring an educated mind capable of concentration and effective target-setting. A partly completed puzzle was a failure. Solving the final clue demanded many of the same skills as a successful professional, entrepreneurial or even, as it appeared, espionage career.[40] Yet it was fundamentally unnecessary and unproductive. It had economic value for the newspapers and book publishers, but otherwise belonged to the realm of idleness. Whilst it might display a familiarity with literary culture, it lacked the imaginative or intellectual profit of serious reading. A finished crossword was a personal achievement that had no lasting meaning once it had been checked in the next day's paper. As Stephen Gelber has argued, such pastimes at once reflected the growing divorce between work and play and endorsed disciplines associated with economic endeavour.[41] In common with other hobbies, whether mental or manual, they celebrated the achievement of the twentieth-century economy in providing more opportunity to escape labour, and more income to invest in alternative activities. They displayed free choice in the consumption of leisure, but were also oriented towards regular, disciplined outcomes.[42] The crossword was one amongst a range of distractions that gave shape to the hours that, for men at least, surrounded the ever-more sharply defined working day. And unlike more practical spare-time activities, the puzzle was essentially portable. As more time was spent commuting to work, or spending salaries on travel to distant holidays, so the crossword held boredom at bay.

The crossword was unusual amongst popular pastimes in that it was almost free. The newspaper might well have been bought anyway, and at a time when correspondence was still the principal means of networking over distance, despite the gradual arrival of the telephone, there were bound to be writing instruments in the house. Elsewhere, solitary pleasures increasingly were an emblematic form of consumption. They constituted an arena in which individuals expressed their identity by the purchase of goods. In the case of collecting, material acquisition was the central objective. Whilst, as we have seen, a range of secondary purposes could be associated with, say, stamp collecting, at the heart of the activity was the potentially limitless investment of money, which, if well judged, might itself become a source of income. This was most obviously so where the object of the collector was money itself. 'Coin collecting,' explained a guide to the practice, 'is one of the few hobbies one can enjoy over the years and still stand to make a profit.'[43] Even where the central purpose was itself non-financial, there were continual demands on the pocket of the enthusiast. The hobby magazines were full of advertisements not just for the particular project but for a wide range of tools and associated materials. Entrepreneurs such as Frank Hornby quickly realized that the key to commercial success was to ensure that no set-up was ever complete. Always there was an extra model to be purchased, a further addition to a track layout, an extension into ancillary model-making of buildings and landscapes.

In its more extreme form, particularly with outdoor pursuits such as fishing, there developed a fetishization of objects, the pleasure of possession of instruments or clothing because they were the latest, best designed or most expensive, or because through their ownership practitioners could demonstrate their superior discernment. It was a means of both self-display and policing the boundaries of the collective pursuit. The multitude of fishing memoirs in the early decades of the twentieth century, for instance, contained descriptions of watery contests which must have been incomprehensible to contemporary non-enthusiasts, let alone later readers. John Waller Hills's *Summer on the Test*, first published in 1924, was exclusively concerned with one man, the river and his kit. 'At last there was movement under my bank,' he wrote, 'it might be a rat, but let us try my dark olive quill; its size was 0, and my gut 3x. The first cast was swept aside by the wind, but at the second there was a confident rise and a good fish careered downstream.'[44] The making and selection of flies to catch salmon and trout became a literary genre in its own right.[45] In all these solitary pursuits, indoors or out, the claim of mere self-indulgence was evaded by the purposeful nature of the activity and, unlike drinking, the avoidance of obvious harm to the practitioners or those around them.

The multiplying opportunities for personal consumption facilitating time alone reflected the growing specialization of leisure. Activities which once had been part of the daily round of managing a home or earning a living increasingly were seen as discrete forms of behaviour. Gardening, for instance, had for centuries been both a source of pleasure and a critical means of supplementing a stressed family economy through the provision of home-produced vegetables. The satisfaction of growing your own remained and took on new forms, but the allotment movement reached its peak during the Depression, and after the government-inspired drive for self-sufficiency in the Second World War, vegetable gardening gradually ceased to be a material necessity.[46] By the early twenty-first century, it was calculated that around twenty-five million adults regularly engaged in the pastime.[47] It fell into the increasingly capacious category of a hobby, which embraced both time-honoured pastimes and new technically based tasks such as chemistry or radio construction. In the first decade of the post-war boom, identifiable expenditure on sports and hobbies increased by 50 per cent.[48]

'The range of pastimes, which are collectively known as hobbies,' observed Ferdynand Zweig his 1952 study *The British Worker*, 'is enormous and satisfies a great variety of interests.'[49] 'Useful crafts,' reported a contemporary survey of working-class families, 'find a surprising number of devotees. There is a lot of satisfaction expressed in "pottering", "tinkering", "fiddling about".'[50] Projects requiring serious individual concentration away from the rest of the family were promoted in the burgeoning periodical literature.[51] The lead item in the 1959 edition of *Hobbies Annual* was a detailed plan for the construction of a 'Musical Swiss Clock'. This told the time, played tunes, had an illuminated clock-face and could be used for holding 'trinkets or cigarettes'. 'It can easily be made up by even the average worker,' assured the journal, 'with but a few simple tools, and makes an excellent choice as a gift.'[52] Undertaking odd jobs around the house took on a new identity with the emergence of the 'do-it-yourself' movement in the mid-1950s. As with the related notion of hobbies, there was an element of continuity in the activities the term embraced. What was new was the sense of an historical change in the relation of householders to their accommodation. The occupants of the publicly financed estates did not wait for council workmen to mend faults or improve the decorations, but set about improving their living space.[53] Owner-occupation generated rising spending on furnishings and fittings. In October 1955, Newnes launched a journal, *Practical Householder*, to cater for the market. Within less than two years it claimed a circulation of over a million.[54] In the rapidly expanding medium of television, the resident DIY expert Barry Bucknell received up to thirty-five thousand inquiries a week, and needed ten secretaries to respond to them.[55] The illustrations of *Practical Householder* often featured all the family, including children, 'making and repairing things and doing jobs around the home'.[56] In the more home-centred society, there was a greater sense of a collective project in the expenditure of time and money on projects such as making 'garden chairs and a garden swing', or constructing a 'studio couch'.[57] The decision-making may more often have been shared, as also the enjoyment of the completed task, but with the possible exception of painting and decorating, the actual labour for the most part remained separate and gendered.

Pedestrian locomotion also could be found under the heading of a hobby. Older forms of walking were slow to decline. Casual strolling out of the house became increasingly feasible for women, particularly with the expanding provision of municipal parks.[58] Despite the use of trains and buses, travelling to work in the towns and cities long remained a matter of physical exercise. Mass Observation surveys during and just after the Second World War indicated that around a third of male breadwinners left home in the morning on foot and another fifth on a bicycle. Only those earning over £10 a week used their own vehicle for travel to their employment office.[59] By the end of the post-war boom, access to personal transport had been transformed. There were two million cars on the road in 1950 and nearly ten million two decades later.[60] Ownership became sufficiently widespread for manual workers who had been dispersed to the suburbs by slum clearance to begin to enjoy the most private and solitary of all journeys: the commute to work in a car occupied only by its driver, with or without a radio playing.[61]

In one regard, nineteenth-century practices of solitary strolling continued to grow. Urban dog-walking showed a relentless increase, with four million animals requiring exercise in the 1960s and eight million by 2012.[62] Essentially these were lone practices, although they could provide opportunities for social encounters between dog-owners in streets and parks.[63] Elsewhere, however, changes were taking place towards the world Rebecca Solnit has described in which 'walking ceased to be part of the continuum of experience and instead became something consciously chosen'.[64] This might mean an essentially social activity. Pedestrian exercise as an organized weekend activity expanded with the aid of urban clubs and improving train services.[65] There was a class distinction between hikers, who set off with a minimum of specialized clothing, and ramblers, who inherited the high intellectual purpose of Leslie Stephen and his colleagues and changed into knee-breeches and tailored jackets for their expeditions.[66] Whatever the dress, the continuing proliferation of printed guides enabled those who chose their own company safely to reach a destination on foot. Solo walking that was neither a necessary element of everyday living nor directed to a particular place gained a higher profile.

In 1927, Virginia Woolf celebrated the possibility of women joining the established tradition of the urban flâneur. She described an expedition whose ostensible goal was merely the purchase of a pencil. 'As we step out of the house on a fine evening between four and six,' she wrote, 'we shed the self our friends know us by and become part of that vast republican army of anonymous trampers, whose society is so agreeable after the solitude of one's own rooms.'[67] As with Dickens, the pleasure lay in the contactless contact with a cast of strangers. Knowledge was constructed by means of a deliberate bricolage. Random mobility revealed fleeting biographies which enriched and entertained without compromising the privacy of the passer-by. It exposed patterns in urban living that were concealed by the formal language of planners and the objective depictions of maps. In our own time, Will Self decries the steady decline since the early twentieth century when '90% of journeys fewer than six miles were taken on foot'.[68] Where in his youth he had walked because he could afford no other means of travel, now he made long expeditions on foot solely for pleasure. Iain Sinclair, the leading modern practitioner of this mode of urban exploration, insists on the synthesizing function of directionless strolling. 'Walking,' he writes, 'is the best way to explore and exploit the city; the changes, shifts, breaks in the cloud helmet, movement of light on water. Drifting purposefully is the recommended mode, tramping asphalted earth in alert reverie, allowing the fiction of an underlying pattern to reveal itself.'[69]

Hobbies, home improvement and other domestic recreations were voluntary activities undertaken in free time. They were at once a celebration of growing prosperity and a compensation for the stultifying means by which the increased income was often gained. 'Work is often simply something which gives him a living,' Ferdynand Zweig observed of the post-war employee, 'something he dislikes and would not do unless he is forced to it. But in his hobbies he regains his freedom; they are often the last thing left to modern man in which he can find freedom.'[70] There was, however, a less positive aspect to the proliferating forms of leisure activity. In 1925, the *Manchester Guardian* published an article on the crossword 'epidemic' that was sweeping through the United States and beginning to reach Europe. It quoted the judgement of Ruth Hale, President of the newly formed National Crossword Puzzle Association. 'When life is entirely without satisfactions,' she explained, 'as it is most of the time even for the best of us, there is nothing to do but leave it – temporarily, of course, but completely. Now a game of bridge will do a little and a ball game will do even better, but a cross-word puzzle does best of all.'[71] Tackling the daily puzzle was a defence against unfulfilled time or unproductive company. It was embraced when there was no profit in conversation, and no immediate prospect of taking up arms against a sea of discontents.

Alongside the crossword, the jigsaw puzzle became a widespread diversion between the wars. Unlike the new word game, the pastime had a long history in British culture. Its origin lay in the dissected map invented by John Spilsbury in 1769, principally as an educational amusement for the children of prosperous families.[72] During the nineteenth century it was embraced by upper-class women, including Queen Victoria, seeking a decorous means of consuming the acres of empty time with which they were faced. Hand-cut wooden puzzles remained an expensive toy, but technical advances in between the wars, particularly in the mass production of die-cut cardboard versions, made the recreation more broadly available just as the workers in the family found themselves with unwanted time on their hands.[73] Thereafter it enjoyed a popularity unconfined by age, class, or gender. It remained a toy for young children, but was widely attempted by all those in possession of a flat surface which could be undisturbed for a period of time. As with stamp collecting, it continued to enjoy the patronage of royalty, including the Duke of Windsor and Queen Elizabeth, but otherwise met a wide range of tastes ranging from photographs of holiday views to reproductions of the best of the world's art constructed out of thousands of pieces.

In common with other long-term projects, such as knitting, the composition of puzzles could be accompanied by intermittent conversation. Other members of the family might share the task or even, to entertain themselves, engage in competitive puzzle making. Essentially, however, it was a personal project, a form of concentrated withdrawal from company or the consumption of long periods when no society was available. When Margaret Drabble turned aside from fiction to the composition of a memoir, she structured her account around her lifelong passion for jigsaws. In common with crosswords, their attraction lay partly in the finite quality of the endeavour. Unlike more serious tasks in life, there was a frame, a given picture and, with sufficient application, a guarantee of completion. Where knitting might fail through some mistake, or a handicraft reveal shortcomings in skill, there was no inherent reason why a puzzle once commenced should not be finished. Although some professional writers embraced word games as a relaxation, Drabble found the non-verbal nature of the task a relief from her working life. There was the additional pleasure afforded by high-end boxes of an education in art history. At the same time, the immersion in what she termed 'a solitary time killer' had a deeper purpose.[74] 'Doing jigsaws,' Drabble explained in the preface to her account, 'and writing about them has been one of my strategies to defeat melancholy and avoid laments.'[75] At a given moment, personal relationships were as much a cause of as a solution to depression. Drabble revived an earlier enthusiasm for puzzles at the death of her parents. To be by herself for hours on end, making frames and patterns without the immediate distraction of other people, was a necessary device for managing her spirits and maintaining her social identity.

Many other solitary pastimes offered similar possibilities of therapeutic absorption. Hunter Davies's lifelong passion for stamp collecting continued throughout the travails of a busy writing life. The essence of its appeal was the enclosed order of the pursuit. 'So far,' he wrote, 'I've had endless pleasure out of stamps, and I can think of no other hobby which is so harmless, so easy to organise, so neat and tidy, which upsets nobody else and doesn't frighten the horses.'[76] He was intimidated by the 'big wide professional stamp world', celebrating instead the privacy of the time spent managing and reviewing his collection.[77] Simon Garfield's memoir, *The Error World*, is similarly insistent on the attraction of a universe from which messy, sometimes unmanageable social relationships were excluded. The usual pressures of adolescence were compounded by the early deaths of his older brother and his mother, and he early found comfort in the dependable silence of his stamp collection. 'Whatever else was happening around me,' he recalled, '– the family disintegrations, pressures of exams and then work, romantic complications – here was a comforting and reliable constant. It was flat, stowable, secret. Stamps seldom disappointed and never left you.'[78] A hobby common to many schoolchildren gained extra meaning as he began to concentrate his collecting on misprinted stamps. 'The period of greatest involvement and expenditure on errors,' he wrote, 'coincided with the strongest feelings of grief over the loss of my family.'[79] He made increasing use of dealers, but kept the larger community of collectors at bay. His was a private solution to personal needs. In adult life his enthusiasm faded but returned as his marriage failed, his retreat into what became an expensive pastime at once a cause of and a response to relationship problems.

Most of the multiplying solitary recreations required, as we have seen, expenditure both on the immediate materials and on the time and space needed to enjoy them. Important though their activities were to middle-class practitioners such as Drabble and Garfield, it can be argued that the benefit was in inverse proportion to opportunity. There was a difference between those spending increasing spare income game fishing on Highland estates or consuming empty hours in country houses completing jigsaws or tapestries, and poor working-class women desperate to find any opportunity for a moment of private leisure. The interviews collected by Margery Spring Rice painted 'a picture in which monotony, loneliness, discouragement and sordid hard work are the main features'.[80] She began her chapter on 'The Day's Work' with a case history of a woman finally driven to a complete breakdown by the absence of any relief from her solitary toil of raising five children.[81] In these circumstances, it was the fleeting moments of personal leisure that had the greatest impact on physical or mental survival.

Some were sociable in the form of encounters with other women on the doorstep or in the corner shop. But many were valued because of the absence of company in the form of wailing children or an uncommunicative husband home from work. Loneliness turned into solitude when the woman was able to take pleasure from her own company in the course of a freely chosen walk, or half an hour with a book or a newspaper, or needlework undertaken for some purpose other than keeping the family's meagre stock of clothing in working order. Even at this level of society, additional diversions were becoming available with some of Spring Rice's witnesses getting hold of cheap jigsaws, or attempting crosswords compiled by less demanding taskmasters than Torquemada.[82]

The most significant of these new recreations was the cinema, which between the wars transformed the opportunities for evading the confines of the home. Men, women, and children of every level of society bought tickets to the newly constructed dream palaces, with annual attendance approaching a billion by 1939.[83] Nearly a third of the population were going at least once a week, with higher proportions amongst the working class, and amongst women.[84] Motives for spending an afternoon or an evening in front of a screen were mixed. With so many in the audience buying tickets irrespective of the programme, and as much as a quarter of some working-class neighbourhoods attending two or more times a week, the attraction was not confined to the appeal of a particular film or actor. Mothers took children to divert them and keep them quiet. Lovers courted out of sight of parents. Couples shared uninterrupted time together. Less welcome contact was made by men who preyed on single women in the dark. Gladys Langford, escaping 'the black dog of melancholy' that visited her solitary life at home, regularly found herself the victim of groping hands, which continued even when she told her assailant that if he could see how old she was he might not bother.[85]

Beneath the social aspects of buying a ticket was the more profound attraction of letting the mind evade all its pressing concerns. Reading had always been valued as a means of escape from immediate conditions and company. 'It's a great blessing,' wrote Nella Last in her Mass Observation diary, 'when one can lose all sense of time, all worries, if only for a short time, in a book.'[86] The same function was performed by repetitive manual recreations. 'I sit and turn things over in my mind,' Last recorded, 'as my fingers fly over my sewing.'[87] This abstracted solitude was nowhere more available than in the midst of the film audience. Many of the women who walked to their often richly designed cinemas sought only a break from their solitary labour. 'She sits on a thoroughly comfortable seat,' wrote Margaret Eyles of the first generation of cinema-goers, 'and hears quite good, popular music. . . . And so the mother rests.'[88] Other than sex, cinema-going was the only popular recreation undertaken principally in the dark. In this it differed from its main successor activity from the 1950s onwards, watching television. Once the lights went down, the confines of the real world were dissolved. In the enveloping blackness, lit only by the flickering projector, every hardship in the home, every shortcoming in relations with family and neighbours, ceased for a while. The relaxing viewer might choose to enter the world of the film, or might otherwise wander through such private landscapes as appealed to the imagination.

A Companion to Me in Solitude

Post-war reconstruction took place in a haze of cigarette smoke. As the welfare state was being constructed, four-fifths of men and two-fifths of women were regular smokers.[89] Unlike most other recreational activities, which were undertaken at particular times or in specific spaces, smoking was pervasive and almost inescapable.[90] It blurred the increasing distinction between the working and domestic arenas, and between the hours of labour and leisure. Those who themselves did not light up were exposed to smoke around the house, on trains, trams and buses, in offices and on shop floors, in cinemas and dance halls. In larger houses, the consumption of cigars had been confined to dedicated smoking rooms, but the portable, instant cigarette transcended such restrictions. The only escape was an outdoor pursuit – gardening or fishing, a solitary walk in the country, driving alone where a car could be afforded.

The sheer ubiquity of tobacco reflected two key characteristics of recreational solitude in the modern era. Firstly it was a product of economic change and mass communication. Cigars and briar and clay pipes had long histories, but all depended on preparation by hand. The turning point in the consumption of tobacco was the adoption in 1883 by the Bristol firm of W. D. and H. O. Wills of an American machine capable of rolling three hundred cigarettes a minute.[91] It launched the unfiltered, high-tar Woodbine at five for a penny in 1888. Over the succeeding sixty years, smoking lost any association with income or class, and increasingly with gender. Sales were driven upwards by energetic advertising, both exploiting and subsidizing the expanding market for reading matter. The passion for collecting was appropriated by the widespread issuing of cigarette cards from the end of the nineteenth century, aimed in part at seeding demand amongst those notionally still too young to smoke themselves.

The second characteristic was the inherent binary quality of the activity. Smoking belonged to the large group of recreations which according to context and inclination were variously social or solitary. Walking, card playing, puzzle making, handicrafts, pet keeping, stamp collecting, cinema going, reading, all had their personal or collective forms, with practitioners able to move between them or concentrate more at one end of the spectrum than the other. With smoking, as with other pastimes, what mattered was the freedom to choose the mode of activity. There was a notorious advertising disaster when a new brand named 'The Strand' was launched in 1959, with an image of a lonely figure, only able to attract attention by opening a packet. Customers wanted to see themselves not as perpetual outsiders, but as agents capable of choosing their own mode of company.[92] The extent to which nicotine addiction compromised free will was not recognized until the 1980s. All were aware of the social attraction. Growing boys wanted to imitate a defining characteristic of their father.[93] According to the major study Mass Observation conducted in the heyday of consumption, the tobacco habit began as a form of emulation:

> Roughly every second smoker attributes his first experiments to some sort of social motive – to the desire to imitate or impress others, to gain social ease and confidence or to avoid the feeling of being left out. Not more than a third, at the outside, give similar reasons for continuing to smoke in later life. Women – who tend to start smoking at a later age than men – are particularly susceptible to social pressure; their first step in smoking is often accepting offered cigarettes, their second buying a packet to proffer in return; and their initiation tends to be set

in parties, social gatherings, and war-time air-raid shelters or First Aid posts.[94]

The transition from the era of cigars and pipes to packets of twenty cigarettes democratized the sociable function. The smoking room in the prosperous household or in the London club was a site of male bonding.[95] It defined a masculine sphere in opposition to women, who were supposed to be unable to tolerate the fumes of tobacco. The temporary withdrawal in order to engage in the sybaritic pleasures of managing pipes and curating and consuming cigars at once defined these men's privilege and recharged their energy for the labour of their public lives. The writer J. M. Barrie described the serious trivia of such practices. 'Once I was a member of a club for smokers,' he recalled, 'where we practised blowing rings. The most successful got a box of cigars as a prize at the end of the year. Those were days. Often I think wistfully of them. We met in a cosy room off the Strand. How well I can picture it still; time-tables lying everywhere, with which we could light our pipes.'[96] In the Woodbine era, the rituals of group bonding were more often performed in cafés and public houses. As Stephen Graham observed, 'there is no doubt that smoking in company is a social grace. It gives a sense of unity, and at the same time, it is a source of some pleasure.'[97]

The affordable gesture of offering a cigarette helped negotiate the gap between acquaintance and friendship. Moments of uncertainty were covered by the interval in conversation imposed by lighting or drawing on a cigarette. Unlike a pipe, which was impossible to share, or the expensive indulgence of a cigar, a cigarette was easily translated from a personal to a social pleasure.[98] By the middle of the twentieth century, it was deployed in rituals in all levels of the economy, and in every recreational space. 'Smoking,' observed Mass Observation, 'is an effective way of procuring introductions, easing contacts both in business and on formal occasions, establishing a general air of relaxation.'[99] Wartime intensified the need for such gestures. Within the forces, cigarettes were a currency of exchange and an instrument of camaraderie in the midst of boredom and danger.[100] On the home front, they compensated for the manifold threats to networks of intimacy and friendship. 'Numerous current surveys,' reported Mass Observation in 1941, 'have shown that at the present time many people are feeling particularly in need of social contacts and socialised interests, which have become less accessible and more desirable because of the war. Here again, smoking acts in some sense as a solution or substitute.'[101]

There was little intimation in the surveys of the epidemiological research that began to be published by Richard Doll and his colleagues in 1950. Protests by doctors and non-smokers had long been made on the grounds of smell, hygiene, and a variety of impacts on health, but neither addiction nor cancer featured in the studies of the scale of war-time and post-war consumption.[102] 'To the medical profession,' concluded Mass Observation's 1949 report, '. . . the cigarette represents a possible source of ill-health and infection, and numerous experiments have been undertaken to prove or disprove the possible evil effects of inhaling, of extra-strong tobacco, etc. For the most part such experiments have come to no vital conclusions, but insurance assessors at any rate do not believe that smoking impairs the health.'[103] The long struggle to establish the connection with lung cancer and other fatal diseases eventually drove consumption down to its current levels of just under 20 per cent of men and 15.3 per cent of women.[104] The mid-nineteenth-century association with income has been reversed, with those earning less than £10,000 a year twice as likely to smoke as those earning above £40,000. Growing medical and social disapproval, reinforced by legislation in 2006 and 2007 banning smoking in public places, has reshaped the spirit of community amongst smokers.[105] Huddled together in the wind and rain in designated outdoor areas, they are bound together by a shared sense of persecution.

Nevertheless, despite these aspects of social bonding, a cigar, pipe, or cigarette has always been smoked alone. Throughout the modern era, the culture of consumption celebrated the association between tobacco and the solitary user. 'I love thee,' proclaimed Captain Marryat in 1832, 'whether thou appearest in the shape of a cigar, or diest away in sweet perfume enshrined in the Mereshaum bowl; I love thee with more than woman's love! Thou art a companion to me in solitude.'[106] Unlike many other recreations, there was no question of smoking creating some further product that could be shared by others. Lighting up left only ash. The activity could be viewed in opposition to the multiplying forms of sociability. The growth in cigarette smoking took place alongside the expansion in collective forms of leisure. 'In an increasingly gregarious world,' reported Mass Observation,

> where fewer and fewer habits and pastimes are entirely individual – we relax in large cinemas and theatres, eat in large restaurants, even tend to live with more and more people in the same building – the cigarette remains for most people a pleasure that, whatever its social significance, can also be enjoyed in entire solitude, and a pleasure that remains entirely individual.[107]

Smoking was a defining example of abstracted solitude, the capacity to remove the self from present company. This was the case even when the group was convened specifically in order to share the pleasure. An early celebration of the club smoking room pictured each of the occupants lost in his private world. 'When those curls of cloud go wafting slowly upwards,' it explained,

> perhaps they sometimes obscure for the moment a misfortune, or shut out for the time some of the worries of life; or it may be that the smoker, his head thrown back and his eye turned up towards the sky and to the ceiling, beholds a whole panorama of splendid castles in the air. But they begin in smoke and they end in smoke.[108]

The drifting, shape-shifting course of the burning tobacco was a visual image of the mental processes it engendered. The more rapidly consumed cigarette might foreshorten the daydream, but it remained the most immediately available means of withdrawal without overtly rejecting the society of others.

At a physical level, smoking provided occupation for the hands and the mouth independently of conversation with others in the room. As with other leisure pursuits such as fishing or collecting, there were opportunities at the high end for a personal connoisseurship not just of the tobacco but of all the accoutrements, including varieties of pipes, cleaners, lighters, cases, racks and humidors, pouches and jars, ashtrays and specialized clothing.[109] Their manipulation was itself an evasion of social exchange. The intercourse was between person and object. A well-worn pipe that could be caressed in a pocket when unlit, or emptied and cleaned between smokes, was a comforting distraction. The frequently renewed cigarette was a source of endless fingering, whether or not it was actually being smoked. 'Another of the sensual enjoyments of the cigarette,' wrote Mass Observation, 'that must be inferred rather than verbally proved, is the pleasure of manipulating the cigarette. Smokers seem to enjoy the sight and feel of the cigarette, the toying with matches, case and lighter, . . . and the presence of the cigarette, even unlit, between the lips.'[110]

There was no fixed boundary between abstraction as a relaxation and as a therapy in the face of difficulty. 'To a solitary man,' concluded the first social history of smoking, 'the well-seasoned tube is an invaluable companion. If he happen, once in a way, to have nothing special to do and plenty of time in which to do it, he naturally fills his pipe as he draws the easy-chair on to the hearthrug, and knows not that he is lonely.'[111] It was a means of preparing the mind for a forthcoming task, or, as a series of writers confessed, of reinforcing concentration whilst at work.[112] Together with alcohol, which could also be consumed in company or alone, it was a widely recognized means of relieving stress. 'Smoking,' concluded Mass Observation, 'quite clearly can for some people be not so much a luxury as a *compensatory* pleasure, a solitary indulgence making good the inadequacies of life; someone has to sweeten the pill and if it is not the publican it will have to be the tobacconist.'[113] Women found that cigarettes were a more accessible means than alcohol of coping with the pressures of managing an under-resourced and often lonely domestic arena.[114] In the post-war era, the increasingly pessimistic epidemiological research on the physical implications of smoking did battle with growing interest in the psychology of stress, for which smoking appeared a valid remedy.[115] As a pathway to inner calm, cigarettes were seen to achieve outcomes associated with spiritual reflection, which will be examined in the next chapter. 'They have served generations of men and women, in periods of acute distress,' writes Richard Klein, 'as an incomparable tool for managing and mitigating anxiety and as a variety of prayer.'[116]

Smoking performed a range of functions in times when human company and material conditions were wanting. In a much-quoted passage, Charles Kingsley described the achievement of the early Indian discoverers of tobacco: 'none was made better than this; to be a lone man's companion, a bachelor's friend, a hungry man's food, a sad man's cordial, a wakeful man's sleep, and a chilly man's fire'.[117] It stood as a restorative actor in the face of social deprivation. Charles Dickens deployed the mid-nineteenth-century term for depression in his depiction of the survival of Magwitch in the wilds of Australia. 'Similarly, I must have my smoke,' explained the convict. 'When I was first hired out as a shepherd t'other side of the world, it's my belief I should ha' turned into a molloncolly-mad sheep myself, if I hadn't a had my smoke.'[118] As the clay pipe was superseded by the cigarette, and the occasions for transitional solitude multiplied in the urbanizing society, smoking remained an accessible and affordable response to loneliness. Mass Observation interviewed a woman who was a newcomer to the metropolis: 'I have several months alone in London,' she replied. 'I was very unhappy and ill, and too ignorant of urban life to know how to get into touch with my own sort of people. . . . I used to sit alone in my own room smoking and watching people in the flats opposite dashing about in cars, with dogs, children, and friends. From then on smoking became compulsive.'[119]

Fishing and the Universe

In 2016, the BBC presenter Claudia Hammond, in conjunction with the Wellcome Trust, conducted 'The Rest Test', in which over eighteen thousand people from 134 countries were asked to rank the activities they found most restful. The top ten were, in order of popularity: 'reading'; 'sleeping or napping'; 'looking at, or being in, a natural environment'; 'spending time on my own'; 'listening to music'; 'doing nothing in particular'; 'walking'; 'taking a bath or a shower'; 'daydreaming'; 'watching TV'.[120] The bulk of these undertakings comprised everyday ways of relaxing. 'Doing nothing in particular' had always been a basic resource in the often narrow space between toil and sleep. Walking, as has been argued throughout this study, was the commonplace, unsung form of active recreation. Modern plumbing, recorded music, and television had enriched the agenda, but most of the ways of spending downtime in the international survey were not dependent on technological innovation. It is striking that all of these quiet pursuits either were wholly solitary, or could readily be undertaken in the absence of company (the eleventh activity was 'meditating or practising mindfulness', which will be discussed in Chapter 6). Engaging with people required some level of energy.

In Britain, the opportunities for quiet recreation multiplied over the course of the twentieth century, gradually, if unevenly, drawing in wider sections of society. Taking time for yourself overlapped with the history of consumption, driven by the same forces of disposable income, technological improvements in manufacture and the home, mass communication and the separation of the domestic and occupational spheres. The expanding category of the hobby expressed the privacy of the undertaking, with value and achievement defined by the practitioner. It also reflected its structural identity, with all kinds of activity sustained by and sustaining a vigorous economy of goods and services. In this sense, smoking in its mid-twentieth-century heyday was at once the emblem of a mass-marketed consumer society and a direct inheritor of the most basic form of abstracted solitude.

The more structured pursuits, including tobacco, were active agents. Individuals engaged their hands and their minds on some chosen task. 'One of the basic feelings in smoking,' concluded Mass Observation, 'is contained in the idea that the cigarette *does things* to the smoker.'[121] The practice performed services for the user that might otherwise be expected of an intimate acquaintance: 'it quietens his nerves, soothes him out of depressions and bad temper, gives him comfort and consolation for what he has not got – and at the same time it fills him with purposiveness, with the ability – real or imagined – to cope with life and chop off heads'.[122] The depth of absorption in a pastime became a constructive force, valued where casual social exchange failed to meet pressing bodily or emotional needs, or where peace of mind demanded a temporary withdrawal from the company of others.

Until addiction in the consumption of alcohol and tobacco became medically defined, recreational solitude could be seen as an exemplification of Zimmermann's prescription that withdrawal was only beneficial when the actor could freely return to social life. Many of the activities surveyed in this chapter had their personal and collective forms. The societies which began to appear in the last quarter of the nineteenth century multiplied and in some cases acquired international dimensions. Print, and later television and then digital communication, ensured that lone practitioners could always feel themselves networked to a larger community of enthusiasts. The weight of the meaning attached to a particular pastime was in the end more a matter of state of mind than physical interaction.

Angling was a case in point. There was a literature, there was expenditure on equipment, there were clubs and competitions especially amongst coarse fishermen, but at the moment of casting a line, the individual was alone.[123] 'Some assert,' wrote the novelist Morley Roberts in 1932, 'that they are not fishermen but a crowd. . . . But I do maintain that the true fisherman is essentially a solitary.'[124] As with many recreations, there was more than a hint of misogyny about the culture, with isolation embraced as an escape from gendered company. 'We wish to be alone,' observed Roberts. 'Our wives and sweethearts, our mistresses, may exist. They cease to be while we fish. If, greatly daring, any such come and speak to us they should be firmly checked. If not there is no end to their interference.'[125] Nonetheless the point was not people and their temporary absence but the consciousness of the figure on the river bank. 'Our philosophy is a kind of solipsism,' explained Roberts. 'When I fish I am the universe. There is none but me. We may club together as against others, but by the water we divide.'[126] So it was with every category of withdrawal that required skill, concentration and, however infrequent the catch, a defined outcome.

THE SPIRITUAL REVIVAL

The Immense Indifference of Things

In 1904, Joseph Conrad published *Nostromo*. The novel is set in the port of Sulaco in the Occidental Province of the fictitious South American state of Costaguana, loosely modelled on Colombia. It is a story of high drama. Charles Gould develops the San Tomé silver concession outside Sulaco, using his increasing wealth to support attempts by the dictator Ribiera to bring stability to a country riven with disunity and disorder, and then to promote the secession of the province. Political and personal adventure suffuse the narrative. At the climax of the novel, the fledgeling independent state is invaded by government forces arriving over the mountains and by sea. Conspiracy is everywhere. Lives are threatened by violence. And then, in an unexpected twist in the plot, a central character, the journalist Martin Decoud, dies of solitude.

Together with Nostromo, the foreman of the dock workers and general factotum of the Gould enterprise, Decoud loads the output of the mine onto a lighter to carry it away from the incoming troops. In the dark, the boat is accidentally run down by the invading government steamer. Nostromo manages to beach the treasure on Great Isabel, an island in the bay of Sulaco, and swims back to the mainland, leaving Decoud to await rescue. Left alone, Decoud's mental health rapidly deteriorates, and on the eleventh day he puts four ingots of silver in his pockets, rows the lighter's dinghy into the bay, and shoots himself. Conrad leaves the reader in no doubt about the cause of the tragedy: 'the truth was that he died from solitude, the enemy known but to few on this earth, and whom only the simplest of us are fit to withstand'.[1] This explanation reversed the assumption of earlier authorities that educated men could be trusted with their own company whilst women and the manual classes lacked the depth of mind to cope with its threat. Decoud is vulnerable because his sceptical, unmoored intelligence is incapable of withstanding the absence of both society and conversation.[2] His troubles begin as soon as he is left by Nostromo:

> At the end of his first day on the Great Isabel, Decoud, turning in his lair of coarse grass, under the shade of a tree, said to himself –
>   'I have not seen as much as one single bird all day.'
>   And he had not heard a sound, either, all day but that one now of his own muttering voice. It had been a day of absolute silence – the first he had known in his life. And he had not slept a wink.[3]

The journalist was a native of Costaguana, but had grown up in Paris. He returned to his homeland a 'plump dandy', as Conrad describes him, believing in nothing except his own wits and advancement.[4] His eventual commitment to the revolutionary cause is presented as a self-promoting affectation rather than an embrace of a fundamental principle or political community.[5] 'The brilliant "Son Decoud",' writes Conrad,

> the spoiled darling of the family, the lover of Antonia and journalist of Sulaco, was not fit to grapple with himself single-handed. Solitude from mere outward condition of existence becomes very swiftly a state of soul in which the affectations of irony and scepticism have no place. It takes possession of the mind, and drives forth the thought into the exile of utter unbelief.[6]

Nostromo, by contrast, lacks both 'intellectual existence or moral strain' and endures his own solitary adventure without difficulty.[7] 'In our activity alone,' concludes Conrad, 'do we find the sustaining illusion of an independent existence as against the whole scheme of things of which we form a helpless part.'[8]

Although the novel was set in South America, Conrad was writing for a Western audience whose cultural inheritance embraced a restorative spatial solitude. An empty landscape was a place to which the troubled mind could retreat in the face of the corrupting affairs of urban civilization. There it would find a spiritual solace which in time might permit re-entry into social life with a renewed moral integrity and sense of purpose. By the beginning of the twentieth century, however, such a view was becoming more difficult to sustain. The Darwinian revolution described a natural world indifferent to the wellbeing of any individual member of a species. The blind reproductive struggle favoured only those fitted by chance to survive. Further, the tradition of the desert fathers was increasingly fading. Chapter 4 described the general failure of the earlier nineteenth-century drive to deploy forms of religious solitude, whether voluntary or enforced, as a means of renewing the authority of the churches in a secularizing society. As a consequence, those retreating into nature encountered merely their own inadequacy. This 'merciless solitude', as Conrad described it, could destroy those incapable of a faith in themselves or some larger destiny.[9] Decoud has no means of salvation in his sleepless sojourn on the island. 'A victim of the disillusioned weariness,' concludes Conrad's obituary for his character, 'which is the retribution meted out to intellectual audacity, the brilliant Don Martin Decoud, weighted by the bars of San Tomé silver, disappeared without a trace, swallowed up in the immense indifference of things.'[10]

Yet the thirst for an escape from the press of modern social relations did not disappear with the suicidal journalist. The new century witnessed the search for new pathways to solitude, largely in the absence of a unifying religious authority or an overarching vision of the natural world. The balance was recast between the personal pilgrimage, however it was conceived, and the mass media in which increasingly it was embodied and communicated. What survived from Conrad's pessimism was the emphasis on spiritual or ideological belief as the means of navigating the experience of solitude. The less choice there was in a withdrawal from company, the greater the importance of an inner sense of mission. The more choice, the larger the risk of a depth of self-discovery that would test to destruction the individual's sense of purpose. In this chapter, the continuing attraction of solitude as an essentially oppositional response to the pressures of modern society will be explored in five contexts: new encounters with the natural world; lone circumnavigation; the persistence of solitary confinement; the final revival of monastic withdrawal; and reimagined forms of spiritual retreat.

Exploring Nature

At a quotidian level, the long tradition of finding comfort in empty countryside continued into the new century, both as a practice and as a literary form. W. H. Hudson's affectionate recreation of the life of a shepherd in 1910 was suffused with the pleasure he took in his lone exploration of the rural landscape in which his subject earned his living:

> That emptiness seemed good for both mind and body. I could spend long hours idly sauntering or sitting or lying on the turf, thinking of nothing, or only of one thing – that is was a relief to have no thought about anything. But no, something was secretly saying to me all the time, that it was more than what I have said which continued to draw me to this vacant place – more than the mere relief experienced on coming back to nature and to solitude, and the freedom of a wide earth and sky.[11]

As agriculture shrank to the margins of the urbanizing society, it retained a fascination for those no longer living on the land. Raymond Williams writes that 'there is almost an inverse proportion, in the twentieth century, between the relative importance of the working rural economy and the cultural importance of rural ideas'.[12] Walkers poured out of the towns and cities on summer evenings and at weekends, often in organized groups, but still also as solitary figures seeking private encounters with what they imagined to be timeless landscapes.[13] In *The Gentle Art of Tramping* of 1927, the journalist and prolific travel-writer Stephen Graham celebrated the consequent reordering of the spirit:

So when you put on your old clothes and take to the road, you make at least a right gesture. You get into your right place in the world in the right way. Even if your tramping expedition is a mere jest, a jaunt, a spree, you are apt to feel the benefits of getting into a right relation toward God, Nature and your fellow man. You get into an air that is refreshing and free. You liberate yourself from tacit assumption of your everyday life.[14]

There were those, however, for whom the 'right relation toward God, Nature and your fellow man' required a fundamental reconsideration of sociability and its antithesis in the modern world. The most strident voice was that of John Cowper Powys, himself a vigorous lone walker, who, in 1933, published the first attempt at a full-scale philosophy of solitude in English since Zimmermann's treatise had been translated in the late eighteenth century.[15] Unlike the Swiss doctor, Powys was not seeking an appropriate balance in modes of association. All forms of everyday social interaction were condemned. 'The drifting, brainless, gregariousness of so many human beings,' he insisted, 'imitating one another, conciliating one another, admiring, desiring, envying, competing, tormenting one another, is an attempt to escape from this inherent loneliness of the self.'[16] He had explored some of these ideas in his *Defence of Sensuality* three years earlier, where he dismissed 'certain gregariously human traditions among us, such as seem to be slowly assassinating all calm ecstatic happiness, the only kind of happiness that really is worthy of organisms with the long history and large hopes of ours'.[17] Now he sought to reverse what he viewed as the dominant emphasis in social theory. 'There are many modern thinkers,' he wrote, 'who emphasize the individual's dependency upon society. It is, on the contrary, only the cultivation of interior solitude, among crowded lives, that makes society endurable.'[18]

In constructing his vision, Powys bypassed the obstacles posed by 'the immense indifference of things' by grounding his philosophy in a pre-Christian epoch and in a form of pantheism where natural selection had no purchase. He established his own intellectual tradition which took the reader past Wordsworth, Rousseau, the medieval schoolmen, the desert hermits, Marcus Aurelius, Epictetus and the Stoics, and Heraclitus, ending with Chinese Taoism. The Taoists appealed to Powys because of their emphasis on unstructured contemplation rather than individual or collective action, and their desire to transcend the boundary between the self and the not-self and thus to achieve a complete harmony with nature.[19] Powys had no interest in organized religion or in the concept of an anthropomorphized deity. He rejected the communal element of church worship and believed that the tradition of solitary mystics had run its course. 'What is advisable for us now,' he argued, 'is to cultivate some definite substitute for the lives of hermits and hermit-saints.'[20] His substitute for Christianity was what he termed a 'planetary elementalism'.[21] He sought to establish a new connection between the 'hard, resistant, inviolable self' and the vestiges of 'this mysterious, primordial earth-mood' which could be encountered in the winds, the grass, and the rocks.[22] The source of spiritual renewal lay beyond human existence. His nature was essentially unpeopled. 'In an English landscape,' he wrote, 'you find the brooding inanimate presence of the primeval elements intertwined with the whole complicated atmosphere of a long local history.'[23] It was the duty of modern citizens to cease talking one to another and instead practise the silence that the soul needs for 'the murmur of the long centuries to grow audible, for the mystery of the cosmic procession to make itself felt'.[24]

A Philosophy of Solitude embraced the past on a scale which emptied it of all chronological specificity. Powys was an heir to the tradition of nature writing that had been promoted by the Georgian poetry movement earlier in the century. This combined a close observation of the countryside with a growing fascination with the myths, legends, and pagan traditions which they imagined could still be found there. The expanding towns and cities had paved over this ancient history, which could only be recaptured by classically educated observers attuned to its cultural and physical traces. Such an approach deflected attention away from the specific moment of both urban and rural living in the decades since 1900. The critique of modernity in the *Philosophy of Solitude* was couched in the most general terms. Powys denounced the 'Gargantuan monstrosities and Dantesque horrors of our great modern cities'.[25] Despite his rejection of institutional religion, his analysis of current ailments had all the emotional force and temporal vagueness of a hell-fire preacher. He contrasted the 'flowing, innocent, ancient calm' of nature with the 'ambitions, the greeds, the jealousies, the treacheries, the hot furies of the human race'.[26] His critique of contemporary social relations began and ended with the all-purpose vice of 'gregarious', which represented the whole spectrum of superficial human discourse. He nowhere addressed the particular character of urban life in the era of maturing industrial capitalism, and of rural society as the inter-war workforce struggled with low wages, inadequate investment, and impoverished services. Rather than illuminating the present, history clouded it in an apocalyptic darkness.

By contrast, the surviving accounts by those earning their living on the land in this period described movements between solitude and sociability that were at once particular to the era and closely related to the values and behaviours of Victorian Britain. It was a world in which walking was still a fundamental means of moving about. The railway system reached its peak around 1911, but long-distance travel remained a rare privilege for the bulk of the labouring poor. Cars were the toys of the seriously wealthy and occasional threats to the safety of those using highways for their original purpose. Most of the journeys for pleasure and necessity were by pedestrians in the lanes in the immediate vicinity of homes and places of work.[27] The mechanization of agriculture had begun in the final quarter of the nineteenth century, and petrol-driven tractors were starting to appear in the Edwardian period. But the real drive to replace horse-power on the land did not commence for another three decades. As late as 1940, there were ten horses for every tractor on British farms.[28] Labourers trudged behind their plough-teams and across the fields caring for their herds and flocks. At best they rode in horse-drawn waggons transporting produce and occasional passengers.

The management of the boundary between solitary and communal behaviours had much in common with the strategies of John Clare and his successors described in Chapter 2. The essence was the ease with which it was possible to pass from one condition to another. The crowded society of a home could be escaped by opening a door into a garden or fields. Conversely, a solitary walk could be joined by neighbours out for the air, or other workers heading to the still labour-intensive farms. Whether or not the pedestrian excursions were planned, the degree of association they embodied was rarely fixed. In the fields, workers moved between collective tasks such as weeding or harvesting crops to more isolated activities such as ploughing or tending sheep.

Then, as had always been the case, the loneliest in all rural society was the lad during or after school days standing in a field scaring birds. In 1940, encouraged by the collective endeavour of a Workers' Education Association class, the farm labourer Fred Kitchen wrote his memoir. *Brother to the Ox* captured a particular moment in the rural economy when participation in a low-paid occupation was challenged by the higher wages in industrial labour, in this case coal-mining in the nearby urban villages. For much of his adult life, however, Kitchen stayed true to his proudly earned skills as a horseman, and he provides a persuasive account of how working closely with animals could compensate for the absence of human company. And as with many nineteenth-century country people, nature was at once the everyday source of the family income and a freely accessible source of private aesthetic pleasure. Towards the end of his narrative, Kitchen describes a moment born of the entirely practical task of growing food for his family:

> The gaffer had a bit of land on the plough right out on the moors. It was too far away from home to be worked properly and too far from the manure heap to grow much produce; but that summer I put it in with potatoes, taking my dinner along and staying in the field all day. Sitting under a stonewall at dinner-time, what a sight it was, mile upon mile of uninterrupted view of field and meadow, and gently rising hills with little farmsteads dotted here and there. At my back was a grim and mighty hill, all purple-topped, and though the country had no leafy woods, it had a stream, which made music, all its own.[29]

With the accelerating displacement of horses by tractors and other machinery after the Second World War, even farm workers stopped using their feet as they earned their living. As car-ownership spread across society, there was a diminishing requirement to engage in pedestrian activity to get to work, to the shops, to school, or to places of leisure. Although casual strolling remained a common every-day recreation,[30] walking over any distance became an increasingly self-conscious activity, undertaken, if at all, for a chosen purpose. It became statistically invisible in the National Travel Surveys, which excluded journeys of less than a mile.[31] The more artificial the practice of extended walking, the more it was the subject of specialist writing, especially over the last three decades.[32] There was a reaction against the sociable forms of walking in the countryside, which was now the most salient form of excursion. The late nineteenth-century insistence on solitary endeavour was revived. '*Always walk alone*' was the first rule in John Merrill's *Walking My Way* of 1984: 'Only you yourself know your capabilities. To go with someone whose pace is slower or faster than yours makes the walk more tiring. Five miles (8 km) is the furthest you should go with another person. A companion distracts your concentration and interferes with your enjoyment of the scenery.'[33] Eventually the activity acquired its own extended philosophy in the writings of Frédéric Gros. His injunctions had echoes of Powys's pantheism in their mistrust of conversation between purposeful pedestrians. The human voice obstructed the task of listening to the rhythms of nature. 'In the silence of a walk,' he wrote, 'when you end up losing the use of words because by then you are doing nothing but walk (and here one should beware of those expedition guides who recode, detail, inform, punctuate the walk with names and explanations . . .), in that silence you hear better, because you are finally hearing what has no vocation to be retranslated, recoded, reformatted.'[34]

For all that modern mass communication systems had brought nature closer to the home of every potential explorer, geography was as relevant in this discourse as it had been in the nineteenth century.[35] 'We headed west,' wrote Lucy Ellmann in her debut novel, 'which in America would take a week, and in Britain can be accomplished in three hours.'[36] The United States and Canada possessed what could still be termed 'wilderness', albeit requiring legislative protection, active conservation, and managed networks of long-distance trails. Encounters between the lone walker and the immense empty spaces possessed a spiritual resonance that was difficult to replicate in the domesticated scenery of most of Western Europe.[37] 'Fierce landscapes,' wrote Belden Lane of the deserts of the southern United States, 'offer a strange solace, yet they require a silence and solitude necessary for entry, as well as a discipline (or *habitus*) capable of disclosing meaning.'[38] The shedding of sociable intercourse was a prior requirement and a desired outcome of such ventures. However well marked the paths, the distances were so vast that it was easy to escape the company of other walkers. In Cheryl Strayed's best-selling account of her 1995 journey along part of the 2,650-mile Pacific Crest Trail which stretches up the west coast from Mexico to Canada, it is striking how rapidly she found herself with only her own thoughts for company, despite the popularity of the hike and the provision of recuperative way-stations.[39] Her ambition was confined to that of finding time and space in which to re-focus a life that had become dispersed by bereavement and failed relationships.

At the outer edges of the nature-walking genre were full-scale rejections of what was construed as political order. In the 1960s, Edward Abbey wrote a widely read account of his time as a seasonal park ranger in the Arches National Monument in Utah. His response to the emptiness of his world once the tourists had driven back to their urban homes reflected the continuing appeal of a pre-social nature. 'I dream of a hard and brutal mysticism,' he wrote, 'in which the naked self merges with a non-human world and yet somehow survives still intact, individual, separate.'[40] But this was an armed solitude, a descendant of Henry Thoreau's 1849 essay 'Civil Disobedience' and its claim 'that government is best which governs least'. Abbey conceived the network of national parks as 'a refuge from authoritarian government, from political oppression. Grand Canyon, Big Bend, Yellowstone and the High Sierras may be required to function as bases for guerrilla warfare against tyranny.'[41]

There was a reckless innocence about much of this literature, which stretched from Cheryl Strayed filling a rucksack for her first ever solitary hike into the wilderness with so much kit she could not lift it, to Chris McCandless, the subject of Jon Krakauer's biography, who died alone in a cabin in Alaska from food poisoning, having deliberately abandoned the maps which might have shown him the way back to nearby medical assistance.[42] The British way was more one of managed discomfort. 'Wilderness' was crucially abbreviated to 'wildness', areas in the interstices of modern life where shaping human intention was absent. This could embrace the spatial fringe of Great Britain. 'In a land as densely populated as Britain,' wrote Robert Macfarlane in his best-seller *Wild Places*,

openness can be hard to find. It is difficult to reach places where the horizon is experienced as a long unbroken line, or where the blue of distance becomes visible. Openness is rare, but its importance is proportionately great. Living constantly among streets and houses induces a sense of enclosure, of short-range sight. . . . A region of uninterrupted space is not only a convenient metaphor for freedom and openness, it can sometimes bring those feelings fiercely on.[43]

Or it could take the form of a micro-engagement with a facet of wildlife, whether or not it was to be found in remote country. Helen Macdonald's prize-winning *H for Hawk* described how she dealt with her grief at the sudden death of her father by raising a goshawk in what she later described as 'a sort of monkish seclusion', partly in a flat in Cambridge, and partly in the nearby countryside.[44]

The scope of the late twentieth- and early twenty-first-century engagement with the wild was extended by the discovery of the borderland between the town and the country, where the landscape took on the unplanned, unvisited characteristics traditionally associated with the natural world. Richard Mabey's pioneering 1973 study *The Unofficial Countryside* celebrated the flora and fauna that flourished amidst urban margins: 'none of these places is the countryside proper, nor were they ever intended to provide bed and board for wildlife. They are all habitats which have grown out of human need.'[45] Approached in the right frame of mind, however, such fragments of wildlife served the same function as conventional rural landscapes. 'That homely canalside stroll,' Mabey recalled, 'was as good an antidote to the workday blues as some real and solitary countryside would have been.'[46] Paul Farley and Michael Symmons Roberts took this approach a stage further by locating what they termed 'Edgelands', 'those places where overspill housing estates break into scrubland . . . unobserved parts of our shared landscape as places of possibility, mystery, beauty'.[47]

The resonance of pedestrian experiences was enhanced by the intervention of applied psychology. Attention restoration theory, or ART, demonstrated that what was termed 'the restorative qualities of being alone with nature' included a stronger memory, greater attentiveness, and improved cognition. For those not wishing to engage in effortful exercise, it was also found that just looking at pictures of the countryside would generate a measurable effect.[48] A more energetic innovation was the practice of psychogeography, described by one of its leading proponents as 'minutely detailed, multi-level examinations of select locales that impact upon the writer's own microscopic inner-eye'.[49] The movement borrowed its terminology from the social sciences, but its roots lay in the writings of Guy Debord, Walter Benjamin, and, most specifically in the British context, the long-distance urban pedestrian Charles Dickens.[50] As with the mid-nineteenth-century ramblings of the novelist, the activity combined physical effort and intense observation with the deliberate absence of a necessary destination. 'Drifting purposefully is the recommended mode,' explained Iain Sinclair.[51] Hardships were invented rather than imposed. Thus Will Self opened his book *Psychogeography* with a lengthy account of catching a plane at Heathrow, and choosing to walk to the airport through the streets from his home in south London rather than using a car or the abundant public transport.[52] Any spatial encounter would suffice, but the most characteristic location of the purposeless drift was the modern city. The objective was not to pattern what was already mapped, but rather to treat the urban landscape as a series of fictions whose identities were revealed through the interaction between the walker's imagination and the narratives embedded in streets, buildings, and their glimpsed residents.

There was a gulf between this intensely literary mode of walking and what remained the true location of random lone pedestrianism, walking the dog.[53] The more physical exercise was promoted and analysed, the more fragmented the practice became. 'Isn't the sordid truth,' pondered Will Self, 'that by turning walking, that most primal of physical activities, into a recreational pursuit like paragliding or motocross, the roaming lobby – quite inadvertently – participate in the downgrading of more workday ambulatory activity?'[54] There remains little consideration of the purpose and states of mind of those who slip out of their house in moments of leisure to encounter the familiar made strange by constant repetition and to engage in an activity requiring so little thought that it leaves space for every kind of reflection. Still less is there an appreciation of the most prolific recent innovation in the field of solitary exercise. The health club, observes Mark Greif, 'is the atomized space in which one does formerly private things, before others' eyes, with the lonely solitude of a body acting as if it were still in private.'[55] At the end of progress is the individual on their personal treadmill, whether in a room at home or in an isolated bubble in a gym, going nowhere, looking at nothing except perhaps the images on a television screen.[56]

Nautical Solitude

There have long been books and magazines about looking after animals and exercising the human body, but these have mostly been consumed by practitioners. At the other end of the spectrum have been the explorers of extreme nature, where the spectators of the activity have vastly outnumbered the participants. In the nineteenth century, as we saw in Chapter 2, the principal theatre of suffering and achievement was the mountain summit. This remained a location of public interest, particularly in the failed Everest expedition of 1924, and the final conquest by Tenzing Norgay and Edmund Hillary in 1953. In the recent past, however, the lengthening queues at the Everest base camp and on the major Alpine ascents have diverted attention to individual, un-roped rock-climbing. Alex Honnold, who made a solo climb of El Capitan in Yosemite National Park in 2017, has become an international media star, the subject of several books and of an Oscar-winning documentary which explored both the skill and courage of the endeavour and its impact on his intimate relationships.[57]

The significant innovation in extreme solitary endeavour in the twentieth century concerned what once had been a commonplace and essentially social practice. In 1900, Joshua Slocum published *Sailing Alone Around the World*, an account of the first single-handed circumnavigation of the globe.[58] He had set out in the *Spray* from Boston in 1895, completing his voyage in three years with frequent landfalls along the way. His book was an instant best-seller, its royalties together with lecturing fees enabling Slocum to buy a farm for his retirement. Both his adventure and the printed narrative were an inspiration for successive generations of lone sailors.[59] The Slocum Society was formed in 1955 to encourage long-distance sailing in small boats.[60] The literary celebration of the voyage was no accident. Like his near contemporary Joseph Conrad, Slocum had spent many years as a professional merchant seaman. But he had always wanted to write, supplementing his maritime income with occasional journalism, and the solo expedition was partly funded by his editor. Slocum exploited what was already a global information network, ensuring that each leg of his voyage was fully reported as it took place. The telegraph enabled his journey to be tracked as it happened and wherever it took him. Thus, for instance, his arrival in Chile was eagerly anticipated. 'They had all heard of the voyage of the *Spray*,' Slocum wrote, 'through the papers of Valparaiso, and were hungry for news concerning it.'[61]

From Slocum onwards, lone sailing was an intensely intertextual activity. The Golden Globe race of 1968–9, which ushered in the great age of solo circumnavigation, was invented by a journalist and was as much a competition between newspapers as between yachtsmen. In their forensic account of the most famous tragedy of the event, the death of Donald Crowhurst, to which we will return below, Nicholas Tomalin and Ron Hall found that the initial logbook of the voyage was a composite of literary tropes gathered from 'the sailing books he had read with such passionate attention'.[62] This was solitude as public spectacle, articulated in a form that could be readily comprehended by an audience which would rarely if ever venture from dry land.

The template was established by Joshua Slocum. It comprised four main features. The first was the sheer toil of the enterprise. Slocum had invented a primitive mode of self-steering without which solo navigation was impossible. All his successors were dependent upon such mechanisms, constantly tinkering with them lest they break down in the middle of the ocean. In rough seas, keeping the boat afloat and on course tested energies to breaking point. Calmer days were consumed by endless minor repairs to sails and equipment. Sleep deprivation was a dominant theme of every account through to the most famous sailor of this century, Ellen MacArthur. 'As I sit here now,' she wrote in her log, 'I feel worse than I have ever felt in my l[i]fe before. Physically i am totally exhausted, and mentally – not so far off.'[63]

The second element of the template was the dependency on books as companions. Lone sailors usually assembled a library before commencing their voyage. Alone on the high seas, their engagement with literature represented a high point of networked solitude, the sense of companionship with distant persons and minds. Slocum made essential use of the volumes donated by his editor. As he recalled, 'my books were always my friends, let fail all else'.[64] There was a circular element to the presence of the reading matter. The sailors were navigating texts as much as boats, and their literary associates were often the source of the books which enabled the completion of the voyage. Thus the Golden Globe competitor John Ridgway, already famous for rowing across the Atlantic with Chay Blyth, acquired the leading literary agent A. D. Peters to secure contracts with a newspaper, a television network, and Hodder & Stoughton, the principal publisher of solo endeavours. In turn the staff of the agency assembled a panel of authors, 'all clients of A. D. Peters, to list the books they would recommend for a year alone'.[65]

The third element was the company of sea-life. The essence of the drama of lone sailing was the overwhelming threat of the wind and the waves. There was a limit to the preparations that could be made against the storms that would be encountered on so long a voyage. Calculation and courage offered no guarantee of survival. Every successive book confirmed that nature was uninterested in the wellbeing of the solitary voyager, however cocooned by media contracts. At the same time, the sailors took a simple pleasure in the wildlife they encountered away from human habitation. As Tomalin and Hall noted, amongst the 'stock themes' of single-handed sailing was 'the companionship of dolphins, sea-birds, porpoises, and other marine creatures'.[66] From Slocum onwards, a particular welcome was given to flying fish, at once a striking natural phenomenon and a conveniently delivered source of fresh food. As many on dry land had discovered, the presence of other living creatures was a compensation for the absence of human society. 'One could not be lonely in a sea like this,' wrote Slocum as he described the birds and fishes he observed from the *Spray*.[67] Even when far from coasts and the shipping lanes, there were actively curious living creatures circling the boat. 'People talk about the empty sea and the sky,' wrote Robin Knox-Johnston, the winner of the first global race, 'but in my experience, more often than not, some form of life is in view. There are many varieties of seabirds which spend their whole lives, apart from the breeding season, living miles away from land. Most common during my voyage were petrels and albatross.'[68]

The final element of the template was solitude itself. There were still occasional instances of unintentional lone voyages, such as Steven Callahan's seventy-six days adrift after his boat was damaged in a race in 1982.[69] For the most part, however, the voyages represented a deliberate commitment to prolonged isolation. 'A prisoner at Dartmoor doesn't get hard labour like this,' wrote Knox-Johnston, 'the public wouldn't stand for it and he has company, however uncongenial. I wonder how the crime rate would be affected if people were sentenced to sail round the world alone, instead of going to prison. It's ten months of solitary confinement with hard labour.'[70] The public fascination was centred on the absolute nature of the enterprise. Solitude was both the condition that was embraced and the experience that was reported back to an ever-widening audience. It is striking, therefore, how fragmentary and often inconsequential are the accounts that were written of the months alone on the oceans of the world. Part of the reason lies in the first of the templates. Solitude was best confronted in tranquillity. Bad weather was so arduous and so all-consuming of mind and body that there was no space for reflecting on the lack of human support beyond the enhanced danger it posed. Joshua Slocum, who had comparatively short spells alone on the many legs of his long voyage, at first found the lack of company a cause of stress. But then the weather turned. 'The loneliness of my state,' he wrote, 'wore off when the gale was high and I found much work to do. When fine weather returned, then came the sense of solitude, which I could not shake off.'[71] For his successors, a calm sea was both a welcome respite and a time of intensified psychological risk.

A further problem was the personality of those who set out on solo voyages. For most of them solitude was an accepted risk, like a sail tearing, rather than a defining spiritual purpose. They were practical men (until women entered the races around the turn of the twenty-first century) whose prime attributes were physical toughness, navigational competence, and a capacity to organize sponsorship. The British amongst them had been schooled by their culture not to take any mental suffering too seriously. The first modern round-the-world sailor, Francis Chichester, was asked at the press conference when he broke his journey in Australia, 'When were your spirits at their lowest ebb?' 'When the gin gave out' was his immediate reply.[72] Such a cast of mind was instinctively wary of negative reflection. 'Despite what I have written I do not allow myself to get maudlin about being alone,' wrote Knox-Johnston.[73] The yachtsmen varied in their social backgrounds and educational attainments, but few were proficient at self-analysis. Knox-Johnston was described as 'distressingly normal' in initial psychiatric tests, and during his voyage was not much troubled by inner debates about the purpose of his venture.[74] Chay Blyth, who made a career of nautical record-breaking, left school at eighteen to join the Parachute Regiment as a private. His attempt to describe the experience of solitude was made persuasive by the sheer absence of articulate insight:

> These feelings, which I tried to argue out with myself, taught me a lot, I think, about why men choose solitary avocations, become hermits, or go off on singlehanded adventures. They taught me too, perhaps, a good deal about myself. I was not sure that I liked it all. I learned at any rate that there were certain things against which I should have to be on guard. I don't want to imply that I was constantly occupied with this sort of introspection. I wasn't. For the most part I thought of practical things – what sails to drop or set to get the best out of the yacht, the most profitable course to steer, how to tackle repair jobs, what to have for dinner. But a man can't be alone with himself without sometimes thinking deeply about life. I don't say that my thoughts were all that profound. But they are part of the record of my voyage.[75]

The major exception amongst the first cohort of competitive solo circumnavigators was the Frenchman Bernard Moitessier. From the outset, he celebrated his solitary engagement with the ocean. 'Wind, sea, boat and sails,' he wrote as his voyage commenced,

> a compact, diffuse whole, without beginning or end, a part and all of the universe . . . my own universe, truly mine. I watch the sun set and inhale the breath of the open sea, I feel my being blossoming and my joy soars so high that nothing can disturb it. The other questions, the ones that used to bother me at times, do not weigh anything before the immensity of a wake so close to the sky and filled with the wind of the sea.[76]

To enhance his sense of isolation, he refused to equip his boat with a modern radio transmitter, preferring to keep in touch with the wider world through occasional catapulted mail when passing another vessel. He took an especially intense pleasure in the wildlife he encountered, which at once alleviated and gave a sense of purpose to his solitude. 'The days go by, never monotonous,' he recorded. 'Even when they appear exactly alike they are never quite the same. That is what gives life at sea its special dimension, made up of contemplation and very simple contrasts. Sea, winds, calms, sun, clouds, porpoises. Peace, and the joy of being alive in harmony.'[77] Eventually the latent tension between record-breaking with the attendant media circus, on the one hand, and the fundamental satisfaction of solitary voyaging, on the other, became unmanageable. Moitessier was an experienced sailor in a well-found boat, and as the Golden Globe race reached its final leg he was a potential winner, although, in the absence of radio reports, no one knew exactly where he or his rivals were. However, instead of setting a course across the Atlantic to Europe, he abandoned the competition and his lucrative contracts with the French press, and sailed half-way round the world again, eventually making landfall in Tahiti six months later.[78]

Public fascination with solitary sailing continued to grow. It was not just a matter of consuming the multiplying media reports from the comfort of home. There was a thirst to get as physically close to the experience as possible. A quarter of a million people assembled on Plymouth Hoe in 1967 to see solitude made manifest as Francis Chichester sailed home, and a similar number greeted Robin Knox-Johnston as he crossed the finishing line at the end of the first Golden Globe race two years later.[79] In 2002, almost a million spectators came to visit the boats assembled to take part in the transatlantic Route du Rhum race in St Malo.[80] The ratio of observers to participants was far higher than in extreme mountaineering. Nearly nine thousand climbs have been made to the summit of Everest since 1953, whereas only about two hundred sailors have completed lone round-the-world voyages.[81] The easier international travel has become, the greater the interest in those who take the hardest possible route around the globe. It has, however, become increasingly difficult to manage the contradictions inherent in the enterprise. There has been no resolution to Moitessier's protest at the subordination of solitude to mass media. Over the decades, the costs of the activity have grown as the boats have become more specialized. Whereas Knox-Johnston sailed a thirty-two-foot schooner he had built with his own hands, modern competitors require multi-hulled vessels costing several million pounds and the services of a back-up team similar to Formula 1 racing. This in turn has increased the dependency on sponsors and their demands for constant publicity. As the radio telephone and traditional navigational devices have been superseded by GPS mapping and digital communication, so the sense of being alone on the seas for any part of any day has been severely compromised. Earlier solo sailors spent long periods with only their own thoughts to keep them company: Knox-Johnston, was completely out of touch for five months during his global voyage. By the end of the twentieth century, a watching audience knew exactly where the sailors were from day to day and the support teams were in constant contact with them. Ellen MacArthur's books on her voyages were records of great personal courage and skill, but had virtually nothing to say about solitude. During her races she was continually discussing with her land-based colleagues the problems posed by the weather, the correct course, and the endless running repairs.

The entire effort of solitary escape to the natural world of the oceans had an ambiguous relation to technical progress. It was a product of the contemporary mass media and required mechanical innovations in order that yachts could be under single-handed control twenty-four hours a day. Later in the twentieth century and into the twenty-first, the boats became monuments of cutting-edge design in both their hulls and their equipment. At the same time, solo record-breaking represented a turning back to a mode of transport that was already redundant at the end of the nineteenth century. Slocum went round the world in *Spray* because it was no longer possible to practise the skills of adjusting sails to the wind in the merchant marine where he had spent his working life. The first generation of British solo circumnavigators openly celebrated a native tradition of nautical prowess. Chichester was knighted with Francis Drake's sword. Knox-Johnston cited Drake, Frobisher, Grenville, Anson, Nelson, and Captain Scott as his inspirations: 'it is a continuation of the same traditions – and notice how it is mostly Britons who have responded to the challenge'.[82] In a postcolonial age, the British could still master the waves, even if they could no longer rule over distant territories. As with the nineteenth-century mountaineers, an assertion of national superiority was embedded in the enterprise. That the competition in the early years was mostly between sailors from Britain and France, or sometimes Spain, only added to the sense of ancient wars being refought. It happened that the first Golden Globe race coincided with the climax of the space race, with Knox-Johnston arriving back in Falmouth in his home-made boat just three months before Neil Armstrong landed on the moon. The contrast between the national registers of heroic achievement could not have been more acute.

This form of a solitary embrace of nature was intrinsically unstable. The most famous literary sailor of the inter-war period was another Frenchman, Alain Gerbault, who described his lone voyages in *The Firecrest* in a series of books. His response to the oceans was reminiscent of the first Alpine climbers. 'In the course of my travels,' he wrote, 'those impressions engraved most deeply and vividly on my memory are of Nature when it has not been altered by the hand of man.'[83] At the ends of the world, God's creation was still visible in its original unspoilt form. By the final third of the twentieth century, this illusion was becoming difficult to sustain. Moitessier's rejection of the concept of solitary racing was partly driven by his anger against the global commercial pressures of which the structures of sponsorship and mass communication were a manifestation. 'I charge the Modern world,' he wrote, '– that's the Monster. It is destroying our earth, and trampling the soul of men.'[84] As time passed, it became all too apparent that the watery expanses were also becoming a victim of the Monster. They were no longer the pristine alternative to the environmental disaster of urban civilization. Increasingly, the sailors were aware of the effects of global warming and the spread of pollution, particularly sea-borne plastics. When Ellen MacArthur, the outstanding lone British sailor of her generation, retired from competition, she used her fame and wealth to establish a foundation dedicated to the promotion of circular economics, with its focus on sustainable production and consumption.[85]

The inherent risk of absolute solitude in empty spaces also became apparent. After Martin Decoud, the most famous nautical suicide of the twentieth century was that of the Golden Globe contestant Donald Crowhurst. The discovery of his boat sailing unmanned in the Atlantic has been the subject of intense public interest ever since. Several non-fiction accounts, novels, plays, and an opera have dealt with the tragedy.[86] Two feature films were made about the event as recently as 2017.[87] Crowhurst had entered the race in the hope that success would generate a financial return sufficient to rescue his failing marine equipment business. As it became apparent that his ill-prepared boat was not sufficiently sea-worthy to meet the challenge of going around the world, he took the fateful decision to pretend to be in the lead, although he had failed to get further than the South Atlantic. It was an action made possible by the particular stage of communications technology, with intermittent radio reports but no global positioning devices. What elevated the drama from one of mere deception and looming discovery was his spiritual journey, which has been pieced together from his surviving logbooks. A glimpse of the latent danger of total immersion in an unpeopled world was supplied by his fellow competitor Bernard Moitessier. 'Sailing in these waters,' he wrote, 'if man is crushed by his feeling of insignificance, he is borne up and protected by that of his greatness. It is here, in the immense desert of the Southern Ocean, that I feel most strongly how much man is both atom and god.'[88] The lone sailor was at once utterly vulnerable and wholly the master of his world. All intervening distraction had been removed. There was a hint of Powys's pantheism here: the sense that by intense communion with the void of nature it would be possible to grasp its primordial meaning.

Peter Anson, in his survey of 'modern hermits' in 1932, wrote of

> maritime hermits, who have managed to find their 'solitary vocations'. Indeed the call of 'the lonely sea and the sky' is but the voice of Eternity, for the sea drowns out humanity and time – it has no sympathy with either; for it belongs to Eternity, and it sings its monotonous song of Eternity for every and ever. Nowhere better than on the sea can one learn what is meant by the 'Loneliness of God'.[89]

In Crowhurst's case, prolonged, lonely meditation on his untenable future drove him towards a complete breakdown in which the atom became merged with the Almighty.[90] He wrote in his log on 25 June 1969, just before he walked off his boat, 'I am very close to God and should, by the methods I claim are available, move at last to prophecy.'[91] Maintenance of his earthly form would only delay his salvation.

Modern Solitary Confinement

On 30 May 2018, Her Majesty's Inspector of Prisons sent an 'Urgent Notification' to the Ministry of Justice on conditions in Exeter Prison. He was particularly concerned about the 'designated segregation unit', where

> there was a special cell which was completely bare and contained no furniture, toilet or bed. Prison and regional managers had approved the use of this cell for those judged to be so vulnerable as to be in need of constant observation, and it had been so used 17 times in the previous six months. There was supposedly an inflatable bed available for use in this cell, but it could not be found by staff during the inspection, and inspectors saw video of a prisoner on constant watch being located in the cell without it.[92]

Solitary confinement had become representative of all that was delinquent and destructive in the prison system. It had long since lost its place as a spiritually informed mode of deterrence and reform. The practice persisted in Britain until the inter-war period, and thereafter 'segregation', as it came to be called, was limited to those who had broken prison rules or who required protection from other prisoners.[93] In 2015, there were 1,586 segregation cells across the prison estate, in which about 10 per cent of the inmates spent at least one night during their incarceration.[94] Unlike the American system, where prolonged segregation has once more become a deliberate element of punishment, particularly in the 'supermax' institutions which now contain more than eighty thousand inmates in solitary confinement, British prisons displayed a toxic mixture of inconsistency and neglect in the management of isolation.[95]

Shorn of its original religious framework, there was little coherent strategy in removing a prisoner from the company of fellow inmates. Although chaplains were still employed in prisons and their work was praised by inspectors, the effect of conducting conversations through the cell door was at best marginal.[96] Decades of studies on the impact of enforced solitude had identified a range of consequent psychological disorders, and as in the pioneering regimes of the 1840s, there was a widespread apprehension of self-harm and suicide. By the early twenty-first century, it was well established that mental illness was as much a cause as a consequence of incarceration, the more so with inmates whose behaviour required them to be isolated from the wider prison population.[97] The practice was condemned by a joint statement of leading medical authorities in 2018.[98] There was a general sense that periods of segregation should be leavened by physical exercise and mental stimulation, but too often these proved absent or insufficient. 'The regime on the unit was poor,' reported an inspection of Wormwood Scrubs, 'particularly for the few prisoners who stayed for long periods, with no opportunity for any activity either on or off the unit. Segregated prisoners were allowed to exercise together but exercise periods were too short, at around 30 minutes.'[99] It was not that the system was unaware of the basic needs of those denied the company of others. Rather there was a widespread failure to deliver such services. 'Segregated prisoners (kept apart from other prisoners because they are disruptive or require protection),' observed the Chief Inspector's 2017–18 annual report, 'should have daily access to the telephone, a shower and time outside for exercise, and be encouraged to access purposeful activities. This was not the case in most establishments, and segregation unit regimes and conditions were poor for many prisoners. In only a quarter of prisons visited could we evidence meaningful work to re-integrate segregated prisoners back to normal.'[100]

The requirement for a purposeful, consistent regime of penal solitude was everywhere frustrated by a growing crisis in resources. After 1990, a 'punitive turn' in the political discourse led to a doubling of the UK prison population to the current level of 92,500.[101] Following the financial crash of 2008–9, the expanding numbers collided with a long-term contraction in public expenditure.[102] Inadequate staffing and physical maintenance impacted on segregation at two levels. Most directly, it meant that the maintenance of some cells was grossly inadequate. In the autumn of 2018, the treatment of segregated prisoners in Bedford Prison was heavily criticized in official reports. 'Despite numerous attempts at refurbishment,' wrote the Independent Monitoring Board, 'the environment of the segregation unit is simply appalling. It is a dungeon. The toilets frequently block, there has been a consistent infestation of cockroaches and, during the summer, there has been a plague of rats.'[103] Prison managers, whether in the public or private sector, varied widely in their capacity to cope with limited funding. The Victorian mission to impose uniformity in standards of punishment was everywhere absent, despite the vocal efforts of the prison inspectorate.

More generally, the levels of violence and drug-taking in the under-resourced prisons as a whole distorted what little rationality there was in the policy of segregation. Alongside those undergoing punishment for rule-breaking or requiring protection because of the nature of their crimes were prisoners manipulating solitary confinement out of self-interest or self-protection. Some deliberately misbehaved in the hope that a period in a segregation unit would lead to their transfer to a preferred alternative prison.[104] Others reacted against the pervasive threat of physical harm in the prisons either by trying to get sent to the units or, in desperation, by creating their own form of segregation. 'We found prisoners isolating themselves in their cells,' the inspectors reported of Birmingham Prison,

> refusing to emerge because of their fear of violence. The prison did not know how many men were in this position and virtually nothing was being done to support them. All of those we found were locked up for over 23, sometimes 24 hours a day, occasionally being unlocked to have a shower. Some told us they felt unsafe even behind the locked cell door, and described ongoing intimidation including other prisoners squirting urine or throwing faeces through their broken observation panels.[105]

A recent critical report by the Children's Commissioner for England held gang involvement partly responsible for the rise in the use of segregation for young offenders, 'which means that teenagers may be unable to associate safely with other children in the establishment'.[106] Where once solitary confinement had been the penal system's new device for reforming prisoners, now it was the prisoners' last resort in staying unharmed behind bars.

During the second half of the twentieth century, insight into how to manage the effects of enforced solitude came not from the institutions of the liberal state but largely from those who had suffered in various forms of totalitarian regime. In 1952, Christopher Burney published *Solitary Confinement*, a widely read account of the eighteen months he spent alone in a French prison during the Nazi occupation in the Second World War. For Frieda Fromm-Reichmann, opening up the field of loneliness as a psychological subject later in the decade, Burney's reported experience demonstrated the key function of intention in the experience of solitude. The capacity to resist prolonged isolation was deeply influenced by a sense of purpose. 'I believe,' she wrote, 'his unquestioned matter-of-fact belief in the spiritual validity of the political convictions which were the cause of his imprisonment may have worked as an additional factor which helped him to survive his ordeal without becoming mentally sick.'[107] Burney, who had been engaged in anti-Nazi espionage, coped by constructing his own routines of eating and exercise in his cell, and by exploiting the enforced absence of practical distractions. 'I had been left free to drop the spectacles of the near-sighted,' he wrote, 'and to scan the horizon of existence. And I believed I had seen something there.'[108] A similar strategy was described by Edith Bone, a left-leaning doctor whom the new Hungarian communist regime sentenced to fifteen years' imprisonment in 1949 for spying for England. She spent her seven years in solitary confinement in a state of unremitting hostility to her captors. 'My life in this prison,' she wrote, 'I regarded as a battle I had to fight with these very inferior people. I had to convince them that the ideas that had been put into their heads by their superiors had no validity in the higher sphere of civilization from which I had come.'[109] She went on a speech strike, a hunger strike, and a cleaning strike, and, like Burney, made use of the empty time. 'In the dark,' she explained, 'there is little one can do except think, and the absence of anything to divert one's thoughts gives them an intensity seldom experienced in normal conditions.'[110] Eventually the Hungarian uprising of 1956 secured her release, and she arrived back in London to be met by a publisher anxious to exploit growing public interest in extreme forms of solitude.

In the British market, the best-selling prison memoir of the early 1990s was Terry Waite's account of his four years' solitary incarceration in Beirut between 1987 and 1991.[111] He endured almost medieval conditions, chained to the floor in a small cell, always aware that the next people to open the door could be his executioners. Two features of his experience resonated with other accounts of prolonged isolation.

The first was the networking effect of literature. Once his captors began to allow him books, he found himself connected to other minds. As with those who had exiled themselves on the seas, the written word was a critically important resource:

> Reading in captivity is sheer delight. I have time to enter into the mind of the writer, and to be caught up in the flow of her thoughts without interruption is a great pleasure. Modern life is fragmented, full of distractions. Here I can really read. Here I can discover how to convert my loneliness into creative solitude. Part of the secret, I think, is to make a companion of the experience. Although much of my life has been spent alone, the real beauty of solitude is only now becoming apparent to me. If ever I leave captivity, I will take this precious gift with me.[112]

In his autobiography, the author John Le Carré reported the singular event of coming face-to-face with another Beirut hostage, Jean-Paul Kauffmann, who had formed a similar relationship with his most popular novel. 'During my three years of misery,' Kauffmann told him, 'I experienced intense moments of joy. *The Spy Who Came in from the Cold* was one of those moments.'[113] It was not just the text, but the person of the writer who penetrated the solitude. 'In this book I found reasons to hope,' said Kauffman. 'The most important is a voice, a presence. Yours. The jubilation of a writer who describes a cruel and colourless world and delights in rendering it so grey and hopeless. You feel it almost physically. Someone is talking to you, you are no longer alone. In my jail, I was no longer abandoned.'[114]

The second resonant feature of Waite's account was the importance of a larger faith as a means of enabling survival. The year before his memoir was published, Stephanie Dowrick reflected on the nature of imprisonment in her study *Intimacy and Solitude*. 'It is surely not by chance,' she observed, 'that the worst punishment likely to be given to a prisoner is solitary confinement, although whether this is, in fact, a nightmare beyond imagining or something which can be tolerated depends not on the crime but on the sense of inner empowerment of the unfortunate prisoner.'[115] This resource was, however, both a strength and a vulnerability. In the long silence of captivity, the precipitating mission was subject to intense scrutiny. Although Terry Waite was an emissary of the Archbishop of Canterbury, he was not himself a theologian, or even an ordained priest. He had a basic belief, which he deployed at the beginning of the day. 'Each morning,' he wrote, 'I wake early. On waking I say my prayers. I don't make special pleas or ask favours. As simply as I can, I try to enter the mystery that is God.'[116] At the beginning of his imprisonment, his faith-driven captors supplied him with a Bible, but he found it an unreliable support. The era of textual criticism had rendered the work and its truths opaque and ambiguous. 'Perhaps the desire for tangible reality leads me to take the Bible too literally,' he confessed. 'I know it can be read on several levels, as a history or literature, but now more than ever I need to be able to read it with the eyes of faith. My faith has been exposed for what it is – uncertain, questioning, vulnerable.'[117] Waite was honest enough in his account to admit to his difficulties, despite the overarching role of the Anglican Church in the drama. His cell was a place of spiritual trial which offered no easy outcome. 'I do not feel the presence of God,' he wrote.

> I wish I didn't have to say that, but it is true. All I do is cling to a simple hope and belief, very simple, very basic. I will be sustained and sup-ported from within, and I will not be destroyed. If this is the dark night of the soul, so be it. One day I will find the light.[118]

The Monastic Revival

As with solo journeys into the wilds of nature, there was an almost limitless market for published accounts of extreme solitude, whether chosen or imposed. In the case of both explorers and prisoners, this genre stretched back well into the nineteenth century. The most sur-prising innovation of the second half of the twentieth came from inside the Christian church itself. In 1948, an American Trappist monk, Thomas Merton, published a memoir of his conversion.[119] The first edition was endorsed by Graham Greene and edited for the English market by Evelyn Waugh, who later visited and corresponded with Merton.[120] *The Seven Storey Mountain* was an instant success. A hun-dred thousand copies were sold on both sides of the Atlantic within a year, and in the following quarter of a century over three and a half million English language volumes, together with more than fifteen translations, were published. Merton became the celebrity monk of his era, a prolific writer of books, articles, and poetry before his premature death in 1968.

There was little in the form of Merton's memoir to suggest such success.[121] It followed the conventional structure of a devotional biography, tracing his education at a French *lycée* and a minor English public school, a debauched year as an undergraduate in Cambridge, a summons to the United States by his worried guardians, and, as war broke out in Europe, a growing awareness of his sinful state. 'Here I was,' he wrote, 'scarcely four years after I had left Oakham and walked out into the world that I thought I was going to ransack and rob of all its pleasures and satisfactions. I had done what I intended, and now I found that it was I who was emptied and robbed and gutted.'[122]

What made the account distinctive was Merton's overwhelming emphasis on the spiritual value of solitude, and its accompanying discipline of silence. He described his first visit to the Cistercian Abbey of Strict Observance at Gethsemani in Kentucky:

> I had entered into a solitude that was an impregnable fortress. And the silence that enfolded me, spoke to me, and spoke louder and more eloquently than any voice, and in the middle of that quiet, clean-smelling room, with the moon pouring its peacefulness in through the open window, with the warm night air, I realized truly whose house that was, O glorious Mother of God![123]

The book contributed to a renewed interest in religious houses after 1945 on both sides of the Atlantic.[124] Recruits flocked into hitherto moribund monasteries and nunneries, and Merton found himself having to deal with an avalanche of correspondence from curious outsiders.[125] In his memoir, he associated his personal sense of sin with the moral bankruptcy of the West in the 1930s, which had led to the devastation of the Second World War. Conversely, the revitalized Christian communities were an exemplar of the spiritual reconstruction that was now required. 'These men,' he wrote, 'hidden in the anonymity of their choir and their white cowls, are doing for their land what no army, no congress, no president could ever do as such: they are winning for it the grace and the protection and the friendship of God.'[126]

The Trappist way of life offered more than merely self-denial. It embraced a conception of a God who was himself solitary, and whose deepest form of communication took place in silence.[127] At the centre of the act of wordless prayer was a shared condition.[128] 'Man's loneliness,' Merton insisted, 'is, in fact, the loneliness of God.'[129] The mystical union between the Deity and the believer was only possible if the supplicant recognized their own solitude. Merton took a stark position on the long debate about the inherent sociability of the human subject. 'Every man is a solitary,' he wrote, 'held firmly by the inexorable limitations of his own aloneness. Death makes this very clear, for when a man dies, he dies alone.'[130] Conversation, inside or outside the church, was at best a precondition for, at worst a distraction from, the act of prayer. Merton rejected the whole corpus of the modern social sciences, and what he termed 'dead, selfish rationalism'.[131] 'Social life,' he wrote, 'tends to form and educate a man, but generally at the price of a simultaneous deformation and perversion.'[132]

By the same measure, the post-Reformation Church stood condemned for its tendency to collective action and its affinity with external forms of organizational activity. The figure of the desert solitary, a continuing presence in theology, stood as a perpetual correction to the temptation of sociable discourse. 'The hermit,' warned Merton, 'remains to put us on our guard against our natural obsession with the visible, social and communal forms of Christian life which tend at times to be inordinately active, and often become deeply involved in the life of the secular, non-Christian society.'[133] Equally distracting was the Protestant preoccupation with what Merton termed 'the smokescreen of words', whether printed or spoken.[134] As by far the most prolific writer within the modern monastic tradition, Merton could scarcely decry the value of written discourse. But poetry, memoir, theological exegesis, to say nothing of a mountain of correspondence, were at best means of enhancing the understanding of those seeking to express their belief. Reading and the liturgy were no more than preparation for the essential act of prayer.

Although Merton claimed he immediately found his true home in a Trappist community, he was from the outset an ill-fitting member of the Abbey at Gethsemani. Evelyn Waugh wrote a foreword to Merton's essays on silence in 1950 in which he expressed his surprise that the Cistercians were so relaxed about one of their monks writing a volume 'designed to popularise the idea of the contemplative life'. 'It is not for us,' he sniffed, 'living in the world, to cavil at this generous decision.'[135] Merton's books required the permission of his superiors before they could be published. Whilst increasingly he enjoyed a reputation as an international scholar, he was not allowed to behave like one. His letters were opened and read before they were released to him, much as they might be in prison, and requests to attend conferences outside the Abbey were usually denied. At a practical level, he found his profound desire for solitary prayer and contemplation constantly opposed by the volume of administrative and teaching duties, and by the stream of letters and calls from spiritual tourists, eager to take inspiration from this exemplary monk, much as the fourth-century hermits were visited from nearby towns. More fundamentally, the Abbey, in common with the monastic tradition stretching back to St Benedict, was deeply unenthusiastic about Merton's professed ambition to lead the life of a solitary. Whilst they took inspiration from the desert hermits, the cenobitic communities were instinctively apprehensive about allowing their members to detach themselves from the structures of ritual and authority.[136] They did not trust the capacity of any penitent to exercise without restraint the licence of absolute solitude. Only God could withstand the pressure of such isolation. Those who wrote and implemented the rules of monastic life from the Benedictines onwards feared a path to heresy or mental collapse. Thus despite informing the world of his commitment to solitude only a year after he had finished his novitiate, it was not until 1965 that Merton was finally allowed to move out of the main community to his own primitive accommodation in the woods.

Merton did not help his case by taking an almost masochistic pleasure in the suffering engendered by his commitment to solitude. 'The terror of the lonely life,' he wrote in his 'Notes for a Philosophy of Solitude', 'is the mystery and uncertainty with which the will of God presses upon our soul.'[137] It was not merely a matter of the constructed discomfort of the Trappist regime. As with the broader tradition of monasticism, Merton was alert to inauthentic solitude. The enclosed communities had to repel superficial pilgrims who sought a temporary, ego-centred escape from the noise of everyday living. A touchstone for distinguishing the true recluse from the false was the willingness to undergo spiritual pain and danger. 'There is no need to say that the call of solitude (even though only interior) is perilous,' Merton wrote. 'Everyone who knows what solitude means is aware of this. The essence of the solitary vocation is precisely the anguish of an almost infinite risk. Only the false solitary sees no danger in solitude.'[138] The traveller and writer Patrick Leigh Fermor published a well-received guide to contemporary monasticism in 1953, in which he drew attention to what he termed 'those hazardous mystical journeys of the soul which culminate, at the end of the purgative and illuminative periods, in blinding moments of union with the Godhead'.[139] Where Merton gloried in the immanence of a total spiritual collapse, his superiors took a more cautious view. Novices were assessed for their balance of mind and, once admitted to the community, kept under supervision lest they succumbed to the perils inherent in intense solitary prayer.

A longer-term difficulty was Merton's engagement with the outside world. The Carolingian monastic tradition turned its back on secular society, encouraging its monks to confine their time between spiritual duties to the manual tasks required to feed and clothe the religious community. The function of prayer was union with God, not the welfare of a fallen society. The point was made by a colleague, the Benedictine Dom Jean Leclercq, in his *Alone with God* in 1962: 'To turn from God's love and the loving of God (which is contemplation) to the process of loving one's neighbour is not an upward but a downward movement. We do not love God for the sake of our neighbour, but our neighbour for the sake of God.'[140] In the initial enthusiasm of his conversion, Merton gloried in his withdrawal from the world. If his solitude had a wider function, it was only that it enabled him better to understand the essential solitude of every sinner. But from the outset his irrepressible desire to write for what became a worldwide audience collided with the essentially private, inward-looking nature of the Cistercian community.[141]

Over time, Merton's wide reading and engagement with a range of literary forms caused increasing friction with his superiors.[142] He came to resent the petty controls on his life exercised by men whose moral

authority no longer appeared beyond question. Interference in his mail
was resented to the point of paranoia. In his diary, he compared the
refusal to allow the publication of an article he had written on Teilhard
de Chardin to the behaviour of the contemporary Russian state against
its dissidents.[143] Further, he gradually came to accept a duty to engage
with the problems of the secular society. He wrote in 1962 that 'the
only justification for a life of deliberate solitude is the conviction that it
will help you to love not only God but also other men'.[144] As his contacts with authors and activists grew, the range of his writings expanded
beyond the purely spiritual. He began to comment on the problems
of his age, including the conflict in Vietnam, race relations, poverty,
the atomic bomb, and the environment. Attempts to write about the
Vietnam War were directly forbidden by the Carthusian censors on
grounds Merton thought as much political as spiritual.[145] 'I am to be
in effect silenced on this subject,' he noted, 'for the main reason that
it is not appropriate for a monk, and that it "falsifies the message of
monasticism".'[146]

The New Spiritualism

Thomas Merton was still based at Gethsemani at the time of his
accidental death in 1968, but was ceasing to attach importance to membership of a religious community for its own sake. Spiritual solitude, he
was beginning to recognize, need not be the monopoly of his Order,
or of Christianity more broadly. He was curious about Buddhism and
Hinduism and their traditions of non-institutional contemplation.
Whilst prayer had been central to his entire life since his conversion, it
had taken the form of a personal, improvised conversation with God.
'Merton never offers us any surefire technique as a solution to prayer,'
observed his former pupil James Finley. 'There is no Merton method
to prayer.'[147] The routines of the community provided the space for
solitary communion, but there were few ordered techniques that were
transferable to secular contexts. Such an approach has remained a
commonplace within Catholicism. The best-known British monk of
the later twentieth century, the Benedictine Cardinal Basil Hume, was
modest about the core activity of his faith: 'Oh I just keep plugging
away. At its best, it's like being in a dark room with someone you

love. You can't see them, but you know they're there.'[148] However, for Merton towards the end of his life, and subsequently within and beyond Catholicism, there was an attraction in Eastern faiths which had developed over the centuries a range of practices that could be exercised outside the authority structures of religious bodies.

The search for alternative forms of what was coming to be called meditation was a response to the loss of momentum in the post-war revival of monasticism as both a practice and an object of public fascination. The flow of recruits into the Cistercian monasteries worldwide slowed and their membership began to decline after the mid-1960s.[149] In Britain, the Benedictines, the largest religious community, saw their numbers fall from 530 monks and 136 nuns in the early 1970s to the current figure of around 280 monks and 35 nuns, with fewer than a dozen novices in training.[150] Religious belief more broadly continued to shrink, with the Anglicans losing half their strength between 1960 and 1985.[151] Just three years after Merton's death, Philip Larkin wrote an obituary for the entire enterprise of solitary spiritual contemplation in his poem 'Vers de Société':

> *All solitude is selfish.* No one now
> Believes the hermit with his gown and dish
> Talking to God (who's gone too); the big wish
> Is to have people nice to you, which means
> Doing it back somehow.
> *Virtue is social.*[152]

Larkin was both perceptive and fundamentally wrong in his verdict. The renewed appeal of the traditional religious community had run its course. Whatever prospect the Catholic Church had of a further revival of enclosed institutions, in Britain or globally, was undermined by the series of sexual scandals that began to surface in the early twenty-first century, exposing behaviour that went back to the 1960s and 1970s. The secrecy that had been claimed for the monasteries and their substantial educational activities was revealed to be fatally open to abuse.[153] As we have seen, the Victorian critics of the new monasteries had argued in vain that their activities should be exposed to the same regime of inspection as schools, prisons, and asylums.[154] Only in the second decade of this century are there signs that the church hierarchies are beginning to respond to the moral catastrophe by accepting the need for external scrutiny of the behaviour of their celibate monks. The glamour of Merton's high-wire drama of intense solitude conducted within walled spaces has been irrecoverably lost.

At the same time, Larkin's assertion that henceforth all virtue was social was ill founded. A withdrawal into some form of spiritual solitude had an appeal which has expanded and diversified since the final quarter of the twentieth century. The millions who had once read about monastic life now began to seek versions of their own, if only in the interstices of their continuing secular lives. What was everywhere missing from the new spiritualism were the structures of control that Merton was beginning to find so frustrating. Solitude was becoming detached from authority. At the same time, the journey to solitary communion was no longer seen as inevitably uni-directional and irreversible. Henceforth, a multiplicity of forms of retreat flourished, with varying levels of transcendental belief, and widely differing boundaries between individual and communal practice.

Within conventional churches, an indication of changing demand was apparent in the contrasting experience of religious buildings. Attendance at neighbourhood Sunday services continued to decline, but by contrast, visits to cathedrals have grown.[155] The attraction, it appeared, was a combination of the immense space within which reflection could expand beyond the immediate moment, and the relative anonymity of the individual worshipper. It was easier to be alone with your thoughts and God in a cathedral than in a smaller, local building.[156] Elsewhere, the energies of the churches were not necessarily sympathetic to wordless discourse with larger spiritual entities. The Pentecostal revivals were essentially noisy, collective activities, closely associated with the textual authority of the Gospels. From within established religion, meanwhile, the most creative response to changing demands for solitary communion has been to continue along the path which Merton was beginning to explore.

Larkin's 'hermit with his gown and dish' had been a marginal figure in Christian practice since the Middle Ages. There was, however, a much stronger tradition of wandering holy men in the Eastern religions from which Western Christianity had parted company in the first millennium. During the 1924 Everest expedition, there was a reveal-ing moment when the climbers making their way to the base camp encountered Tibetan monks living in lonely cells in the countryside. There followed a comedy of mutual incomprehension, with the hermits unable to understand why anyone should risk their lives in the impious and pointless task of scaling the summit, and the teams of mountaineers bemused by the monks' isolated discomfort.[157] Later in the twentieth century, however, a new view was forming in the West of the value of individualized, democratically practised spiritual contemplation. A more sympathetic interest was shown in Buddhist hermit practices, including the career of an Englishwoman, Tenzin Palmo, originally Diane Perry from Hertfordshire, who spent twelve years from 1976 in a small cave high in the Indian Himalayas. 'Here,' writes her biographer,

> perched like an eagle on the top of the world, she would most definitely not be bothered by the clamour and clutter of human commerce. She would have the absolute silence she yearned for. The silence that was so necessary to her inner search, for she knew, like all meditators, that it was only in the depth of silence that the voice of the Absolute could be heard.[158]

Common to many variants of Buddhism was an insistence on a relation between body and mind in the experience of enlightenment. Beyond kneeling for prayer, the limited menu of Christian meditative techniques had generally paid little attention to the corporeal aspects of spiritual contemplation. Amongst those still working within the framework of Christian belief at the end of the twentieth century, there was an increasing interest in methods borrowed from other faiths which combined physical and mental disciplines. In Britain, Esther de Waal kept the flag flying for Thomas Merton and the Catholic monas-tic tradition more broadly through her publications and supervised retreats. Her approach to prayer was inflected not only with a concern for the arrangement of the body, but also with an intense awareness of its demands and rhythms.[159] 'There are certain entirely practical things you can do,' she wrote in *A Retreat with Thomas Merton*. 'First of all decide in what position you can best pray. . . . Then when you are completely relaxed (don't rush, there's all the time in the world),

concentrate on your breathing. Take deep, slow breaths.'[160] The built
surroundings of the activity were of diminishing relevance. All that was
required, de Waal insisted, is 'a place in which it is possible to be quiet
and on my own'.[161]

'Mind, Body, Spirit' became the new trinity, spreading out from
formal structures of transcendental belief to embrace a proliferating
menu of practices and observations. A consumer industry of courses,
retreats, and associated literature and digital media grew up.[162] It
embraced activities principally focused on psychological renewal and
forms of alternative medicine which relied on states of mind as much as
therapeutic interventions. Common to all versions of this spiritual turn
was an inward gaze.[163] Every individual was negotiating with his or her
private self, whether to comprehend or transcend the limits of the ego.
It was axiomatic that they already possessed the resources for renewal
and lacked only the techniques to release them. The objective, as the
British Buddhist Stephen Bachelor writes, was not 'a transhuman absolute value' but 'the optimum mode of being that man himself is capable
of realizing'.[164] Belief in any form of divine being was optional. Nature
survived on the border between ecology and pantheism. Ignoring the
natural world, writes a Mindfulness guide, 'has led us to deprive ourselves of the simple joy of living, with harmful consequences for our
own happiness and well-being, as well as for the well-being of the rest
of life on Earth'.[165] Otherwise, nature functioned as a prop for specified
practices. Retreats tended to be held in rural locations rather than cities,
but largely because it was easier to concentrate on the inner being when
not distracted by the noise of urban living, and, given the costs which
were often involved, more feasible to present the process as a holiday
from everyday life if it were held in an attractive surrounding.[166]

The balance between sociability and solitude varied between and
within activities. Many involved some kind of instructor or practitioner
and a period of collective association. But they also specified at least a
temporary withdrawal from everyday life, and in most cases stressed
the importance of accompanying periods of silence. Whilst there was a
proliferating body of written guidance for every undertaking, the actual
conduct tended to be wordless. It is no accident that by far the most
successful of the spiritual therapies in the recent past, Mindfulness,
is based on a combination of solitary contemplation and collective

support.[167] As we saw in the discussion of private prayer in Chapter 4, there were serious practical problems facing those who wished to withdraw from the increasingly complex routines of home and work for the purposes of spiritual meditation. Mindfulness proposes a framed, structured solution to the task. At its heart is a secularized exercise of silent meditation which has roots in both monastic Christianity and Buddhism. 'The basic idea,' explained its founder, Jon Kabat-Zinn, 'is to create an island of being in the sea of constant doing in which our lives are usually immersed, a time in which we allow all the "doing" to stop.'[168] It commences with a learned technique of listening to the body and managing its breathing. Gradually the subjects separate themselves from the myriad anxieties and commitments in their external lives and begin to deepen trust in their own feelings and authority.

Effort is required. Kabat-Zinn stresses that 'it would be incorrect to think of meditation as a passive process. It takes a good deal of energy and effort to regulate your attention and to remain genuinely calm and nonreactive.'[169] But as soon as the daily exercise is complete, social life can be resumed. Training and support are always available for the skills and discipline that are required. The practitioner is for the moment wholly detached from all external structures, and at the same time supported by participation in a theorized, documented, and organized movement. All but the most hard-pressed worker or household manager can afford the forty-five minutes a day that need to be devoted to the exercise. Unlike organized retreats, which impose substantial costs of time and money on participants, there are few material obstacles to its practice.[170]

'The immense indifference of things' that had killed Martin Decoud on Great Isabel was evaded by the intense subjectivity of the new spiritual culture. Structures of religious or institutional authority that once had supplied or policed solitary withdrawal lost their purchase over the succeeding century. Where Darwinian evolution had questioned whether nature was a benign source of moral renewal, now global pollution terminated the pristine escape from urban civilization. Instead the search for a release from the press of social living turned inward. Mindfulness is solitude tailored to late modernity – eclectic, privatized, and readily commodified.[171] The UK Amazon site currently lists over fifty thousand versions of books containing 'Mindfulness' in their title. The practice is promoted as an additional resource for reducing personal stress, whatever the cause. Its relation to specific structures of social or economic inequality or injustice is at best optional, at worst non-existent.

THE 'EPIDEMIC OF LONELINESS' REVISITED

The Rise of Loneliness

While this book was being written, the British Conservative government appointed Tracey Crouch as the world's first 'Minister for Loneliness'. In October 2018, she published her strategy, entitled *A Connected Society*.[1] The then Prime Minister, Theresa May, took the time to launch the document on a day when she faced another crisis over Brexit. In the accompanying press release, she described the scale of the problem: 'Up to a fifth of all UK adults feel lonely most or all of the time.'[2] This was an inflation of the estimate contained in the strategy itself 'that between 5% and 18% of UK adults feel lonely often or always'.[3] The higher figure was derived from a study commissioned by the Co-operative Society and the British Red Cross in 2016, which concluded that 4 per cent of those aged sixteen and over always felt lonely, and a further 14 per cent often did. Only 20 per cent of the adult population were found never to have suffered from loneliness.[4] The source of the lower figure was the government's own research body. As part of the preparation for the loneliness strategy, the Office for National Statistics was asked to conduct a reanalysis of data collected for its regular *Community Life Survey*. When asked the question, 'How often do you feel lonely?', 5 per cent of the sample replied 'often/always'.[5]

The gap between the official finding and the Prime Minister's four-fold summary was about eight million lonely people. The reluctance to abandon the more alarming calculation reflected the broader discourse about the issue. The Co-op/Red Cross figure had been adopted by the principal pressure group in the field, The Campaign to End Loneliness, founded in 2011. 'The Facts on Loneliness' section of its website at the time of the publication of *A Connected Society* stated that 'over 9 million people in the UK across all adult ages – more than the population of London – are either always or often lonely'.[6] The Jo Cox Loneliness Commission, set up by the MP before her murder in June 2016 and carried forward by parliamentary colleagues, lobbied for the creation of a loneliness minister and strategy on the basis of the same data.[7] The most recently published figure derives from a transnational study supported by the Wellcome Trust for a BBC Radio 4 series on *The Anatomy of Loneliness*, which was broadcast as the government's strategy was launched. A self-selected sample of 55,000 people from 237 countries generated a finding that 'a third of people often or very often feel lonely'.[8]

The statistical pessimism was accompanied by an inflation in the rhetoric of the debate. On the basis of an extensive literature review, the historian Keith Snell concludes that 'Loneliness is now widely diagnosed as a modern "epidemic" or "plague".[9] The claim that the condition is comparable to a mass health crisis stretches back at least as far as the closing decade of the last century and formed the basis of a 2016 BBC television documentary on *The Age of Loneliness*.[10] The programme also stated that 'the country has been described as the loneliness capital of Europe'. This striking finding was derived from another Office for National Statistics report, *Measuring National Well-being: European Comparisons, 2014*. The document confined itself to printing a series of figures ranking European Union countries by their response to propositions such as 'Support needed about a serious personal or family matter', or 'Feeling close to people in the local area'.[11] It was left to a broadsheet journalist to calculate that across the tables, the United Kingdom fared on aggregate worse than any other nation, and to invent the phrase 'loneliness capital', which immediately entered the bloodstream of public debate.[12] The claim was repeated later in 2014 by the writer George Monbiot in an article entitled 'The Age of

Loneliness is Killing Us', which cited a range of findings demonstrating that 'severe loneliness in England . . . is rising with astonishing speed'.[13] The assertion parallels the assertion in the most recent survey of solitude that in the United States 'rates of loneliness have jumped from 14 per cent in the 1970s to over 40 per cent today'.[14]

It is difficult to establish a reliable time series on the incidence of loneliness. The published findings are largely dependent on self-reported states of mind or experience in relation to categories which alter from survey to survey. Immense variations rest on subjective distinctions between 'always' or 'most' or 'some' of the time. Faced with the range of data in its own document, it is no surprise that amongst the recommendations of the government's new strategy is the construction of 'a stronger evidence base'.[15] There is, however, a scattering of research stretching back to the 1940s which allows us to form some estimation of the scale and direction of change. The most consistent evidence relates to the elderly, who initially were supposed to be most at risk from this form of suffering. It suggests that reported levels were at the lower end of the range now circulating in public debate, and that there has been no significant growth in percentages over two-thirds of a century. Christina Victor and colleagues concluded in 2003 that

> there appears to be little strong or compelling evidence to suggest that we are either experiencing an epidemic of loneliness in old age or that rates of loneliness have increased markedly over time. . . . Self-reported significant loneliness ('very/often lonely') is experienced by about 5–15 per cent of the population aged 65 years and over and this has remained stable over the past 60 years.[16]

The data on a range of Western countries since 1948 collected by Clare Wenger and colleagues revealed a similar spread of findings.[17] In this context, the 2018 Office for National Statistics 'often/always' figure of 5 per cent, although relating to the whole adult population, does not look like an outlier.

Two questions therefore arise. The first is the nature of the rising concern about loneliness, which has come to be seen as an emblematic failing of our times. A combination of demographic, political, cultural, ideological, and medical factors have together created a category of experience which in its outlines is as broad as the pathology of melancholy which was so widely deployed before the twentieth century.[18] The panic has also occurred at a personal level. 'Loneliness anxiety,' claimed the first full-length study of the topic in 1961, 'is a widespread condition in contemporary society.'[19] In her 2015 survey of 'Loneliness Past and Present and Its Effect on Our Lives', Amy Rokach writes that 'we all experience its searing pain, social alienation, and negative effects on our self-esteem'.[20] Whether or not it was avoided, fear of falling out of company has been seen as a shaping force in twentieth and early twenty-first society.

The second question, which will be the subject of the final section of this chapter, is the critical boundary between loneliness and solitude. The government's new strategy is based on the widely used 1981 formulation by Daniel Perlman and Letitia Anne Peplau, which describes 'a subjective, unwelcome feeling of lack or loss of companionship. It happens when we have a mismatch between the quantity and quality of social relationships that we have, and those that we want.'[21] This construction has the advantage of differentiating between loneliness, as a felt condition, and social isolation, as a physical event; however, it fails to clarify the critical distinction between time alone that is valued and embraced and the absence of intimate company that is a cause of negative emotions ranging from nagging regret to intense suffering.[22] Stephanie Dowrick usefully distinguishes between solitude, being 'reasonably comfortable with your own self', and loneliness, as 'uncomfortably alone without someone'.[23] 'In solitude,' writes Thomas Dumm, 'we are each of us by our self, but not yet alone, because we are more or less happily occupied with our self, beside our self in a positive way.'[24] The absence of such absorption is the beginning of loneliness. 'Our language has wisely sensed those two sides of man's being alone,' wrote Paul Tillich. 'It has created the word "loneliness" to express the pain of being alone. And it has created the word "solitude" to express the glory of being alone.'[25] The most succinct definition of loneliness is failed solitude.[26] This foregrounds the critical issue of why, in virtually all the surveys going back to the 1940s, a substantial majority of people who were temporarily or permanently living alone do not report being lonely. Given the steep rise in the elderly and single households, the question is not why there was so much acute loneliness but why there was so little.

The Panic

Loneliness was first identified as a modern problem during the conflict with Hitler. In the long period between Dunkirk and the Normandy landings, the Home Front was seen as critical to the defence of the country. For the first time in a liberal democracy, the government began to take a systematic interest in how ordinary people felt about their lives. Where once it had been enough that they obeyed the law, observed the basic tenets of Christianity, and reproduced successive generations of disciplined workers, now it was important to know about what was loosely termed their 'morale'. The fear was that early military defeats combined with the bombing of population centres and the rationing of basic necessities would sap the will to resist. Of particular concern was the outlook of women amidst the social dislocation of conflict. As their husbands were conscripted and their children evacuated, there was a danger that they would turn against the national effort, undermining the discipline of troops and diminishing their contribution to the wartime economy.

Research was commissioned, particularly from Mass Observation, whose pre-war foundation was seized upon by anxious politicians. Attention was focussed on a category of experience which had rarely been named or recognized. 'In cases where conscription closely affects women,' reported a 1940 study, 'their anxiety and loneliness becomes the main subject of their thoughts. In diaries, conversations, letters come stories of mothers left alone, and apparently unable to adapt themselves to the situation.'[27] They lost their menfolk to the armed forces, and then their children were sent away. If they maintained their role as mothers, they had to abandon their familiar, supportive networks in the towns and cities. 'To most of them,' Mass Observation discovered, 'to all but the very youngest or most adaptable, this meant, not the beginning of a new social life, but simply the destruction of the old, leading to nothing but isolation and loneliness.'[28]

The investigations did not, however, conclude that the absence of company was leading to a turn against the wartime endeavour. To the contrary, it was generating a shift in emphasis from the private to the public domain. 'With husbands and sons called up, many children evacuated,' reported Mass Observation, 'there was little incentive for any woman to want to remain in the solitude of her battered and uncomfortable home, cut off from society – the focal points of modern society being . . . found in offices, factories and workshops, not among the homes.'[29] Forms of war effort varied from an extension of roles traditionally performed by young women in particular to male-replacement labour in heavy industry.[30] Alongside manifold types of voluntary activity, conscription of women into the armed forces began in 1940.

A common response to the new duties was a sense of escape from the monotonous isolation of home life. 'It may be that they are lonely, or bored,' observed a 1940 report on 'Women in the War Effort', '. . . the desire to be among others is particularly noticeable.'[31] Rather than loneliness proving an obstacle to the collective struggle, its avoidance became an incentive for action. Nella Last, who kept one of the most detailed diaries of the war years, found herself increasingly depressed at the beginning of the conflict. Life at home was both arduous and lonely. Her grown-up sons were in the forces; she had little supportive communication with her husband, whom she thought should never have left his mother; and the toil of managing the household economy on wartime rations eroded her spirit and energies. But then she joined the Women's Voluntary Service (WVS) in her native Barrow-in-Furness, which ran a centre supporting a range of public endeavours in the town. The escape from domestic silence was immediately celebrated. 'I've found companionship,' she wrote in her diary in September 1940, 'and unexpected laughter and gaiety, understanding and sympathy. They have brought out unsuspected little gifts of money making ideas and organising. . . . I've found a serenity of mind and purpose that this time last year was, or seemed to be, impossible, and I thank God and pray I may keep it and that it will increase as need arises.'[32] She was one amongst many for whom the end of the conflict meant a returning sense of social poverty. In retrospect, the WVS community effort was the high tide of her life in the town.

The wartime discovery of loneliness expanded in two connected areas after 1945. Planning for the new society envisaged a growing problem of social relations amongst the elderly.[33] During the nineteenth century, the proportion of the population aged sixty-five and over was stable at between 4 and 5 per cent. It began to grow between the wars and reached almost 12 per cent by 1961, on its way to the current level of just over 18 per cent.[34] The first major examination of this section of society was conducted by J. H. Sheldon as early as 1948. 'Loneliness,' he explained, '. . . is of considerable importance, not only because of its inherent pathos, but also because there appear to be some reasons for supposing that loneliness may help to precipitate a breakdown of mental health in the old people affected.'[35] His basic conclusion was confirmed by further studies in the 1950s and 1960s.[36] Those who reported being lonely varied in the intensity of their experience. At the core of the problem was bereavement. 'Loneliness of some degree,' Sheldon noted,

> affected approximately one-fifth of the old people in the sample. It ranges in severity from an intermittent feeling to a desolation of spirit that is heart-rending to encounter. The latter is nearly always found where an old person has recently lost his or her spouse and has then to live alone, or is the sole survivor of a family of siblings who previously lived together.[37]

The most influential of the post-war studies of the elderly was conducted by Peter Townsend in 1957. He found that 'the underlying reason for loneliness in old age is desolation rather than isolation'.[38] The destruction of health and spirits was a function of the irreversible loss of a long-term intimate partner. Amongst this group the suffering was acute. 'I get so lonely,' reported one of his witnesses, 'I could fill up the teapot with tears.'[39] In a subsequent cross-national survey, between 2 and 3 per cent of the elderly were discovered to be living without any significant human contact at all.[40] The qualitative research was reinforced by demographic change. As was noted in Chapter 5, the post-war era saw the remorseless rise of the single-person household.[41] The change was particularly dramatic amongst the elderly. By the late 1960s, a quarter of men and just over a half of women aged sixty-five and over were living alone. Amongst this group, the most common determinant of household structure was the transition to widowhood.[42]

The second generator of the post-war concern with loneliness was the revived programme of slum clearance. As the council estates received their new tenants and the Labour Party lost a series of elections in the 1950s, investigators sought to comprehend the consequences of the rapid change in urban living. It was claimed that the move out of the inner city generated new forms of social distance. The focus of family life was reported to have shifted to the domestic interior. In exchange for more rooms, indoor plumbing, and gardens, the occupants of the new houses were seen to have lost contact with their neighbours. Men travelled further to their employment, and back at home, shops and other community resources were slow to develop. The surveys radically compressed the transition from a street- to a home-based culture which had been visible in towns and cities since at least the later nineteenth century, and over-stated the communal warmth of the older neighbourhoods, to which few of the new tenants wished to return. There was, however, substance in their discussion of the plight of the transplanted wives, who found themselves lacking adult company during the long days in their new houses. A post-war survey of working-class marriage found that 'In many homes, especially those in sprawling suburbs, one saw the loneliness and isolation of women cut off even from relatives, and the consequent monotony of their lives.'[43] In the most influential study, published in 1957, and selling half a million copies as a Penguin paperback throughout the 1960s, Michael Young and Peter Willmott discovered that in their reference council estate of 'Greenleigh' (Debden), women were particularly vulnerable. 'Those who do not follow their husbands into the society of the workplace,' they reported, '– and loneliness is one of the common reasons for doing so – have to spend their day alone, "looking at ourselves all day," as they say.'[44]

The social investigations reflected a growing concern that the forces of modernity were generating unanticipated problems of sociability. A combination of the welfare state and the post-war consumer boom was placing individual gratification at odds with intimate relationships. What Mark Abrams described in 1959 as the 'home-centred society' was creating new risks of isolation.[45] Loneliness was seen as a visible symptom of an increasingly unmanageable tension between the pursuit of material comfort and the conduct of stable and satisfying personal relations. In this process, the welfare state was an ambiguous good. If the ambition was to repair the deprivation of the Slump and the domestic dislocation of wartime, the outcome was a new category of victim. A set of reforms ranging from the destruction of long-established

communities to the creation of an enlarged and more powerful official bureaucracy left the most vulnerable in society, including young
mothers and the elderly, powerless to prevent the destruction of supportive networks. The most iconic depiction of this process was the
1966 television play *Cathy Come Home*, directed by Ken Loach from
a script by Jeremy Sandford.[46] In the drama, Cathy's young family is
gradually dismantled by a combination of a feckless husband, increasingly unsupportive neighbours, and a series of hard-faced officials. She
is left distraught and alone in the last scene as her children are forcibly
taken from her by the social services.

The resonance of loneliness was enhanced by contemporary developments in the burgeoning discipline of psychiatry. Increasingly large
claims were made for the impact of states of mind on physical wellbeing. As medical advances at last promised victory over tuberculosis and
other hitherto unpreventable fatal illnesses, attention was turned to the
potential gains to be made by treating mental illness. 'Once infectious
disease was the principal cause of death and disability,' proclaimed
G. M. Carstairs in the 1962 Reith Lecture, 'but now it is from other
sources that we encounter threats to life and to the fullness of being.'[47]
At the same time, the notion of psychological malfunction was broadened to embrace conditions that might affect large sections of society.
The discourse built upon the experience of two world wars, both on the
front line and at home.[48] New kinds of suffering were identified whose
incidence was widespread and whose origins lay in extremes of everyday experience. No longer was the concern of the profession confined
to those committed to asylums, which contained a hundred and fifty
thousand patients in the 1950s.[49] To the contrary, a growing body of
research, particularly associated with the work of Erving Goffman,[50]
argued that prolonged incarceration was itself an engine of suffering.
Both the location of mental health and causes of breakdown were to be
found in the family and in the community in which it was embedded.[51]
Investigation was required into the social relations patients had endured
in their childhood or into the structures in which they now lived.[52]

In 1959, a posthumously published paper by the distinguished
German-American psychologist Frieda Fromm-Reichmann introduced
the condition of loneliness to the growing list of mental illnesses. She
claimed that 'fear of loneliness is the common fate of the people of our

Western culture'.[53] As a consequence, resistance strategies were embedded in the conduct of social relations. 'Loneliness,' Fromm-Reichmann wrote, 'seems to be such a painful, frightening experience that people do practically everything to avoid it.'[54] Fear of being alone at once shaped the conduct of social relations and impeded a clear-sighted view of its characteristics. The actual incidence of loneliness was capable of limitless destruction of the individual's inner being. 'Real loneliness,' Fromm-Reichmann explained, '. . . leads ultimately to the development of psychotic states. It renders people who suffer it emotionally paralyzed and helpless.'[55] The nineteenth-century category of melancholy was reborn as a lethal condition which both was caused by the absence of social exchange and prevented the sufferer from engaging in effective interpersonal communication.[56] The psychologist was faced with a patient who was forced into silence by their experience. 'This loneliness,' wrote Fromm-Reichmann, 'in its quintessential form, is of a nature that is incommunicable by the one who suffers it.'[57] The very practice of the psychiatrist's profession was at risk. The patient on the couch could no longer give an account of their breakdown.

Loneliness was a special case of a failure of social relations that everywhere threatened the post-war citizen. Its roots were increasingly sought in child development, particularly in the influential work of John Bowlby. Manifold forms of adult delinquency and psychological suffering were traced back to the nature of the attachment of the infant to its mother. 'Amongst the most significant developments in psychiatry during the past quarter of a century,' wrote Bowlby in 1952, 'has been the steady growth of evidence that the quality of parental care which a child receives in his earliest years is of vital importance for his future mental health.'[58] He shared with contemporary social investigators the conclusion that forms of modernity were eroding wider support systems for the most vulnerable in society. 'It is probably only in communities in which the greater family group has ceased to exist,' he explained, 'that the problem of deprived children is found on a serious scale. This condition characterizes many communities of Western civilization.'[59] The solution did not lie in attempts to substitute for lost collective endeavour. No social or medical service, however well meaning, could replicate the critical bond with the mother-figure, who, Bowlby wrote, stands 'in contrast to the almost complete deprivation which is still not uncommon in institutions, residential nurseries, and hospitals, where the child often has no one person who cares for him in a personal way and with whom he may feel secure'.[60] What mattered to Bowlby was not just the physical presence of the mother but the intimate relationship that was developed with the growing infant. Another adult could perform this role, providing they were a constant and caring presence. The damage, which could last a lifetime, was caused when the child felt alone with its mother, lacking the intimate framework within which it could work through early feelings of anxiety and guilt. After the first six to twelve months, it was very difficult to repair the harm. Instead the psychiatrist was faced with the double bind outlined by Fromm-Reichmann, with an asocial adult unable to interact with their contemporaries or with the professional seeking to ameliorate their condition.

Until the publication of Anthony's Storr's pioneering study in 1989,[61] few psychologists were interested in the boundary between loneliness and solitude. The major exception was Bowlby's contemporary Donald Winnicott. He reacted against the dominant emphasis on the negative condition amongst his colleagues and in society more generally.[62] 'It is probably true to say,' he observed in 1960, 'that in psycho-analytical literature more has been written on the *fear* of being alone or the *wish* to be alone than on the *ability* to be alone. . . . It would seem to me that a discussion on the *positive* aspects of the capacity to be alone is overdue.'[63] His own research suggested that the capacity to be content with their own company was a normal and necessary feature of the growing child. Being alone was redefined as a positive condition. Empirical observation indicated that 'many people do become able to enjoy solitude before they are out of childhood, and they may even value solitude as a most precious possession'.[64] The key to this achievement lay in how the infant learned to be alone in the presence of their mother. At the heart of successful development was a paradox. The child could only learn to be alone if a trusted adult was present. Winnicott's work laid the foundation for later explorations of solitude, but in its own time it did nothing to relieve the apprehension about the consequences of distant parenting. Everything revolved around the quality of communication between intimate family members. Successful development remained 'dependent on the infant's awareness of the continued existence of a reliable mother whose reliability makes it possible for the infant to be alone and to enjoy being alone, for a limited period'.[65] Breakdowns of domestic relationships, particularly in the critical early years, remained a major threat to subsequent adult mental health.

Alongside the concern with psychological ill-health and associated forms of anti-social behaviour, there has been a more recent growth in studies of the bodily consequences of loneliness. The origins of the current research can again be traced back to the post-war decades. The creation of the National Health Service together with a commitment to supply adequate housing and income for the expanding elderly population raised the still unanswered question of whether the state was generating more costs that it would ever fully be able to meet. Early studies by J. H. Sheldon, Jeremy Tunstall, and others began to grapple with the health implications of survival into old age, particularly amongst those who were widowed and living alone.[66] At the same time, the discipline of epidemiology, still in its infancy in the late 1940s, began to supply the tools for measuring the interaction between social behaviours and medical outcomes for complete populations. A further, more recent development was the growth of interest in the interface between psychological and physiological heath, specifically whether states of mind could cause specific biological effects up to and including early mortality. What Judith Shulevitz has termed 'the lethality of loneliness' became the subject of widespread commentary amongst politicians, pressure groups, and the press.[67] The list of possible outcomes grew rapidly. By the time the British government launched its loneliness strategy in 2018, the condition was associated with practically every contemporary medical crisis. 'Its health impact,' claimed the document,

> is thought to be on a par with other public health priorities like obesity or smoking. Research shows that loneliness is associated with a greater risk of inactivity, smoking and risk-taking behaviour; increased risk of coronary heart disease and stroke; an increased risk of depression, low self-esteem, reported sleep problems and increased stress response; and with cognitive decline and an increased risk of Alzheimer's.[68]

The alarmist language conflated a number of unresolved complexities in the research. As with all commentary in this field, it was dependent on the self-description of the target population in response to questionnaire surveys. Thus, for instance, John and Stephanie Cacioppo, who published widely in the field of social neuroscience, insisted in *The Lancet* that a third of the population of industrial countries were afflicted by loneliness, and one in twelve 'severely' so. On the basis of this finding, they claimed that the effects 'are not attributable to some peculiarity of the character of a subset of individuals, they are a result of the condition affecting ordinary people'.[69] Moreover, the condition was 'contagious', thus giving support to those freely referring to an 'epidemic' of loneliness. But unlike earlier public health concerns, such as smoking and obesity, with which the new crisis was associated, there was no objective measure of suffering. Cigarettes could be counted, people could be weighed. In the case of loneliness, however, the distinctions between severe and less severe remained for the most part a construct of the researchers, applying adjectival categories as a means of ordering their data.[70] The UCLA Loneliness Scale, which, since 1978, has been the basis of 80 per cent of empirical research in the United States, requires respondents to assign themselves to one of four boxes: 'never', 'rarely', 'sometimes', or 'often'.[71] The scale is internally consistent and generates statistics which can be measured over time and against other phenomena. It does not, however, reflect the complexity of the experience over the life-course. There is no inherent reason why loneliness, as with any emotional state, should increase in step changes, however they are labelled and by whom. Nor, at a more granular level, does loneliness necessarily progress on a single scale of intensity. Some forms of loneliness are not more or less than others, just different.

Solitude itself has rarely been the subject of quantifiable measurement. We saw in Chapter 4 how the imposition of solitary confinement was undermined by the inability of chaplains to count the number of prisoners who had been successfully converted.[72] Loneliness has become and is likely to remain a statistical event, for all the methodological shortcomings, because since the Second World War it has increasingly been seen as a matter for political debate and intervention. The limited attempt that has so far been made to establish a solitude scale has succeeded only in demonstrating that amongst a group of undergraduates, those with a preference for solitude tend to spend more time by themselves.[73]

A second complexity was the issue of causality. If there was an association of loneliness with failing health, it was not clear which was leading to the other. Early surveys of the burgeoning problem frequently drew attention to the impact of reduced mobility on sociability.[74] Physical constraints on leaving the home, problems of communication caused by poor eyesight or hearing, all increased the difficulty of maintaining supportive personal contact. These factors were in turn exacerbated by issues such as inadequate local transport, remote medical facilities, and failing social services. 'Those who reported having a long-term illness or disability,' concluded the recent Office for National Statistics survey, 'were significantly more likely to report feeling lonely "often/always" and "some of the time".'[75] Suggestive recent medical research has drawn attention to a direct link between states of mind and physiological conditions that can increase the risk of illness and death. Loneliness has been found to have an impact on vascular resistance, on the immune system, on anti-inflammatory activity, and on the production of dopamine.[76] The forms of lethality surveyed by Judith Shulevitz are wide-ranging. 'A partial list of the physical diseases thought to be caused or exacerbated by loneliness,' she writes, 'would include Alzheimer's, obesity, diabetes, high blood pressure, heart disease, neurodegenerative diseases, and even cancer – tumors can metastasize faster in lonely people.'[77]

Much of this work is at an early stage, and is hampered by the reliance on cross-sectional studies which fail to establish long-term interactions between physical and psychological factors.[78] Where there is a demonstrated effect on the body, its direct impact on mortality is difficult to measure. Further, the boundary between behavioural and biological factors remains unclear. It has long been argued, for instance, that ill-health amongst the self-described lonely was influenced by their failure to go to a doctor with their symptoms. Those with no-one to watch over them were less likely to seek help when it was first needed.[79] A raft of 'health behaviours' have been identified amongst the lonely, including poor sleep patterns, excessive alcohol consumption, insufficient exercise, and a general inability to look after themselves.[80] The recent, widely cited, large-scale literature review by Julianne Holt-Lunstad and colleagues insists on an association between loneliness and morbidity, but is careful to leave open the direction of travel. 'Future researchers,' it warns, 'will need to confirm the hypothesis that when individuals are ill (and ostensibly needing support) their risk for mortality increases substantially when lacking social support.'[81]

A final difficulty is the nature of public discourse. There is a confusion between reported direct consequences of loneliness and attention-generating analogies. On the one hand there are epidemiological findings that state that whatever the causal flow, there is, as the 2018 *Lancet* article by John and Stephanie Cacioppo claims, 'a 26% increase in the risk of premature mortality' amongst the third of the population that they deem to be lonely.[82] On the other there is a growing propensity to appropriate anxieties about well-established public health threats such as cigarettes, obesity, substance abuse, and dementia. Thus, for instance, Theresa May's introduction to the government loneliness strategy states that 'research now shows that loneliness is as damaging to our physical health as smoking'.[83] There is a widely circulated claim that the condition is specifically as dangerous as consuming fifteen cigarettes a day. Such a statement belongs to the realm of rhetoric rather than diagnosis. The range of possible variations on both sides of the equation renders the association meaningless. Its circulation can partly be explained by the dynamics of pressure group activity. Bodies seeking to raise funding and enhance their public profile associate themselves with the authority of campaigns which, in the case of smoking, go back over two-thirds of a century. There is a drive to medicalize the agenda of protest, despite warnings that there are no pills to cure loneliness.[84] The pressure groups, however, are the product of a larger sense of panic. The constant tendency to fly to extremes of negative estimation has its roots in a wider apprehension about the failings of late modernity.

The sense of crisis is manifest at two levels. In government, there is a concern that the lonely citizen is an unintended consequence of the necessary pursuit of individual gain in a society of weakening social networks. It is prudent to pay more attention to those who are insufficiently supported by families or communities, or by the public services designed to respond to such shortcomings. The failings have long histories but threaten short-term consequences, particularly at the ballot box. *A Connected Society* is nothing if not a wide-ranging document. It generalizes the issue of loneliness, engaging with the still broader topic of how people connect with each other. Agencies responsible for action include not only the state and local government but also community organizations and spaces, businesses in their personnel practices, and a host of voluntary and charitable organizations. The strategy explains that it 'recognises that government can't make that change alone, and sets out a powerful vision of how we can all play a role in building a more socially connected society'.[85] There is a modest investment in ventures such as the 'Building Connection Fund', and a commensurate hope that community ventures will reduce the cost pressures on the National Health Service. The document revived David Cameron's 'Big Society' project, thought by commentators to be long buried, and was perhaps the nearest Theresa May came to implementing her inaugural Downing Street commitment to social justice.

For critics of the Conservatives' approach, the challenge is more fundamental. Loneliness is the representative pathology of high modernity. It is not a niche social problem or a passing challenge to public policy, but reflects the comprehensive inability of contemporary forms of intimacy to withstand what George Monbiot describes as 'competitive self-interest and extreme individualism'.[86] Monbiot has started his own loneliness project, deploying a range of digital media, in a campaign against what he sees as the wholesale destruction of what it is to be a sociable human. All the data on medical and psychological morbidity are corralled into a case against rampant neo-liberalism. Loneliness is a consequence of a process by which 'we have ripped the natural world apart, degraded our conditions of life, surrendered our freedoms and prospects of contentment to a compulsive, atomising, joyless hedonism, in which having consumed all else, we start to prey upon ourselves. For this, we have destroyed the essence of our humanity: our connectedness.'[87] The army of lonely people, threatened with impoverished lives and premature death, is at once a measure of late capitalism's failure and a source of energy for fundamental reform. Numbers matter in this discourse. The risks of community breakdown are immense; the chances of avoiding the negative consequences are slight and diminishing. Social disconnection is the malaise; collective protest is the solution.

Loneliness and Solitude

In the discourse about loneliness, solitude appears as a double negative. It is the condition of those who are not in company and who are not feeling alone. The experience is infrequently addressed by name, despite the fact that it constitutes the majority of responses in most surveys. Keith Snell refers to it as 'a desired and non-lonely situation, akin to an outcome of satisfied privacy'.[88] As Sara Maitland has observed, the intense public debate about loneliness has had the effect of obscuring the positive function of solitude.[89] It may be argued, however, that the impact of late modernity on social relations lies at the boundary between solitude and loneliness.[90] When Johann Zimmermann considered the matter in the late eighteenth century, he stressed, as we have seen, the importance of the movement between being alone and being in company.[91] Safe, productive solitude was a function of choice. The individual should be able to move freely into and out of a solitary condition. As with most of his contemporaries, Zimmermann did not deploy the term 'loneliness'; however, destructive solitude, which he discussed at length, largely corresponded to the modern use of the word. The harm was caused when the individual was forced out of company against their will, or embraced a form of solitude, such as a monastic vow or intense melancholy, from which there was no escape. In conformity with the prevailing view of the subject, Zimmermann assumed that only a particular category of educated males could be trusted to navigate safely between creative and damaging solitude. The canvas has widened in our own time to include men and women of every age and class, but the emphasis on managing the transition between the conditions remains wholly valid. As psychologists Christopher Long and James Averill conclude, 'the voluntariness or degree of control a person has in a situation may be the most important factor that tips the balance between an experience of positive solitude and an experience of loneliness'.[92]

The steep growth of single-person households since the Second World War has fuelled much of the current sense of crisis.[93] However, a succession of surveys have challenged the association between the physical condition of living alone and the emotional pain of loneliness.[94] From the research of Peter Townsend in the 1950s and 1960s to that of Christina Victor and her colleagues more recently, it has been established that the elderly, whose living patterns first raised the alarm about social isolation, were for the most part exploiting opportunities rather than suffering deprivation.[95] Letitia Peplau, who led research on the topic in the United States in the 1980s, argued that the wide-spread belief that the lone elderly 'lead impoverished social lives' was 'mythic'.[96] It was not that after 1945 the older generation developed a new ambition for living apart from their children or other relatives for as long as they could. Rather, as in the related case of privacy, a set of material conditions made it increasingly possible to realize long-held aspirations.[97] The desire for autonomous living became easier to fulfil with the introduction of adequate pensions in 1948, and associated improvements in life-time income, housing conditions, and medical and social support. Couples put off moving in with their offspring, and surviving widows continued to run their own households whilst they were physically capable of doing so.[98]

The fear of losing independence was increasingly a more powerful force amongst the elderly than the fear of loneliness. Amongst younger cohorts, whose inclination and ability to maintain separate social units have grown more recently, there was a wider range of needs and cir-cumstances, but common to all was the capacity to determine how to live. At every age there were perceived gains, ranging from those in their twenties who wished neither to return to the parental home nor to share accommodation with relative strangers, to those in middle age who sought untrammelled autonomy in between relationships or were temperamentally inclined to enjoy their own company more than living with a partner.[99]

The feasibility of living alone was enhanced by the increasing flexibility of social networks. In the early post-war decades, physical location and forms of emotional and material support were closely associated in most communities. Sheldon's pioneering survey of the lone elderly found that 'comparatively few old people live a life of com-plete isolation, the great majority living in contact with their children so that they have to be considered as part of a family unit rather than as separate individuals'.[100] Four per cent of his sample were actually living next door to a child. Despite the subsequent transitions from inner-city slums to suburban estates, as late as the 1980s, the elderly remained on average no further from their nearest offspring than in early nineteenth-century communities.[101] Over time the distances grew, but the capacity of families to both recognize and fulfil obligations to potentially isolated members remained largely intact.[102] Grandparents retained an involvement in the lives of children and grandchildren, and in turn could expect material and emotional assistance if they ran into difficulty.[103] The role of family members was enhanced, rather than replaced, by the growth in engagement with unrelated friends, whether in the locality or workplace or further afield.[104] The spread of car ownership among the working class in the third quarter of the century meant that physical contact was no longer constrained by walking distance or the availability of public transport. Well before the digital revolution, networked solitude, the capacity of those physically alone to enjoy supportive contact with distant relations or friends, was becoming more significant. The telephone finally overtook correspondence in the mid-1970s, and it remained the most widely used form of making connection until as late as a decade ago. In 2007, the British Social Attitudes Survey asked respondents about the means by which they maintained 'contact with a close friend, relative or someone else close to you (apart from your spouse or partner) about how you're feeling or just to catch up'. For women, face-to-face conversation was still the most widely used medium, 51 per cent talking to intimates 'every day or about every day'. The second most deployed channel was the telephone at 47 per cent. Text-messaging and emails still lagged behind at 35 per cent and 29 per cent. With all forms, men were worse communicators, though less so with digital devices.[105]

Whether or not they were talking to friends and family, those living alone had a wider range of diversions within their homes. As Chapter 5 discussed, improvements in domestic space, household prosperity, and communication systems expanded the pastimes which engaged attention in the absence of society. Whether the individual was seeking space within a household or consuming time when dependent on their own company, there was a richer agenda of diversion. At the beginning of the twenty-first century, Chris Phillipson and colleagues revisited the communities which had been the subject of the classic post-war surveys. They identified a total of 139 leisure activities being undertaken by the elderly. These embraced a number of long-standing activities which were now more accessible and more recent innovations such as watching the television or travelling on holiday. The ancient pastime of reading was still the most common diversion, with going for a walk, the basic leisure resource down the centuries for rich and poor alike, the fourth most common.[106] As the single-person household ceased to be a marginal social presence and became a recognized feature of an increasingly diverse range of living arrangements, so the market gradually adjusted to a new category of consumer demand. Supermarkets sold food packaged for individual needs. Coffee shops supplied refreshment without invading the bubble of personal privacy surrounding their customers. Home delivery services catered for those unwilling to eat or shop by themselves in public places.[107] Package holidays were arranged, at an enhanced cost, for single travellers.

The desire to live alone was further enhanced by what Anthony Giddens has termed the reflexive project of late modernity.[108] More choice in forms of intimacy both permitted and required greater consideration of self-identity. A continuing review of personal values and aspirations was a condition of open, trusting intimacy. There was no necessary requirement for this reflection to be undertaken in physical isolation, but finding some space in which to audit or develop the sense of self became an increasingly attractive proposition, as was noted in the preceding chapter. The withdrawal might be temporary, or undertaken as a longer-term plan. In accounts captured by Mass Observation during the Second World War it is possible to glimpse amidst the intense privation a sense of excitement about the increasing feasibility of independent living. 'Home to me is the place where I can be a complete individual,' explained one witness. 'At present it is a complete flat which I run myself, which I have enured with my own personality – where I can receive my friends, where I can retire into solitude doing what I like, eating when I like – in short a place where I have perfected the art of being successfully alone.'[109]

The central argument of Anthony Storr's study of solitude was that the condition was necessary to the development of identity in ways which had been consistently overlooked by his own profession of psychology. 'It seems to me,' he wrote, 'that what goes on in the human being when he is by himself is as important as what happens in his interactions with other people.'[110] For women in particular, there was an attraction in escaping what once had been the overwhelming demands of children and domestic labour in order to give focussed consideration to who they were and wished to become. In the introduction to her edited collection of essays *The Center of the Web: Women and Solitude*,

Delease Wear found that 'many of the writers think of solitude as a respite for reflection on identities. Within these inquiries, solitude is often a condition/place to refurbish our spirits, to distill our thoughts, to confront the way we live and often to work – separate from the other lives we live within the many kinds of families we've created.'[111] Attention has also been paid to the value of solitude in the transition to adulthood. The studies of adolescents by Reed Larson and colleagues have stressed the importance to the development of self-identity of the ability to withdraw at will from the company of adults and peers.[112] Whether it is retreating behind a locked door within the parental home, or setting up in a separate room in college or an apartment, the fiercely asserted solitude is not a rejection of society but a necessary resource for learning how to participate in it.

There are grounds for arguing, therefore, that living alone is less a pathology of late modernity and more often a direct and frequently valued consequence of its defining strengths. The key question is under what circumstances solitude tips over into loneliness. There is an implicit determinism in many of the accounts of the topic. Quantifiable demographic changes since 1945, particularly the ageing society and the rapid growth of single-person households, are seen to lead directly to forms of mental and physiological suffering associated with the absence of company. It is helpful to focus instead on the issue of free will. As Jon Lawrence has recently argued, 'it is important to recognize that this massive increase in living alone is largely a consequence of personal choices made possible by increased affluence'.[113] Seeking to make space for yourself within a relationship or withdrawing from it altogether have always been strategies for living. They were calculated risks which did not always result in intended outcomes. A satisfying private hobby pursued in the home could set up unanticipated barriers with a partner. Simon Garfield commenced his account of his passion for philately with a sorrowful if humorous preamble. 'I told my wife of my affair [with stamps] in a straightforward way, on a walk along the Kent coast one afternoon,' he wrote, 'and things moved swiftly from there. Within a week I was sleeping in my office, within a month in a rented flat.'[114] A decision to leave an unsatisfactory relationship in the hope of finding something better could lead to a much longer period alone than had been anticipated. In other circumstances, expected benefits were set against known costs. Ray Pahl, in his study of the expanding role of friendship, summarized the risk assessment that lies at the heart of every act of association with others. Taking the example of a woman who 'prefers to be solitary and have the space to live her life her way', he argues,

> that, surely, is a decision she has to make. She will recognize that this may involve loneliness from time to time, but some loneliness is part of the human condition. Those trapped all day with young children can feel so lonely that they become clinically depressed; others who are married to a kind, worthy, but basically dull and boring partner may feel acutely lonely at times.[115]

Time itself is a critical factor. One definition of loneliness is that it is solitude that has continued for longer than was intended or desired.[116] Recent research has suggested that the condition represents a U-shaped curve, with the peaks of suffering amongst those in their early and concluding years.[117] This finding is related to the growth in the number of transitions in most people's lives. At the beginning of the period covered by this book, there were likely to be few significant changes in an individual's social or economic circumstances. During childhood, productive labour and such schooling as was available would be interleaved. There might be a move to an apprenticeship or a period of in-service domestic labour at around fourteen, then marriage and in short order a family, with at best a few years of the couple together once their children had left. Whilst individual jobs might be brief, there was unlikely to be a major change of occupation, and movements from a place of birth would be to nearby towns with which the migrant would already be familiar.

By contrast, late modernity has seen a multiplication of what the recent government strategy described as 'trigger points', and with it an expansion of the range of choices about forms of sociability.[118] These include changing schools in childhood, leaving home for university, moving between places and between careers over a lifetime, a greater propensity to begin and end intimate relationships, and the lengthening period beyond child-rearing, which might in turn entail further changes of location or activity. At each of these points, there is a prospect of periods of isolation as the individual maps out a new relationship landscape. Their meaning depends on the cost–benefit calculation which underpins a change, with expected gains set against periods of loss or uncertainty. The result might be experienced as solitude if the outcomes of the transformation are enjoyed, or loneliness if the period of adjustment goes on too long or the offsetting gains are too few. There are now so many occasions for change that surveys have had difficulty in finding respondents who have never encountered moments of loneliness in their lives. Such experiences are also conditioned by expectation. One of the reasons why those in their late teens and early twenties feature so strongly in tables of loneliness is that they find it more difficult to estimate how long a period alone will last, and have equipped themselves with fewer tools to cope with it.[119] The young think the present will never end; the old know that most things pass, even the bad times.[120]

At many of these transition points the encounter with loneliness is itself so short-lived that the suffering is slight and the contrast with what Andersson terms 'voluntary, temporary, self-induced solitude' without great significance. [121] It begins to matter when the element of choice is constrained by necessity, and when there is no likelihood of escape in any foreseeable future. This is when time is at its most threatening. Gladys Langford was one of Mass Observation's most prolific diarists, recording her daily thoughts and activities in the years between 1936 and 1940. Her marriage had been ended by her husband's desertion shortly after it began. Now in her late forties, never having remarried and taking no pleasure in her career as a teacher, she bitterly described her unending loneliness, which was broken only by the occasional visit of Leonard, a married lover. 'The black dog of melancholy lies on my shoulders today,' she wrote.

> I'm short of money and have even less inclination to stir out of the house. I thought perhaps Leonard might have come today, but of course he didn't, so I've lain in a chair, reading or writing and deploring the passage of time and the passing of friends. I make no new ones. How can I? I belong to no 'body' and if I visit I am usually the sole guest while the hatred of leaving my home grows ever more pronounced. I feel as though I'm already half dead.[122]

A contemporary diarist, Nella Last, whom we encountered earlier seeking the society of wartime voluntary work in Barrow, was still married, but to a man with whom she could not communicate. With her children departed, she was left isolated in a half-empty house. In a memorable image, she described how attempts to break the silence by getting her husband interested were 'like trying to strike a match on a patch of damp moss'.[123] Both Gladys Langford and Nella Last were disempowered women, unable to escape the long-term consequences of a mistaken choice of a husband and the prevailing conventions of marital conformity. Nella Last could still find moments of pleasurable solitude in day trips to the nearby Lake District, but at the heart of her life was a profound, timeless loneliness.

Where the intimate relationship was successful over a prolonged period, the pain of eventual bereavement was all the greater.[124] At this point, every meaningful choice lay in the past. There was no prospect of reconsideration, no means of striking a new balance between welcome and unwelcome states of being alone. Attempts at condolence by surviving friends and relatives reinforced rather than relieved the sense of grief. Reaching out to others could seem a betrayal of the lost partner.[125] As Harriet Martineau had explained in the middle of the nineteenth century, the suffering of those engaged with death and dying was best consumed in silence.[126] The most that could be attempted was what might be termed bereavement solitude, when the survivor kept going through the worst of their grief by continuing to converse with the departed lover. The experience might end with a gradual return to society, or it could be concluded by increasing ill-health or death, especially within the first two years. During the post-war era, a range of organizations began to supplement the traditional role of the church in offering support to those in mourning. Cruse Bereavement Care was founded in 1959, and other voluntary bodies, including the Marriage Guidance Council, offered advice to those marooned either by death or by the breakdown of a relationship.[127] The threat was not just to peace of mind. Amidst the claims for the association of loneliness with physical health, the impact of bereavement on mortality is well established.[128]

Consideration of the often porous boundary between loneliness and solitude generates two broad conclusions. The first is that loneliness in some form is not exclusively the product of the failings of the recent past.

The later twentieth and the early twenty-first centuries did not invent bereavement and its consequences. At most they postponed the event for most of the population further into old age. Neither did they witness for the first time forms of isolation within established partnerships. To the contrary, the rise of the companionate marriage, however many qualifications need to be attached to the concept, probably increased the incidence of face-to-face discourse in most homes. The major change that has taken place is in the multiplication of the 'trigger points' generated by educational, occupational, and geographical movements, and by the increasing diversity and instability of intimate relationships. In this regard, the argument of the more alarmist accounts of loneliness that it is becoming a near universal experience has some substance.[129] The question, however, is the depth of the suffering which it entails. Loneliness in this sense has been woven into the human condition, integral to the strategies for living that all have to negotiate, and almost all fail at some point to manage successfully.[130]

The second conclusion is that the association of loneliness with the failings of late modernity originated less from the interface between intimacy and individualism and more from the incidence of material inequality and the constraints in the public finances that have become more pronounced since the financial crash of 2008. In one way or another, the expansion of forms of recreational solitude that were explored in Chapter 5 were a function of increasing household prosperity, better access to communication systems, and the introduction of a welfare state. There was more money to spend on solitary diversions, more space within homes, better technology, improved pensions, and enhanced support from local and national social and health services. The changes saw not so much the invention of new desires as a widening capacity to fulfil them. Finding the time, space, and resources to enjoy solitude was, however, still conditional on a range of physical and social assets.[131] This was particularly the case for women, whose ability to enjoy the forms of recreational withdrawal developed by men was one of the features of the twentieth century, particularly in the post-war era. The constraints of Virginia Woolf's *A Room of One's Own* never entirely disappeared. In her 1998 celebration of women's solitude, Delease Wear cautioned that the writers she had discussed were for the most part 'white, privileged and without immediate dependants'.[132]

The difficulty of enjoying solitude whilst containing loneliness increased as personal and collective prosperity fell.[133] Although there are also problems of definition and measurement in this field, recent data suggest that fourteen million people, over a fifth of the population, are in poverty and one and a half million are destitute.[134] The reversal of the post-war reduction in inequality has had multiple effects in the field of social relations. Deprivation has impacted directly on solitude with regard to inadequate housing, insufficient surplus cash to spend on personal pastimes, and exclusion from physical and virtual mobility in the form of transport systems and the use of the internet.[135] As Eric Klinenberg has recently argued, an impoverished social infrastructure renders the elderly and immobile more vulnerable to isolation and consequent mental and physical hardship.[136] At best, individuals have to turn back to the more basic forms of solitary pleasure that were discussed in the conclusion to Chapter 5, such as taking walks, reading, or watching the near ubiquitous television.[137] The poor are also less likely to have access to the services which can relieve the experience or threat of loneliness. Amongst the still provisional explorations of the interaction of mental and physical suffering, it has long been known that serious ill-health and disability are causes of loneliness, particularly, but not exclusively, amongst the elderly.[138] *A Connected Society* endorses the claim of Scope, the disability charity, that 45 per cent of those of working age, and 85 per cent of young disabled adults, experience some form of loneliness.[139] This immediately raises the question of the quality of access to surgeries and hospitals in poorer areas, and the provision of long-term support in the locality.

The post-2010 austerity programme challenges any attempt to develop a government strategy in this field. In the post-war period, a mixed economy of support developed.[140] Alongside commercial endeavours, such as dating services, and national and local welfare provision, a set of voluntary bodies emerged, supplementing collective endeavour and urging improvement. By the 1970s, the agony aunts in the flourishing women's magazines were beginning to deal with complaints not only from those unable to form relationships, but also from those who found themselves alone inside marriage or stranded by desertion or divorce. Anna Raeburn in *Woman* routinely responded by directing correspondents to a proliferating body of local and networked voluntary organizations, such as the National Federation of Solo Clubs, the National Council for the Divorced and Separated, or the Samaritans, and to municipal services such as libraries, meeting spaces, and educational classes.[141] The scope of the voluntary bodies has since widened with the development of web-based support, connecting the lonely to each other and to sources of assistance.

However, with the state unable to spend significant sums overcoming the still incomplete access to the internet, and continuing disinvestment in critical facilities such as public libraries, communal recreational facilities, and adult social services, the prospect of an effective, integrated attack on even the more acute forms of loneliness seems remote. The subject has become a proxy not for contradictions in the social relations of our times, but for the intensifying crisis in the distribution of wealth and the provision of public services.

8

CONCLUSION:
SOLITUDE IN THE DIGITAL ERA

Passengers on modern-day public transport are likely to find themselves sitting amid distant company. Alongside them, across tables and aisles, will be travellers absorbed with their mobiles, or wearing noise-cancelling headphones that deliver an isolating silence more absolute, if more sterile, than was available to almost anyone in the past. Empty rooms in domestic interiors then were rarely insulated from life elsewhere in the house. The solitary walker in fields and woods was surrounded by birdsong and the rustle of wind through the grass and trees. Perhaps only the monk's cell offered such an absence of sound, although there were occasional sandals slapping on the stone floors of cloisters, and bells marking the canonical hours.

The digital revolution represents the culmination of the search not only for sociability but, as important, also for its absence. At the outset of this history, it was suggested that there were three categories of solitude as a practice: physical, networked, and abstracted. Since the nineteenth century, the latter two have become more salient. On an increasingly crowded island, the difficulties of finding space have grown, making alternative means of withdrawal from company correspondingly more attractive. The earlier debate about solitude engaged an audience that could readily imagine an alternative to urban living. Despite the rapidly expanding capital city, four-fifths of the population still lived in the countryside, in sight of fields or less cultivated landscapes. The subsequent urbanization and expansion of transport networks could not fail to put pressure on what had appeared at the end of the eighteenth century to be the most obvious theatre of solitude. As a consequence, in a host of social and recreational endeavours, individuals have harnessed the communications technology of their era not only to connect with distant friends, relations, and other enthusiasts but also to withdraw from the life going on in crowded interiors and external spaces in order to concentrate on private thoughts and activities.

The invention of the World Wide Web in 1991, and the subsequent development of software and hardware to exploit its capacities, met deep-seated demands for both networked and abstracted solitude. Noise-cancelling headphones, designed initially for the benefit of aeroplane pilots and passengers, could be used either to enjoy silence or as a more efficient, and expensive, version of the Sony Walkman.[1] They became part of the arsenal of consumer products designed to enable connections with distant people and bodies of information and entertainment. A reason why the take-up of networks and devices has been so rapid and irreversible in the early twenty-first century is that they provide a solution to the perennial problem of how to be alone yet also in company.

The key innovations are not much more than a decade old. The launch of the smartphone in 2007, and its increasing use for asynchronous text-messaging rather than conversation, has created the emblematic figure of our times, silently hunched over a hand-held object, either in a separate space or mentally withdrawn from the immediate press of people. If nothing else, the iPhone and its competitors have supplied activity for the fingers missing since the decline of smoking. By 2018, digital communication was reaching saturation point amongst those under fifty-five, and smartphones were increasingly replacing computers as the means of access to the internet. Nearly 90 per cent of British adults are online and are spending an average of twenty-four hours a week on their devices.[2] Amongst the young, on both sides of the Atlantic, use is pervasive. In the United States, teenagers are sending an average of thirty or more texts a day, and 45 per cent of the cohort were recently found to be 'online on a near-constant basis'.[3] Technology and consumer markets have been agents of change throughout this study.

They drove the conscious experience of solitude from a privilege of the educated male to the practice of all but the poorest or least interested in the late modern era. In this sense, the smartphone has not been a disruptive innovation but rather the culmination of a journey through correspondence, print, telephone, film, and television. Earlier generations could only dream of a device that allowed the individual at will to be apart from society but instantly in contact with selected groups and individuals.

The speed of recent change makes it difficult to conduct an audit of its consequences. Johann Zimmermann was debating the implications of solitude with Petrarch across four centuries, and Petrarch in turn was talking to pre-Christian authorities about shared dilemmas in the withdrawal from society. The first appearance of texting phones was barely a moment ago in this long chronology, and their saturated presence in developed countries yet more recent. Although some research has been conducted into the concurrent behaviours of different age groups, it is too soon to mount long-term studies of its impact over the life-course.[4] There is a preoccupation with the potential psychological and physiological damage caused to teenage users of digital media which is reminiscent of the long obsession with the solitary vice categorized by Tissot in the mid-eighteenth century.[5] We cannot yet know how the digital natives will perform as they grow up to be lovers, parents, and pensioners and face new challenges in moving between electronic and verbal communication.[6]

It is, however, possible to draw a parallel between the immersive presence of new technology and the evolution of patterns of withdrawal from society. As digital devices and their use are now commonplace, so also, over a much longer time-frame, withdrawing from company has ceased to be a deviation or a novelty. Solitude has become normal. It is built into the techniques for living of most men and women, so commonplace as at times to seem scarcely worth naming or discussing. The adversarial drama of Zimmermann's treatise has been transformed into a rich and varied set of everyday narratives. The 'little intervals of accidental solitude' that Abraham Cowley recognized have grown and diversified, becoming available to those he termed 'the very meanest of people'.[7] Men and women, teenagers and still younger children, have the capacity to move between their own company and chosen social groups with a freedom and fluidity that was rarely available at the end of the eighteenth century. People have enjoyed more domestic space, found more time to devote to their own activities, and had more disposable income to spend on private pastimes. Since 1800, the average consumption per head of market goods and services has grown tenfold in advanced Western countries.[8] There were many ways in which this prosperity manifested itself in collective pastimes and social engagements. But it also encouraged all kinds of withdrawal into empty, heated, lighted domestic spaces where, as the epochal Parker Morris report of 1961 advocated, different members of the family could move between shared and solitary pursuits.

Growth has reset the polarities of solitude. At the beginning of this study, the meaning of the condition was seen in relation to its antithesis. Its salience at the end of the eighteenth century reflected the anxieties generated by the Enlightenment endorsement of sociability. More recent developments have witnessed not the triumph of one alternative over the other, but rather a reconsideration of how the relation between them should be understood.

Over much of the period, networked solitude was seen as a necessary and increasingly productive companion to physical solitude. As a larger proportion of the population lived in the bustling streets of expanding towns and cities, so the capacity of communication technologies mentally to free them from pressing company was welcomed. Of all the ways of being alone described in this history, the vicarious form was perhaps the most widely practised. From the desert fathers through to Robinson Crusoe, the Romantic poets, Frankenstein, narratives of solo exploration, print and later media on quiet recreations, guides to solitary undertakings, texts on revived monasticism, and mind, body, and spirit publications, the proportion of the population that has enjoyed solitude from the comfort of their armchairs far outweighs those who have actually experienced it, particularly in the more extreme forms.

At their most creative, digital data and narratives have further expanded the capacity of networked solitude to abstract users from their immediate surroundings and allow them to engage with distant people and alternative worlds. The growing use of the internet, however, has raised two urgent concerns. In the first case, with increasing awareness of the surveillance capacities of digital media, the function of solitude as the last realm of personal independence has been counterposed to the use of communication systems to extend its reach. Rather than enriching the realm of withdrawal, the smartphone connected to search engines and social media may impoverish it altogether. The facial-recognition technologies now being introduced threaten to abolish the very concept of solitude. There will no longer be a space in which individuals can talk to themselves without being seen or overheard by corporate or state agencies.

Secondly, immersion in the internet universe revives Zimmermann's apprehension that there were forms of withdrawal that constituted a one-way journey. Doubts have been raised about the impact of digital communication on an appropriate balance between the solitary and the social. It has been argued that the online universe locks the user into a realm where neither true solitude nor effective interpersonal relations can be enjoyed.[9] As terms such as obsession and addiction are applied, particularly to younger internet users, so worries have surfaced that the skills of face-to-face interaction are being lost.[10] Those spending as much as a day a week text-messaging will have neither the time nor the capacity to talk to each other. In the view of Sherry Turkle, the effects are mutually destructive. The hours spent online prevent the development of the sense of inner being required for effective personal relations, and in turn the decay of spoken communication impedes the creation of a fuller identity. 'Solitude,' Turkle writes, 'reinforces a secure sense of self, and with that, the capacity for empathy. Then, conversation with others provides rich material for self-reflection. Just as alone we prepare to talk together, together we learn how to engage in more productive solitude.'[11]

There are problems of historical perspective in this analysis. In particular, we lack systematic knowledge of the scale of face-to-face interaction in past societies. As we have seen, for instance, a housewife in the nineteenth and much of the twentieth centuries often spent long hours in enforced isolation, with no-one to talk to except young children, or servants, whose topics of conversation were limited by the social relations in which they stood. Her returning husband might well have lacked the interest or energy to discuss her day, or have preferred to unburden himself to male friends in the club or the public house. If the subsequent growth of the companionate marriage increased the possibility of sociable exchange, the parallel expansion of separate bed-rooms for adolescent children, and of private spaces for adult activities within the home, created further obstacles to casual talking. Equally, the rapid rise in single-person households since 1945 has formed new islands of silence in domestic living. Whether there was a moment in late modernity when peak conversation was reached and passed requires further investigation.

A consequence of the debate has been a renewed emphasis on older categories of withdrawal. If solitary and sociable behaviours have a shared enemy, they also have a joint remedy. In both cases, healthy practice consists in conducting life with the mobile and the laptop turned off. Physical solitude has a newly enhanced attraction, as net-worked and abstracted forms are threatened by excessive dependency on digital communication. Surveillance is best avoided by disconnec-tion from networks and escaping the reach of cameras. The difficulty is that in the early twenty-first century, many of the practices associated with a bodily absence from the company of others have forever lost their lustre.

Lone walking through unpeopled countryside, which has been a theme throughout this study, can less readily be experienced and cel-ebrated in our own times. The last great literary pedestrian journey of the twentieth century in Britain was W. G. Sebald's walk down the Suffolk coast from Lowestoft. *The Rings of Saturn* is a meditation on the decline of communities, families, and empires. The most extensive description of a place is an account of Dunwich, which was overcome by waves in the Middle Ages. The pollution of the land and the sea is a recurring theme. 'Every year,' Sebald writes, 'the rivers bear thousands of tons of mercury, cadmium and lead, and mountains of fertilizer and pesticides, out into the North Sea. A substantial proportion of the heavy metals and other toxic substances sink into the waters of the Dogger Bank, where a third of the fish are now born with strange deformities and excrescences.'[12] There is no compensation to be found in farmland, which is mechanized and almost completely devoid of people. Towards the end of the book, Sebald turns inland from Orford:

I walked for nearly four hours, and in all that time I saw nothing apart from harvested cornfields stretching away into the distance under a sky heavy with clouds, and dark islands of trees surrounding the farmsteads which stood well back from the road, a mile or two apart from each other. I encountered hardly any vehicles while treading this seemingly unending straight, and I knew then as little as I know now whether walking in this solitary way was more of a pleasure or a pain.[13]

Such expeditions had always required the walker to render invisible those who worked on the land they travelled through. Now the emptiness of the fields is a measure not of free space but of the continuing displacement of people by machines.

At the same time, exploration of extreme nature, long the subject of public fascination and literary celebration, is irredeemably compromised. None of the early-twenty-first-century adventurers suppose they travel in search of a prelapsarian creation. At best they are using whatever publicity they can attract to draw attention to problems of pollution and global warming that are not readily visible from within urban societies. A recent contribution to this genre of travel literature, Dan Richards' *Outpost: A Journey to the Wild Ends of the Earth*, begins by citing Jack Kerouac: 'no man should go through life without once experiencing healthy, even bored solitude in the wilderness'.[14] It then recognizes that such an enterprise can only be justified if it is used to bear witness to the harm being caused to the remotest corners of the planet:

> For better or worse *homo sapiens* are a questing, consuming, destructive species. We have now entered the age of Anthropocene – humans are ruining the planet. It might be better for the Earth if we stopped exploring, lest the human litter which now blights the top of Everest and the depths of the sea spread to every part of the world. . . . I believe the more we know about our world, the more we see, the more deeply we engage with it, understand its nature, the more likely we are to be good custodians and reverse our most selfish destructive behaviour.[15]

Competitive solo endeavours have retreated from the heroic to the trivial or the wilfully perverse. No longer do they represent the last appeal to an imperial past. As technology robs the Golden Globe yacht race of much of its original fascination, a retro fiftieth-anniversary competition was recently organized, with competitors confined to monohulls and to the communication devices used by Knox-Johnston and his fellow yachtsmen in 1968–9. Only five of the eighteen competitors completed the race, which was won by 'French sailing legend' Jean-Luc Van Den Heede, who took almost three times as long as the current record.[16] Ever-more obscure tasks have to be invented to attract the attention of donors. In 2018, John Farnworth from Lancashire made his way to the Everest Base Camp whilst continually juggling a football. He later walked sixty miles alone across the Sahara Desert performing keepie-uppies. Elsewhere, John Ketchell from Hampshire completed the first solo circumnavigation of the world by gyrocopter in 2019, and earlier in the year a Frenchman, Jean-Jacques Savin, became the only man to float across the Atlantic in a tub without the aid of oars or sails.

The long-term growth of possessive individualism has complicated the role of physical solitude as a response to modernity. On the one hand, improvements in consumption and communication have done much to democratize the experience of lone behaviours. On the other, they have kept alive the role of solitude as a critical response to the materialism of the age. Withdrawal from excessive spending and overheated social intercourse has a renewed appeal. However, the institutional means of accommodating and supporting such retreats have lost much of their influence.

The return of enclosed orders in Britain in the middle of the nineteenth century, and the revived interest in monastic seclusion after the Second World War, generated both fascination and repulsion, partly because of the buildings in which they were housed and the religious hierarchies that controlled them. Myths flourished about the monasteries and convents when the doors were locked against outsiders, and their inmates took vows of obedience to their superiors. The most famous hermit of the post-1945 era, Thomas Merton, fought increasingly against both the abbot in his Trappist community and the broader Catholic system of censorship. The millennia-long attraction of the desert hermits was finally undermined by the relentless spread of communication systems which destroyed prolonged attempts to keep secret the sexual abuse that had flourished in uninspected institutions. At the same time, the internet helped to open up Christian traditions to information about alternative spiritual practices. The emerging culture of retreats and meditation both reflected and was sustained by the absence of authority in the digital universe. Any individual on their phone or computer could explore a preferred mode of spiritual self-examination and discover the means of creating their own set of practices or participating in those of others. Information was at once eclectic and centred on the interests of the enquirer, who was free to choose whether or not to make connections with wider structures of power and inequality.

The tone of the debate about solitude has shifted its emphasis. The anxieties which fill the pages of Zimmermann's treatise and the fierce arguments about forms of total isolation in the following decades are now often difficult to comprehend. In part this is because of the diminishing role of institutions. The intensity of the nineteenth-century debates about prolonged solitary meditation reflected a bid for power by organized religion in conjunction with the state. Both the attraction of solitary confinement and the reaction against it were consequences of the attempt by governments to construct a national system of punishment using the personnel and doctrines of the Church of England. The theology and architecture of the monastic tradition were appropriated to serve an urgent secular purpose. The outcome of the long experiment that began in Pentonville in 1842 was a terminal loss of confidence in the effects of enforced, enclosed religious reflection. Ambitions of character-changing biblical discourse between prisoners and chaplains were eventually replaced by continuing concern about basic issues of mental health, educational deprivation, and inadequate hygiene and security. Where once separation was the solution to the process of deterrence, punishment, and rehabilitation, now it has become an emblematic weakness of the entire penal system. Even here, digital communication plays its role. Amongst the critical shortcomings of twenty-first-century prisons is the apparent ease with which inmates can smuggle phones into their cells and use them to organize drug supplies and other contraband.

The risk register of solitude has changed. In the pioneering texts of modern psychology, religious mania was an especially pernicious consequence of intense private prayer in isolation from the collective forms of Christian worship. The advocates of a renewed eremitical tradition gloried in the perils inherent in their lone conversations with a solitary, silent Deity. By the beginning of the present century, however, the mere act of withdrawing from company was no longer seen as a pathology of prevailing forms of intercourse. Instead the tendency to panic about the condition of interpersonal relations has become focused on the category of loneliness, which may be seen as a failure of solitude rather than of sociability. Critics of the digital revolution have included in their charge sheet the accusation that it has increased the incidence of this form of suffering.[17] It is partly that heavy users may lose the skills of maintaining intimate personal relations or the opportunity to practise them, and partly that at times of adjustment and insecurity they can be thrust into depression by the apparently flourishing lives of those they encounter on social networks.[18]

As with the impact of smartphones more generally, there is a problem of measurement. Whereas solitude is still rarely counted, loneliness, in common with digital media, is constantly translated into numbers. Thus, according to a recent American study of teenage internet users, 'a stunning 31% more 8th and 10th graders felt lonely in 2015 than 2011, along with 22% more 12th graders'.[19] The preceding chapter reviewed the uncertainty of this kind of arithmetic, and stressed the high incidence of relatively minor transitional loneliness as individuals negotiate the increasingly complex developmental stages of their lives. There is also a misleading tendency to generalize across the population from the experience of a narrow cohort of teenagers. It is perhaps not surprising that a recent study of those who had survived the emotional maelstrom of adolescence and later formed long-term, intimate relationships attributed only a minor role to digital devices. It reported that '10% of internet users who are married or partnered say that the internet has had a "major impact" on their relationship, and 17% say that it has had a "minor impact". Fully 72% of married or committed online adults said the internet has "no real impact at all" on their partnership.'[20]

For the most part, particularly amongst the elderly, computers and mobile phones are performing the role of earlier communication technologies of helping individuals to stay on the right side of the line between solitude and loneliness. It is easier to be content with the absence of physical company if virtual contact can readily be made with friends and family, which remains the primary reported function of internet use.[21] Digital media are especially useful for those who are prevented by incapacity or other forms of ill-health from leaving their homes and mixing with others.[22] The question then becomes one of inequalities of resource as the poor and less educated struggle to manage relatively expensive and complex equipment.

As with any emotion, solitude has a recognizable identity over time, even as its features are reshaped by historical circumstances.[23] Despite the impact of a wide range of cultural and material forces, it is still possible to conduct a conversation with the writers who devoted renewed attention to the topic around the end of the eighteenth century. The digital present informs our own perspective. 'As we adapt to evolving technological environments,' notes Michael Harris in the most recent survey of the topic, 'as we respond to shifts in living arrangements, as we inhale the rhetoric and poetics of our own time, our relationship to solitude keeps changing.'[24] An effect of these alterations, however, is to throw renewed emphasis on the continuities over time. For all the debate, despite the major shifts in the polarities of withdrawal and sociability, there remains a recognizable core to the experience and practice of solitude. Zimmermann's definition, 'a tendency to self-collection and freedom', holds true in our own age.[25]

There is a persisting attraction in the escape from the company of others. Other people are work, however necessary and creative. At one level it is simply a matter of rest, of an opportunity to reflect on relationships and on the broader transactions of life. A chosen moment of retreat makes it possible to find new purpose and recharge the spirit for resumed encounters. Except for those still committed to a silent conversation with a hidden God, there is an awareness of a necessary movement between conversation and its absence. In her recent *Republic of Noise*, Diana Senechal echoes Zimmermann's prescription: 'The greatest strength may lie in a flexible solitude, one that can bear with company and lack of company.'[26] As Daniel Defoe once argued, the healthiest form of solitude is embedded in the busiest of lives.[27] A sense of proportion and value resides in constant transitions between states of private reflection and sociable encounter.

Since the classical philosophers and the desert hermits, solitude has been an intensely intertextual event. From the everyday recreations of walking and fishing to heroic exploits in extreme nature and profound spiritual explorations, actors have had a book in their minds, informing their ambitions and testing their outcomes. Upper-case and lower-case solitude have formed complex patterns over time. From 'Zimmerman on Solitude' onwards, there has been a constant exchange between reading alone and reading about being alone. The spread of literacy and cheap literature since the early nineteenth century, and the current digital revolution, have merely broadened the culture, diversifying the available material, shortening the journeys between print and practice.

At one level, this has been a history of doing nothing at all. Solitary 'peace and quietness' is too easily overlooked as the means by which most people in the past recuperated from their labours in the home or the workplace. At the same time, tracing the subject through its varied forms has highlighted the importance of physical activity in the purpose and effect of solitude. From Wordsworth marching across Europe on his unremarkable legs and 'the Elastic Novice' Dickens striding through the streets of London with random purpose, to the host of men and women strolling out from overcrowded homes, with or without a dog on a leash, exercise has calmed and organized the mind. The same is true of the multitude of quiet recreations that this account has sought to rescue from the neglect of history. Doing things with hands, whether sewing, knitting, and embroidery, turning over playing cards, completing word games, collecting stamps, breeding animals, digging the soil, casting a fishing line, making household items, or, until comparatively recently, lighting a cigarette, were in many ways the substance as well as the form of solitary practices. Such pastimes not only required but also created time and space. They signalled to others that practitioners wanted their own company, whether or not they were physically removed from those around them. Concentration on manipulative tasks permitted the mind to make its own journeys over moments or hours, whether fleeting thoughts and daydreams or more purposeful contemplation. It was an escape from disciplined labour, a device for taking feelings and ideas out to play. If there is an arc of rise and fall in this context, it is in the long-term growth in the range of solitary physical activities culminating in the constant tapping of mobile phones in the presence of others and the use of gym equipment to disconnect solitary exercise from destination and the open air.

The drivers of change across this period have embraced major structural forces. Demography, the consumer market, technological innovation, and communication systems have reshaped the purpose and practice of solitude. For the most part, however, these processes have facilitated rather than limited individual choice as to whether to keep the company of others or withdraw from it. Men and women decided to live alone in increasing numbers after the Second World War because it became practically feasible to do so and because at different times they preferred their own company to that of their parents, or grown-up children, or unsatisfactory partners. The issue of agency raises a caution against the argument that individuals are now, as Sara Maitland writes, 'terrified of being alone with themselves'.[28] More precisely, they are anxious about the denial of free will in their social arrangements. Where they can embrace solitude as an option, they can find many ways of leading as full a life as their age and health permit. It is where desired outcomes are confounded by bereavement or the prolonged failure of personal relationships, or constrained by public and private deprivation, that loneliness sets in, and great suffering can follow.

A final connection with the past lies in the beleaguered presence of the natural world, the time-honoured location of solitary retreat. It may be under every kind of threat, but at the end of the second decade of the twenty-first century, it remains some kind of resource for self-collection and freedom. Despite all the population growth and environmental destruction since the beginning of the industrial revolution, people can still walk away from company into nearby parks and countryside, or work on their gardens in their private plot of Eden.

NOTES

Chapter 1 Introduction: Solitude Considered

1 *The Gentleman's Magazine*, LXI, 2 (1791): 1215.

2 George S. Rousseau, 'Science, Culture and the Imagination: Enlightenment Configurations', in *The Cambridge History of Science, Vol. 4*, ed. Roy Porter (Cambridge: Cambridge University Press, 2003), 768.

3 Jay MacPherson, *The Spirit of Solitude: Conventions and Continuities in Late Romance* (New Haven: Yale University Press, 1982), 56. English editions of Zimmermann's writings, and subsequent discussions of his work, freely anglicized his name to 'Zimmerman'. This text uses his Swiss-German name, although the references and quotations will, where appropriate, keep the spelling adopted by a publisher or commentator.

4 'Zimmerman on Solitude', *The Critical Review*, 3 (1791): 14.

5 The first English versions were based on an edited translation of a French translation made by J. B. Mercier, which omitted eight chapters critical of solitude. These were included in a fuller version published in 1798 which is used here. See 'Advertisement', in Johann Zimmerman, *Solitude Considered with Respect to its Dangerous Influence Upon the Mind and Heart* (London: C. Dilly, 1798); Frederick H. Wilkens, *Early Influence of German*

Literature in America (Reprint No. 1, *Americana Germanica*, III, 2, London: Macmillan, 1900), 49–50; Anne Vila, 'Solitary Identities: Perspectives on the "Contemplative" Life from 18th-Century Literature, Medicine, and Religion (France, Switzerland)', presented 18 July 2019 at the congress of the International Society for Eighteenth-Century Studies in Edinburgh. I am grateful to Anne Vila for advice on the different editions.

6 Zimmerman, *Solitude*, 316.

7 Zimmerman, *Solitude*, 88.

8 Wolf Lepenies, *Melancholy and Society*, trans. Jeremy Gaines and Doris Jones (Cambridge, MA: Harvard University Press, 1992), 62.

9 See Francis Petrarch, *The Life of Solitude*, trans. Jacob Zeitlin ([Urbana]: University of Illinois Press, 1924). Encouraged by the success of Zimmermann's *Solitude*, one of his English publishers, Vernor and Hood, issued a new translation of the life of Petrarch in 1797. Advertisement in *The Times*, 7 April 1797: 2.

10 Samuel-Auguste Tissot, *The Life of Zimmerman* (London: Vernor and Hood, 1797), 3–10.

11 Zimmerman, *Solitude*, 66.

12 Rousseau, 'Science, Culture and the Imagination', 768.

13 Zimmerman, *Solitude*, 75.

14 Zimmerman, *Solitude*, 2.

15 Lawrence E. Klein, 'Sociability, Solitude, and Enthusiasm', in *Enthusiasm and Enlightenment in Europe, 1650–1850*, ed. Lawrence E. Klein and Anthony J. La Vopa (San Marino, CA: Huntingdon Library, 1998), 155–6.

16 Johann Zimmerman, *Aphorisms on Men, Morals and Things: Translated from the Mss Of J. G. Zimmerman* (London: Vernor and Hood, 1800), 40–1.

17 Denis Diderot, *Encyclopédie* (1765), vol. XV, 324. See also Robert Sayre, *Solitude in Society: A Sociological Study in French Literature* (Cambridge MA: Harvard University Press, 1978), 49.

18 Cited in Lepenies, *Melancholy and Society*, 65.

19 Petrarch, *Life of Solitude*, 125

20 Michel de Montaigne, *The Complete Essays*, trans. and ed. M. A. Screech (London: Penguin, 2013), 269.

21 On the context of his essay see Brian Vickers, ed., *Public and Private Life in the Seventeenth Century: The Mackenzie–Evelyn Debate* (Delmar, NY: Scholars' Facsimiles & Reprints, 1986), x–xxxiv.

22 John Evelyn, *Publick Employment and an Active Life Prefer'd to Solitude … In Reply to a late Ingenious Essay of a contrary Title* (London: H. Herringman, 1667), 69.

23 Evelyn, *Publick Employment*, 77.

24 Evelyn, *Publick Employment*, 118.

25 Zimmerman, *Solitude*, 21.

26 Robert Burton ('Democritus Junior'), *The Anatomy of Melancholy* (Oxford: Henry Cripps, 1621), 116.

27 Zimmerman, *Solitude*, 3.

28 *The Gentleman's Magazine*, LXI, 2 (1791): 1215.

29 On the development of the autobiographical form, see, Michael Mascuch, *Origins of the Individualist Self: Autobiography and Self-Identity in England, 1591–1791* (Cambridge: Polity, 1997), 7–23.

30 Jean-Jacques Rousseau, *Reveries of the Solitary Walker*, trans. Russell Goulbourne (1782; Oxford: Oxford University Press, 2011), 7.

31 Zimmerman, *Solitude*, 165–6.

32 Zimmerman, *Solitude*, 164.

33 Sarah Bakewell, *How to Live: Or A Life of Montaigne in One Question and Twenty Attempts at an Answer* (London: Chatto & Windus, 2010), 162.

34 Tissot, *Life of Zimmerman*, 37. On the friendship of Tissot and Zimmermann, see Antoinette Emch-Dériaz, *Tissot: Physician of the Enlightenment* (New York: Peter Lang, 1992), 28.

35 Zimmerman, *Solitude*, 15.

36 Tissot, *Life of Zimmerman*, 91.

37 Zimmerman, *Solitude*, 3.

38 Zimmerman, *Solitude*, 19

39 Jean-Étienne Dominique Esquirol, *Mental Maladies: A Treatise on Insanity*, trans. E. K. Hunt (Philadelphia: Lea and Blanchard, 1845), 199.

40 Matthew Bell, *Melancholia: The Western Malady* (Cambridge: Cambridge University Press, 2014), 54; Stanley W. Jackson,

Melancholia and Depression: From Hippocratic Times to Modern Times (New Haven: Yale University Press, 1986), 4–17; Esquirol, *Mental Maladies*, 199.

41 Edward Shorter, *From Paralysis to Fatigue: A History of Psychosomatic Illness in the Modern Era* (New York: Free Press, 1992), 15–16; Rousseau, 'Science, Culture and the Imagination', 779–80.

42 Lepenies, *Melancholy and Society*, 65.

43 Burton, *Anatomy of Melancholy*, 119.

44 Thomas Trotter, *A View of the Nervous Temperament* (London: Longman, Hurst, Rees, Orme & Brown, 1812), xiv.

45 Zimmerman, *Solitude*, 156–7.

46 William Buchan, *Domestic Medicine; or, The Family Physician* (1769; Edinburgh: no pub., 1802), 230.

47 Philippe Pinel, *A Treatise on Insanity*, trans. D. D. Davies (1801; London: Cadell and Davies, 1806), 136. Also Alexander Crichton, *An Inquiry into the Nature and Origin of Mental Derangement*, 2 vols (London: T. Cadell, Junior, and W. Davies, 1798), vol. 2, 229.

48 Philip Koch, *Solitude: A Philosophical Encounter* (Chicago: Open Court, 1994), 212.

49 Cited in Roy Porter and Dorothy Porter, *In Sickness and in Health: The British Experience 1650–1850* (London: Fourth Estate, 1988), 208.

50 Zimmerman, *Solitude*, 60.

51 John D. Barbour, 'A View from Religious Studies: Solitude and Spirituality', in *The Handbook of Solitude: Psychological Perspectives on Social Isolation, Social Withdrawal, and Being Alone*, ed. Robert J. Coplan and Julie C. Bowker (Chichester: Wiley Blackwell, 2014), 559–60.

52 Zimmerman, *Solitude*, 109.

53 Klein, 'Sociability, Solitude, and Enthusiasm', 164–7.

54 Zimmerman, *Solitude*, 30–1.

55 Cited in Michael Hill, *The Religious Order* (London: Heinemann Educational, 1973), 51.

56 Evelyn, *Publick Employment*, 5–6.

57 John Haslam, *Observations on Madness and Melancholy* (London: J. Callow, 1809), 263. See also Pinel, *Treatise on Insanity*, 142.

58 Haslam, *Observations on Madness*, 265.

59 Richard von Krafft-Ebing, *Text-Book of Insanity*, trans. Charles Gilbert Chaddock (Philadelphia: F. A. Davis, 1904), 302.

60 Zimmerman, *Solitude*, 158.

61 Gordon Campbell, *The Hermit in the Garden* (Oxford: Oxford University Press, 2013), 96–144; Edward S. Harwood, 'Luxurious Hermits: Asceticism, Luxury and Retirement in the Eighteenth-Century English Garden', *Studies in the History of Gardens & Designed Landscapes*, 20, 4 (2000): 274–8. On the hiring of a hermit to occupy the cave complex created on the Hawkstone Estate in 1783, see Robert Macfarlane, *Mountains of the Mind* (London: Granta Books, 2003), 151.

62 Rev. Joseph Milner, *The History of the Church of Christ*, 3 vols (1794–1809; new edn, London: Longman, Brown, Green & Longmans, 1847), vol. 1, 554–5.

63 Louis F. Peck, *A Life of Matthew G. Lewis* (Cambridge, MA: Harvard University Press, 1961), 11–13; Joseph James Irwin, *M. G. 'Monk' Lewis* (Boston: Twayne, 1976), 35–59.

64 On the writing of *The Monk* and its German sources, see Matthew G. Lewis, *The Life and Correspondence of M. G. Lewis*, 2 vols (London: Henry Colburn, 1839), vol. 1, 73; André Parreaux, *The Publication of The Monk: A Literary Event 1796–1798* (Paris: Librarie Marcel Didier, 1960), 26–31; Syndy Conger, *Matthew G. Lewis, Charles Robert Maturin and the Germans* (Salzburg: Institut für Englische Sprache und Literatur, 1977), 12–159; D. L. Macdonald, *Monk Lewis: A Critical Biography* (Toronto: University of Toronto Press, 2000), 76–80, 91–127.

65 Denis Diderot, *Memoirs of a Nun (La Religieuse)*, trans. Francis Birrell (1796; London: George Routledge, 1928), 60.

66 Matthew Lewis, *The Monk* (1796; Oxford: Oxford University Press, 1998), 53–4.

67 Lewis, *The Monk*, 440.

68 Lewis, *Life and Correspondence*, 151–2. See, for instance, the contemporary review by Coleridge: [Samuel Taylor Coleridge], 'Lewis's Romance of the Monk', *The Critical Review*, XIX (February 1797): 195, 197.

69 Parreaux, *Publication of The Monk*, 63–70. On the widespread and

immediate popularity of cheap versions of the novel, see Carolyn Steedman, *An Everyday Life of the English Working Class: Work, Self and Sociability in the Early Nineteenth Century* (Cambridge: Cambridge University Press, 2013), 31.

70 Samuel-Auguste Tissot, *Onanism*, trans. A. Hume (1760; London: T. Pridden, 1766), 22. On the subsequent debate, see Thomas W. Laqueur, *Solitary Sex: A Cultural History of Masturbation* (New York: Zone Books, 2003).

71 Tissot, *Onanism*, 129.

72 Zimmermann's emphasis on this issue is discussed in Margaret Mary Wood, *Paths of Loneliness: The Individual Isolated in Modern Society* (New York: Columbia University Press, 1960), 6–7.

73 Zimmerman, *Solitude*, 62–3.

74 Zimmerman, *Solitude*, 312.

75 Zimmerman, *Solitude*, 169.

76 Zimmerman, *Solitude*, 162.

77 Zimmerman, *Solitude*, 21.

78 Zimmerman, *Solitude*, 169–70.

79 Zimmerman, *Solitude*, 12.

80 Zimmerman, *Solitude*, 193. On his unhappy residence in Brugg, see Tissot, *Life of Zimmerman*, 28. Brugg (often anglicized to Brug) had a population of around a thousand at this time.

81 MacPherson, *The Spirit of Solitude*, 56.

82 Zimmerman, *Solitude*, 90.

83 Klein, 'Sociability, Solitude, and Enthusiasm', 164–7.

84 John Thelwall, *The Peripatetic; Or, Sketches of the Heart, of Nature and Society* (London: for the author, 1793), 8.

85 Michael Harris, *Solitude: In Pursuit of a Singular Life in a Crowded World* (London: Random House, 2017), 7.

86 James Vernon, *Distant Strangers: How Britain Became Modern* (Berkeley: University of California Press, 2014), 19.

87 John Milton, *The Doctrine and Discipline of Divorce* (1643), republished as John Milton, *Divorce: In Two Books* (London: Sherwood, Neely and Jones, 1820), 17.

88 *Oxford English Dictionary*. See also the discussion in Kevin Lewis, *Lonesome: The Spiritual Meanings of American Solitude* (London: I. B. Tauris, 2009), 4.

89 Lord Byron, *Childe Harold's Pilgrimage*, Canto III, verse LXII, lines 590–4.

90 Byron, *Childe Harold's Pilgrimage*, Canto III, verse LXVIII, lines 648–51.

91 On the increasing incidence of the term, which was almost unknown in the eighteenth century, see Fay Bound Alberti, 'This "Modern Epidemic": Loneliness as an Emotion Cluster and a Neglected Subject in the History of Emotions', *Emotion Review*, 10, 3 (July 2018): 3–5.

92 A Christmas Episode from *Master Humphrey's Clock* (11 April 1840), in Charles Dickens, *A Christmas Carol and Other Christmas Writings*, intro. and notes by Michael Slater (London: Penguin Classics, 2010), 20, 22. For a similar discussion of 'solitude' as a friendless state in the metropolis, see William Hazlitt, 'London Solitude', in *New Writings of William Hazlitt*, ed. Duncan Wu, 2 vols (Oxford: Oxford University Press, 2007), vol. 2, 354–5.

93 G. K. Chesterton, 'On Loneliness', in *Come to Think of It . . . : A Book of Essays* (London: Methuen, 1930): 82.

94 Frieda Fromm-Reichmann, 'On Loneliness', in *Psychoanalysis and Psychotherapy: Selected Papers of Frieda Fromm-Reichmann*, ed. Dexter M. Bullard (Chicago: University of Chicago Press, 1959), 326.

95 Anthony Storr, *Solitude* (1989; London: HarperCollins, 1997), ix.

96 Ira J. Cohen, *Solitary Action: Acting on Our Own in Everyday Life* (New York: Oxford University Press, 2016), 2.

97 James Daybell, *The Material Letter in Early Modern England: Manuscript Letters and the Culture and Practices of Letter-Writing, 1512–1625* (London: Palgrave Macmillan, 2012), 20; Gemma Allen, *The Cooke Sisters: Education, Piety and Politics in Early Modern England* (Manchester: Manchester University Press, 2013), 8–9.

98 Susan Whyman, *The Pen and the People: English Letter-Writers 1660–1800* (Oxford: Oxford University Press, 2009), 9–10. Also David Vincent, *Privacy: A Short History* (Cambridge: Polity, 2016), 47.

99 Tissot, *Life of Zimmerman*, 100.

100 David Vincent, *Literacy and Popular Culture: England 1750–1914* (Cambridge: Cambridge University Press, 1993), 32–49.

101 See, for instance, Diana Senechal, *Republic of Noise: The Loss*

of Solitude in Schools and Culture (Lanham, MD: Rowman & Littlefield, 2014), 34.

102 [Daniel Defoe], *Serious Reflections during the Life and Surprising Adventures of Robinson Crusoe: with his Vision of the Angelick World. Written by Himself*, ed. G. A. Starr (1720; London: Pickering & Chatto, 2008). The novel was not a literary success, and was not reprinted in full until 1895.

103 [Defoe], *Serious Reflections*, 61.

104 [Defoe], *Serious Reflections*, 59.

105 [Defoe], *Serious Reflections*, 66.

106 On the association of melancholy with the intellectual endeavours of highly educated men, see George Cheyne, *The English Malady: Or, a Treatise of Nervous Diseases of All Kinds* (London: G. Strahan, 1733), 181–2; Roy Porter, *Madness: A Brief History* (Oxford: Oxford University Press, 2002), 83–6.

107 Thomas Arnold, *Observations on the Nature, Kinds, Causes and Prevention of Insanity*, 2 vols (2nd edn, London: Richard Phillips, 1806), vol. 2, 64. Also Crichton, *An Inquiry into the Nature and Origin of Mental Derangement*, vol. 2, 235.

108 Buchan, *Domestic Medicine*, 119. Also Elizabeth Dolan, *Seeing Suffering in Women's Literature of the Romantic Era* (Aldershot: Ashgate, 2008), 25–7.

109 Trotter, *A View of the Nervous Temperament*, 48.

110 Lady Chudleigh, *Essays Upon Several Subjects in Prose and Verse* (London: R. Bonwicke et al., 1710), 233, 234.

111 Chudleigh, *Essays Upon Several Subjects*, 235, 237.

112 Zimmerman, *Solitude*, 144–5.

113 Abraham Cowley, 'Of Solitude', in *Abraham Cowley, Poetry & Prose* (Oxford: The Clarendon Press, 1949), 80.

114 Cowley, 'Of Solitude', 80.

115 Robert Bloomfield, *The Farmer's Boy: A Rural Poem* (London: Vernor and Hood, 1800), 31.

116 Vincent, *Privacy*, 10–13, 48, 65–6.

117 Leo Marx, *The Machine in the Garden: Technology and the Pastoral Ideal in America* (New York: Oxford University Press, 1964), 4.

118 Philip Koch, *Solitude: A Philosophical Encounter* (Chicago: Open Court, 1994), 101.

119 Senechal, *Republic of Noise*, xv.

120 Cohen, *Solitary Action*, 2.

121 For instance, Richard Holt, *Sport and the British: A Modern History* (Oxford: Oxford University Press 1990); Robert W. Malcolmson, *Popular Recreations in English Society 1700–1850* (Cambridge: Cambridge University Press, 1973); Andrew Davies, *Leisure, Gender and Poverty* (Buckingham: Open University Press, 1992).

122 See, for instance, the biographical account of the well-known pedestrian Mr Foster Powell in *The Sporting Magazine* (October 1792): 7–15. The periodical later carried an extract from Zimmermann's *Solitude*, referring to Sabbath practices in Louis XV's court: (April 1794): 5.

123 Nineteenth-century reprints were usually based on the shorter, French translation by J. B. Mercier, which omitted many of the critical comments on solitude.

124 'D'Egville' was presumably named after James Harvey D'Egville (c.1770–c.1836), a well-known dancer and choreographer.

125 *The Era*, 30 March 1845.

Chapter 2 Solitude, I'll Walk with Thee

1 John Clare to John Taylor, 10 June 1820, in *The Letters of John Clare*, ed. Mark Storey (Oxford: Clarendon Press, 1985), 74.

2 John Clare to Markham E. Sherwill, 24 February 1820, in *Letters of John Clare*, 33.

3 John Goodridge, 'Junkets and Clarissimus: The Clare–Keats Dialogue', *The Keats–Shelley Review*, 25, 1 (2011): 35; Jonathan Bate, *John Clare: A Biography* (London: Picador, 2003), 189; Nicholas Roe, *John Keats: A New Life* (New Haven: Yale University Press, 2012), 365.

4 John Taylor to John Clare, 16 March 1820, in *Letters of John Clare*, 38.

5 27–9 September 1820, cited in Goodridge, 'Junkets and Clarissimus': 44.

6 John Clare, 'Solitude', in *The Village Minstrel*, 2 vols (London: Taylor and Hessey, 1821), vol. 1, 200.

7 Clare, 'Solitude', 202.

8 Roger Sales, *John Clare: A Literary Life* (Basingstoke: Palgrave, 2002), 25.

9 James Thomson, *The Seasons* (1726; London: John Sharpe, 1816), 13.

10 Peter L. Courtier, *Pleasures of Solitude: With Other Poems* (1800; 3rd edn, London: F. C. and J. Rivington, 1804), 19.

11 Clare, 'Solitude', 206.

12 John Clare, *Sketches in the Life of John Clare* (1821), in *John Clare by Himself*, ed. Eric Robinson and David Powell (Manchester: Carcanet Press, 1996), 1–31. 'Pootys' were snails or snail shells.

13 Kim Taplin, *The English Path* (2nd edn, Sudbury: Perry Green Press, 2000), 1; Sales, *John Clare*, 2.

14 Anne D. Wallace, *Walking, Literature, and English Culture: The Origins and Uses of Peripatetic in the Nineteenth Century* (Oxford: Clarendon Press, 1993), 25–6.

15 Clare, *Village Minstrel*, vol. 1, 50.

16 John Clare, 'The Shepherd's Calendar, January', in *John Clare, Selected Poems*, ed. Jonathan Bate (London: Faber & Faber, 2004), 63.

17 Thomson, *The Seasons*, 55.

18 Joseph Arch, *From Ploughtail to Parliament: An Autobiography* (1898; London: Cresset Library, 1986), 32.

19 William Howitt, *The Rural Life of England* (1844; 3rd edn, Shannon: Irish University Press, 1971), 139.

20 Charles Shaw, *When I Was a Child* (1903; Firle: Caliban Books, 1977), 54.

21 [Alexander Somerville], *The Autobiography of a Working Man* (London: Charles Gilpin, 1848), 13.

22 M. K. Ashby, *Joseph Ashby of Tysoe, 1859–1919* (1961; London: The Merlin Press, 1974), 24. See also W. H. Hudson, *A Shepherd's Life* (1910; London: Futura, 1979), 52; Arch, *Ploughtail to Parliament*, 27.

23 Flora Thompson, *Lark Rise to Candleford* (1945; Harmondsworth: Penguin, 1973), 254. On the use of the carrier's cart in semi-rural Lancashire, see Joseph Lawson, *Progress in Pudsey during the Last Sixty Years* (Stanningley: J. W. Birdsall, 1887), 81.

24 Cited in Robert B. Shoemaker, *The London Mob: Violence and*

Disorder in Eighteenth-Century Britain (London: Hambledon and London, 2004), 3.

25 Frédéric Gros, *A Philosophy of Walking* (London: Verso, 2015), 3. Also 162.

26 David Vincent, *Privacy. A Short History* (Cambridge: Polity, 2016), 10.

27 Miles Jebb, *Walkers* (London: Constable, 1986), 84–5.

28 The one attempt to examine the long-run history of walking amongst the lower orders, Morris Marples's pioneering, *Shanks's Pony: A Study of Walking* (London: J. M. Dent, 1959), is now sixty years old. The more recent, sophisticated histories of walking have largely been confined to the activities and writings of literary pedestrians. See Rebecca Solnit, *Wanderlust: A History of Walking* (London: Verso, 2001) and Wallace, *Walking, Literature, and English Culture*.

29 See, for instance, John Clare, *Journal*, in *John Clare by Himself*, 177, 26 September 188; 179, 29 September 1824; 193, 6 November 1824.

30 Francis Place, *The Autobiography of Francis Place (1771–1854)*, ed. Mary Thale (Cambridge: Cambridge University Press, 1972), 108.

31 Patrick Joyce, *The State of Freedom* (Cambridge: Cambridge University Press, 2013), 100–43. Even more so in the United States, where it constituted the most visible presence of the federal government. Wayne E. Fuller, *The American Mail: Enlarger of the Common Life* (Chicago: University of Chicago Press, 1972), 84.

32 Cited in Duncan Minshull, ed., *The Vintage Book of Walking* (London: Vintage, 2000), 74–5.

33 John Clare, 'Autobiographical Fragments', in *John Clare by Himself*, 78.

34 Jebb, *Walkers*, 153.

35 Robert Bloomfield, *The Farmer's Boy* (1800); reprinted in *The Works of Robert Bloomfield* (London: George Routledge and Sons, 1867), 40.

36 Joseph Amato, *A History of Walking* (New York: New York University Press, 2004), 103.

37 Jo Guldi, *Roads to Power: Britain Invents the Infrastructure State* (Cambridge, MA: Harvard University Press, 2012), 20; Philip

S. Bagwell, *The Transport Revolution from 1770* (London: B. T. Batsford, 1974), 35–60.

38 Georges Duby, 'Solitude: Eleventh to Thirteenth Century', in *A History of Private Life: Vol. II, Revelations of the Medieval World*, ed. Georges Duby (Cambridge, MA: The Belknap Press, 1988), 509.

39 Richard Jefferies, *Jefferies' England*, ed. Samuel J. Looker (London: Constable, 1937), 188.

40 Thomas De Quincey, *Recollections of the Lakes and the Lake Poets* (Edinburgh: Adam and Charles Black, 1862), 139.

41 [W. Thom], *Pedestrianism; or, An Account of The Performances of celebrated Pedestrians during the Last And Present Century; with a full narrative of Captain Barclay's Public and Private Matches* (Aberdeen: Brown and Frost, 1813), 46. On the gambling pedestrian culture of the eighteenth century, see Robert W. Malcolmson, *Popular Recreations in English Society 1700–1850* (Cambridge: Cambridge University Press, 1973), 43.

42 Peter Radford, *The Celebrated Captain Barclay* (London: Headline, 2001), 1–10. Barclay achieved his goal after six weeks with twenty-three minutes to spare. Also [Thom], *Pedestrianism*, 122–7; Marples, *Shanks's Pony*, 24–9.

43 Jebb, *Walkers*, 72–73.

44 Amato, *A History of Walking*, 105–7.

45 James Dawson Burn, *The Autobiography of a Beggar Boy*, ed. David Vincent (1855; London: Europa, 1978), 107.

46 [Alexander Somerville], *The Autobiography of a Working Man* (London: Charles Gilpin, 1848), 83. See also the fifty-mile walk undertaken by William Farish in search of employment. William Farish, *The Autobiography of William Farish: The Struggles of a Hand-Loom Weaver* (Privately printed, 1889), 21.

47 Burn, *Autobiography of a Beggar Boy*, 135.

48 Humphrey Southall, 'The Tramping Artisan Revisits: Labour Mobility and Economic Distress in Early Victorian England', *Economic History Review*, XLIV, 2 (1991): 281–294; John Burnett, *Idle Hands: The Experience of Unemployment, 1790–1990* (London: Routledge, 1994), 89–90, 111–14.

49 Benjamin Shaw, *The Family Records of Benjamin Shaw: Mechanic of Dent, Dolphinholme and Preston, 1772–1841*, ed. Alan G. Crosby

(Stroud: Alan Sutton and The Record Society of Lancashire and Cheshire, 1991), 33.

50 Wallace, *Walking, Literature, and English Culture*, 8.

51 Thomson, *The Seasons*, 153.

52 Thomson, *The Seasons*, 48.

53 John Lucas, 'Bloomfield and Clare', in *The Independent Spirit: John Clare and the Self-Taught Tradition*, ed. John Goodridge (Helpston: John Clare Society, 1994), 63.

54 Robert Bloomfield, 'Love of the Country', in *The Works of Robert Bloomfield* (London: George Routledge and Sons, 1867), 202.

55 Clare, *Sketches*, 14–15.

56 Clare, *Sketches*, 15.

57 Clare's library includes a copy of a 1797 edition of Coleridge's poetry, and an 1820 edition of Wordsworth's *Miscellaneous Poems*, inscribed as presented by his father in 1822, although Clare was certainly familiar with his work before then. 'Clare's Library', in *Catalogue of the John Clare Collection in the Northampton Public Library* (Northampton: Northampton Public Library, 1964), 23–34. On Clare and Wordsworth see Bate, *John Clare*, 187–8.

58 William Wordsworth, *The Prelude*, ed. J. C. Maxwell (Harmondsworth: Penguin, 1971), 76.

59 Wordsworth, *The Prelude*, 160.

60 For *The Compleat Angler*, see below, Chapter 3, 85–6, 100–1.

61 See the accounts by working-class autobiographers in David Vincent, *Bread, Knowledge and Freedom: A Study of Nineteenth-Century Working-Class Autobiography* (London: Methuen, 1981), 183–93.

62 Clare, *Sketches*, 18.

63 John Clare, 'The Progress of Rhyme', in *Selected Poems*, 122.

64 John Goodridge, *John Clare and Community* (Cambridge: Cambridge University Press, 2013), 191 and *passim*.

65 John Clare to John Taylor, 19 March 1820, in *Letters of John Clare*, 38–9.

66 Johanne Clare, *John Clare and the Bounds of Circumstance* (Kingston: McGill-Queen's University Press, 1987), 108–9.

67 As he was described on the title page of his first volume of poetry,

Poems Descriptive of Rural Life and Scenery (London: Taylor and Hessey, 1820).

68 'On Going a Journey' first appeared in the *New Monthly Magazine* of 1821, and was then republished in William Hazlitt, *Table Talk; Or, Original Essays* (London: Henry Colburn, 1822), vol. 2, 35–53.

69 On the influence of Hazlitt's essay, see Solnit, *Wanderlust*, 19–20; Marples, *Shanks's Pony*, 47, 146.

70 George Macaulay Trevelyan, 'Walking', in *The Joys of Walking*, ed. Edwin Valentine Mitchell (New York: Dover Publications, 2012), 77.

71 For an early contribution to this literature see, [Thomas West], *A Guide to the Lakes* (London: Richardson and Urquhart, 1778).

72 William Wordsworth, *A Guide through the District of the Lakes in the North of England* (Kendall: Hudson and Nicholson, 1835), 60. Also Marples, *Shanks's Pony*, 32.

73 Richard Holt, *Sport and the British: A Modern History* (Oxford: Oxford University Press 1990), 194; Solnit, *Wanderlust*, 117; Marples, *Shanks's Pony*, 32–3; Wallace, *Walking, Literature, and English Culture*, 63.

74 George Watson, 'The Bliss of Solitude', *Sewanee Review*, 101, 3 (1993): 343.

75 See, for instance the meeting with an 'unhappy rustic', a hay-maker, troubled by bad weather: John Thelwall, *The Peripatetic; Or, Sketches of the Heart, of Nature and Society* (London: for the author, 1793), 25.

76 Solnit, *Wanderlust*, 109–10.

77 Hazlitt, 'On Going a Journey', 35. The construction of never alone/when alone had a long literary lineage. It is attributed to Edward Gibbon. Robert Burton in his *Anatomy of Melancholy* cites Scipio Africanus in Tully: 'never less solitary than when he was alone, never more busy then when he seemed to bee most idle'. Robert Burton ('Democritus Junior'), *The Anatomy of Melancholy* (Oxford: Henry Cripps, 1621), 117.

78 Jeffrey C. Robinson, *The Walk: Notes on a Romantic Image* (Norman: University of Oklahoma Press, 1989), 43.

79 Hazlitt, 'On Going a Journey', 36.

80 Hazlitt, 'On Going a Journey', 37.

81 Hazlitt, 'On Going a Journey', 36–7. The quote is from *Henry V*; 'wrack' should be 'wreck'. For a more extended discussion of the value of walking alone, see Gros, *A Philosophy of Walking*, 53.

82 R. L. Stevenson, 'Walking Tours' [1876], in *The Lore of the Wanderer: An Anthology of the Open-Air*, ed. George Goodchild (London: J. M. Dent & Sons, 1920), 10–11. See also Merlin Coverley, *The Art of Wandering: The Writer as Walker* (Harpenden: Oldcastle Books, 2012), 90.

83 Treveleyan, 'Walking', 77. See also John Burroughs, 'The Exhilaration of the Road', in *In Praise of Walking: Thoreau, Whitman, Burroughs, Hazlitt* (London: Arthur C. Fifield, 1905), 71.

84 Cited in Jebb, *Walkers*, 101.

85 Treveleyan, 'Walking', 66–7. Edward Bowen, a Cambridge Apostle, was actually famous for having walked from Cambridge to Oxford in twenty-six hours, starting at midnight. W. E. Bowen, *Edward Bowen: A Memoir* (London: Longmans, Green, 1902), 51.

86 Jebb, *Walkers*, 101.

87 The Oxford to Cambridge line no longer exists, but its restoration is now in progress.

88 Leslie Stephen, 'In Praise of Walking', in *The Joys of Walking*, ed. Edwin Valentine Mitchell (New York: Dover Publications, 2012), 18.

89 W. H. Hudson, *Afoot in England* (London: Hutchinson, 1909), 2.

90 'Walker Miles' [Edmund Taylor], *Field-Path Rambles (Brighton Series)* (London: Robert Edmund Taylor & Son, 1909), 185. See also John Derry, *Across the Derbyshire Moors: Twelve Rambles Near Sheffield* (Sheffield: Independent Press, 1904); Melanie Tebbutt, 'Rambling and Manly Identity in Derbyshire's Dark Peak, 1880s–1920s', *Historical Journal*, 49, 4 (2006): 1130.

91 'Walker Miles', *Field-Path Rambles (Brighton Series)*, 186.

92 Jebb, *Walkers*, 154–6; Marples, *Shanks's Pony*, 135–6.

93 Geoffrey Murray, *The Gentle Art of Walking* (London: Blackie & Son, 1939), 285–6; Marples, *Shanks's Pony*, 181–2.

94 Arthur Hugh Sidgwick, *Walking Essays* (London: Edward Arnold, 1912), 249. He subsequently took part in the greatest team game of them all, dying of his wounds at Ypres in 1917.

95 Sidgwick, *Walking Essays*, 250.

96 Solnit, *Wanderlust*, 186.

97 John Gay, *Trivia: or, the Art of Walking the Streets of London* (London: Bernard Lintott, [1716]).

98 Cited in Geoff Nicholson, *The Lost Art of Walking* (Chelmsford: Harbour Books, 2010), 41.

99 Solnit, *Wanderlust*, 203. See, for instance, George R. Sims, *How the Poor Live* (London: Chatto & Windus, 1883), 5.

100 Augustus J. C. Hare, *Walks in London*, 2 vols (London: Daldy, Isbister, 1878), vol. 1, xxv.

101 Lauren Elkin, *Flâneuse: Women Walk the City in Paris, New York, Tokyo, Venice and London* (London: Chatto & Windus, 2016), 10.

102 Gros, *Philosophy of Walking*, 175–81. On the fascination of London as a conglomeration of strangers, see Jerry White, *London in the 19th Century* (London: Vintage, 2008), 122–3.

103 Charles Dickens, 'Shy Neighbourhoods', in *The Uncommercial Traveller* (Oxford: Oxford University Press, 2015), 94.

104 The function of walking in Dickens's engagement with the drama of the city is examined in David Vincent, 'Social Reform', in *The Oxford Handbook of Charles Dickens*, ed. Robert L. Patten et al. (Oxford: Oxford University Press, 2018), 428–9. See also Claire Tomalin, *Charles Dickens: A Life* (London: Viking, 2011), 45, 309, 320, 375.

105 Dickens, 'Shy Neighbourhoods', 94–5.

106 Charles Dickens, 'On an Amateur Beat', in *The Uncommercial Traveller*, 338.

107 Dickens, 'On An Amateur Beat', 338.

108 Jeremy Tambling, *Going Astray: Dickens and London* (Harlow: Pearson Education, 2009), 233.

109 Cited in Coverley, *The Art of Wandering*, 77.

110 Deborah Epstein Nord, *Walking the Victorian Streets* (Ithaca, NY: Cornell University Press, 1995), 4; Elkin, *Flâneuse*, 11–13.

111 Sydenham Edwards, *Cynographia Britannica* (London: for the author, 1800), 5. See also Harriet Ritvo, *The Animal Estate: The English and Other Creatures in the Victorian Age* (Cambridge, MA: Harvard University Press, 1987), 85–6.

112 James, A. Serpell, *In the Company of Animals* (Oxford: Basil Blackwell, 1988), 98; Judith M. Siegel, 'Companion Animals:

In Sickness and in Health', *Journal of Social Issues*, 49, 1 (1993): 157–67.

113 Rev. W. Bingley, *Memoirs of British Quadrupeds, Illustrative Principally of Their Habits of Life, Instincts, Sagacity, and Uses to Mankind* (London: Darton and Harvey, 1809), 79–80; Edward Jesse, *Anecdotes of Dogs* (London: Henry G. Bohn, 1858), 24–5; Darcy F. Morey, *Dogs: Domestication and the Development of a Social Bond* (Cambridge: Cambridge University Press, 2010), 207.

114 *Beeton's Book of Poultry and Domestic Animals* (London: Ward, Lock and Tyler, 1871), 545–6.

115 Erica Fudge, *Pets* (Stocksfield: Acumen, 2008), 14.

116 John K. Walton, 'Mad Dogs and Englishmen: The Conflict over Rabies in Late Victorian England', *Journal of Social History*, 13, 2 (1979), 226–39.

117 Philip Howell, *At Home and Astray: The Domestic Dog in Victorian Britain* (Charlottesville: University of Virginia Press, 2015), 150–73. Working rural dogs were exempt from taxation.

118 See, for instance, the court case reported in the *Observer*, 23 June 1878: 3.

119 PP1878, 46, XLVI.15. *Return of the Number of Dogs assessed to the Dog Tax in each Year from the 5th day of April 1866 to the 5th day of April 1868, when the Assessed Tax on Dogs expired; and of the Number of Licenses granted for Dogs during each of the Eleven Years from 1868 to 1877, ending on the 31st day of December in each Year*; Brian Harrison, 'Animals and the State in Nineteenth-Century England', *The English Historical Review*, 88, 349 (October 1973): 786.

120 On estimates of avoidance, see Walton, 'Mad Dogs and Englishmen': 221.

121 Gros, *Philosophy of Walking*, 178.

122 See below, Chapter 3, 71–2.

123 Cited in Tambling, *Going Astray*, 40–1.

124 Raymond Williams, *The Country and the City* (1973; London: Vintage, 2016), 222–38.

125 Byron, *Childe Harold's Pilgrimage*, Canto II, verse XXV, lines 217–25.

126 Byron, *Childe Harold's Pilgrimage*, Canto II, verse XXVI, lines 226–34.

127 Fiona MacCarthy, *Byron: Life and Legend* (London: John Murray, 2002), 157–60.

128 Richard Holmes, *Shelley: The Pursuit* (London: Quartet Books, 1976), 64–5, 300–3.

129 Percy Bysshe Shelley, *Alastor; or, The Spirit of Solitude and Other Poems* (London: Baldwin, Craddock, and Joy, 1816), 6.

130 Shelley, *Alastor*, v–vi.

131 Mary Shelley, *Frankenstein, or The Modern Prometheus* (1818; Ware: Wordsworth, 1999), 17, 43.

132 Shelley, *Frankenstein*, 73.

133 Shelley, *Frankenstein*, 126.

134 Shelley, *Frankenstein*, 78.

135 Shelley, *Frankenstein*, 94.

136 Shelley, *Frankenstein*, 89. On Shelley's use of a sublime landscape as a potential healing resource for the monster, see Elizabeth Dolan, *Seeing Suffering in Women's Literature of the Romantic Era* (Aldershot: Ashgate, 2008), 71.

137 Shelley, *Frankenstein*, 113.

138 Shelley, *Frankenstein*, 169.

139 Leslie Stephen, *The Playground of Europe* (London: Longmans, Green, 1894), 43.

140 Coverley, *The Art of Wandering*, 24–8.

141 Ronald Clark, *The Victorian Mountaineers* (London: B. T. Batsford, 1953), 18–21.

142 See, for instance, John Tyndall, *Mountaineering in 1861* (London: Longman, Green, Longman & Roberts, 1862), 20.

143 James D. Forbes, *Travels through the Alps of Savoy* (Edinburgh: Adam and Charles Black, 1843), 13. See also Edward Whymper's account of a lone seventy-mile walk across the foothills in preparation for serious climbing. *Scrambles amongst the Alps in the Years 1860–69* (London: John Murray, 1871), 13.

144 On the inadvisability of attempting solo climbs in this period, see *Peaks, Passes, and Glaciers: A Series of Excursions by Members of the Alpine Club*, ed. John Ball (3rd edn, London: Longman, Green, Longman & Roberts, 1859), 493–4.

145 Thomas Woodbine Hinchliff, *Summer Months Among the Alps*

(London: Longman, Brown, Green, Longman & Roberts, 1857), 298.

146 On the small number of female climbers in this period, such as Lucy Walker and Miss Brevoort, see Clark, *Victorian Mountaineers*, 174–85.

147 The words of George Barnard, cited by Clark, *Victorian Mountaineers*, 65.

148 Solnit, *Wanderlust*, 134.

149 Stephen, *Playground of Europe*, 48.

150 [George Carless Swayne], 'Mountaineering – the Alpine Club', *Blackwood's Edinburgh Magazine*, 86 (1859): 457. The Alpine Club had been formed in 1857. See the eighteen essays collected in Ball, *Peaks, Passes, and Glaciers*.

151 [Swayne], 'Mountaineering': 457.

152 [Swayne], 'Mountaineering': 456. Also Peter H. Hansen, 'Albert Smith, the Alpine Club, and the Invention of Mountaineering in Mid-Victorian Britain', *Journal of British Studies*, 34, 3 (1995): 300–24; Michael P. Cohen, *The Pathless Way: John Muir and American Wilderness* (Madison: University of Wisconsin Press, 1984), 78–81.

153 Whymper, *Scrambles amongst the Alps*, 407.

154 John Ruskin, cited by Clark, *Victorian Mountaineers*, 32.

155 Gordon T. Stewart, 'Whymper of the Matterhorn', *History Today*, 33, 2 (1983): 5–13.

156 *The Times*, 27 July 1865: 18.

157 [Charles Dickens], 'Foreign Climbs', *All The Year Round*, 14 September 1865: 137. Mont Cervin (which Dickens anglicizes here as Mount Cervin) is the French name for the Matterhorn. For a more recent discussion of this point, see Robert Macfarlane, *Mountains of the Mind* (London: Granta Books, 2003), 98.

158 Richard Jefferies, *The Story of My Heart* (1883; London: Macmillan, 1968), 55.

159 Thomas Miller, *Pictures of Country Life* (London: David Bogue, 1847), xi.

160 Travis Elborough, *A Walk in the Park: The Life and Times of a People's Institution* (London: Jonathan Cape, 2016), 59–111.

Chapter 3 Home Alone in the Nineteenth Century

1 Johann Zimmerman, *Solitude Considered with Respect to its Dangerous Influence Upon the Mind and Heart* (London: C. Dilly, 1798), 264.

2 Zimmerman, *Solitude*, 262

3 See the comprehensive recent survey of demographic research on this topic in K. D. M. Snell, 'The Rise of Living Alone and Loneliness in History', *Journal of Social History*, 42, 1 (2017): 8–17. Also Michael Anderson, *Family Structure in Nineteenth-Century Lancashire* (Cambridge: Cambridge University Press, 1971), 43–4.

4 Thomas R. Cole and Claudia Edwards, 'The 19th Century', in *The Long History of Old Age*, ed. Pat Thane (London: Thames & Hudson, 2005), 220.

5 Richard Wall, 'Elderly Persons and Members of Their Households in England and Wales from Preindustrial Times to the Present', in *Aging in the Past: Demography, Society and Old Age*, ed. David I. Kertzer and Peter Laslett (Berkeley: University of California Press, 1995), 97–100.

6 See also the sample of respondents in Elizabeth Roberts, *A Woman's Place: An Oral History of Working-Class Women 1890–1940* (Oxford: Basil Blackwell, 1984), 172.

7 John Tosh, *A Man's Place: Masculinity and the Middle-Class Home in Victorian England* (New Haven: Yale University Press, 1999), 5, 17–18.

8 John Burnett, *A Social History of Housing, 1815–1985* (2nd edn, London: Methuen, 1980), 156.

9 M. J. Daunton, 'Housing', in *The Cambridge Social History of Britain 1750–1950*, ed. F. M. L. Thompson (Cambridge: Cambridge University Press, 1990), vol. 2, 206.

10 On the use of the parlour, see, M. J. Daunton, *House and Home in the Victorian City: Working-Class Housing 1850–1914* (London: Edward Arnold, 1983), 263–85.

11 Sarah Stickney Ellis, *The Women of England, Their Social Duties, and Domestic Habits* (1839; 11th edn, London: Fisher, Son & Co., n.d.), 11–12. On the dangers of idle hours, see Marianne Farningham, *Life Sketches and Echoes from the Valley, Second Series* (London: James Clarke, 1868), 99.

12 Jean-Étienne Dominique Esquirol, *Mental Maladies: A Treatise on Insanity* (Philadelphia: Lea and Blanchard, 1845), 211.

13 Rozsika Parker, *The Subversive Stitch: Embroidery and the Making of the Feminine* (2nd edn, London: I. B. Tauris, 2010), 2.

14 Florence Nightingale, *Cassandra* (1854; London: Pickering and Chatto, 1991), 211.

15 Parker, *The Subversive Stitch*, 6.

16 Janet E. Mullin, *A Sixpence at Whist: Gaming and the English Middle Classes 1680–1830* (Woodbridge: The Boydell Press, 2015).

17 David Parlett, *A History of Card Games* (Oxford: Oxford University Press, 1991), 159.

18 Catherine Perry Hargrave, *A History of Playing Cards* (New York: Dover Publications, [1966]), 144.

19 Lady Adelaide Cadogan, *Illustrated Games of Patience* (1874; 2nd ser., London: Sampson Low, Marston, Searle, and Rivington, 1887).

20 See, for instance, John L. and Joseph F. Triggey, *The Art of Playing Solitaire, in Thirty-Three Different Ways* (London: W. Kent, 1869); Rev. T. Gaskin, *The Theory and Practice of Solitaire* (Cheltenham: J. Lillywhite, 1881). Versions of the game elsewhere in Europe were played on slightly larger boards, with thirty-six or more counters. To confuse matters further, card Patience is known as Solitaire in the United States and Solitaire has become the standard name for modern electronic versions of the game.

21 David Parlett, *The Penguin Book of Patience* (London: Allen Lane, 1979).

22 'Tarbart', *Games of Patience Illustrated by Numerous Diagrams* (2nd edn, London: Thos. De La Rue, 1921), 99.

23 Walter Wood, *The Book of Patience; or, Cards for a Single Player* (London: W. H. Allen, 1887), 43. See also 'Tarbart', *Games of Patience*, 62–3.

24 Charles Dickens, *Great Expectations* (1860–1; Harmondsworth: Penguin, 1965), 352.

25 Dickens, *Great Expectations*, 353.

26 Miss Whitmore Jones, *Games of Patience for One or More Players* (London: L. Upcott Gill, 1888), 7.

27 Jones, *Games of Patience*, 8.

28 Triggey and Triggey, *The Art of Playing Solitaire*, v–vi.

29 Colin Narberth, *An Introduction to Stamp Collecting* (London: Arthur Barker, 1970), 7; W. J. Hardy and E. D. Bacon, *The Stamp Collector* (London: George Redway, 1898), 12; James Mackay, *Stamp Collecting* (London: Park Lane Press, 1980), 68; Simon Garfield, *The Error World: An Affair with Stamps* (London: Faber & Faber, 2008), 84–5; Frederick Booty, *The Stamp Collector's Guide; Being a List of English and Foreign Postage Stamps, with 200 Facsimile Drawings* (Brighton: H. & C. Treacher; London: Hamilton, Adams & Co., 1862); Bertram T. K. Smith, *How to Collect Postage Stamps* (London: George Bell, 1907), 156. It was preceded by a French catalogue published the previous year by Alfred Potiquet. Narberth, *Introduction to Stamp Collecting*, 7.

30 Booty, *The Stamp Collector's Guide*, n.p.

31 John Edward Gray, *The Illustrated Catalogue of Postage Stamps for the Use of Collectors* (3rd edn, London: E. Marlborough, 1865), v. For similar claims to a classless hobby, see Edward J. Nankivell, *Stamp Collecting as a Pastime* (London: Stanley Gibbons, 1902), 4, 10–11; Stanley Phillips, *Stamp Collecting* (London: Sampson Low, Marston, [1936]), 4.

32 *Cassell's Household Guide*, 49; Hardy and Bacon, *The Stamp Collector*, 25.

33 Chas. J. Phillips, *Fifty Years of Philately: The History of Stanley Gibbons, Ltd.* (London: Stanley Gibbons, 1906), 119.

34 A world record at the time but perhaps a good investment. A Mauritius two-pence blue was sold at auction in London in 2011 for just over a million pounds. Duncan Campbell-Smith, *Masters of the Post: The Authorized History of the Royal Mail* (London: Allen Lane, 2011), 136. On a starter's collecting kit, see George Beal, *The Superbook of Stamp Collecting* (London: Kingfisher Books, 1986), 4.

35 Nankivell, *Stamp Collecting as a Pastime*, 4.

36 Nankivell, *Stamp Collecting as a Pastime*, 12.

37 Phillips, *Fifty Years of Philately*, 21.

38 Nankivell, *Stamp Collecting as a Pastime*, 44; Phillips, *Stamp Collecting*, 266; Arthur Blair, *The World of Stamps and Stamp Collecting* (London: Hamlyn, 1972), 116–20.

39 T. G. Brown and R. S. Sanderson, *A History of the Sheffield Philatelic Society 1894–1994* (Sheffield: Sheffield Philatelic Society, 1994), 8.

40 Nankivell, *Stamp Collecting as a Pastime*, 3.

41 On the long tradition of needlework see, 'Sempronia' [Mary Lamb], 'On Needle-Work' (1815), in *The Works of Charles and Mary Lamb*, ed. E. V. Lucas (London: Methuen, 1903), vol. 1, 180.

42 On Berlin wool-work see, Wilton, *The Art of Needle-work*, 297–9; *The Ladies' Hand-book of Knitting, Netting, and Crochet* (London: H. G. Clarke and Co., 1842), 12–13; Pamela Warner, *Embroidery: A History* (London: B. T. Batsford, 1991), 147–9; Barbara Morris, *Victorian Embroidery* (London: Herbert Jenkins, 1962), 7; Mary Eirwen Jones, *A History of Western Embroidery* (London: Studio Vista, 1969), 42–3; Therle Hughes, *English Domestic Needlework 1660–1860* (London: Lutterworth Press, 1961), 27; Geoffrey Warren, *A Stitch in Time: Victorian and Edwardian Needlecraft* (Newton Abbot: David & Charles, 1976), 33–6.

43 Morris, *Victorian Embroidery*, 7–26.

44 Wilton, *The Art of Needle-work*, 5. On the suitability of embroidery as a pastime for young women, see *The Young Lady's Book: A Manual of Elegant Recreations, Exercises and Pursuits* (2nd edn, London: Vizetelly, Branston, 1829), 291.

45 Warren, *A Stitch in Time*, 58.

46 Miss A. Lambert, *The Handbook of Needlework* (Philadelphia: Willis P. Hazard, 1851), 15. For a similar stress on colour selection as being the location of individual creativity, see *The Ladies' Hand-book of Knitting, Netting, and Crochet*, 56.

47 W. G. Paulson Townsend, *Embroidery, Or the Craft of the Needle* (London and New York: Truslove, Hanson & Comba, 1899), iv.

48 *The Ladies' Hand-book of Knitting*, ix.

49 Mrs Beeton, *The Housewife's Treasury of Domestic Information* (London: Ward Lock, [1884]), 809.

50 Maud Pember Reeves, *Round About a Pound a Week* (1913; London: Virago, 1979), 162, 166, 168.

51 Surveyed in Victoria Cooper and David Russell, 'Publishing for Leisure', in *The Cambridge History of the Book: Volume VI 1830–1914*, ed. David McKitterick (Cambridge: Cambridge University Press, 2009), 475–99.

52 Kathryn Hughes, *The Short Life & Long Times of Mrs Beeton* (London: Fourth Estate, 2005), 162–79.

53 Mrs R. Valentine, *The Home Book of Pleasure and Instruction* (London: Frederick Warne, 1868); *Cassell's Household Guide* (London: Cassell, Petter, & Galvin, 1873); Beeton, *The Housewife's Treasury*. See also *The Young Ladies Journal* (9th edn, London: E. Harrison, 1892). On the consumption of this literature, see Yaffa Claire Draznin, *Victorian London's Middle-Class Housewife: What She Did All Day* (Westport, CT: Greenwood Press, 2001), 150.

54 Beeton, *Housewife's Treasury*, 787.

55 Osmund Lambert, *Angling Literature in England* (London: Sampson Low, Marston, Searle & Rivington, 1881); Walter John Turrell, *Ancient Angling Authors* (London: Gurney and Jackson, 1910).

56 W. Carew Hazlitt, *Old Cookery Books and Ancient Cuisine* (London: Elliot Stock, 1886); Arnold Whittaker Oxford, *English Cookery Books to the Year 1850* (London: Henry Frowde, 1913).

57 [Maria Eliza Rundell], *A New System of Domestic Cookery; Formed upon Principles of Economy: and Adapted to the Use of Private Families* (1806; London: John Murray, 1811). On the importance of the book to Murray's business, see Fiona MacCarthy, *Byron: Life and Legend* (London: John Murray, 2002), 148. On the sales, see Janet Morgan's Preface to the 2009 reprint (London: Persephone Books), and Oxford, *English Cookery Books*, 135–6.

58 The Countess of Wilton, *The Art of Needle-work* (1840; 3rd edn, London: Henry Colburn, 1841).

59 Richard Rutt, *A History of Hand Knitting* (London: B. T. Batsford, 1987), 113–15.

60 Izaak Walton, *The Compleat Angler. Or; The Contemplative Man's Recreation* (1653: London: Arcturus, 2010).

61 Jonquil Bevan, *Izaak Walton's The Compleat Angler: The Art of Recreation* (Brighton: Harvester, 1988), ix–x.

62 Bernard S. Horne, *The Compleat Angler 1653–1967: A New Bibliography* (Pittsburgh: University of Pittsburgh, 1970).

63 On its popularity despite its obsolescence, see Francis Francis, *Angling* (London: 'The Field' Office, 1877), v.

64 On the textual antecedents of Walton's text, see John R. Cooper,

The Art of The Compleat Angler (Durham, NC: Duke University Press, 1988), 167–70.

65 Walton, *The Compleat Angler*, 67.

66 Turrell, *Ancient Angling Authors*, xi, 7–22.

67 *The treatise of fysshynge wyth an Angle* (1486), in D. L. Braekman, *The Treatise on Angling in The Boke of St Albans (1496)* (Brussels: Scripta, 1980), 60.

68 J. J. Manley, *Notes on Fish and Fishing* (London: Sampson Low, Marston, Searle & Rivington, 1881), iv–v.

69 To Mrs Wright, March 1825, in *The Natural History Prose Writings of John Clare*, ed. Margaret Grainger (Oxford: Clarendon Press, 1983), 170.

70 'Clare's Library', in *Catalogue of the John Clare Collection in the Northampton Public Library* (Northampton: Northampton Public Library, 1964), 23–34; *The Natural History Prose Writings of John Clare*, Appendix Va, 258–9.

71 Thomas Tusser, *Five Hundred Points of Good Husbandry . . . Together with a Book of Huswifery, new edition, with notes, georgical, illustrative, and explanatory, a glossary, and other improvements. By William Mavor* (1557; London, 1812).

72 J. H. Plumb, 'The Commercialisation of Leisure in Eighteenth-Century England', *The Stenton Lecture 1972* (Reading: University of Reading, 1973).

73 Benjamin Whitmil, *Kalendarium Universale: or, The Gardiner's Universal Kalendar* (London: J. Clarke, 1748).

74 Thomas Mawe and John Abercrombie, *Every Man His Own Gardener, Being a New and More Complete Gardener's Calendar and General Directory than Any One Hitherto Published* (17th edn, London: J. Johnson, 1803). Early editions of the work were published under the name of the gardener of the Duke of Leeds, Thomas Mawe, whom Abercrombie believed would help sales but who otherwise played no part in their compilation.

75 Clare had also come into the possession of two posthumously published compilations of Abercrombie's material: John Abercrombie, *The Gardener's Companion or Horticultural Calendar . . . Being a monthly index or remembrancer, according to the divisions of Abercrombie 'Practical Gardener' . . . To which is annexed . . . The Garden-Seed and*

Plant Estimate . . . Edited from an original manuscript of J. Abercrombie . . . by J. Mean, Horticulturist (London: T. Cadell, 1822); James Abercrombie, *Abercrombie's Practical Gardener, or Improved System of Modern Horticulture: Adapted either to Small or Large Gardens* (2nd edn, London: T. Cadell and W. Davies, 1817).

76 James Maddock, *The Florist's Directory, A Treatise on the Culture of Flowers* (1792; London: John Harding, 1822); James Edward Smith, *A Compendium of English Flora* (2nd edn, London: Longman, Rees, Orme, Green & Longman, 1836). For a similar treatise in the 1790s, see Charles Marshall, *An Introduction to the Knowledge and Practice of Gardening* (London: for the author, 1796).

77 Thomas Hogg, *A Concise and Practical Treatise on the Growth and Culture of the Carnation . . . and other Flowers* (1820; 3rd edn, London: G. & W. B. Whittaker, 1824); Isaac Emmerton, *A Plain and Practical Treatise on the Culture and Management of the Auricula* (London: Baldwin, Craddock and Joy, 1815); [Elizabeth Kent], *Flora Domestica, or The Portable Flower-Garden* (London: Taylor and Hessey, 1823).

78 The library of the servant examined by Jan Fergus included two gardening books. Jan Fergus, 'Provincial Servants' Reading in the Late Eighteenth Century', in *The Practice and Representation of Reading in England*, ed. James Raven et al. (Cambridge: Cambridge University Press, 1996), 202–25.

79 For instance, J. C. Loudon, *Encyclopaedia of Gardening: Comprising the Theory and Practice of Horticulture, Aboriculture, and Landscape-Gardening, Including All the Latest Improvements; a General History of Gardening in All Countries* (London: Longman, Hurst, Rees, Orme & Brown, 1822) and successive editions; Charles McIntosh, *The Book of the Garden*, 2 vols (Edinburgh: William Blackwood, 1853–5); James Anderson, *The New Practical Gardener and Modern Horticulturalist* (London: William Mackenzie, 1875).

80 For instance, J. C. Loudon, *The Suburban Gardener and Villa Companion* (London: for the author, 1838); James Shirley Hibberd, *The Town Garden: A Manual for the Management of City and Suburban Gardens* (London: Groombridge and Sons, 1855).

81 On the growth of the gardening periodicals, see Geoffrey Taylor, *The Victorian Flower Garden* (London: Skeffington, 1952), 110;

Miles Hadfield, *A History of British Gardening* (3rd edn, London: John Murray, 1979), 303–59.

82 John Worlidge, *A Compleat System of Husbandry and Gardening; or, the Gentleman's Companion, in the Business and Pleasures of a Country Life* (London: J. Pickard, 1716), title page.

83 *The Gardener's Chronicle*, 1, nos 1–2, 2–9 January 1841.

84 Mawe and Abercrombie, *Every Man His Own Gardener*, iv.

85 Mawe and Abercrombie, *Every Man His Own Gardener*, iv.

86 Susan Whyman, *The Pen and the People. English Letter-Writers 1660–1800* (Oxford: Oxford University Press, 2009).

87 The general outcome of reform is discussed in David Vincent, *Literacy and Popular Culture. England 1750–1914* (Cambridge: Cambridge University Press, 1993), 38–49; Howard Robinson, *Britain's Post Office* (London: Oxford University Press, 1953), 155; Campbell-Smith, *Masters of the Post*, 140.

88 *Forty-Seventh Annual Report of the Postmaster General on the Post Office* (London, 1901), Appendix A.

89 David Vincent, *I Hope I Don't Intrude: Privacy and Its Dilemmas in Nineteenth-Century Britain* (Oxford: Oxford University Press, 2015), 190–8.

90 Cited in Joe Bray, *The Female Reader in the English Novel: From Burney to Austen* (Abingdon: Routledge, 2009), 10. See also 'Hints on Reading', *The Lady's Magazine* (April 1789): 178.

91 On the supposed propensity of private readers to engage in forms of sexual misconduct, see Thomas W. Laqueur, *Solitary Sex: A Cultural History of Masturbation* (New York: Zone Books, 2003), 314–5.

92 Jane Austen, *Northanger Abbey* (1818; Ware: Wordsworth Editions, 2007), 33; Ann Radcliffe, *The Mysteries of Udolpho* (1794; London: Penguin, 2001).

93 Thomas Trotter, *A View of the Nervous Temperament* (London: Longman, Hurst, Rees, Orme & Brown, 1812), 93.

94 Kate Flint, *The Woman Reader 1837–1914* (Oxford: Clarendon Press, 1993), 208–9.

95 Sarah Stickney Ellis, *The Mothers of England* ([London]: 1843), 338–9.

96 Naomi Tadmor, '"In the Even My Wife Read to Me": Women,

Reading and Household Life in the Eighteenth Century', in *The Practice and Representation of Reading in England*, 162–74; Jacqueline Pearson, *Women's Reading in Britain, 1750–1835: A Dangerous Recreation* (Cambridge: Cambridge University Press, 1999), 170–5.

97 Abigail Williams, *The Social Life of Books: Reading Together in the Eighteenth-Century Home* (New Haven: Yale University Press, 2017), 36–63.

98 Elizabeth M. Sewell, *The Autobiography of Elizabeth M. Sewell* (London: Longmans, Green, 1907), 16. Also, Annabel Huth Jackson, *A Victorian Childhood* (London: Methuen, 1932), 13; The Viscountess Rhondda, *This Was My World* (London: Macmillan, 1933), 35.

99 Paul Thompson and Trevor Lummis, *Family Life and Work Experience Before 1918, 1870–1973* (data collection) (7th edn, 2009), UK Data Service, SN: 2000, *http://dx.doi.org/10.5255/UKDA-SN-2000-1*, Mr Mulligan.

100 Alice Foley, *A Bolton Childhood* (Manchester: Manchester University Extra-Mural Department, 1973), 12, 25.

101 Thompson and Lummis, *Family Life and Work Experience*, Miss Pool.

102 Thompson and Lummis, *Family Life and Work Experience*, Mr Wildman.

103 George R. Sims, *How the Poor Live* (London: Chatto & Windus, 1883), 5.

104 Sims, *How the Poor Live*, 7.

105 Stephen Constantine, 'Amateur Gardening and Popular Recreation in the 19th and 20th Centuries', *Journal of Social History*, 14, 3 (1981): 388.

106 Hogg, *Concise and Practical Treatise*, xv–xvii.

107 Keith Thomas, *Man and the Natural World* (London: Allen Lane, 1983), 236.

108 Mrs Loudon, *Instructions in Gardening for Ladies* (London: John Murray, 1840). See also G. W. Francis, *The Little English Flora or a Botanical and Popular Account of All Our Common Field Flowers* (London: Simpkin Marshall, 1839), which was dedicated to 'the Young Ladies of England'.

109 Louisa Johnson, *Every Lady Her Own Flower Gardener* (3rd edn, London: W. S. Orr, 1840), 4.

110 Loudon, *Suburban Gardener*, 6.

111 James Shirley Hibberd, *The Town Garden: A Manual for the Management of City and Suburban Gardens* (London: Groombridge and Sons, 1855), 6.

112 On the Nottingham allotments, see William Howitt, *The Rural Life of England* (1844; 3rd edn, Shannon: Irish University Press, 1971), 551–3. On the late nineteenth-century spread of allotments, see S. Martin Gaskell, 'Gardens for the Working Class: Victorian Practical Pleasure', *Victorian Studies*, 23, 4 (1980): 484–7.

113 The competitive nature of working-class recreational culture is discussed in Richard Holt, 'Introduction', in *Sport and the Working Class in Modern Britain*, ed. Richard Holt (Manchester: Manchester University Press, 1990), 5; Constantine, 'Amateur Gardening and Popular Recreation': 393.

114 Margaret Willes, *The Gardens of the British Working Class* (New Haven: Yale University Press, 2014), 97–106.

115 Ruth Duthie, *Florists' Flowers and Societies* (Princes Risborough: Shire Publications, 1988), 25.

116 Michael Worboys, Julie-Marie Strange and Neil Pemberton, *The Invention of the Modern Dog: Breed and Blood in Victorian Britain* (Baltimore: Johns Hopkins, 2018), 45–7.

117 Harriet Ritvo, 'Pride and Pedigree: The Evolution of the Victorian Dog Fancy', *Victorian Studies*, 29, 2 (1986): 227–53; John K. Walton, "Mad Dogs and Englishmen: The Conflict over Rabies in Late Victorian England", *Journal of Social History*, 13, 2 (1979): 222–6. On the emerging culture of breeding and judging, see Charles Henry Lane, *All About Dogs* (London: John Lane, 1900).

118 Harrison Weir, *Our Cats and All About Them* (Tunbridge Wells: R. Clements, 1889), 1–5; Miss Frances Simpson, 'All About Cats', in Herbert Compton et al., *Home Pets* (London: Greening & Co, 1907), 38. On the money to be made from breeding fancy pigeons in this period, see Percival Bretton, *Pigeons for Profit* (London: C. Arthur Pearson, 1914), 13.

119 On the rise of the pigeon Fancy, see Erich Müller and Dr Ludwig

Schrag, *Fancy Pigeons* (Hengersberg: Schober Verlags, 1985), 15–16.

120 Meredith Fradd, 'Rabbits and Rabbit Keeping', in Compton et al., *Home Pets*, 65.

121 'An Old Fancier', *Fancy Mice: Their Varieties, Management and Breeding* (4th edn, London: L. Upcott Gill, 1896).

122 'Old Fancier', *Fancy Mice*, 1.

123 Gordon Stables, *Dogs* (London: Dean & Son, [1909]), 40.

124 Worboys et al., *Invention of the Modern Dog*, 225.

125 Weir, *Our Cats and All About Them*, 5.

126 George Ure, *Our Fancy Pigeons* (London: Elliot Stock, 1889), 11.

127 Lambert, *Angling Literature in England*, 1; John Lowerson, 'Brothers of the Angle: Coarse Fishing and English Working-Class Culture, 1850–1914', in *Pleasure, Profit, Proselytism: British Culture and Sport at Home and Abroad 1700–1914*, ed. J. A. Mangan (London: Frank Cass, 1988), 105–27.

128 Manley, *Notes on Fish and Fishing*, 71–2. On the social range of the pastime, see W. C. Stewart, *The Practical Angler or The Art of Trout-Fishing* (3rd edn, Edinburgh: Adam and Charles Black, 1857), 3.

129 Adrian Franklin, *Animals and Modern Cultures* (London: Sage, 1999), 111.

130 Richard Holt, *Sport and the British. A Modern History* (Oxford: Oxford University Press 1990), 55.

131 Holt, *Sport and the British*, 189.

132 Martin Johnes, 'Pigeon Racing and Working-Class Culture in Britain, c. 1870–1950', *Cultural and Social History*, 4 (2007): 370–1.

133 *Cassell's Household Guide*, 118.

134 John Matthews Eaton, *A Treatise on the Art of Breeding and Managing the Almond Tumbler* (London: for the author, 1851), v.

135 Eaton, *A Treatise on the Art of Breeding and Managing the Almond Tumbler*, v. 'Hippochondriasis', now more usually spelled hypochondriasis, is an early version of hypochondria, a form of mental breakdown that imagines the affliction of non-existent physical maladies.

136 Manley, *Notes on Fish and Fishing*, 93.

137 Cited in Cooper, *The Art of The Compleat Angler*, 172.

138 Walton, *The Compleat Angler*, 14.

139 Walton, *The Compleat Angler*, 31.

140 For an early nineteenth-century example of the intricate techniques of fishing, see [Robert Salter], *The Modern Angler: Being a Practical Treatise on the Art of Fishing, &c. in a Series of Letters to a Friend* (Oswestry: J. Salter, [1811]).

141 [Charles Kingsley], 'Chalk-Stream Studies', *Fraser's Magazine*, 58, 345 (1858): 324. Also Manley, *Notes on Fish and Fishing*, 88.

142 Howitt, *The Rural Life of England*, 547.

143 As, for instance, is the case in Holt, *Sport and the British*, 189.

144 T. F. Salter, *The Angler's Guide* (6th edn, London: Sherwood, 1825), 342.

145 Lowerson, 'Brothers of the Angle', 121.

146 The Angling Trust, *Model Match Rules* (2014), rules 2 and 6; National Federation of Anglers, *Match Rules* (2017).

147 For instance, F. Greville, *The Rail and the Rod, No. III. South-Western Railway* (London: Horace Cox, 1867).

148 Miriam Bailin, *The Sickroom in Victorian Fiction. The Art of Being Ill* (Cambridge: Cambridge University Press, 1994), 5–35.

149 Alex Innes Shand, 'The Pleasures of Sickness', *Blackwood's Edinburgh Magazine*, 145, 882 (1889): 548.

150 *Christian Meditations; or The Believer's Companion in Solitude* (London: Hamilton, Adams, 1846), 485.

151 G. W. Mylne, *The Sick Room; or, Meditations and Prayers, in the Simplest Form, For the Use of Sick Persons* (London: Wertheim and Macintosh, 1850), 44–5.

152 *The Solace of an Invalid* (London: J. Hatchard and Son, 1823), viii–ix.

153 John Thornton, *A Companion for the Sick Chamber: Or, The Uses of Affliction* (London: Frederick Westley and A. H. Davies, 1835), title page.

154 Thornton, *A Companion for the Sick Chamber*, 86. See also *Gleanings from Invalids: A Companion for the Sick Room* (London: The Religious Tract Society, 1875); 'An Invalid', *The Cup of Consolation: Or, Bright Messages from the Sickbed* (London: Hodder & Stoughton, 1880); Rev. William March, *A Companion for the Sick Chamber* (London: Simpkin, Marshall, 1843).

155 William Buchan, *Domestic Medicine; or, The Family Physician* (1769;

Edinburgh: no pub., 1802), 230; Trotter, *A View of the Nervous Temperament*, 37–8. See above, Chapter 1, 8–9.

156 Esquirol, *Mental Maladies*, 212.

157 Elaine Showalter, *The Female Malady: Women, Madness and English Culture 1830–1980* (London: Virago, 1987), 134.

158 Dinah Maria Craik, *A Woman's Thoughts About Women* (London: Hurst and Blackett, 1858), 13.

159 The house, at 57 Front Street, is now the Martineau Guest House.

160 On Nightingale's health, see Mark Bostridge, *Florence Nightingale: The Woman and Her Legend* (London: Viking, 2008), 324–9.

161 R. K. Webb, *Harriet Martineau: A Radical Victorian* (London: Heinemann, 1960), 193–225; Valerie Kossew Pichanick, *Harriet Martineau: The Woman and Her Work 1802–76* (Ann Abor: University of Michigan Press, 1980), 121–2.

162 Cited in Bostridge, *Florence Nightingale*, 326.

163 The book was published anonymously, but the identity of its author was soon discovered. On its composition and reception, see Harriet Martineau, *Harriet Martineau's Autobiography*, 3 vols (London: Smith, Elder & Co., 1877), vol. 2, 170–2. For favourable reviews, all naming the author, see 'Life in the Sick-Room: Essays by an Invalid', *Tait's Edinburgh Magazine*, vol. 11 (February 1844): 131–5; Edward Moxon, 'Life in a Sick Room', *Westminster Review*, 41, 2 (1844): 608–11; 'Thoughts of an Invalid', *Chambers's Edinburgh Journal* (7 February 1844): 107–9.

164 Harriet Martineau, *Life in the Sick-Room: Essays by an Invalid* (London: Edward Moxon, 1844), 30–1.

165 Jane Austen, *Mansfield Park* (1814; Harmondsworth: Penguin, 1966), 416.

166 Martineau, *Life in the Sick-Room*, 34.

167 Alison Winter, 'Harriet Martineau and the Reform of the Invalid in Victorian England', *Historical Journal*, 38, 3 (1995): 608. See by contrast later accounts of the power exercised over the invalid by the 'oracular' doctor or consultant. A. B. Ward, 'The Invalid's World – the Doctor, the Nurse, the Visitor', *Scribner's Magazine*, 5, 1 (1889): 58; Shand, 'The Pleasures of Sickness'; George Whyte Melville, 'A Week in Bed', *Fraser's Magazine*, 69, 411 (1864): 330.

168 Anthony Todd Thomson, *The Domestic Management of the Sick*

Room (London: Longman, Orme, Brown, Green & Longmans, 1841), 465.

169 Martineau, *Life in the Sick-Room*, 326

170 Florence Nightingale, *Notes on Nursing: What It Is, and What It Is Not* (London: Harrison & Sons, 1859), 54.

171 Letter to Henry Crabbe Robinson, 1842, cited in Pichanick, *Harriet Martineau*, 123.

172 Letter dated 28 May 1845. Elizabeth Barrett Browning, *Kind Words from a Sick Room* (Greenock: privately printed, 1891), 6. On Elizabeth Barrett's control of her own domestic space, see George Pickering, *Creative Malady: Illness in the Lives and Minds of Charles Darwin, Florence Nightingale, Mary Baker Eddy, Sigmund Freud, Marcel Proust, Elizabeth Barrett Browning* (London: George Allen & Unwin, 1974), 253.

173 Martineau, *Harriet Martineau's Autobiography*, vol. 2, 151–2.

174 To Anna Jameson, 15 June 1841, in Harriet Martineau, *Selected Letters*, ed. Valerie Sanders (Oxford: Clarendon Press, 1990), 59.

175 Valerie Sanders, *Reason over Passion: Harriet Martineau and the Victorian Novel* (Brighton: Harvester Press, 1986), 92.

176 Cited in Maria H. Frawley, *Invalidism and Identity in Nineteenth-Century Britain* (Chicago: University of Chicago Press), 138.

177 Letter to Richard Monckton Milnes, Tynemouth, May 28, 1843, in Martineau, *Selected Letters*, 77; Webb, *Harriet Martineau*, 195–6.

178 Cited in Margaret Forster, *Elizabeth Barrett Browning* (London: Vintage, 2004), 96.

179 Martineau, *Life in the Sick-Room*, 32.

180 Winter, 'Harriet Martineau and the Reform of the Invalid': 606.

181 Pichanick, *Harriet Martineau*, 123; Webb, *Harriet Martineau*, 194–5.

182 Martineau, *Life in the Sick-Room*, 85–6.

183 Martineau, *Life in the Sick-Room*, 85–6.

184 Martineau, *Life in the Sick-Room*, 6–7.

185 E. Lynn Linton, *The Girl of the Period and other Social Essays* (London: Richard Bentley & Son, 1883), vol. 2, 209.

186 To Catherine Macready, 29 December 1841. Martineau, *Selected Letters*, 64.

187 Deborah Anna Logan, *The Hour and the Woman: Harriet Martineau's*

'Somewhat Remarkable' Life (DeKalb: Northern Illinois University Press, 2002), 71–4.

188 Martineau, Harriet Martineau's Autobiography, vol. 2, 414–15.

Chapter 4 Prayers, Convents, and Prisons

1 Matthew 6:6 (Authorized Version).

2 Alan Stewart, 'The Early Modern Closet Discovered', Representations, 50 (1995): 83.

3 Diarmaid MacCulloch, Silence: A Christian History (London: Allen Lane, 2013), 136.

4 Ian Green, 'New for Old? Clerical and Lay Attitudes to Domestic Prayer in Early Modern England', Reformation and Renaissance Review, 10, 2 (2008): 198.

5 William Roberts, The Portraiture of a Christian Gentleman, by a Barrister (London: J. A. Hessey, 1829), 9.

6 John Frere, A Manual Intended to Aid the Pious Christian in the Duty of Family Prayer and Private Devotion (Cambridge: 1851), x–xi.

7 Frere, Manual Intended to Aid the Pious Christian, xii.

8 [Robert Hawker], Ten Minutes Recommendation of Private Prayer, Considered as to Its Pleasures and Advantages [London: 1815?], 271.

9 Frere, Manual Intended to Aid the Pious Christian, vi.

10 Arthur Benoni Evans, Personal Piety, Or Aids to Private Prayer for Individuals of All Classes (London: Longman, Brown, Green & Longmans, 1851), advertisement.

11 F. O. Morris, Plain Sermons for Plain People: Private Prayer (London: Macintosh, [18--]), n.p.

12 Evans, Personal Piety, iii. Also T. T. Carter, A Book of Private Prayer for Morning, Mid-day, Night and Other Times, with Notes, for those who would Live to God amid the Business of Daily Life (London: Joseph Masters, 1861), 1.

13 [Hawker], Ten Minutes Recommendation of Private Prayer, 291.

14 Morris, Plain Sermons for Plain People, n.p.

15 Rev. Edward Bickersteth, A Treatise on Prayer (London: R. B. Seeley and W. Burnside, 1839), 22. Also [Hawker], Ten Minutes Recommendation of Private Prayer, 275.

16 Mrs M. L. M. Dawson, Communion with God or Aids to Private Prayer (London: Suttaby & Co., 1887), v.

17 Rev. R. C. Moberly, *Enrichment of Private Prayer* (London: SPCK, 1897), 3.

18 H. C. G. Moule, *Secret Prayer* (London: Seeley & Co., 1890), 25.

19 Moule, *Secret Prayer*, 26.

20 Sir James Stonhouse, *Prayers for the Use of Private Persons, Families, Children and Servants* (18th edn, London: SPCK, 1815), 19.

21 Charles F. Harford-Battersby, *Daily: A Help to Private Prayer* (London: Marshall Brothers, 1897), 5.

22 Bickersteth, *A Treatise on Prayer*, 22.

23 [Hawker], *Ten Minutes Recommendation of Private Prayer*, 281–2.

24 *The Book of Private Prayer* (London: J. Whittaker, 1879), v–vi.

25 Harford-Battersby, *Daily*, 5.

26 Carter, *A Book of Private Prayer*, 1.

27 Alfred Dale, *Looking Upward; A Little Hand-book of Prayer for Private or Family Use* (London: S. W. Partridge, 1871), 7.

28 Morris, *Plain Sermons for Plain People*, n.p.

29 Moule, *Secret Prayer*, 18.

30 Moule, *Secret Prayer*, 17.

31 Rev. Edwin Hobson, *From Strength to Strength: A Manual of Private Prayer for Home Use* (London: Roper and Drowley, 1889), 10.

32 Bickersteth, *A Treatise on Prayer*, 23.

33 *English Convents, What are They?* (London: Macintosh, 1870), 3; A. M. Allchin, *The Silent Rebellion: Anglican Religious Communities 1845–1900* (London: SCM Press, 1958), 60–5.

34 Evelyn Bolster, *The Sisters of Mercy in the Crimean War* (Cork: The Mercier Press, 1964), xviii.

35 Maria Trench, 'English Sisterhoods', *The Nineteenth Century*, 16, 90 (1884): 340–1; Edward Norman, *The English Catholic Church in the Nineteenth Century* (Oxford: Clarendon Press, 1984), 220; Susan Mumm, ed., *All Saints Sisters of the Poor* (Woodbridge: The Boydell Press, 2001), xi.

36 Owen Chadwick, *The Victorian Church, Part 1* (3rd edn London: Adam & Charles Black, 1971), 287.

37 *English Convents*, 3; Susan O'Brien, '*Terra Incognita*: The Nun in Nineteenth-Century England', *Past & Present*, 121 (1988): 110; John Nicholas Murphy, *Terra Incognita, or The Convents of the United Kingdom* (London: Longmans, Green, 1873), 338–70.

38 Mumm, ed., *All Saints Sisters of the Poor*, xi.

39 Alexander Penrose Forbes, *A Plea for Sisterhoods* (London: Joseph Masters, 1849).

40 Bridget Hill, 'A Refuge from Men: The Idea of a Protestant Nunnery', *Past & Present*, 117 (1987): 130; Susan P. Costeras, 'Virgin Vows: The Early Victorian Artists' Portrayal of Nuns and Novices', *Victorian Studies*, 24, 2 (1981): 158; Kathrin Levitan, 'Redundancy, the "Surplus Woman" Problem, and the British Census, 1851–1861', *Women's History Review*, 17, 3 (2008): 363–5.

41 [Anne Mozley], 'Convent Life', *Blackwood's Edinburgh Magazine*, 105, 643 (1869): 607–8.

42 Anna Jameson, *Sisters of Charity: Catholic and Protestant: Abroad and at Home* (London: Longman, Brown, Green & Longmans, 1855), 10. See also [Diana Mulock Craik], 'About Sisterhoods', *Longman's Magazine*, 1, 3 (1883): 308–9.

43 See above, Chapter 3, 105–11.

44 For contemporary British evaluations of Kaiserswerth, see 'Deaconesses or Protestant Sisterhoods', *Edinburgh Review*, 87 (1848), 441–6; Jameson, *Sisters of Charity*, 46–51.

45 On Nightingale at Kaiserswerth, see Mark Bostridge, *Florence Nightingale: The Woman and Her Legend* (London: Viking, 2008), 140–7, 155–60.

46 [Florence Nightingale], *The Institution on the Rhine, for the Practical Training of Deaconesses, etc.* (London: for the inmates of the London Ragged Colonial Training School, 1851), 8. On the influence of this account on the subsequent foundations of sisterhoods, see Rev. R. J. Hayne, *Church Deaconesses* (London: John Henry and James Parker, 1859), 6–9.

47 Walter L. Arnstein, *Protestant versus Catholic in Mid-Victorian England: Mr Newdegate and the Nuns* (Columbia: University of Missouri Press, 1982), 222.

48 Cardinal Wiseman, *Convents: A Review of Two Lectures on This Subject by the Rev. M. Hobart Seymour* (London: Thomas Richardson and Son, 1852), 22.

49 See, for instance, the criticism from experience in [Mary Frances Cusack], *Five Years in a Protestant Sisterhood and Ten Years in a*

Catholic Convent: An Autobiography (London: Longmans, Green, 1869).

50 Rev. Joseph Milner, *The History of the Church of Christ*, 3 vols (1794–1809; new edn, London: Longman, Brown, Green & Longmans, 1847), vol. 1, 555. On the influence of Milner's book on nineteenth-century evangelicals, see John Wolffe, *The Protestant Crusade in Great Britain 1829–1860* (Oxford: Clarendon Press, 1991), 111.

51 John Henry Newman, *The Church of the Fathers* (1840; Leominster: Gracewing, 2002), 97.

52 Michael Hill, *The Religious Order* (London: Heinemann Educational, 1973), 108–27.

53 'The Convents of the United Kingdom', *Fraser's Magazine*, 9, 49 (1874): 14.

54 'Deaconesses or Protestant Sisterhoods': 446.

55 Peter F. Anson, *The Call of the Cloister* (London: SPCK, 1955), 220–479.

56 Rev. James Spurrell, *Miss Sellon and 'The Sisters of Mercy': An Exposure of the Constitution, Rules, Religious Views and Practical Workings of their Society* (London: Thomas Hatchard, 1852), 2.

57 Jameson, *Sisters of Charity*, vi. On the scale of the campaign in popular literature, see Rene A. Kollar, *Foreign and Wicked Institution: The Campaign Against Convents in Victorian England* (Eugene, OR: Pickwick Publications, 2011), 21.

58 Arnstein, *Protestant versus Catholic*, 212.

59 Alfred Wesley Wishart, *A Short History of Monks and Monasteries* (London: John Lane, The Bodley Head, 1900), 396.

60 *The English Churchman*, 26 June 1845: 403.

61 'The Convents of the United Kingdom', *Fraser's Magazine*, 9, 49 (1874): 15.

62 Arnstein, *Protestant versus Catholic*, 62.

63 On Matthew Lewis, see above, Chapter 1, 12–14.

64 *The Awful Disclosures of Maria Monk: The Secrets of a Nun's Life in a Convent* (1836; London: World Distributors, 1965), 26, 37, 80. On the circulation of the book in Britain, see Wolffe, *The Protestant Crusade in Great Britain*, 125.

65 Cited in Wiseman, *Convents*, 5.

66 *English Convents*, 5.

67 Mumm, ed., *All Saints Sisters of the Poor*, 90.

68 Margaret Goodman, *Sisterhoods in the Church of England* (London: Smith, Elder, 1863), vii.

69 *English Convents*, 6.

70 The exclusion of religious orders from inspection by the Charity Commission is examined in the *Report from the Select Committee on the Law Respecting Conventual and Monastic Institutions* (1870), 1–10.

71 Cited in Kollar, *Foreign and Wicked Institution*, 43. Also Goodman, *Sisterhoods*, vii.

72 Costeras, 'Virgin Vows': 158. On the consequences of exchanging a 'birth mother' for a mother superior, see Rev. W. M. Colles, *Sisters of Mercy, Misters of Misery: or Miss Sellon in the Family* (London: T. Hatchard, 1852), 6.

73 General Sir Robert Phayre, *Monasticism Unveiled* (London: John Kensit, 1890), 5.

74 Cited in *English Convents*, 15.

75 Cited in Arnstein, *Protestant versus Catholic*, 109. On the case see [Cusack], *Five Years in a Protestant Sisterhood*, xv. Cf. Denis Diderot's mid-eighteenth-century novel, *La Religieuse*, discussed above, Chapter 1, 12–13.

76 *The Times*, 10 February 1869: 7.

77 She was also known under her married name of Mrs Edith O'Gorman Auffray. On her lectures as 'The Escaped Nun', see Sister Mary Agnes, *Nunnery Life in the Church of England* (London: Hodder & Stoughton, 1890), ix. On the argument with her rival sufferer, see *What the Escaped Nun Says About the Rescued Nun* (London: Catholic Truth Society, 1894).

78 Edith O'Gorman, *Convent Life Unveiled* (32nd edn, West Norwood: Truslove and Bray, 1913).

79 For a protest against this fictive accusation, see Rev. Herbert Thurston, S. J., *Mr Rider Haggard and the Myth of the Walled-Up Nun* (London: Catholic Truth Society, [1894?]).

80 Cited in Arnstein, *Protestant versus Catholic*, 222.

81 Ester Schaler Buchholz, *The Call of Solitude: Alonetime in a World of Attachment* (New York: Simon & Schuster, 1997), 64; Andrew Jotischky, *The Perfection of Solitude: Hermits and Monks in the*

Crusader States (University Park: Pennsylvania State University Press, 1995), 175–7.

82 Hill, *The Religious Order*, 52.

83 On Newman's view of the monastic tradition see John Henry Newman, 'The Mission of St Benedict', *The Atlantis*, January 1858.

84 Ian Ker, *John Henry Newman: A Biography* (Oxford: Oxford University Press, 2010), 328–9, 426, 430, 438; Arnstein, *Protestant versus Catholic*, 63; Chadwick, *The Victorian Church*, 288.

85 Susan Mumm, *Stolen Daughters, Virgin Mothers: Anglican Sisterhoods in Victorian Britain* (London: Leicester University Press, 1999), 6; Rev. T. T. Carter, *Harriet Monsell: A Memoir* (2nd edn, London: J. Masters, 1884), 58; Thomas Jay Williams, *Priscilla Lydia Sellon* (London: SPCK, 1965), 90–8.

86 [Craik], 'About Sisterhoods': 311. On Craik's support for female communities, see Anna Stenson Newnum, 'Single but not Solitary: Dinah Mullock Craik's Vision of a Protestant Female Community', *Women's Writing*, 20, 3 (2013): 309–15.

87 O'Brien, '*Terra Incognita*': 112; Mumm, ed., *All Saints Sisters of the Poor*, xiii; Mother Francis Raphael Drane, *Life of Mother Margaret Mary Hallahan* (London: Longmans, Green, 1929), 293.

88 Trench, 'English Sisterhoods': 351. Also [Anne Mozley], 'Convent Life', *Blackwood's Edinburgh Magazine*, 105, 643 (1869): 608.

89 Hill, 'A Refuge from Men': 128.

90 U. R. Q. Henriques, 'The Rise and Decline of the Separate System of Prison Discipline', *Past & Present*, 54 (1972): 62.

91 Luigi Cajani, 'Surveillance and Redemption: The *Casa di Correzione* of San Michel a Ripa in Rome', in *Institutions of Confinement: Hospitals, Asylums, and Prisons in Western Europe and North America, 1500–1950*, ed. Norbert Finzsch and Robert Jütte (Cambridge: Cambridge University Press, 1996), 301–18; Ian O'Donnell, *Prisoners, Solitude, and Time* (Oxford: Oxford University Press, 2014), 5–6; Michael Ignatieff, *A Just Measure of Pain* (London: Macmillan, 1978), 53.

92 John Howard, *The State of the Prisons in England and Wales* (Warrington: William Eyres, 1777), 119, 123.

93 Howard, *State of the Prisons*, 43.

94 Jonas Hanway, *Solitude in Imprisonment* (London: J. Bew, 1776), 4.

95 Hanway, *Solitude in Imprisonment*, 4.

96 Hanway, *Solitude in Imprisonment*, 70–1.

97 Hanway, *Solitude in Imprisonment*, 44. On Hanway's penal theory, see Randall McGowan, 'The Well-Ordered Prison: England, 1780–1865', in *The Oxford History of the Prison: The Practice of Punishment in Western Society*, ed. Norval Morris and David J. Rothman (New York: Oxford University Press, 1995), 86.

98 Jonas Hanway, *Distributive Justice and Mercy* (London: J. Dodsley, 1781), 102–3. On Hanway's own Christian beliefs, see John H. Hutchins, *Jonas Hanway 1712–1786* (London: SPCK, 1940), 11.

99 Hanway, *Solitude in Imprisonment*, 102–3.

100 Ignatieff, *Just Measure of Pain*, 78.

101 Hanway, *Solitude in Imprisonment*, 104.

102 Gustave de Beaumont and Alexis de Tocqueville, *On the Penitentiary System in the United States*, trans. Francis Lieber (1833; New York: Augustus M. Kelley, 1970), 5.

103 See, for instance, William Simpson, 'Solitary Confinement and the Silent System', *The Lancet*, 40, 2 (1840): 370.

104 [Robert Ferguson], 'Reports of the Commissioners for Pentonville Prison', *Quarterly Review*, 82, 163 (1847): 181. On the Auburn experiment, see O'Donnell, *Prisoners, Solitude, and Time*, 8–9.

105 For commentary on the tone of the debate on both sides of the Atlantic, see Samuel Gridley Howe, *An Essay on Separate and Congregate Systems of Prison Discipline* (Boston: William D. Ticknor, 1846), 8; George Laval Chesterton, *Revelations of Prison Life*, 2 vols (London: Hurst and Blackett, 1856), vol. 1, 320.

106 *The New Regulations for Prisons in England and Wales* (London: Shaw and Sons, 1843), 40. The Regulations, first issued in 1840, were designed to ensure local prisons consistently conformed to relevant practice in the convict prisons.

107 Sir Richard Vyvyan, *A Letter from Sir Richard Vyvyan, Bt, MP to the Magistrates of Berkshire, on their Newly-Established Practice of Consigning Prisoners to Solitary Confinement before Trial* (London: Ridgway, 1845), 9.

108 Henry Mayhew and John Binny, *The Criminal Prisons of London and Scenes of Prison Life* (London: Charles Griffin, 1862), 103.

109 Their duties were set out in the contemporary regulations. See

Regulations for Prisons in England and Wales (London: W. Clowes and Sons, 1840), 40–3; *Rules for the Government of Pentonville Prison* (London: W. Clowes, 1842), 46–9. Also Henriques, 'The Rise and Decline of the Separate System': 78; Neil Davie, '"Nothing Kept Back, Nothing Exaggerated": Piety, Penology and Conflict: Joseph Kingsmill, Prison Chaplain (1842–1860)', in *Law, Crime and Deviance since 1700*, ed. Anne-Marie Kilday and David Nash (London: Bloomsbury Academic, 2017), 276.

110 Rosalind Crone, *Illiterate Inmates: Educating Criminals in 19th-Century England* (Oxford: Oxford University Press, forthcoming).

111 *Sixth Report of the Commissioners for the Government of the Pentonville Prison*, PP 1847–8, XXXIV, 29.

112 De Beaumont and de Tocqueville, *On the Penitentiary System in the United States*, 51.

113 De Beaumont and de Tocqueville, *On the Penitentiary System in the United States*, 93.

114 Walter Lowe Clay, *The Prison Chaplain: A Memoir of the Rev. John Clay, B. D.* (Cambridge: Macmillan, 1861), 301.

115 *Extracts from the Second Report of [William Crawford and Whitworth Russell Esqs,] the Inspectors of Prisons for the Home District* (London: W. Clowes and Sons, 1837), 27.

116 Davie, '"Nothing Kept Back, Nothing Exaggerated"': 273.

117 Eric Stockdale, 'A Short History of Prison Inspection in England', *The British Journal of Criminology*, 23, 3 (1983): 214–16. Ireland already had an inspectorate.

118 Charles Dickens, *American Notes* (1842; London: Penguin, 2004), 111.

119 Dickens, *American Notes*, 111.

120 Dickens, *American Notes*, 113. On Dickens and prisons, see David Vincent, 'Social Reform', in *The Oxford Handbook of Charles Dickens*, ed. Robert L. Patten et al. (Oxford: Oxford University Press, 2018), 435–6.

121 Rev. J. Field, *Prison Discipline and the Advantages of the Separate System of Imprisonment*, 2 vols (London: Longman, Brown, Green & Longmans, 1848), vol. 1, 105–8.

122 Joseph Adshead, *Prisons and Prisoners* (London: Longman, Brown, Green & Longman, 1845), 114.

123 [Charles Dickens], 'Pet Prisoners', *Household Words*, 27 April 1850: 101. On Dickens's visits to the London prisons, see Anne Schwan, 'Crime', in *Charles Dickens in Context*, ed. Sally Ledger and Holly Furneaux (Cambridge: Cambridge University Press, 2011), 303.

124 [Dickens], 'Pet Prisoners': 100.

125 Charles Dickens, *David Copperfield* (1850; London: Everyman's Library and Alfred A. Knopf, 1991), 848.

126 Dickens, *David Copperfield*, 850.

127 Dickens, *David Copperfield*, 851.

128 Dickens, *David Copperfield*, 851.

129 De Beaumont and de Tocqueville, *On the Penitentiary System in the United States*, 57.

130 Sir Peter Laurie, *'Killing No Murder'; or, The Effects of Separate Confinement on the Bodily and Mental Condition of Prisoners in the Government Prisons* (London: John Murray, 1846), 42.

131 Mayhew and Binny, *The Criminal Prisons of London*, 111.

132 *Rules for Pentonville Prison*, 48.

133 *Reports of the Directors of Convict Prisons ... For the Year 1854* (London: HMSO, 1855), 30. Also Joseph Kingsmill, *Chapters on Prisons and Prisoners* (London: J. H. Jackson, 1850), 122.

134 *Sixth Report of the Commissioners for the Government of the Pentonville Prison*, 33. See also *Reports of the Directors of Convict Prisons ... For the Year 1862* (London: HMSO, 1863), 16.

135 *Sixth Report of the Commissioners for the Government of the Pentonville Prison*, 33.

136 Hepworth Dixon, *The London Prisons* (London: Jackson and Walford, 1850), 160.

137 *Reports of the Directors of Convict Prisons ... For the Year 1866* (London: HMSO, 1867), 10.

138 *Extracts from the Second Report of [William Crawford and Whitworth Russell ESQS,] the Inspectors of Prisons for the Home District*, 8.

139 Dixon, *The London Prisons*, 156.

140 *Reports of the Directors of Convict Prisons ... For the Year 1854*, 13–14.

141 Laurie, *'Killing No Murder'*, 35.

142 Ignatieff, *Just Measure of Pain*, 9, 178.

143 See, for instance, Thomas J. Clarke, *Glimpses of an Irish Felon's Prison Life* (Dublin and London: Maunsel & Roberts, 1922), 71;

Jeremiah O'Donovan Rossa, *Irish Rebels in English Prisons* (1882; Dingle, Co. Kerry: Brandon Book Publishers, 1991), 117, 119.

144 *Report of the Commissioners Appointed to Inquire into the Workings of the Penal Servitude Acts, Vol. 1, Commissions and Report* [Kimberley] (1879). C2369.

145 Theodore M. Porter, *The Rise of Statistical Thinking 1820–1900* (Princeton: Princeton University Press, 1986), 5–11; Lawrence Goldman, 'The Origins of British "Social Science": Political Economy, Natural Science and Statistics, 1830–1835', *Historical Journal*, 26, 3 (1983): 590–1.

146 Ian Hacking, *The Taming of Chance* (Cambridge: Cambridge University Press, 1990), 2. Also, Harald Westergaard, *Contributions to the History of Statistics* (London: P. S. King & Son, 1932), 136–71.

147 On the quantitative construction of literacy, see David Vincent, 'The Invention of Counting: The Statistical Measurement of Literacy in Nineteenth-Century England', *Comparative Education*, 50, 3 (2014): 266–81.

148 *Sixth Report of the Commissioners for the Government of the Pentonville Prison*, 3.

149 The 1875 report for Pentonville contained twenty pages of tables on the labour of inmates: *Reports of the Directors of Convict Prisons . . . For the Year 1875* (London: HMSO, 1876), 318–37.

150 Laurie, *'Killing No Murder'*, 2.

151 *Reports of the Directors of Convict Prisons . . . For the Year 1862*, 16.

152 Lambert Adolphe Jacques Quetelet, *A Treatise on Man and the Development of His Faculties* (Edinburgh: William and Robert Chambers, 1842), vii. On the search for mathematical laws governing society, see Mary Poovey, 'Figures of Arithmetic, Figures of Speech: The Discourse of Statistics in the 1830s', *Critical Inquiry*, 19, 2 (1993): 268.

153 Lieut. Col. Joshua Jebb, *Report on the Discipline and Management of the Convict Prisons, and Disposal of Convicts, 1851* (London: HMSO, 1852), 7.

154 *Reports of the Directors of Convict Prisons . . . For the Year 1854*, 27.

155 Seán McConville, 'The Victorian Prison: England, 1865–1965', in *The Oxford History of the Prison: The Practice of Punishment in*

Western Society, ed. Norval Morris and David J. Rothman (New York: Oxford University Press, 1995), 148.

156 *Reports of the Directors of Convict Prisons ... For the Year 1869* (London: HMSO, 1870), 12.

157 John Sibley, *A Letter on the Superior Advantages of Separate Confinement over the System of Prison Discipline ... Addressed to Benjamin Hawes Esq., MP* (London: John Hatchard and Son, 1838), 72.

158 On the infrequency of chaplains' visits at Millbank, see [Edward Callow], *Five Years' Penal Solitude, By One Who Has Endured It* (London: Richard Bentley & Son, 1878), 100.

159 Sharon Shalev, *A Sourcebook on Solitary Confinement* (London: Mannheim Centre for Criminology, 2008), 17–18; Peter Scharff Smith, 'The Effects of Solitary Confinement on Prison Inmates: A Brief History and Review of the Literature', *Crime and Justice*, 34, 1 (2006): 451.

160 John Charles Bucknill and Daniel H. Tuke, *A Manual of Psychological Medicine* (London: John Churchill, 1858), 166–9.

161 'The Horrors of Pentonville Prison. I Life', *The Examiner*, 3703 (18 January1879): 79.

162 See, for instance, 'A Ticket of Leave Man', *Convict Life* (London: Wyman and Sons, 1880), 201. Also Jabez Spencer Balfour, *My Prison Life* (London: Chapman and Hall, 1907), 66–72; F[rederick] Brocklehurst, *I Was in Prison* (London: T. Fisher Unwin, 1898), 22. These memoirs have formed the basis of several studies, including Philip Priestley, *Victorian Prison Lives: English Prison Biography 1830–1914* (London: Methuen, 1985) and O'Donnell, *Prisoners, Solitude, and Time*, which have difficulty balancing the narratives of those who survived the silence with those who did not.

163 Clarke, *Glimpses of an Irish Felon's Prison Life*, 93.

164 See, for instance, Michael Davitt, *Leaves from a Prison Diary*, 2 vols (London: Chapman & Hall, 1885).

165 *Report from the Departmental Committee on Prisons (Gladstone)*, PP 1895, LVI, I (C7702), 384.

166 Jeremiah O'Donovan Rossa, *My Years in English Jails* (1874; Tralee, Co. Kerry: Anvil Books, 1967), 164–78; Jeremiah O'Donovan

Rossa, *Irish Rebels in English Prisons* (1882; Dingle, Co. Kerry: Brandon Book Publishers, 1991), 175–263.

167 Smith, 'The Effects of Solitary Confinement on Prison Inmates': 442. On the early twentieth-century regime of solitary confinement, see Alyson Brown, *English Society and the Prison: Time, Culture and Politics in the Development of the Modern Prison 1850–1920* (Woodbridge: The Boydell Press, 2003), 19–20.

168 *Report from the Select Committee of the House of Lords, Appointed to Inquire into the Provisions and Operation of the Act 16 & 17 Vict. Cap. 99, intituled, 'An Act to Substitute, in certain Cases, other Punishment in lieu of Transportation'*, 26 July 1856.

169 *Reports of the Directors of Convict Prisons … For the Year 1885–86* (London: HMSO, 1886), ix.

170 *Report of the Commissioners Appointed to Inquire into the Operation of the Acts Relating to Transportation and Penal Servitude*, PP 1863 (3190), XXI, I, 40.

171 *Reports of the Directors of Convict Prisons … For the Year 1875*, 339.

172 John Joseph Gurney, *Observations on the Religious Peculiarities of the Society of Friends* (London: J. and A. Arch, 1824), 235.

173 Caroline Emelia Stephen, *Quaker Strongholds* (London: Kegan Paul, Trench, Trübner, 1890), 21.

174 Stephen, *Quaker Strongholds*, 59.

175 Caroline Emelia Stephen, *Light Arising: Thoughts on the Central Radiance* (Cambridge: W. Heffer & Sons, 1908), 68.

176 On Elizabeth Fry and penal reform, see Anne Isba, *The Excellent Mrs Fry* (London: Continuum, 2010), 49–173.

177 PP 1818 (275), *Report from the Committee on the Prisons Within the City of London and Borough of Southwark* (1818), 35.

178 Elizabeth Fry, *Observations on the Visiting, Superintendence, and Government, of Female Prisoners* (London: John and Arthur Arch, 1827), 23.

179 PP 1818 (275), *Report from the Committee on the Prisons*, 41.

180 PP 1835 (438). *First Report from the Select Committee of the House of Lords Appointed to Inquire into the Present State of the Several Gaols and Houses of Correction in England and Wales* (1835), 339.

181 See, for instance, Walter Walsh, *The Secret History of the Oxford Movement* (London: Swan Sonnenschein, 1897).

Chapter 5 Solitude and Leisure in the Twentieth Century

1 Margery Spring Rice, *Working-Class Wives: Their Health and Conditions* (1939; 2nd edn, London: Virago, 1981), 114.

2 Claire Langhamer, *Women's Leisure in England 1920–1960* (Manchester: Manchester University Press, 2000), 133.

3 Pearl Jephcott, *Married Women Working* (London: George Allen & Unwin, 1962), 3. Also David Kynaston, *Family Britain 1951–57* (London: Bloomsbury, 2009), 460.

4 Andrew Davies, *Leisure, Gender and Poverty* (Buckingham: Open University Press, 1992), 35.

5 Robert Roberts, *The Classic Slum* (Harmondsworth: Penguin, 1973), 49–50. Also James Winter, *London's Teeming Streets 1830–1914* (London: Routledge, 1993), 67.

6 E. Wight Bakke, *The Unemployed Man: A Social Study* (London: Nisbet and Co., 1933), 189.

7 John Burnett, *Liquid Pleasures: A Social History of Drinks in Modern Britain* (London: Routledge, 1999), 137–9; David Kynaston, *Modernity Britain, 1957–62: Books 1 and 2* (London: Bloomsbury, 2015), 62.

8 Virginia Woolf, *A Room of One's Own* (1929; London: Chatto & Windus, 1984), 97.

9 Kathleen Dayus, *Her People* (London: Virago, 1982), 3.

10 Local Government Boards for England and Wales, and Scotland, *Report of the Committee appointed by the President of the Local Government Board and the Secretary for Scotland to consider questions of building construction in connection with the provision of dwellings for the working classes in England and Wales, and Scotland, and report upon methods of securing economy and despatch in the provision of such dwellings* [Tudor Walters Report] (1918) Cd 9191, 25.

11 *Report of the Committee appointed by the President of the Local Government Board*, 25.

12 A. H. Halsey with Josephine Webb, eds, *Twentieth-Century British Social Trends* (3rd edn, Basingstoke: Macmillan, 2000), 477.

13 K. D. M. Snell, 'The Rise of Living Alone and Loneliness in History', *Journal of Social History*, 42, 1 (2017): 9; Ray Hall et al., 'The Pattern and Structure of One-Person Households in

England and Wales and France', *International Journal of Population Geography*, 3 (1997): 162–3.

14 Gavin Weightman, *Children of Light: How Electricity Changed Britain Forever* (London: Atlantic Books, 2011), 225.

15 Spring Rice, *Working-Class Wives*, 132; Hannah Gavron, *The Captive Wife: Conflicts of Housebound Mothers* (London: Routledge & Kegan Paul, 1966), 49. Also Elizabeth Roberts, *Women and Families: An Oral History, 1940–1970* (Oxford: Blackwell, 1995), 22–7; Alison Light, *Common People: The History of an English Family* (London: Fig Tree, 2014), 240.

16 Alan Johnson, *This Boy* (London: Corgi, 2014). More generally on London housing see Jerry White, *London in the Twentieth Century: A City and Its People* (London: Viking, 2001), 235–6.

17 David Vincent, *Privacy: A Short History* (Cambridge: Polity, 2016), 79–80.

18 Ministry of Housing and Local Government, *Homes for Today & Tomorrow* (London: HMSO, 1961), 1, 2.

19 Ministry of Housing and Local Government, *Homes for Today & Tomorrow*, 15. Also John Burnett, *A Social History of Housing* (London: Methuen, 1986), 304–8.

20 Ministry of Housing and Local Government, *Homes for Today & Tomorrow*, 2.

21 David Vincent, *Literacy and Popular Culture. England 1750–1914* (Cambridge: Cambridge University Press, 1993), 28–9.

22 Chris Phillipson, Miriam Bernard, Judith Phillips and Jim Ogg, *The Family and Community Life of Older People* (London: Routledge, 2001), 243.

23 Cynthia White, *Women's Magazines 1693–1968* (London: Michael Joseph, 1970); Joan Barrell and Brian Braithwaite, *The Business of Women's Magazines* (London: Kogan Page, 1988); Richard Hoggart, *The Uses of Literacy* (1957; London: Penguin, 2009), 103–11, 182–97; James Curran and Jean Seaton, *Power without Responsibility: The Press, Broadcasting and New Media in Britain* (6th edn, London: Routledge, 2003), 69–92.

24 Eileen Green, Sandra Hebron and Diana Woodward, *Women's Leisure, What Leisure?* (Houndmills: Macmillan, 1990), 84.

25 A. B. Creeke, *Stamp Collecting: A Guide for Beginners* (London:

Thomas Nelson and Sons, [1915]), 273; Also James Mackay, *Stamp Collecting* (London: Park Lane Press, 1980), 74; F. J. Melville, *Stamp Collecting* (4th edn, London: Hodder & Stoughton, 1978), 200; Hunter Davies, *The Joy of Stamps* (London: Robson Books, 1983), 18–21.

26 Terry Davy, *The Hobbies Story* (Dereham: Nostalgia Publications, 1998), 19–25; Ross McKibbin, 'Work and Hobbies in Britain, 1880–1950', in *The Ideologies of Class: Social Relations in Britain, 1880–1950* (Oxford: Clarendon Press, 1990), 141.

27 On the subsequent growth of literature for model train enthusiasts, nationally and globally, see Peter McHoy, *The World Guide to Model Trains* (London: Ward Lock, 1983), 16.

28 Cited in Anthony McReavy, *The Toy Story: The Life of Times of Inventor Frank Hornby* (London: Ebery Press, 2002), 165.

29 White, *Women's Magazines*, 96.

30 Asa Briggs, *The BBC: The First Fifty Years* (Oxford: Oxford University Press, 1985), 278.

31 A. M. Carr-Saunders, D. Caradog Jones and C. A. Moser, *A Survey of Social Conditions in England and Wales* (Oxford: Clarendon Press, 1958), 246–7.

32 Asa Briggs and Peter Burke, *A Social History of the Media: From Gutenberg to the Internet* (3rd edn, Cambridge: Polity, 2009), 213.

33 John Ellis, *Seeing Things: Television in the Age of Uncertainty* (London: I. B. Tauris, 2000), 41; Kynaston, *Family Britain*, 670–1.

34 Laurie Taylor and Bob Mullan, *Uninvited Guests: The Intimate Secrets of Television and Radio* (London: Coronet, 1987), 184.

35 Taylor and Mullan, *Uninvited Guests*, 183. Also Peter Collett and Roger Lamb, *Watching People Watching Television* (Oxford: Department of Experimental Psychology, 1986), 15; Joe Moran, *Armchair Nation: An Intimate History of Britain in Front of the TV* (London: Profile Books, 2013), 272.

36 *Report of the Committee on Broadcasting, 1960* [Pilkington], Cmnd 1763 (London: HMSO, 1962), 21.

37 John Halpern, *The History of the Crossword* (London: Andre Deutsch, 2016), 15.

38 Michelle Arnot, *A History of the Crossword Puzzle* (London: Papermac, 1982), 67.

39 Sandy Balfour, *A Clue to our Lives: 80 Years of the Guardian Crossword* (London: Guardian Books, 2008), 4.

40 Completion of the *Daily Telegraph* crossword became an integral element of the selection process for the government's security centre, GCHQ.

41 Steven M. Gelber, *Hobbies: Leisure and the Culture of Work in America* (New York: Columbia University Press, 1999), 2–5.

42 McKibbin, 'Work and Hobbies in Britain, 1880–1950', 142.

43 Burton Hobson, *Coin Collecting as a Hobby* (London: Oak Tree Press, 1967), 11.

44 John Waller Hills, *A Summer on the Test* (1924; Ellesmere: The Medlar Press, 2016), 38.

45 See, for instance, G. E. M. Skues, *The Way of a Trout with a Fly* (London: A. C. Black, 1921).

46 Joanna Bourke, *Working-Class Cultures in Britain 1890–1960. Gender, class and ethnicity* (London: Routledge, 1994), 86.

47 Leisure Industries Research Centre, *Leisure Forecasts 2011–2015* (Sheffield: Leisure Industries Research Centre, 2012), 32.

48 Carr-Saunders et al., *A Survey of Social Conditions*, 249.

49 Ferdynand Zweig, *The British Worker* (Harmondsworth: Penguin, 1952), 149–53.

50 Eliot Slater and Moya Woodside, *Patterns of Marriage: A Study of Marriage Relationships in the Urban Working Classes* (London: Cassell, 1951), 86.

51 White, *Women's Magazines*, 156–62.

52 *Hobbies Annual, 1959* (Dereham: Hobbies Ltd, 1959), 37.

53 Jephcott, *Married Women Working*, 123.

54 *The Practical Householder* (July 1957): 659.

55 Joe Moran, *Queuing for Beginners: The Story of Daily Life from Breakfast to Bedtime* (London: Profile Books, 2007), 133.

56 *The Practical Householder* (October 1955): 15.

57 *The Practical Householder* (July 1955): passim.

58 Travis Elborough, *A Walk in the Park: The Life and Times of a People's Institution* (London: Jonathan Cape, 2016), 228.

59 Mass Observation, *File Report: Work and Leisure* (1948), 3. Also Mass Observation, *An Enquiry into People's Homes* (London: John Murray, 1943), 200.

60 Halsey with Webb, eds, *Twentieth-Century British Social Trends*, 442.

61 See, for instance, the transformative effect the purchase of a Ford Anglia in 1959 had on the life of Alan Johnson in his new estate. Alan Johnson, *Please, Mister Postman: A Memoir* (London: Transworld Publishers, 2014), 124.

62 Leisure Industries Research Centre, *Leisure Forecasts 2011–2015*, 38; Adrian Franklin, *Animals and Modern Cultures* (London: Sage, 1999), 89.

63 John Bradshaw, *The Animals Among Us: The New Science of Anthrozoology* (London: Allen Lane, 2017), 94–6.

64 Rebecca Solnit, *Wanderlust. A History of Walking* (London: Verso, 2001), 267.

65 Sir Hubert Llewellyn Smith, *The New Survey of London Life and Labour*, 9 vols (London: P. S. King, 1930–35), vol. IX, 61; D. Caradog Jones, ed., *The Social Survey of Merseyside*, 3 vols (Liverpool: University Press of Liverpool, 1934), vol. 3, 294.

66 Richard Holt, *Sport and the British: A Modern History* (Oxford: Oxford University Press 1990), 199–200.

67 Virginia Woolf, 'Street Haunting: A London Adventure', in *Street Haunting and Other Essays*, ed. Stuart N. Clarke (1927; London: Vintage Books, 2014), 225–6. Also Lauren Elkin, *Flâneuse: Women Walk the City in Paris, New York, Tokyo, Venice and London* (London: Chatto & Windus, 2016), 86. For a contemporary male perspective, see Arthur Machen, *The London Adventure: Or the Art of Wandering* (London: Martin Secker, 1924).

68 Will Self et al., '"Would That All Journeys Were on Foot": Writers on the Joy of Walking', *Guardian*, 18 September 2018.

69 Iain Sinclair, *Lights Out for the Territory* (London: Penguin, 2003), 4.

70 Zweig, *The British Worker*, 150.

71 'Epidemic in the United States: "Cross-Words"', *Manchester Guardian*, 21 January 1925: 9.

72 Linda Hannas, *The English Jigsaw Puzzle 1760–1890* (London: Wayland, 1972), 14–28; Tom Tyler, *British Jigsaw Puzzles of the Twentieth Century* (Shepton Beauchamp: Richard Dennis, 1997), 9–10.

73 Chris McCann, *Master Pieces: The Art History of Jigsaw Puzzles* (Portland, OR: Collector's Press, 1998), 7–8.

74 Margaret Drabble, *The Pattern in the Carpet: A Personal History with Jigsaws* (London: Atlantic Books, 2009), 6.

75 Drabble, *The Pattern in the* Carpet, xiii.

76 Hunter Davies, *The Joy of Stamps* (London: Robson Books, 1983), 12.

77 Davies, *The Joy of Stamps*, 13.

78 Simon Garfield, *The Error World: An Affair with Stamps* (London: Faber & Faber, 2008), 91.

79 Garfield, *The Error World*, 212.

80 Spring Rice, *Working-Class Wives*, 94.

81 Spring Rice, *Working-Class Wives*, 94. On the persisting isolation of non-working mothers in the home, see Dorothy Hobson, 'Housewives: Isolation as Oppression', in *Women Take Issue*, ed. the Women's Study Group, University of Birmingham (London: Hutchinson, 1978), 85–90.

82 Spring Rice, *Working-Class Wives*, 109, 112.

83 Kathleen Box, *The Cinema and the Public* (London: Mass Observation, 1946), 1–2; Jeffrey Richards, *The Age of the Dream Palace: Cinema and Society in 1930s Britain* (London: I. B. Tauris, 2010), 12–15; Davies, *Leisure, Gender and Poverty*, 73.

84 Jones, ed., *The Social Survey of Merseyside*, vol. 3, 275–80.

85 Patricia and Robert Malcolmson, *A Free-Spirited Woman: The London Diaries of Gladys Langford, 1936–1940* (Woodbridge: The London Record Society and The Boydell Press, 2014), 18, 28, 47, 49.

86 Nella Last, *The Diaries of Nella Last*, ed. Patricia and Robert Malcolmson (London: Profile Books, 2012), 244.

87 Last, *Diaries*, 238.

88 Margaret Leonora Eyles, *The Woman in the Little House* (London: Grant Richards, 1922), 117.

89 Mass Observation, *Man and His Cigarette* (December 1949), 1–2; Moran, *Queuing for* Beginners, 101.

90 Kynaston, *Family Britain*, 173.

91 Matthew Hilton, *Smoking in British Popular Culture 1800–2000* (Manchester: Manchester University Press, 2000), 5.

92 Stephanie Dowrick, *Intimacy and Solitude* (London: The Women's Press, 1992), 159; Kynaston, *Modernity Britain*, 385.

93 See, for instance, Compton Mackenzie, *Sublime Tobacco* (London: Chatto & Windus, 1957), 1.

94 Mass Observation, *Man and His Cigarette*, 103–4. Also Matthew Hilton, 'Smoking and Sociability', in *Smoke: A Global History of Smoking*, ed. Sander L. Gilman and Zhou Xun (London: Reaktion Books, 2004), 126.

95 G. L. Apperson, *The Social History of Smoking* (London: Martin Secker, 1914), 159–68.

96 J. M. Barrie, *My Lady Nicotine* (London: Hodder & Stoughton, 1890), 12.

97 Stephen Graham, *The Gentle Art of Tramping* (London: Robert Holden, 1927), 163.

98 Mass Observation, *File Report 818: Smoking Trends* (August 1941), 1–2.

99 Mass Observation, *Man and His Cigarette*, 144–5.

100 Richard Klein, *Cigarettes are Sublime* (Durham, NC: Duke University Press, 1993), 3.

101 Mass Observation, *File Report 818: Smoking Trends*, 6.

102 For a survey of mid-nineteenth-century medical hostility to smoking, see 'To Smoke, or Not to Smoke?', *All The Year Round*, 27 May 1865: 413–18.

103 Mass Observation, *Man and His Cigarette*, 4.

104 Office for National Statistics, *Adult Smoking Habits in the UK: 2015* (7 March 2017), 3–4.

105 Linda Bauld, *The Impact of Smoking Legislation in England: Evidence Review* (University of Bath and Department of Health, March 2011),10; Katrina Hargreaves et al., 'The Social Context of Change in Tobacco Consumption Following the Introduction of "Smokefree" England Legislation: A Qualitative, Longitudinal Study', *Social Science & Medicine*, 71, 3 (2010): 459–66.

106 Captain Marryat, *Newton Forster, or, The Merchant Service* (1832; London: Richard Bentley, 1838), 42.

107 Mass Observation, *Man and His Cigarette*, 12.

108 'The Smoking-Room at the Club', *The Cornhill Magazine*, 6, 34 (1862): 513.

109 Hilton, 'Smoking and Sociability', 127–8.

110 Mass Observation, *Man and His Cigarette*, 133.

111 Apperson, *Social History of Smoking*, 200.

112 See the anthology of writers' practices in George Redway, *Tobacco Talk and Smokers' Gossip* (London: G. Redway, 1884), 63–91.

113 Mass Observation, *Man and His Cigarette*, 136.

114 Penny Tinkler, *Smoke Signals: Women, Smoking and Visual Culture* (Oxford: Berg, 2006), 62, 206.

115 The conflict is explored in Mark Jackson, 'Stress in Post-War Britain: An Introduction', in *Stress in Post-War Britain, 1945–85*, ed. Mark Jackson (London: Pickering & Chatto, 2015), 9; and Mark Jackson, *The Age of Stress: Science and the Search for Stability* (Oxford: Oxford University Press, 2013), 246–51.

116 Klein, *Cigarettes are Sublime*, 138.

117 Charles Kingsley, *Westward Ho!* (1855; London, Collins, 1953), 164.

118 Charles Dickens, *Great Expectations* (1860–61; Harmondsworth: Penguin, 1965), 346.

119 Mass Observation, *Man and His Cigarette*, 138.

120 Claudia Hammond and Gemma Lewis, 'The Rest Test: Preliminary Findings from a Large-Scale International Survey on Rest', in *The Restless Compendium: Interdisciplinary Investigations of Rest and Its Opposites*, ed. Felicity Callard et al. (Basingstoke: Palgrave Macmillan, 2016), 63. See also Claudia Hammond, *The Art of Rest: How to Find Respite in the Modern Age* (Edinburgh: Canongate, 2019).

121 Mass Observation, *Man and His Cigarette*, 140.

122 Mass Observation, *Man and His Cigarette*, 140.

123 See above, Chapter 3, 102 for the regulations specifying the distance fishermen had to keep from each other on the river bank.

124 Morley Roberts, *A Humble Fisherman* (London: Grayson & Grayson, 1932), 24. Also Jeremy Paxman, *Fish, Fishing and the Meaning of Life* (London: Michael Joseph, 1994), 444.

125 Roberts, *A Humble Fisherman*, 25.

126 Roberts, *A Humble Fisherman*, 24.

Chapter 6 The Spiritual Revival

1 Joseph Conrad, *Nostromo* (1904; Oxford: Oxford University Press, 2007), 356.

2 Ian Watt, *Joseph Conrad: Nostromo* (Cambridge: Cambridge University Press, 1988), 63–4; Ursula Lord, *Solitude versus Solidarity in the Novels of Joseph Conrad* (Montreal: McGill-Queen's University Press, 1998), 209, 228–9, 242–5, 281.

3 Conrad, *Nostromo*, 356.

4 Conrad, *Nostromo*, 227.

5 Henry Marten, 'Conrad's Skeptic Reconsidered: A Study of Martin Decoud', *Nineteenth-Century Fiction*, 27, 1 (1972): 81–94; Joyce Carol Oates, '"The Immense Indifference of Things": The Tragedy of Conrad's "Nostromo"', *Novel*, 9, 1 (1975): 11; Jacques Berthoud, *Joseph Conrad: The Major Phase* (Cambridge: Cambridge University Press, 1978), 111; Owen Knowles and Gene M. Moore, eds, *Oxford Reader's Companion to Conrad* (Oxford: Oxford University Press, 2000), 101.

6 Conrad, *Nostromo*, 356–7.

7 Conrad, *Nostromo*, 300.

8 Conrad, *Nostromo*, 356.

9 Conrad, *Nostromo*, 359.

10 Conrad, *Nostromo*, 359.

11 W. H. Hudson, *A Shepherd's Life* (1910; London: Futura, 1979), 34.

12 Raymond Williams *The Country and the City* (1973; London: Vintage, 2016), 370–1.

13 Geoffrey Murray, *The Gentle Art of Walking* (London: Blackie & Son, 1939), 285; Morris Marples, *Shanks's Pony: A Study of Walking* (London: J. M. Dent, 1959), 144–5, 183.

14 Stephen Graham, *The Gentle Art of Tramping* (London: Robert Holden, 1927), 2. In similar vein, see John Burroughs, 'The Exhilaration of the Road', in *In Praise of Walking* (London: Arthur C. Fifield, 1905), 67.

15 Janina Nordius, *'I Am Myself Alone': Solitude and Transcendence in John Cowper Powys* (Göteborg: Acta Universitatis Gothoburgensis, 1997), 22–42.

16 John Cowper Powys, *A Philosophy of Solitude* (London: Jonathan Cape, 1933), 39.

17 John Cowper Powys, *In Defence of Sensuality* (London: Victor Gollancz, 1930), 9. See also Peter F. Anson, *The Quest of Solitude* (London: J. M. Dent, 1932), 107.

18 Powys, *A Philosophy of Solitude*, 55.

19 Morine Krissdottir, *John Cowper Powys and the Magical Quest* (London: Macdonald General Books, 1980), 27.

20 Powys, *A Philosophy of Solitude*, 76.

21 Powys, *A Philosophy of Solitude*, 79.

22 Powys, *A Philosophy of Solitude*, 49, 66.

23 Powys, *A Philosophy of Solitude*, 12.

24 Powys, *A Philosophy of Solitude*, 51.

25 Powys, *A Philosophy of Solitude*, 3.

26 Powys, *In Defence of Sensuality*, 278.

27 Kim Taplin, *The English Path* (2nd edn, Sudbury: Perry Green Press, 2000), 1.

28 Paul Brassley, 'Output and Technical Change in Twentieth-Century British Agriculture', *Agricultural History Review*, 48, 1 (2000): 73–4.

29 Fred Kitchen, *Brother to the Ox* (1940; Toller Fratrum: Little Toller Books, 2015), 154.

30 Jonathan, I. Gershuny and Kimberly Fisher, *Leisure in the UK across the 20th Century* (Colchester: Institute for Social and Economic Research, 1999), 28.

31 Joe Moran, *Queuing for Beginners. The Story of Daily Life from Breakfast to Bedtime* (London: Profile Books, 2007), 133.

32 Merlin Coverley, *The Art of Wandering: The Writer as Walker* (Harpenden: Oldcastle Books, 2012).

33 John M. Merrill, *Walking My Way* (London: Chatto & Windus, 1984), 159.

34 Gros, *A Philosophy of Walking*, 62.

35 See above, Chapter 2, 69.

36 Lucy Ellmann, *Sweet Desserts* (London: Penguin, 1989), 81.

37 Richard Mahler, *Stillness: Daily Gifts of Solitude* (Boston, MA: Red Wheel, 2003), 125–6.

38 Belden C. Lane, *The Solace of Fierce Landscapes* (New York: Oxford University Press, 1998), 212.

39 Cheryl Strayed, *Wild: A Journey from Lost to Found* (London:

Atlantic Books, 2015). The book was made into a film in 2017.

40 Edward Abbey, *Desert Solitaire: A Season in the Wilderness* (1968; London: Robin Clark, 1992), 6.

41 Abbey, *Desert Solitaire*, 130.

42 Jon Krakauer, *Into the Wild* (London: Macmillan, 1996). The book was made into a film in 2007.

43 Robert Macfarlane, *The Wild Places* (London: Granta Books, 2007), 76.

44 Helen Macdonald, *H is for Hawk* (London: Jonathan Cape, 2014). See also Helen MacDonald, *H is for Hawk: A New Chapter* (BBC Two, 19 October 2017).

45 Richard Mabey, *The Unofficial Countryside* (London: Collins, 1973), 12.

46 Mabey, *Unofficial Countryside*, 10.

47 Paul Farley and Michael Symmons Roberts, *Edgelands: Journeys into England's True Wilderness* (London: Jonathan Cape, 2011), 5–6.

48 Kaleva Korpola and Henk Staats, 'The Restorative Qualities of Being Alone with Nature', in *The Handbook of Solitude: Psychological Perspectives on Social Isolation, Social Withdrawal, and Being Alone*, ed. Robert J. Coplan and Julie C. Bowker (Chichester: Wiley Blackwell, 2014), 351; Marc G. Berman et al., 'The Cognitive Benefits of Interacting with Nature', *Psychological Science*, 19, 2 (2008): 1211; Nicholas Carr, *The Shallows: How the Internet is Changing the Way We Think, Read and Remember* (London: Atlantic Books, 2010), 219.

49 Will Self with Ralph Steadman, *Psychogeography* (London: Bloomsbury, 2007). See also Geoff Nicholson, *The Lost Art of Walking* (Chelmsford: Harbour Books, 2010), 46–53.

50 See above, Chapter 2, 54–5.

51 Iain Sinclair, *Lights Out for the Territory* (London: Penguin, 2003), 4

52 Self, *Psychogeography*, 20–38

53 See above, Chapter 2, 57–8, 70–1.

54 Self, *Psychogeography*, 157.

55 Mark Greif, *Against Everything* (London: Verso, 2016), 5.

56 For discussion of this point see Rebecca Solnit, *Wanderlust: A History of Walking* (London: Verso, 2001) 264–5.

57 See the books, Alex Honnold and David Roberts, *Alone on the Wall: Alex Honnold and the Ultimate Limits of Adventure* (London: Macmillan, 2015) and Mark Synnott, *The Impossible Climb: Alex Honnold, El Capitan and the Climbing Life* (London: Allen & Unwin, 2019), and the film, *Free Solo* (2018), directed by Jimmy Chin and Elizabeth Chai Vasarhelyi.

58 Joshua Slocum, *Sailing Alone Around the World* (1900; London: Century Publishing, 1984).

59 See, for instance, Alain Gerbault, *The Flight of the 'Firecrest'* (London: H. F. & G. Witherby, 1926), 40, 45; Robin Knox-Johnston, *A World of My Own* (London: Cassell, 1969), 130; Chay Blyth, *The Impossible Voyage* (London: Hodder & Stoughton, 1971), 37.

60 On the Society and Slocum's influence more generally, see Valentine Howells, *Sailing into Solitude* (no place: Landsker Publications, 2011), 255–9.

61 Slocum, *Sailing Alone Around the World*, 134.

62 Nicholas Tomalin and Ron Hall, *The Strange Voyage of Donald Crowhurst* (London: Hodder & Stoughton, 1970), 104.

63 Ellen MacArthur, *Taking on the World* (London: Michael Joseph, 2002), 283.

64 Slocum, *Sailing Alone Around the World*, 141.

65 John Ridgway, *Journey to Ardmore* (London: Hodder & Stoughton, 1971), 193.

66 Tomalin and Hall, *The Strange Voyage of Donald Crowhurst*, 104.

67 Slocum, *Sailing Alone Around the World*, 227.

68 Knox-Johnston, *A World of My Own*, 82.

69 Steven Callahan, *Adrift: Seventy-Six Days Lost at Sea* (New York: Bantam Press, 1986).

70 Knox-Johnston, *A World of My Own*, 70.

71 Slocum, *Sailing Alone Around the World*, 51.

72 Francis Chichester, *Gipsy Moth Circles the World* (London: Hodder & Stoughton, 1967), 110.

73 Knox-Johnston, *A World of My Own*, 56.

74 Peter Nichols, *A Voyage for Madmen* (London: Profile Books, 2001), 255.

75 Blyth, *The Impossible Voyage*, 130.

76 Bernard Moitessier, *The Long Way*, trans. William Rodarmor (London: Adlard Coles, 1974), 4.

77 Moitessier, *The Long Way*, 62.

78 Chris Eakin, *A Race Too Far* (London: Ebury Press, 2009), 179–201.

79 Tomalin and Hall, *The Strange Voyage of Donald Crowhurst*, 39; Eakin, *A Race Too Far*, 212.

80 Ellen MacArthur, *Full Circle* (London: Michael Joseph, 2010), 15–16.

81 *The Himalayan Database* (1 July 2019), *http://www.himalayandata base.com/2018 Season/Lists/2018/Spring/A1.html*.

82 Knox-Johnston, *A World of My Own*, 54. The importance to Knox-Johnston and other competitors of nautical patriotism is explored in J. R. L. Anderson, *The Ulysses Factor: The Exploring Instinct in Man* (London: Hodder & Stoughton, 1970), 245–9.

83 Alain Gerbault, *In Quest of the Sun* (London: Hodder & Stoughton, [1929]), 77.

84 Moitessier, *The Long Way*, 163.

85 See, for instance, her recent publication *Reuse: Rethinking Packaging* (Ellen MacArthur Foundation, 2019).

86 For a survey of the aftermath in various media, see Edward Renehan, *Desperate Voyage: Donald Crowhurst, The London Sunday Times Golden Globe Race, and the Tragedy of Teignmouth Electron* (Wickford, RI: New Street Communications, 2016), 105–6.

87 *The Mercy*, starring Colin Firth, and *Crowhurst*, starring Justin Salinger.

88 Moitessier, *The Long Way*, 171.

89 Peter F. Anson, *The Quest of Solitude* (London: J. M. Dent, 1932), 262–3.

90 Eakin, *A Race Too Far*, 240–60.

91 Tomalin and Hall, *The Strange Voyage of Donald Crowhurst*, 249; Nichols, *A Voyage for Madmen*, 265–74; Michael Bender, 'Yachting and Madness', *Journal for Maritime Research*, 15, 1 (2013): 83–93.

92 HM Inspector of Prisons, *Urgent Notification: HM Prison Exeter* (30 May 2018).

93 Peter Scharff Smith, 'The Effects of Solitary Confinement on

Prison Inmates: A Brief History and Review of the Literature', *Crime and Justice*, 34, 1 (2006): 468–9.

94 Sharon Shalev and Kimmett Edgar, *Deep Custody: Segregation Units and Close Supervision Centres in England and Wales* (London: Prison Reform Trust, October 2015), v.

95 Lorna A. Rhodes, *Total Confinement: Madness and Reason in the Maximum Security Prison* (Berkeley: University of California Press, 2004), 21–60; Jeffrey L. Metzner and Jamie Fellner, 'Solitary Confinement and Mental Illness in US Prisons: A Challenge for Medical Ethics', *Journal of the American Academy of Psychiatry and the Law*, 38 (2010): 104–7. The figures for the American prisoners in solitary do not include those in immigrant detention centres, county jails, and juvenile facilities.

96 Shalev and Edgar, *Deep Custody*, 40.

97 Sharon Shalev, *A Sourcebook on Solitary Confinement* (London: Mannheim Centre for Criminology, 2008), 10.

98 The British Medical Association, the Royal College of Psychiatrists, and the Royal College of Paediatrics and Child Health. See British Medical Association, 'Our Joint Position Statement on the Medical Role in Solitary Confinement' (London: March 2018).

99 HM Inspector of Prisons, *Report on an Announced Inspection of HMP Wormwood Scrubs, 31 July–11 August 2017* (2017).

100 HM Chief Inspector of Prisons for England and Wales, *Annual Report 2017–18* (11 July 2018), 15.

101 *UK Prison Population Statistics* (23 July 2019), *https://researchbriefings.parliament.uk/ResearchBriefing/Summary/SN04334#fullreport*; Vicky Pryce, *Prisonomics* (London: Biteback, 2013), 249.

102 Alison Liebling, *Prisons and Their Moral Performance* (Oxford: Oxford University Press, 2005), 456.

103 Independent Monitoring Board, *HMP Bedford – IMB Statement in Response to Urgent Notification* (13 September 2018). Also HM Inspectorate of Prisons, *Debriefing Paper: Full Inspection of: HMP Bedford, 28 August–6 September 2018* (2018).

104 Shalev and Edgar, *Deep Custody*, vi.

105 HM Chief Inspector of Prisons, *Urgent Notification: HM Prison Birmingham* (16 August 2018).

106 Children's Commissioner for England, *Report on the Use of*

Segregation in Youth Custody in England (London: October 2018), 7. It was reported at the beginning of March 2019 that Aylesbury Young Offenders Institution has been put in special measures following the discovery that inmates were being held in its segregation unit for up to three months at a time.

107 Frieda Fromm-Reichmann, 'On Loneliness', in *Psychoanalysis and Psychotherapy: Selected Papers of Frieda Fromm-Reichmann*, ed. Dexter M. Bullard (Chicago: University of Chicago Press, 1959), 333. On her work on loneliness, see below, Chapter 7, 228–9.

108 Christopher Burney, *Solitary Confinement* (London: Clerke and Cockeran, 1952), 150. On Burney and his use of enforced free time, see Philip Koch, *Solitude: A Philosophical Encounter* (Chicago: Open Court, 1994), 107–8.

109 Edith Bone, *Seven Years Solitary* (Oxford: Bruno Cassirer, 1966), 101.

110 Bone, *Seven Years Solitary*, 103.

111 Terry Waite, *Taken on Trust* (London: Hodder & Stoughton, 1993), 117. See also three other books by Waite: *Footfalls in Memory: Reflections on Solitude* (London: Hodder & Stoughton, 1996); *Out of the Silence: Memories, Poems, Reflections* (London: SPCK, 2016); *Solitude: Memories, People, Places* (London: SPCK, 2017).

112 Waite, *Taken on Trust*, 117. Waite subsequently published an anthology of extracts from the books he had read in solitary confinement. See Waite, *Footfalls in Memory*.

113 John Le Carré, *The Pigeon Tunnel* (London: Viking, 2016), 252–3.

114 Le Carré, *The Pigeon Tunnel*, 254.

115 Stephanie Dowrick, *Intimacy and Solitude* (London: The Women's Press, 1992), 153. For a recent example of survival in the American solitary confinement system, see Albert Woodfox, *Solitary* (New York: First Grove Atlantic, 2019), the memoir of a former Black Panther who was sustained by his political commitment and his sense of injustice at his murder conviction, which eventually was overturned.

116 Waite, *Taken on Trust*, 108.

117 Waite, *Taken on Trust*, 196.

118 Waite, *Taken on Trust*, 218.

119 Thomas Merton, *The Seven Storey Mountain* (1948; London:

Sheldon Press, 1975). On the initial reception of the book, see Monica Furlong, *Merton: A Biography* (London: Collins, 1980), 153–62.

120 Mary Frances Coady, *Merton and Waugh: A Monk, a Crusty Old Man, & the Seven Storey Mountain* (Brewster, MA: Paraclete Press, 2015).

121 On the conventional nature of the structure, see Diarmaid MacCulloch, *Silence: A Christian History* (London: Allen Lane, 2013), 229.

122 Merton, *The Seven Storey Mountain*, 163–4.

123 Merton, *The Seven Storey Mountain*, 321.

124 On the English revival, and the influence upon it of Thomas Merton, see Mother Mary Clare, 'Eremitical Revival in the Anglican Church in the Twentieth Century', in *Solitude and Communion: Papers on the Hermit Life*, ed. A. M. Allchin (1977; 2nd edn, Oxford: SLG Press, 2014), 78–94.

125 On the post-war expansion of Cistercian communities, see Louis J. Lekai, *The Cistercians: Ideals and Reality* (Kent, OH: Kent State University Press, 1977), 209–10.

126 Merton, *The Seven Storey Mountain*, 325.

127 Alain Corbin, *A History of Silence*, trans. Jean Birrell (2016; Cambridge: Polity, 2018), 42–8.

128 For a more recent exploration of this understanding, see Rachel Muers, *Keeping God's Silence* (Oxford: Blackwell, 2004), 11.

129 Thomas Merton, 'Notes for a Philosophy of Solitude', in *Disputed Questions* (London: Hollis and Carter, 1961), 190.

130 Merton, 'Notes for a Philosophy of Solitude', 180–1. Also Thomas Merton, *Thoughts in Solitude* (London: Burns & Oates, 1958), 69; Diana Senechal, *Republic of Noise: The Loss of Solitude in Schools and Culture* (Lanham, MD: Rowman & Littlefield, 2014), 22.

131 Merton, *The Seven Storey Mountain*, 190.

132 Merton, 'Notes for a Philosophy of Solitude', 183.

133 Merton, 'Notes for a Philosophy of Solitude', 190.

134 Merton, *Thoughts in Solitude*, 72.

135 Thomas Merton, *The Waters of Silence*, with a Foreword by Evelyn Waugh (London: Hollis and Carter, 1950).

136 A. M. Allchin, 'The Solitary Vocation: Some Theological Considerations', in *Solitude and Communion*, 9.

137 Merton, 'Notes for a Philosophy of Solitude', 204.

138 Merton, 'Notes for a Philosophy of Solitude', 185.

139 Patrick Leigh Fermor, *A Time to Keep Silence* (1953; London: John Murray, 1982), 33.

140 Dom Jean Leclercq, *Alone with God* (London: Hodder & Stoughton, 1962), 38.

141 MacCulloch, *Silence*, 229; Lekai, *The Cistercians*, 213.

142 Furlong, *Merton: A Biography*, 239.

143 Thomas Merton, *Turning Toward the World: The Pivotal Years*, ed. Victor A. Kramer (San Francisco: HarperSanFrancisco, 1997), 64, entry for 14 November 1960.

144 Thomas Merton, *New Seeds of Contemplation* (London: Burns & Oates, 1962), 41.

145 Furlong, *Merton: A Biography*, 244.

146 Merton, *Turning Toward the World*, 216.

147 James Finley, *Merton's Palace of Nowhere* (Notre Dame, IN: Ave Maria Press, 1978).

148 Cited in Peter Stanford, *Cardinal Hume and the Changing Face of English Catholicism* (London: Geoffrey Chapman, 1999), 196.

149 Lekai, *The Cistercians*, 210.

150 Catherine Pepinster, 'Crucial Test for Benedictine Monks' New Leader as Order Faces Sex Abuse Scrutiny', *Guardian*, 13 October 2017.

151 Grace Davie, *Religion in Britain: A Persistent Paradox* (2nd edn, Chichester: John Wiley, 2015), 37.

152 Philip Larkin, 'Vers de Société', *The New Statesman*, 18 June 1971: 854.

153 Richard Scorer, *Betrayed: The English Catholic Church and the Sex Abuse Crisis* (London: Biteback, 2014); Pepinster, 'Crucial Test for Benedictine Monks' New Leader'; MacCulloch, *Silence*, 203–4.

154 See above, Chapter 4, 128, 130, 151–2.

155 On church attendance, see Peter Brierley, *The Tide is Running Out: What the English Church Attendance Survey Reveals* (London: Christian Research, 2000), 27; Paul Heelas and Linda Woodhead,

The Spiritual Revolution: Why Religion is Giving Way to Spirituality (Oxford: Blackwell, 2005), 51.

156 Report by the Bishop of Chelmsford to the 2018 National Cathedrals Conference.

157 Wade Davis, *Into the Silence* (London: The Bodley Head, 2011), 279, 300–1.

158 Vicki Mackenzie, *Cave in the Snow: Tenzin Palmo's Quest for Enlightenment* (London: Bloomsbury, 1998), 79. The cave was so small that Tenzin Palmo was unable to lie down to sleep at night.

159 Esther de Waal, *Seeking God: The Way of St Benedict* (London: HarperCollins, 1996), 26.

160 Esther de Waal, *A Retreat with Thomas Merton* (3rd edn, London: Canterbury Press, 2010), 14–15.

161 Esther de Waal, *Living with Contradiction: Benedictine Wisdom for Everyday Living* (Norwich: Canterbury Press, 2003), 13.

162 For a useful survey of this world, see Heelas and Woodhead, *The Spiritual Revolution*.

163 Giselle Vincett and Linda Woodhead, 'Spirituality', in *Religions in the Modern World: Traditions and Transformations*, ed. Linda Woodhead et al. (2nd edn, London: Routledge, 2009), 320–2.

164 Stephen Batchelor, *Alone with Others: An Existential Approach to Buddhism* (New York: Grove Weidenfeld, 1983), 69. Also Graham Turner, *The Power of Silence: The Riches that Lie Within* (London: Bloomsbury 2014), 175–98.

165 Claire Thompson, *Mindfulness and the Natural World: Bringing Our Awareness Back to Nature* (London: Leaping Hare Press, 2018), 8.

166 Roger Housden, *Retreat: Time Apart for Silence & Solitude* (London: Thorsons, 1995).

167 Paul Salmon and Susan Matarese, 'Mindfulness Meditation: Seeking Solitude in Community', in *The Handbook of Solitude*, 335–50.

168 Jon Kabat-Zinn, *Full Catastrophe Living* (London: Piatkus, 2004), 20.

169 Kabat-Zinn, *Full Catastrophe Living*, 23.

170 On the costs of retreats and the tendency for them to be patronized by the educated middle class, see de Waal, *Retreat with Thomas Merton*, 13; Heelas and Woodhead, *The Spiritual Revolution*, 93.

171 Ronald E. Purser, *McMindfulness: How Mindfulness became the New Capitalist Spirituality* (London: Repeater Books, 2019), 14–34; David Forbes, *Mindfulness and Its Discontents: Education, Self and Social Transformation* (Black Point, NS: Fernwood Publishing, 2019), 25–45.

Chapter 7 The 'Epidemic of Loneliness' Revisited

1 HM Government, *A Connected Society: A Strategy for Tackling Loneliness – Laying the Foundations for Change* (London: Department for Digital, Culture, Media and Sport (October 2018). The strategy was for England only. Tracey Crouch resigned from the government a fortnight later on an unrelated issue of principle.

2 Gov UK, 'Prime Minister Theresa May Launches Government's First Loneliness Strategy' (London: Prime Minister's Office, 15 October 2018).

3 HM Government, *A Connected Society*, 6.

4 Co-op and British Red Cross, *Trapped in a Bubble: An Investigation into Triggers for Loneliness in the UK* (December, 2016), 17.

5 Office for National Statistics, *Loneliness – What Characteristics and Circumstances are Associated with Feeling Lonely?* (April 2018), 2–3. The survey covered England only.

6 *https://www.campaigntoendloneliness.org/the-facts-on-loneliness/*.

7 Jo Cox Commission on Loneliness, *Combatting Loneliness One Conversation at a Time: A Call to Action* (2017), 8.

8 The findings were first broadcast in a BBC Radio 4 *All in the Mind* programme on 1 October 2018.

9 K. D. M. Snell, *Spirits of Community: English Senses of Belonging and Loss, 1750–2000* (London: Bloomsbury Academic, 2016). Also K. D. M. Snell, 'Agendas for the Historical Study of Loneliness and Lone Living', *The Open Psychology Journal*, 8, Suppl 2-M2 (2015): 62.

10 *The Age of Loneliness*, BBC One, 18 October 2016; Colin Killeen, 'Loneliness: An Epidemic in Modern Society', *Journal of Advanced Nursing*, 28, 4 (1998): 762–70.

11 Chris Randall and Ann Corp, *Measuring National Well-being: European Comparisons, 2014* (Office for National Statistics, June 2014), figs 2 and 6.

12 John Bingham, 'Britain the Loneliness Capital of Europe', *Daily Telegraph*, 18 June 2014. See also Radhika Sanghani, 'Generation Lonely: Britain's Young People Have Never Been Less Connected', *Daily Telegraph*, 28 December 2014. It is cited without comment in a recent review of loneliness: Olivia Sagan and Eric Miller, 'Introduction', in *Narratives of Loneliness: Multidisciplinary Perspectives from the 21st Century*, ed. Olivia Sagan and Eric D. Miller (London: Routledge, 2018), 1.

13 George Monbiot, 'The Age of Loneliness is Killing Us', *Guardian*, 14 October 2014. See also George Monbiot, 'Why I Wrote an Album of Anthems for All the Lonely People', *Guardian*, 3 October 2016.

14 Michael Harris, *Solitude: In Pursuit of a Singular Life in a Crowded World* (London: Random House, 2017), 32.

15 HM Government, *A Connected Society*, 60.

16 Christina Victor et al., 'Loneliness, Social Isolation, and Living Alone in Later Life', Research Findings no. 17, Growing Older Programme. Economic and Social Research Council, 2003, *http://www.growingolder.group.shef.ac.uk/ChristinaVic_F17.pdf*, 1.

17 G. Clare Wenger et al., 'Social Isolation and Loneliness in Old Age: Review and Model Refinement', *Ageing and Society*, 16 (1996): 336. See also Joan Fidler, 'Loneliness. The Problems of the Elderly and Retired', *The Journal of the Royal Society for the Promotion of Health*, 96, 1 (1976): 39–41; Letitia Anne Peplau et al., 'Being Old and Living Alone', in *Loneliness: A Sourcebook of Current Theory, Research and Therapy*, ed. Letitia Anne Peplau and Daniel Perlman (New York: John Wiley, 1982), 332.

18 For a late discussion of the pathology of melancholy, see Edwin L. Hopewell-Ash, *Melancholia in Everyday Practice* (London: John Bale, 1934).

19 Clark E. Moustakas, *Loneliness* (Englewood Cliffs, NJ: Prentice Hall, 1961), 25.

20 Ami Rokach, 'Editorial: Loneliness Past and Present, and Its Effects on Our Lives', *The Open Psychology Journal*, 8, Suppl 2-M1 (2015): 59.

21 HM Government, *A Connected Society*, 18. The reference is to Daniel Perlman and Letitia Anne Peplau, 'Toward a Social

Psychology of Loneliness', in *Personal Relationships: 3. Relationships in Disorder*, ed. Steve Duck and Robin Gilmour (London: Academic Press, 1981), 32. See also Daniel Perlman and Letitia Anne Peplau, 'Loneliness Research: A Survey of Empirical Findings', in *Preventing the Harmful Consequences of Severe and Persistent Loneliness*, ed. Letitia Anne Peplau and Stephen E. Goldston (Rockville, MD: US Department of Health and Human Services, 1984), 15; Liesl M. Heinrich and Eleonora Gullone, 'The Clinical Significance of Loneliness: A Literature Review', *Clinical Psychology Review*, 26 (2006): 698.

22 Daniel W. Russell et al., 'Is Loneliness the Same as Being Alone?', *The Journal of Psychology*, 146, 1–2 (2012): 21; Robert S. Weiss, *Loneliness: The Experience of Emotional and Social Isolation* (Cambridge, MA: MIT Press, 1973), 15–22.

23 Stephanie Dowrick, *Intimacy and Solitude* (London: The Women's Press, 1992), 141. Also Peter Townsend, *The Family Life of Old People* (London: Routledge & Kegan Paul, 1957), 166. For a converse view which moves between positive and negative aspects of the same condition of solitude, see Kenneth H. Rubin, 'Foreword: On Solitude, Withdrawal, and Social Isolation', in *The Handbook of Solitude: Psychological Perspectives on Social Isolation, Social Withdrawal, and Being Alone*, ed. Robert J. Coplan and Julie C. Bowker (Chichester: Wiley Blackwell, 2014), xiii–xvii.

24 Thomas Dumm, *Loneliness as a Way of Life* (Cambridge, MA: Harvard University Press, 2008), 40–1. Also Fay Bound Alberti, 'This "Modern Epidemic": Loneliness as an Emotion Cluster and a Neglected Subject in the History of Emotions', *Emotion Review*, 10, 3 (2018): 2.

25 Paul Tillich, *The Eternal Now: Sermons* (London: SCM Press, 1963), 11.

26 See, *inter alia*, Evangelina Galanaki, 'The Origins of Solitude: Psychoanalytic Perspectives', in *The Handbook of Solitude*, 71; Reed Larson and Meery Lee, 'The Capacity to Be Alone as a Stress Buffer', *The Journal of Social Psychology*, 136, 1 (1996): 6; Sherry Turkle, *Alone Together: Why We Expect More from Technology and Less from Each Other* (New York: Basic Books, 2012), 288; Brian Beach and Sally-Marie Bamford, *Isolation: The Emerging Crisis*

for Older Men. A Report Exploring Experiences of Social Isolation and Loneliness among Older men in England (London: Independent Age and International Longevity Centre, 2014), 3; Lars Svendsen, A Philosophy of Loneliness (London: Reaktion Books, 2017), 107–8.

27 Mass Observation, File Reports: Women in Wartime (June 1940), 18.

28 Mass Observation, File Reports: The Crisis (June 1944), 68; also 70.

29 Mass Observation, File Reports: The Crisis, 96.

30 Penny Summerfield, Reconstructing Women's Wartime Lives (Manchester: Manchester University Press, 1998), 78–113.

31 Mass Observation, File Reports: Women and the War Effort (December 1940), 28.

32 Nella Last, The Diaries of Nella Last, ed. Patricia and Robert Malcolmson (London: Profile Books, 2012), 25.

33 See, for instance, Emily D. Samson, Old Age in the New World (London: The Pilot Press, 1944), 6–7.

34 Jeremy Tunstall, Old and Alone: A Sociological Study of Old People (London: Routledge & Kegan Paul, 1966), 1–2; Office for National Statistics, Overview of the UK Population: November 2018 (2018); Pat Thane, Old Age in English History: Past Experiences, Present Issues (Oxford: Oxford University Press, 2000), 333.

35 J. H. Sheldon, The Social Medicine of Old Age (London: Oxford University Press for the Nuffield Foundation, 1948), 190.

36 Jim Ogg, Living Alone in Later Life (London: Institute of Community Studies, 2003), xii.

37 Sheldon, Social Medicine of Old Age, 135. See also Peter Marris, Widows and Their Families (London: Routledge & Kegan Paul, 1958), 55; Marilyn J. Essex and Sunghee Nam, 'Marital Status and Loneliness among Older Women: The Differential Importance of Close Family and Friends', Journal of Marriage and Family, 49, 1 (1987): 101; Chris Phillipson et al., The Family and Community Life of Older People (London: Routledge, 2001), 5–6; Robert L. Rubinstein, Singular Paths: Old Men Living Alone (New York: Columbia University Press, 1986), 199.

38 Townsend, Family Life of Old People, 182.

39 Townsend, Family Life of Old People, 175.

40 Peter Townsend, 'Isolation, Desolation and Loneliness', in Ethel Shanas et al., *Old People in Three Industrial Societies* (London: Routledge & Kegan Paul, 1968), 262.

41 See above, Chapter 5, 157.

42 Ogg, *Living Alone in Later Life*, 26.

43 Eliot Slater and Moya Woodside, *Patterns of Marriage: A Study of Marriage Relationships in the Urban Working Classes* (London: Cassell, 1951), 91–2.

44 Michael Young and Peter Willmott, *Family and Kinship in East London* (Harmondsworth: Penguin, 1962), 149. For a re-evaluation of this study, see Jon Lawrence, 'Inventing the "Traditional Working Class": A Re-Analysis of Interview Notes from Young and Willmott's *Family and Kinship in East London*', *Historical Journal*, 59, 2 (2016): 567–93.

45 Mark Abrams, *Beyond Three-Score Years and Ten: A First Report on a Survey of the Elderly* (Mitcham: Age Concern, 1978).

46 It was voted by the magazine *Broadcast* in 2005 the most influential British television programme ever made.

47 G. M. Carstairs, *This Island Now* (London: The Hogarth Press, 1963), 21.

48 Mark Jackson, *The Age of Stress: Science and the Search for Stability* (Oxford: Oxford University Press, 2013), 6; Ali Haggett, *Desperate Housewives, Neuroses and the Domestic Environment, 1945–1970* (London: Pickering & Chatto, 2012).

49 Andrew Scull, *Madness in Civilization: A Cultural History of Insanity, from the Bible to Freud, from the Madhouse to Modern Medicine* (London: Thames & Hudson, 2016), 362. Figures for England and Wales.

50 Erving Goffman, *Asylums: Essays on the Condition of Mental Patients and Other Inmates* (New York: Vintage Books, 1961).

51 Roy Porter, *Madness: A Brief History* (Oxford: Oxford University Press, 2002), 198.

52 L. Andersson, 'Loneliness Research and Interventions: A Review of the Literature', *Aging & Mental Health*, 2, 4 (1998): 264–74.

53 The paper was in draft form at her death in 1957, and was prepared for publication two years later. Frieda Fromm-Reichmann, 'On Loneliness', in *Psychoanalysis and Psychotherapy: Selected Papers*

of Frieda Fromm-Reichmann, ed. Dexter M. Bullard (Chicago: University of Chicago Press, 1959), 332.

54 Fromm-Reichmann, 'On Loneliness', 325.

55 Fromm-Reichmann, 'On Loneliness', 326.

56 This theory is further explored in Michael Hughes and Walter R. Gove, 'Living Alone, Social Integration, and Mental Health', *American Journal of Sociology*, 87, 1 (1981): 48–74; Liesl M. Heinrich and Eleonora Gullone, 'The Clinical Significance of Loneliness: A Literature Review', *Clinical Psychology Review*, 26 (2006): 695–6.

57 Fromm-Reichmann, 'On Loneliness', 327.

58 John Bowlby, *Maternal Care and Mental Health* (Geneva: World Health Organization, 1952), 11. See also John Bowlby, *Attachment and Loss, Vol. 2: Separation: Anxiety and Anger* (Harmondsworth: Pelican Books, 1975), 43.

59 Bowlby, *Maternal Care and Mental Health*, 72.

60 Bowlby, *Maternal Care and Mental Health*, 12.

61 Anthony Storr, *Solitude* (1989; London: HarperCollins, 1997).

62 Dowrick, *Intimacy and Solitude*, 141–62.

63 D. W. Winnicott, 'The Capacity to Be Alone' (1960), in *The Maturational Processes and the Facilitating Environment* (London: The Hogarth Press, 1965), 30.

64 Winnicott, 'The Capacity to Be Alone', 33.

65 Winnicott, 'The Capacity to Be Alone', 30.

66 Sheldon, *Social Medicine of Old Age*; Tunstall, *Old and Alone*. See also Ogg, *Living Alone in Later Life*, 50–1.

67 Judith Shulevitz, 'The Lethality of Loneliness', *The New Republic*, 27 May 2013: 21–9.

68 HM Government, *A Connected Society*, 18.

69 John T. Cacioppo and Stephanie Cacioppo, 'The Growing Problem of Loneliness', *The Lancet*, 391 (3 February 2018): 426.

70 The limitations of this form of counting are surveyed in Svendsen, *A Philosophy of Loneliness*, 49–53.

71 Andersson, 'Loneliness Research and Interventions': 265.

72 See above, Chapter 4, 144–6.

73 Jerry M. Burger, 'Individual Differences in Preference for Solitude', *Journal of Research in Personality*, 29 (1995): 85–108.

74 Christina R. Victor and Keming Yang, 'The Prevalence of Loneliness Among Adults: A Case Study of the United Kingdom', *The Journal of Psychology*, 146, 1–2 (2011): 100.

75 Office for National Statistics, *Loneliness*, 7–8. See also Thane, *Old Age in English History*, 398.

76 Ye Luo et al., 'Loneliness, Health, and Mortality in Old Age: A National Longitudinal Study', *Social Science & Medicine*, 74 (2012): 907. Also G. A. Matthews et al., 'Dorsal Raphe Dopamine Neurons Represent the Experience of Social Isolation', *Cell*, 164, 4 (2016); research cited in Erica Buist, 'All by Myself', *Guardian*, 28 April 2018.

77 Shulevitz, 'The Lethality of Loneliness', 24.

78 See the discussion in Claudia Hammond, *http://www.bbc.com/future/story/20180213-five-myths-about-loneliness*.

79 Katherine King, 'Social Isolation', in *Cultural Sociology of Mental Illness*, ed. Andrew Scull (London: Sage, 2014), vol. 2, 817.

80 Denis Campbell, 'Loneliness Among Over-50s "is Looming Public Health Concern"', *Guardian*, 25 September 2018.

81 Julianne Holt-Lunstad et al., 'Loneliness and Social Isolation as Risk Factors for Mortality: A Meta-Analytic Review', *Perspectives on Psychological Science*, 10, 2 (2015): 233.

82 Cacioppo and Cacioppo, 'The Growing Problem of Loneliness': 426. On this claim, see also Holt-Lunstad et al., 'Loneliness and Social Isolation': 232. For a broader account of the physiological consequences of loneliness, see John T. Cacioppo and William Patrick, *Loneliness: Human Nature and the Need for Social Connection* (New York: W. W. Norton, 2009).

83 HM Government, *A Connected Society*, 2.

84 Amy J. McLennan and Stanley J. Ulijaszek, 'Beware the Medicalisation of Loneliness', *The Lancet*, 391, 10129 (14–20 April 2018): 1480. See also Moya Sarner, 'Mindfulness by Itself Won't Cure Loneliness – Ending Austerity is the Key', *Guardian*, 8 June 2018.

85 HM Government, *A Connected Society*, 6.

86 George Monbiot, 'Neoliberalism is Creating Loneliness. That's What's Wrenching Society Apart', *Guardian*, 12 October 2016.

87 Monbiot, 'The Age of Loneliness is Killing Us'.

88 Snell, 'Agendas for the Historical Study of Loneliness and Lone Living': 63.

89 Sara Maitland, *How to Be Alone* (London: Macmillan, 2014), 29.

90 On the importance of considering the terms separately from each other, see Jo Griffin, *The Lonely Society* (London: Mental Health Foundation, 2010), 3.

91 See above, Chapter 1, 15–16.

92 Christopher R. Long and James Averill, 'Solitude: An Exploration of Benefits of Being Alone', *Journal for the Theory of Social Behaviour*, 33, 1 (1997): 31.

93 See above, Chapter 5, 157.

94 See, for instance, the summary in Ray Hall et al., 'The Pattern and Structure of One-Person Households in England and Wales and France', *International Journal of Population Geography*, 3 (1997): 162.

95 Townsend, *Family Life of Old People*, 172; Townsend, 'Isolation, Desolation and Loneliness', 258; Christina Victor et al., *The Social World of Older People: Understanding Loneliness and Social Isolation in Later Life* (Maidenhead: Open University Press, 2009), 209–16; Wenger et al., 'Social Isolation and Loneliness in Old Age': 334.

96 Peplau et al., 'Being Old and Living Alone', 329, 342.

97 David Vincent, *Privacy: A Short History* (Cambridge: Polity, 2016), 79–110; Pat Thane, 'Old Women in Twentieth-Century Britain', in *Women and Ageing in British Society Since 1500*, ed. Lynn Botelho and Pat Thane (Harlow: Pearson Education, 2001), 215–16; Robert T. Michael et al., 'Changes in the Propensity to Live Alone: 1950–1976', *Demography*, 17, 1 (1980): 40; Phillipson et al. *The Family and Community Life of Older People*, 87.

98 Ogg, *Living Alone in Later Life*, 5.

99 Eric Klinenberg, *Going Solo: The Extraordinary Rise and Surprising Appeal of Living Alone* (London: Duckworth Overlook, 2013), 31; Michael Hughes and Walter R. Gove, 'Living Alone, Social Integration, and Mental Health', *American Journal of Sociology*, 87, 1 (1981): 48–74.

100 Sheldon, *The Social Medicine of Old Age*, 128. See also Elizabeth Roberts, *A Woman's Place: An Oral History of Working-Class Women 1890–1940* (Oxford: Basil Blackwell, 1984), 172.

101 Richard Wall, 'Relationships Between the Generations in British

Families Past and Present', in *Families and Households: Divisions and Change*, ed. Catherine Marsh and Sara Arber (Houndmills: Macmillan, 1992), 72–6.

102 Phillipson et al., *The Family and Community Life of Older People*, 87, 4; Peter Willmott, *Friendship Networks and Social Support* (London: Policy Studies Institute, 1987), 96–7.

103 Elaine Wethington and Karl Pillener, 'Social Isolation Among Older People', in *The Handbook of Solitude*, 243–4.

104 Ray Pahl, *On Friendship* (Cambridge: Polity, 2000), 167–8.

105 *British Social Attitudes Survey, 2007*, cited in Office for National Statistics, *Social Trends, No. 39* (2009), 203–4.

106 Phillipson et al., *The Family and Community Life of Older People*, 242.

107 Anneli Rufus, *Party of One* (New York: Marlowe and Company, 2003), 19.

108 Anthony Giddens, *The Transformation of Intimacy: Sexuality, Love and Eroticism in Modern Societies* (Cambridge: Polity, 1992), esp. 184–9.

109 Mass Observation, *File Reports: Some Psychological Factors in Home Building* (March 1943), 3.

110 Storr, *Solitude*, xiv.

111 Delease Wear, 'Introduction', in *The Center of the Web: Women and Solitude*, ed. Delease Wear (Albany: State University of New York Press, 1993), xiv.

112 Reed W. Larson, 'Secrets in the Bedroom: Adolescents' Private Use of Media', *Journal of Youth and Adolescence*, 24, 5 (1995): 353; Reed W. Larson, 'The Uses of Loneliness in Adolescence', in *Loneliness in Childhood and Adolescence*, ed. Ken J. Rotenberg and Shelley Hymel (Cambridge: Cambridge University Press, 1999), 244–62.

113 Jon Lawrence, *Me Me Me? The Search for Community in Post-War England* (Oxford: Oxford University Press, 2019), 231.

114 Simon Garfield, *The Error World: An Affair with Stamps* (London: Faber & Faber, 2008), 2.

115 Pahl, *On Friendship*, 168.

116 Rubinstein, *Singular Paths*, 195.

117 Office for National Statistics, *Loneliness*, 4; BBC Radio 4, *The Anatomy of Loneliness*, Episode 1, BBC Radio 4, 2 October 2018.

118 HM Government, *A Connected Society*, 20.

119 Long and Averill, 'Solitude: An Exploration of Benefits of Being Alone': 31.

120 On the greater resilience of the old to periods of loneliness, see Reed W. Larson, 'The Solitary Side of Life: An Examination of the Time People Spend Alone from Childhood to Old Age', *Developmental Review*, 10, 2 (1990): 176–7.

121 Andersson, 'Loneliness Research and Interventions': 265.

122 Patricia and Robert Malcolmson, *A Free-Spirited Woman: The London Diaries of Gladys Langford, 1936–1940* (Woodbridge: The London Record Society and The Boydell Press, 2014), 49.

123 Last, *The Diaries of Nella Last*, 346.

124 Colin Killeen, 'Loneliness: An Epidemic in Modern Society', *Journal of Advanced Nursing*, 28, 4 (1998): 765.

125 Marris, *Widows and Their Families*, 55–67.

126 See above, Chapter 3, 105–11.

127 See, for instance, Angela Willans, *Alone Again* (Rugby: National Marriage Guidance Council, 1977).

128 See, for instance, M. S. Stroebe et al., 'Consequences of Bereavement: A Review', *The Lancet*, 370 (8 December 2007): 1960–73.

129 Linda A. Wood, 'Loneliness', in *The Social Construction of Emotions*, ed. Rom Harré (Oxford: Basil Blackwell, 1986), 193.

130 Eliot Deutsch, 'Loneliness and Solitude', in *Loneliness*, ed. Leroy S. Rouner (Notre Dame, IN: University of Notre Dame Press, 1998), 117.

131 On the association of loneliness with lower income groups in the later twentieth century, see Wood, 'Loneliness', 200.

132 Delease Wear, 'A Reconnection to Self: Women and Solitude', in *The Center of the Web*, 10. See also Jo Malin, 'Introduction', in *Herspace: Women, Writing, Solitude*, ed. Jo Malin and Victoria Boynton (New York: The Haworth Press, 2003), 6; Christina Pugh, 'Unknown Women: Secular Solitude in the Works of Alice Koller and May Sarton', in *Herspace*, 73.

133 Alberti, 'This "Modern Epidemic"', 2.

134 Data from the Social Metrics Commission and the Institute of Fiscal Studies, cited in Philip Alston, United Nations Special

Rapporteur on extreme poverty and human rights, *Statement on Visit to the United Kingdom* (16 November 2018), 1.

135 Thomas Scharf et al., 'Social Exclusion of Older People in Deprived Urban Communities of England', *European Journal of Ageing*, 2 (2005): 83.

136 Eric Klinenberg, *Palaces for the People: How to Build a More Equal and United Society* (London: The Bodley Head, 2018), 1–24.

137 See above, Chapter 5, 179–80.

138 Ogg, *Living Alone in Later Life*, 27.

139 HM Government, *A Connected Society*, 30.

140 On the growing 'loneliness industry' in the post-war decades, see Margaret Mary Wood, *Paths of Loneliness: The Individual Isolated in Modern Society* (New York: Columbia University Press, 1960), 8. For an influential survey of the range of voluntary and municipal responses that needed to be made to loneliness, see National Council of Social Services, *Loneliness: An Enquiry into Causes and Possible Remedies* (London: National Council of Social Services, 1964), 53–7.

141 See, for instance, the columns in *Woman:* 3 January 1976: 58; 17 January 1976: 8; 7 February 1976: 62; 14 February 1976: 63; 28 February 1976: 63; 5 June 1976: 59.

Chapter 8 Conclusion: Solitude in the Digital Era

1 See above, Chapter 5, 162.

2 Ofcom, *Adults' Media Use and Attitudes Report* (25 April 2018), *https://www.ofcom.org.uk/__data/assets/pdf_file/0011/113222/Adults-Media-Use-and-Attitudes-Report-2018.pdf*, 2.

3 Amanda Lenhart and Dana Page, *Teens, Social Media & Technology Overview 2015: Smartphones Facilitate Shifts in Communication Landscape for Teens* (Pew Research Center, April 2015), 4, *https://www.pewresearch.org/internet/2015/04/09/teens-social-media-technology-2015/*; Pew Research Center, *Teens, Social Media & Technology* (31 May 2018), *https://www.pewinternet.org/2018/05/31/teens-social-media-technology-2018/*. 'Teenagers' in the Pew study were those aged thirteen to seventeen.

4 See, for instance, Amanda Lenhart and Maeve Duggan, *Couples, the Internet, and Social Media: How American Couples Use Digital*

Technology to Manage Life, Logistics, and Emotional Intimacy within Their Relationships (Pew Research Center, February 2014), *https:// www.pewresearch.org/internet/2014/02/11/couples-the-internet-and-so cial-media/.*

5 See, for instance, Katerina Lup et al., 'Instagram #Instasad? Exploring Associations Among Instagram Use, Depressive Symptoms, Negative Social Comparison and Strangers Followed', *Cyberpsychology, Behavior, and Social Networking*, 18, 5 (2015): 247–52. See also Chapter 1, 14.

6 The most recent reviews of research on the impact of digital media on loneliness find that it is too soon to resolve contradictory findings. Philip S. Morrison and Rebekah Smith, 'Loneliness: An Overview', in *Narratives of Loneliness: Multidisciplinary Perspectives from the 21st Century*, ed. Olivia Sagan and Eric D. Miller (London: Routledge, 2018), 17; Eric D. Miller, 'Cyberloneliness: The Curse of the Cursor?', in *Narratives of Loneliness*, 56–62.

7 See above, Chapter 1, 25–6.

8 Avner Offer, 'Consumption and Well-Being', in *The Oxford Handbook of the History of Consumption*, ed. Frank Trentmann (Oxford: Oxford University Press, 2013), 654.

9 Yair Amichai-Hamburger and Barry H. Schneider, 'Loneliness and Internet Use', in *The Handbook of Solitude: Psychological Perspectives on Social Isolation, Social Withdrawal, and Being Alone*, ed. Robert J. Coplan and Julie C. Bowker (Chichester: Wiley Blackwell, 2014), 319; Sherry Turkle, *Alone Together: Why We Expect More from Technology and Less from Each Other* (New York: Basic Books, 2012).

10 For an early examination of this issue, see Miller McPherson et al., 'Social Isolation in America: Changes in Core Discussion Networks over Two Decades', *American Sociological Review*, 71, 3 (2006): 373.

11 Sherry Turkle, *Reclaiming Conversation: The Power of Talk in a Digital Age* (New York: Penguin Press, 2015), 10.

12 W. G. Sebald, *The Rings of Saturn* (1995; London: Vintage, 2002), 53.

13 Sebald, *The Rings of Saturn*, 241.

14 Dan Richards, *Outpost: A Journey to the Wild Ends of the Earth* (Edinburgh: Canongate, 2019), 8.

15 Richards, *Outpost*, 9–10.

16 The only British competitor, Susie Goodall, generated headlines in December 2018 when her boat capsized end-over-end and lost its mast in the southern Pacific Ocean. Appropriately, the winner, Van Den Heede, was the oldest sailor ever to complete a solo round-the-world voyage.

17 Fay Bound Alberti, 'This "Modern Epidemic": Loneliness as an Emotion Cluster and a Neglected Subject in the History of Emotions', *Emotion Review*, 10, 3 (2018): 9.

18 K. D. M. Snell, 'Agendas for the Historical Study of Loneliness and Lone Living', *The Open Psychology Journal*, 8, Suppl. 2-M2 (2015): 64; Roy Pea et al, 'Media Use, Face-to-Face Communication, Media Multitasking, and Social Well-Being among 8- to 12-Year-Old Girls', *Developmental Psychology*, 48, 2 (2012): 334; Olivia Laing, *The Lonely City: Adventures in the Art of Being Alone* (Edinburgh: Canongate, 2016), 221–2.

19 Jean M. Twenge, *iGen* (New York: Atria Books, 2017), 97. The grades correspond to thirteen- to fourteen-, fifteen- to sixteen-, and seventeen- to eighteen-year-olds in the British school system.

20 Lenhart and Duggan, *Couples, the Internet, and Social Media*, 2.

21 Pew Research Center, *Teens, Social Media & Technology*.

22 Veronique Siegler et al., *Inequalities in Social Capital by Age and Sex, July 2015* (Office for National Statistics, 2015), 6; Amichai-Hamburger and Schneider, 'Loneliness and Internet Use', 325.

23 William M. Reddy, *The Navigation of Feeling: A Framework for the History of Emotions* (Cambridge: Cambridge University Press, 2001), 45.

24 Michael Harris, *Solitude. In Pursuit of a Singular Life in a Crowded World* (London: Random House, 2017), 229.

25 Johann Zimmerman, *Solitude Considered with Respect to its Dangerous Influence Upon the Mind and Heart* (London: C. Dilly, 1798), 21. See Chapter 1, 5.

26 Diana Senechal, *Republic of Noise: The Loss of Solitude in Schools and Culture* (Lanham, MD: Rowman & Littlefield, 2014), 33.

27 See Chapter 1, 23–4.

28 Sara Maitland, *How to Be Alone* (London: Macmillan, 2014), 15.

INDEX

Abbey, Edward, 191
Abercrombie, John, 87, 88
Abrams, Mark, 227
Acts of Parliament
  Penitentiary (1779), 135
  Gaol (1823), 137
  Vagrancy (1824), 56
  Catholic Emancipation (1829),
    122
  Highways (1835), 40
  Small Holdings (1892), 96
agricultural labour, 36–7, 39, 44–5, 97,
    188, 189, 252–3
Alastor, or The Spirit of Solitude, see
    Shelley, Percy Bysshe
Alpine Club, the Alps, 51, 62, 64–6, 67,
    68, 69, 194, 201
America, *see* United States
Anatomy of Melancholy, see Burton,
    Robert
Anglican Church, *see* Protestantism
angling, *see* fishing
Arch, Joseph, 36
Ashby, Joseph, 37
attention restoration theory, 192
Austen, Jane, 90, 106
Averill, James, 235
Awful Disclosures of Maria Monk, The,
    127

Bakke, E. Wight, 154
Barclay, Captain, 42
Barrett, Elizabeth, 107, 108
Barrie, J. M., 175
Beeton, Isabella (Mrs), 84
Beeton, Samuel, 57, 84, 93
Benjamin, Walter, 193
Bentham, Jeremy, 135
bereavement, 7, 72, 191, 226, 243–4,
    259
Berlin wool-work, *see* embroidery
bird-singing, competitive, 99–100
Bloomfield, Robert, 26, 27, 28, 29, 40,
    44–5
Blyth, Chay, 196, 198
Bone, Edith, 206
books, 25, 34, 36, 74, 83–6, 91–3, 95,
    108, 110, 128, 143, 154, 195–6, 207,
    218
Bowlby, John, 229–30
Buchan, William, 9, 25
Buddhism, 213, 216, 217, 218
Burn, James Dawson, 42–3
Burney, Christopher, 205–6
Burton, Robert, 5, 8
Byron, Lord, 20, 59–61, 85,

Cacioppo, John and Stephanie, 232, 234
Campaign to End Loneliness, 221

cars, motor vehicles, 34, 40, 69, 162, 167, 179, 188, 189, 238
Carstairs, G. M., 228
Carthusians, 4, 11
Castle of Otranto, see Walpole, Horace
cat breeding, cat shows, 97
Catholic Church, 10–14, 113, 122–32, 133, 138, 208–15, 254; *see also* monasteries
Cathy Come Home, 228
Chesterton, G. K., 21
Chichester, Francis, 197, 199, 200
Childe Harold's Pilgrimage, see Byron, Lord
children, 6, 26, 39, 46, 56, 58–9, 72, 83, 91, 93, 103, 113, 119, 139, 153, 156, 157, 158, 160, 167, 169, 171–2, 179, 205, 224–5, 228, 229, 232, 237–8, 239, 241, 243, 249–50, 251–2
Christianity, *see* religion
Chudleigh, Mary, 25
cigarettes, *see* smoking
cinema, 155, 161, 172–3, 174, 249
Cistercians, 11, 122, 209, 211
cities, *see* urbanization
Clare, John, 29, 31–4, 35–6, 38–9, 44, 45–7, 56, 58, 61, 65, 70, 86–8, 188
climbing, *see* mountains
Cohen, Ira, 21, 27–8
coin collecting, 160, 165
communication networks, 22, 34, 40, 49, 69, 75, 78, 88–9, 90, 99, 102, 109, 110, 113, 128, 144, 151, 155–63, 173, 180, 190, 200, 201–2, 233, 238, 244, 248–52, 254, 255–6, 258–9; *see also* correspondence, digital communication, telephone
Compleat Angler, The, see Walton, Izaak
Connected Society, A, see Crouch, Tracey
Conrad, Joseph, 182–5, 194, 218
convents, 113, 122–32
conversation, 134, 142–4, 154, 238, 251–2
cooking, cookery books, 73, 84–5, 93, 162
correspondence, 22–3, 39, 64–5, 75, 79–80, 88–9, 105, 108, 109, 128, 143, 148, 160, 163, 164, 209, 210, 211, 224, 238, 249
Courtier, Peter, 32–3

Cowley, Abraham, 25–6, 249
Craik, Dinah, 104–5, 131
crosswords, 163–4, 169, 172
Crouch, Tracey, 220, 221, 234, 235, 241, 245
Crowhurst, Donald, 195, 201–2
Cruse Bereavement Care, 243

David Copperfield, see, Dickens, Charles
Davies, Hunter, 170–1
Davitt, Michael, 148, 149
Dayus, Kathleen, 156, 157
de Beaumont, Gustave, 136, 138, 141
Debord, Guy, 193
Defoe, Daniel, 23–4, 45, 46, 257; *see also Robinson Crusoe*
demography, *see* family structure
De Quincey, Thomas, 41, 43, 54
desert fathers, hermits, 2, 10–12, 17, 67–8, 101, 107, 130, 184, 186, 187, 198, 202, 210–11, 216, 250, 254, 257
de Tocqueville, Alexis, 136, 138, 141
de Waal, Esther, 216–17
Dickens, Charles, 20–1, 54–6, 59, 68, 77–8, 92–3, 139–41, 157, 168, 179, 193, 258
Diderot, Denis, 4, 12–13
digital communication, 238, 247–9, 250–1, 254–5, 256–7, 258
disability, 245, 257
doctors, *see* medicine
dog breeding, dog shows, 97, 98
dog-walking, 56-7, 70, 97, 98, 167–8, 258
Doll, Richard, 176
'do-it-yourself', 158, 162, 166–7
domestic interiors, *see* housing
Dowrick, Stephanie, 207, 223
Drabble, Margaret, 170
Du Cane, Edward, 149

elderly, *see* old age
'Elegy Written in a Country Churchyard', *see* Gray, Thomas
Ellmann, Lucy, 190
emails, *see* digital communication
embroidery, 28, 74, 80–3, 84, 85, 105, 110–11, 258
Encyclopédie, 4
Enlightenment, 3, 4, 12–13, 17, 19, 250

environmental damage, pollution, 201,
    253–4, 259
Esquirol, Jean-Étienne Dominique, 8,
    74, 104
Evelyn, John, 4–5, 11
Everest, Mount, 67, 194, 199, 216, 253,
    254
Eyles, Margaret, 173

family structure, 71–2, 157, 223, 225–6,
    240, 252, 258
'Fancy', 97–100
Farmer's Boy, The, see Bloomfield, Robert
farming, see agricultural labour
Fenians, 148–9
Fermor, Patrick Leigh, 212
fishing, 28, 85–6, 98, 100–2, 165, 171,
    173, 177, 179–81, 257, 258
Foley, Alice, 92–3
Frankenstein, or the Modern Prometheus,
    see Shelley, Mary
friendship, friendship networks, 241
Fromm-Reichmann, Frieda, 206, 228–9,
    230
Fry, Elizabeth, 150-1

gardening, gardens, 28, 48, 69, 73, 84,
    86–8, 94–7, 99, 109, 110, 112,
    161–2, 163, 166, 173, 188, 227, 259
Garfield, Simon, 171, 240
Garve, Christian, 4
Gavron, Hannah, 157
Gay, John, 54
Gerbault, Alain, 201
Gibbons, Stanley, 79, 80
Giddens, Anthony, 239
Goffman, Erving, 228
Golden Globe Race, 195–202, 253–4
Gray, Thomas, 9, 32
Greene, Graham, 208
Gros, Frédéric, 58, 190
guidebooks, maps, 40, 48, 51–2, 54, 70,
    168, 191
Gurney, Joseph John, 150
Guldi, Jo, 40
gyms, 193–4, 258

Hammond, Claudia, 179–80
Hanway, Jonas, 133–5, 147
Harris, Michael, 257
Hazlitt, Carew, 85

Hazlitt, William, 48, 49–50, 53, 55, 70
Helpston, 31, 33, 45, 65
hermits, see desert fathers
hobbies, 28, 78–9, 80, 84, 100, 154,
    158, 159–60, 164, 165, 166–7, 169,
    170–1, 180, 240
Holt-Lunstad, Julianne, 233
Honnold, Alex, 194
Hornby, Frank, 160, 165
horse racing, 30
housewives, housework, 28, 35, 56, 83,
    93, 153, 161
    housing, domestic interiors, 73, 74,
    82, 105, 106, 115, 119, 155–8, 162,
    164, 166, 173, 226–7, 237, 238, 240,
    244, 247
Howard, John, 133
Howitt, William, 36
Hudson, W. H., 51–2, 185
Hume, Cardinal Basil, 213
hypochondria, 14, 105

insanity, 25, 129, 136, 147-8
internet, see digital communication
invalidity, ill health, 75, 103–11
iPhone, mobile phones, smartphones,
    163, 247, 248, 249, 255, 256, 258

Jameson, Anna, 108, 123–4, 126
Jebb, Joshua, 146
Jefferies, Richard, 41, 69
jigsaw puzzles, 169–70, 172
Jo Cox Loneliness Commission, 221
Johnson, Alan, 157

Kabat-Zinn, Jon, 218
Keats, John, 31–2, 46–7
Kingsley, Charles, 101, 178–9
Kingsmill, Joseph, 141–2
Kitchen, Fred, 189
Klein, Lawrence, 18
Klein, Richard, 178
Klinenberg, Eric, 245
knitting, 71, 73, 74, 83, 85, 161, 170, 258
Knox-Johnston, Robin, 196, 197–8,
    199–200, 201, 254
Koch, Philip, 27
Krafft-Ebbing, Richard von, 11

Langford, Gladys, 172, 242, 243
Langhamer, Claire, 153

Larkin, Philip, 214–15
Larson, Reed, 240
Last, Nella, 172, 173, 225, 243
Lawrence, Jon, 240
Le Carré, John, 207
Leclercq, Dom Jean, 212
letters, *see* correspondence, Penny
    Post
Lewis, Matthew, 12–14, 114, 127
libraries, public, 246
Life in the Sick-Room, *see* Martineau,
    Harriet
literacy, illiteracy, 22, 90–1, 93, 116, 137,
    145, 156, 158–9, 258
Loach, Ken, 228
  London, 23, 24, 31, 33, 37, 38–9, 41,
    42, 43, 51, 52, 53, 54, 55, 77, 80, 81,
    102, 106, 107, 137, 140, 141, 153,
    157, 175, 179, 193, 221, 258
London Federation of Rambling Clubs,
    53
loneliness, 'loneliness epidemic', 2, 20–2,
    27, 29, 62, 63, 107, 123, 171, 172,
    179, 186, 197, 202, 206, 207, 210,
    220–46, 256–7, 259
Loudon, J. C., 86, 87
lunacy, *see* insanity

Mabey, Richard, 192
MacArthur, Ellen, 195, 201
Macdonald, Helen, 192
Macfarlane, Robert, 191–2
Mackenzie, George, 4–5
Maitland, Sara, 236, 259
Mansfield Park, see Austen, Jane
Marriage Guidance Council, 243
Marryat, Captain, 176
Martineau, Harriet, 105–11, 124, 243
masturbation, 14, 249
Marx, Leo, 26
Mass Observation, 167, 172, 174, 175–6,
    177, 178, 179, 180, 224, 239
Matterhorn, 67–8
May, Theresa, 220, 221, 234, 235
Mayhew, Henry, 137, 141
McCandless, Chris, 191
medicine, medical profession, 3, 6–7,
    8, 9–10, 11, 14, 19, 21, 103, 106–7,
    146, 147, 176, 206, 217, 233
meditation, 216–19
melancholy, 8–11, 14–15, 16, 19, 21,

    24–5, 60, 74, 100, 104, 147, 170,
    172, 222–3, 229, 236, 242
Merton, Thomas, 208–13, 214, 215, 216,
    254
Milner, Reverend James, 12, 125
Milton, John, 20
Mindfulness, 180, 217–19
model trains, 160, 165
Moitessier, Bernard, 198–9, 202
monasteries, monastic life, 2, 11, 10–14,
    17, 112, 113, 114, 122, 128, 208–13,
    214–15, 247, 250, 254
Monbiot, George, 221–2, 235
Monk, The, *see* Lewis, Matthew
Montaigne, Michel de, 4, 6
Mont Blanc, 63, 64,
mountains, mountaineering, 49, 60,
    63–8, 194, 194, 199, 215, 253
Mysteries of Udolpho, *see* Radcliffe, Ann

National Council for the Divorced and
    Separated, 246
National Federation of Solo Clubs,
    246
nature, countryside, 18, 19–20, 31–55,
    69–70, 93–4, 109, 179, 185–94,
    218, 252–3, 259; *see also* fishing,
    gardening, walking.
needlework, *see* embroidery, knitting,
    sewing
Newman, John Henry, 125, 128, 131
newspapers, 67, 92, 111, 159, 163, 164,
    172, 196
Nightingale, Florence, 74, 105, 107,
    124, 130
Northanger Abbey, *see* Austen, Jane
Nostromo, *see* Conrad, Joseph

old age, 72, 159, 222, 223, 225, 226, 228,
    231, 236, 237, 238, 242, 244, 245,
    256
Office for National Statistics, 220
onanism, *see* masturbation

Pahl, Ray, 241
Palmo, Tenzin (Diane Perry), 216
Parker Morris report, 157–8, 250
Patience, card solitaire, 76–9, 84, 104,
    155
penal policy, reform, *see* prisons
Penny Post, 23, 27, 79, 89, 108, 128

Pentonville Prison, 127, 132, 135, 136–7, 139, 140, 141, 143–5, 147–8, 255

Peplau, Letitia Anne, 223, 236–7

Peripatetic, The, see Thelwall, John

Perlman, Daniel, 223

Petrarch, 2, 4, 5, 16, 47, 65, 249

philately, *see* stamp collecting

Phillipson, Chris, 238–9

Philosophy of Solitude, A, see, Powys, John Cowper

pigeon breeding, 97-9

Pinel, Phillippe, 9

pollution, *see* environmental damage

poverty, 245–6, 257, 259

Powys, John Cowper, 186–8, 190

Practical Householder, 167

prayer, 112–13, 114–22, 132–50, 208–12, 213–14, 218, 255–6

prison chaplains, 135, 137–9, 141–2, 144–6, 147, 149, 151, 152, 203, 232, 255

prisons, 114–15, 127, 129, 132–50, 203–8, 232, 255

privacy, 7, 38, 49, 59, 79, 104, 109, 113, 151–2, 158, 169, 171, 180, 236, 237, 239

Protestantism, 10, 16, 17, 113, 114, 115–22, 124–6, 133, 206–8, 210; *see also* convents, monasteries

psychiatry, 228–30

psychogeography, 192–3

public houses, 38, 47, 55, 97, 154, 251

Quakers, 112, 150–2

Quetelet, Adolphe, 146

Radcliffe, Ann, 12, 90

radio, radio communication, 160, 161, 162, 166, 167, 198, 199, 200, 202, 221

Raeburn, Anna, 245–6

railways, *see* steam trains

ramblers, rambling, rambling associations, 40, 41, 48–59, 69, 70, 168, 193

reading, 46, 47, 48, 61, 74, 77–8, 79, 89–93, 104, 108, 109–10, 116, 131, 140, 151–2, 156, 158–9, 161, 164, 172, 174, 179, 195–6, 207, 210, 238, 242, 245, 258

Reeves, Maud Pember, 83

Reformation, 11, 112, 116, 122, 125, 210

religion, Christianity, 4, 10–14, 17, 103–4, 108, 112–50, 184, 208–19, 224; *see also* Catholic Church, Protestantism, Quakers

Religieuse, La, see Diderot, Denis

Reveries of the Solitary Walker, see Rousseau, Jean-Jacques

Richards, Dan, 253

Ridgway, John, 196

Rings of Saturn, The, see Sebald, W. G.

Roberts, Morley, 181

Roberts, Robert, 154

Robinson Crusoe, 23–4, 35, 45–6, 250

Rokach, Amy, 223

Romantic Movement, poets 18–20, 45, 70, 250

Rousseau, Jean-Jacques, 6–7, 17, 64, 186

Ruskin, John, 67

sailing, round-the-world, 194–202, 253–4

Samaritans, 246

Sandford, Jeremy, 228

Seasons, The, see Thomson, James

Sebald, W. G., 252–3

segregation, penal, *see* prisons

Self, Will, 168, 193

Senechal, Diana, 27, 257

servants, 72, 73, 82, 103, 106, 113, 115–16, 119, 251

Seven Storey Mountain, The, see Merton, Thomas

sexual abuse, 214–15, 254

sewing, 71, 73, 74, 80, 83, 84, 92, 104, 151, 161, 173, 258

Shaftesbury, third Earl, 18

Shaw, Charles, 36

Sheldon, J. H., 226, 231, 237

Shelley, Mary, 62–4, 68, 250

Shelley, Percy Bysshe, 61–2, 68

Showalter, Elaine, 104

Shulevitz, Judith, 231, 233

Sidgwick, Arthur Hugh, 53–4

silence, 13, 27, 45, 50, 75, 89, 102, 112, 130, 133, 142–4, 147–8, 150, 171, 183, 187, 190, 207–11, 216, 217, 225, 229, 243, 247–8, 252

Sinclair, Iain, 168, 193

sisterhoods, *see* convents

Slocum, Joshua, 194–7, 200,
smoking, 173–9, 180, 231, 232, 234, 248
Snell, Keith, 221, 236
social networks, 237–8
social services, 233, 236, 237, 244, 245, 246
solitary confinement, *see* prisons
Solnit, Rebecca, 168
Somerville, Alexander, 36–7, 43
Sony Walkman, 162, 163, 248
Spring Rice, Margery, 153, 157, 171–2
stamp collecting, 28, 78–80, 84, 160, 164, 165, 169, 170–1, 174, 240, 258
statistics, 144–6, 231–2, 256
steam trains, railways, 34, 35, 41, 49, 52, 53, 64, 69, 79, 99, 102, 167, 173, 188
Stephen, Leslie, 51, 52, 64, 66, 168
Stephens, Caroline, 150
Stevenson, Robert Louis, 50, 55, 70
Strayed, Cheryl, 190–1
strolling, *see* walking
Storr, Anthony, 21, 230, 239
suicide, 135, 145, 182–3, 201–4, 218

Taoism, 186
talking, *see* conversation
Taylor, John, 31–2, 46
teenagers, 90, 156, 158, 205, 240, 248, 249–50, 256
telephone, 23, 164, 200, 204, 238, 249
television, 87, 158, 160–2, 167, 173, 179, 180–1, 194, 221, 228, 238, 245, 249
Thelwall, John, 18, 49
Thompson, Flora, 37, 39
Thomson, James, 32, 36, 44
Thoreau, Henry, 191
Thrower, Percy, 162
Tillich, Paul, 223
Tissot, Samuel-Auguste, 6–7, 8, 14, 22–3, 249
towns, *see* urbanization
Townsend, Peter, 226, 236
Trappist monasteries, *see* Merton, Thomas
Treveleyan, G. M., 48, 50, 51, 53
Trivia: or, the Art of Walking the Streets of London, *see*, Gay, John
Trotter, Thomas, 8, 25
Tudor Walters report, 156

Tunstall, Jeremy, 231
Turkle, Sherry, 251

UCLA Loneliness Scale, 232
United States, 26, 85, 136, 138, 139–40, 141, 163, 169, 190, 191, 194, 203, 209, 222, 232, 237, 248, 256
urbanization, 16, 19, 24, 34, 35, 36, 41, 49, 52–3, 54, 56, 58, 66, 87, 101, 102, 121–2, 167, 185, 187, 224, 227, 247–8, 250

Vernon, James, 19
Victor, Christina, 222, 236
Village Minstrel, The, *see* Clare, John
Virgil, 16

Waite, Terry, 206–8
walking (competitive), 28, 41–2
walking, strolling, 18, 20, 28, 32–70, 93, 99, 154, 163, 167–8, 172, 173, 174, 179, 185–6, 188–91, 193, 238–9, 240, 245, 248, 252–3, 257, 259; *see also* ramblers
Wallace, Anne, 44
Walpole, Horace, 12
Walton, Izaak, 46, 85–6
Watson, George, 48
Waugh, Evelyn, 208, 211
Wear, Delease, 239–40, 244
Whyman, Susan, 22
Whymper, Edward, 66–8
wild, wilderness, 59–68, 190–3, 253–4
Williams, Raymond, 185
Willmott, Peter, 227
Winnicott, Donald, 230–1
wireless, *see* radio
Wiseman, Cardinal, 122, 125
Woman, 160, 245–6
Woolf, Virginia, 155–6, 168
Wordsworth, William, 41, 42, 43, 45–6, 48, 49, 186, 258

Young, Michael, 227

Zimmermann, Johann Georg, 1–18, 19, 22–3, 25, 26–7, 28, 29, 61, 68, 70, 71, 109, 113, 180, 186, 236, 249, 251, 255, 257
Zweig, Ferdynand, 166, 169